'This highly analytical... treatise provides an excellent conceptual foundation and reference for the conduct of Foucaultian research in various areas... the text is written with fluency, logically presented, and its arguments are introduced to readers using vivid language... [it] provides an excellent resource for health care professionals... [and] is an important contribution to critical social science research '

Ari Väänänen, *Psychology*

'In an age where arguabl... ...perseded Foucault in terms of scholar... ...is timely and welcome... it will draw... chology, including sociologists, hum... ...ntists... I thoroughly enjoyed this exc... ...ory, and Hook makes for a perceptive and p... ...guide.'

Brendan Gough, *British Journal of Sociology*

'This exciting new text by Derek Hook represents a much needed elaboration of the application of Foucault's analytics of power for use within the discipline of psychology and the social sciences more broadly... Hook's close reading of Foucault's work demonstrates an in-depth knowledge of what is often a very dense body of work, and as a result he renders Foucault's key ideas in ways that are both highly readable and stimulating. The book will definitely be of interest to those working in the field of critical race and whiteness studies who are looking to draw upon the work of Foucault to conduct their own research, and will also provide a useful springboard for those wishing to further critique the functions of racialised power, both within Foucault's work and beyond.'

Damien W. Riggs, ACRAWSA

'Derek Hook has undeniably made a valuable contribution... [and] produced a readable, useable text. Whoever reads through these pages will arrive at a more sophisticated, more radical, and potentially more productive engagement with Foucault in psychology.'

Desmond Painter

'Through his original and provocative engagement with Foucault, Hook sets up an innovative dialogue with thinkers in the fields of sociology, philosophy and social and political theory. He uses Foucault's work as a prism to open up a variety of provocative methodologies to rejuvenate the fields of discourse analysis, the psychology of space-identity and the study of race and racism.'

Professor Catherine Campbell,
London School of Economics, UK

Critical Theory and Practice in Psychology and the Human Sciences

Titles include:

Barnaby Barrett
THE EMERGENCE OF SOMATIC PSYCHOLOGY AND BODYMIND THERAPY

Derek Hook
FOUCAULT, PSYCHOLOGY AND THE ANALYTICS OF POWER

Mary Watkins and Helene Shulman
TOWARD PSYCHOLOGIES OF LIBERATION

Critical Theory and Practice in Psychology and the Human Sciences
Series Standing Order ISBN 978–0–230–52113–1 (hardback) and
978–0–230–52114–8 (paperback)
(*outside North America only*)

You can receive future titles in this series as they are published by placing a standing order. Please contact your bookseller or, in case of difficulty, write to us at the address below with your name and address, the title of the series and the ISBN quoted above.

Customer Services Department, Macmillan Distribution Ltd, Houndmills, Basingstoke, Hampshire RG21 6XS, England

Foucault, Psychology and the Analytics of Power

Derek Hook
London School of Economics, UK

© Derek Hook 2007

All rights reserved. No reproduction, copy or transmission of this
publication may be made without written permission.

No portion of this publication may be reproduced, copied or transmitted
save with written permission or in accordance with the provisions of the
Copyright, Designs and Patents Act 1988, or under the terms of any licence
permitting limited copying issued by the Copyright Licensing Agency,
Saffron House, 6-10 Kirby Street, London EC1N 8TS.

Any person who does any unauthorized act in relation to this publication
may be liable to criminal prosecution and civil claims for damages.

The author has asserted his right to be identified
as the author of this work in accordance with the Copyright,
Designs and Patents Act 1988.

First published 2007
This paperback edition published 2010 by
PALGRAVE MACMILLAN

Palgrave Macmillan in the UK is an imprint of Macmillan Publishers Limited,
registered in England, company number 785998, of Houndmills, Basingstoke,
Hampshire RG21 6XS.

Palgrave Macmillan in the US is a division of St Martin's Press LLC,
175 Fifth Avenue, New York, NY 10010.

Palgrave Macmillan is the global academic imprint of the above companies
and has companies and representatives throughout the world.

Palgrave® and Macmillan® are registered trademarks in the United States,
the United Kingdom, Europe and other countries.

ISBN 978-0-230-00819-9 hardback
ISBN 978-0-230-00820-5 paperback

This book is printed on paper suitable for recycling and made from fully
managed and sustained forest sources. Logging, pulping and manufacturing
processes are expected to conform to the environmental regulations of the
country of origin.

A catalogue record for this book is available from the British Library.

A catalog record for this book is available from the Library of Congress.

10   9   8   7   6   5   4   3   2   1
19 18 17 16 15 14 13 12 11 10

Printed and bound in Great Britain by
CPI Antony Rowe, Chippenham and Eastbourne

For Joan and Derek

It seems to me that the real political task in a society such as ours is to criticize the working of institutions which appear to be both neutral and independent; to criticise them in such a manner that the political violence which has always exercised itself obscurely through them will be unmasked, so that one can fight them.

(Foucault, 1974, p. 171)

Contents

Preface

The 1999 film *The Matrix* portrays a system in which humans experience going to work, having relationships, eating, sleeping and otherwise living out their daily lives, while in fact they are merely imagining or dreaming these realities as part of the energy production system of a machine-controlled earth. Along with the protagonist Neo who chooses to take the pill that allows him to grasp the human situation from a more complete perspective, film audiences are stunned when they confront the truth and the reality of this oppression. For those of us caught up in the machines of modern consciousness in various ways, there exists a similar hard pill to swallow. We must confront the possibility that psychology may have been similarly deluded about the human situation and, more seriously, about its own functions in connection with the machines of power in modern societies.

In the case of psychology, swallowing the 'truth' pill opens up a panorama of the following sort: Psychology, both through its practices and through the concepts that justify its practices, operates for the most part as an ideological apparatus. This means that its array of discourses and activities constructs and sustains systems of domination and oppression even as they appear to support self-understanding and well-being. Therapy, counselling, assessment, research, self-help, prevention work, clinic spaces, case studies and all forms of psy-work *construct* specific forms of understanding and experience as they operate. In so doing, relations of power are worked up, sorted out and established along the lines that existing systems allow. Simultaneously, modes of resistance and counter-systems take shape. These ideological functions of psy-work and their subversion have been noted in previous scholarly work, but it is obvious from the ongoing expansion of the psychology enterprise that the critique is not taking hold.

The critical conceptualization of ideology employed here is still debated extensively even among progressive social theorists, with many arguing that we are doomed to be locked in ideological processes and discourses that reinforce the status quo and should therefore not hold out the possibility that resistance might lead to experience 'beyond ideology'. It may be that solutions to this apparent dilemma are prevented mostly by a lack of clarity about concepts. Yet, should we not insist, as we are engaged in the critical human sciences, on the goal of understanding and transforming social relations that systematically produce human suffering? Should we not at least attempt to participate in the collective dismantling of ideological structures? And if a major scientific discipline and industry such as psychology is part and parcel of such structures, should it not be our task to expose and confront the collusion?

Derek Hook's *Foucault, Psychology and the Analytics of Power* makes a huge contribution towards clarifying both the limits and possibilities of contemporary psychology. In this book, Hook leads readers from the received view of psychology as a helpful science to a glimpse of its foundations in ideological pseudo-realities. In the process, Hook provides critical conceptual tools for digging towards analytic practices that reveal oppressive forms of power. As the title implies, Foucault provides the vessel for this journey.

For several decades now, the work of the French philosopher Michel Foucault (1926–1984) has transformed the perspectives and analytic strategies of numerous disciplines in the human sciences. His work provides a framework as productive and powerful as that of the Frankfurt School of critical social theory associated with Adorno, Horkheimer, Marcuse and Habermas. Derek Hook reminds us that Foucault's work deserves the critical attention of psychologists for a variety of compelling reasons.

First, Foucault saw psychological knowledge and practice as one of modern society's new strategies for disciplining and shaping the action of individuals. His studies of prisons, asylums and therapeutic self-reflection are obvious examples of this interest. But, in fact, Foucault's entire outlook butts up against the realms of human experience addressed by psychological inquiry and his analyses allow us to grasp how changing social relations and institutional practices themselves constitute particular historical forms of subjective experience. So, Foucault describes the structuring and production of modern individual 'consciousness' in ways that turn standard psychological understandings upside down. To put it simply, what we know as experience and consciousness within psychological frameworks are understood in the Foucauldian vision as the effects of discourses and 'disciplinary technologies' in modern society that produce individuals who experience themselves as 'experiencing' and 'being conscious'. Psychological knowledge and psychological modes of assessment and intervention are part of the processes that produce these effects.

Derek Hook argues, however, that we cannot simply explain away 'the psychological' as the effect of modern forms of power. These effects need to be fully understood and such understanding entails a grasp of the workings of power at the level of the individual subject. Hook works to fill in the gaps created by the fact that Foucault was committed to understanding social relations in ways that did not require what we would usually think of as psychological accounts. He takes care to avoid filling in these spaces with problematic psychologizing. Without abandoning the critical lens developed by Foucault, he establishes the grounds for an account of subjectivity that encompasses features of experience such as memory, emotion and self-awareness. These aspects of experience are often seen as irrelevant in Foucault-inspired work, but they are essential to a fully developed critique of power. Hook shows how the apparent contradictions can be thought through.

Finally, this book powerfully develops the idea that Foucault's analytics of power, in particular his methodological contributions (analytics of space, critical history and discourse), raise serious questions about the new orthodoxies of qualitative research in psychology and provide innovative and potentially even complementary directions. These possibilities are exemplified by excerpts from Hook's own studies on racism in contemporary South Africa. Researchers in the human sciences will find plenty of inspiration here, especially with regard to neglected yet fundamental aspects of social relations.

This book will deeply reward the efforts of all readers who seek to escape the matrix and embark on the long journey entailed in exposing, resisting and transforming both the workings of the psychology industry and the systematic forms of oppression that characterize modern and post-modern society.

Tod Sloan
Editor, Palgrave series on Critical Theory in
Psychology and the Human Sciences
Lewis & Clark College
Portland, OR, USA

Acknowledgements

For institutional support I need to thank the Research Office and the School of Human and Community Development at the University of the Witwatersrand; I am particularly grateful to have been offered a research associate position by the latter. I am likewise grateful to the Institute of Public Scholarship at Emory University, to Ivan Karp and Cory Kratz, and indeed, the Rockefeller Foundation, for making my fellowship at Emory possible. I am also thankful to all colleagues and students in the Institute of Social Psychology at the London School of Economics. Thanks is also due to the British Academy for offering funding for the 'Flesh & Blood' conference held at the LSE between 19 and 21 April 2005 which proved of central importance in developing aspects of the arguments presented in this book.

At the level of scholarly input and personal support I am indebted to a large number of people. Some of those whose assistance is directly reflected in this book are: Mark Anderson, Lisa Baraitser, Martin Bauer, Brett Bowman, Erica Burman, Chris Byl, Anthony Collins, Jacqueline Crane, Norman Duncan, Kevin Durrheim, Gill Eagle, Stephen Frosh, David Giles, Ros Gill, Paul Gilroy, Brendan Gough, Grahame Hayes, Caroline Howarth, Simone Huning, Sandra Jovchelovitch, Peace Kiguwa, Daniel Linehan, Carol Long, Alec McHoul, Kareen Malone, Solani Ngobeni, Desmond Painter, Ian Parker, Debbie Posel, Jonathan Potter, Kopano Ratele, Damien Riggs, Nik Rose, Edward Soja, Hank Stam, Kathryn Smith, Martin Terre Blanche, Michele Vrdoljak, Valerie Walkerdine, Nicola Webb-Jenkins, Bruce Williams, Carla Willig, Margie Wetherell and Sue van Zyl. The biggest thank-you of all goes to Merryn Hook.

An earlier version of Chapter 3 appeared in *Theory & Psychology*, under the title of 'Discourse, knowledge, materiality, history' (2001, 11 (4), 521–547) and is reprinted by permission of Sage Publications. Much of the text of Chapter 4 appeared in *Qualitative Research in Psychology* as 'Genealogy, discourse, "effective history"' in 2005 (2, 1–29) and is likewise reprinted by permission of Sage Publications. Certain of the examples of genealogical method used in the chapter are derived from collaborative work with my friend and colleague Brett Bowman. The formulations and argumentative uses of these examples are my own, although I am indebted to Brett for the opportunity to work with him, for his research assistance, and his gathering of the original empirical materials. Chapter 5 is an adaptation of a paper originally co-authored with Michele Vrdoljak; once again I am indebted to my colleague for her research assistance, particularly in terms of gathering the raw data. The formulations I offer here, however are mine. (For versions of the jointly-authored paper, see *Psychology in Society* – where aspects of this material first appeared – 'Fear and loathing in Northern Johannesburg: Security Park as Heterotopia' (2001, 27, 61–83), and also *Geoforum*, 'Gated communities, heterotopia and a "rights" of privilege' (2002, 33, 195–219) for which Elsevier has kindly granted permission to reproduce sections of the text. Aspects of Chapter 6 have appeared both in *Theory & Psychology* as 'Analogues of Power: Reading Psychotherapy through the sovereignty-discipline-government complex' (2003, 13 (5), 605–628), reprinted by permission of Sage Publications, and in *International Journal of Critical Psychology* as 'Affecting whiteness: Racism as technology of affect (1)' (16, 74–99), reproduced by permission of Lawrence and Wishart. The examples of the analysis of psychodynamic psychotherapy discussed in Chapter 1 have been drawn from an article entitled 'Therapeutic discourse, co-construction, interpellation, role-induction: psychotherapy as iatrogenic treatment modality? published in *The International Journal of Psychotherapy* (2001, 6, 1, 47–66) by permission of Taylor & Francis (for further details see http://wwwtandf.co.uk/journals).

Introduction

This series of essays presents a variety of responses to the question of what the genealogical works of Michel Foucault may mean to the domain of critical psychology. This, I think, is an important task given that 20 years after Foucault's death, the discipline of psychology has yet to absorb the full impact of his work. Two particular problems arise here, both of which became apparent to me in relation to teaching. First, although there are several reasonable introductory texts on Foucault (McHoul and Grace, 1997; McNay, 1994; Mills, 2003; Smart, 1985) none focuses on those of Foucault's ideas most important to students/practitioners of psychology and none introduces Foucault from the standpoint of psychology itself. Although certain critical psychology texts have made mention of Foucault (Gough and McFadden, 2001; Hepburn, 2003; Parker, 2003; Tuffin, 2005; Walkerdine, 2002) his work is generally drawn on in a 'mix and match' manner, along with other thinkers – usually under the general rubric of poststructuralism – without the benefit of sustained exposition and/or adequate theoretical and methodological contextualization. Second, despite the importance of Foucault's methodological writings, and, indeed, the need for critical psychology to engage with these lines of critique and analysis, I have found it difficult to prescribe a text which presents a detailed set of Foucauldian methodological frameworks within the context of Foucault's particular theoretical, political and historical objectives.

As neglected as the topic of Foucault and psychology has been – especially so, given the content of Foucault's earliest published work,[1] and in view of his training and practice in the realm of clinical psychology (Macey, 2004; Whitebrook, 2005) – it is not completely novel. Nikolas Rose's (1991, 1996a) seminal studies of the Psy-complex and British psychology usefully extends Foucault's critique of psychology – aspects of which I revisit in the following chapter – although these studies cannot be described as didactic, or as offering easy access to a variety of Foucauldian frames of analysis. May's (1993) *Between Genealogy and Epistemology* does, admittedly, discuss the relation between aspects of Foucault's thought and psychology; once again, however, this treatment does not lend itself to practical application. His predominant focus, moreover, is on Foucault's earlier archaeological writings; it is the later genealogical work between the mid and late 1970s that I, by contrast, believe holds the most potential both for the critique of psychology and for analytical innovation. On the other hand, a book like Kendall and Wickham's (1998) *Using Foucault's Methods*, which does hope to introduce a series of Foucauldian frameworks for analysis in a user-friendly way, lacks the theoretical depth and historical complexity that grounds Foucault's work, and that lends it much of its characteristic urgency. My position, in contrast to such an approach, is that Foucault's methods cannot be simply detached from the political and philosophical concerns that Foucault had with *interrogating the human science disciplines themselves*. The aim of this book is thus to introduce both of these methodological and politico-historical preoccupations together, to put Foucault's genealogical writings to work as a means of critically re-conceptualizing aspects of psychological knowledge and practice, first and, correspondingly, as a means of grounding a set of radical research methods, second.

In terms of the first of these objectives, Foucault certainly enables us to spell out a series of complex links between psychology and power; to understand how psychology is *itself* an indispensable vector of modern power, something typically overlooked in most approaches to the discipline. The themes of such a critique emerge in a variety of ways throughout this book: in the account of the disciplinary role of psychology as a subjectifying form of power-knowledge whose history cannot be divorced from the trajectory of corrective practices essential to modern power; in the interrogation of those psychological notions so central to the philosophy of humanism and to the detouring of critique (e.g. 'individuality' as a naturally emerging category rather than a function of power; interpretative appeals to the truths of consciousness and/or interiority); and in an awareness of how technologies of subjectivity implemented by various Psy-disciplines and institutions enable certain governmental agendas – particular rationalities of the state – to be articulated through the ethical self-knowledge and self-practices of subjects. Foucault's work, provides us with a complex analytics of modern power, indeed, with a multi-dimensional model of the functioning of relations of control, that may be critically applied in a variety of different locations and at a variety of different levels, both within the domain of psychology and further afield.

The book's second key objective is to foreground Foucault's various contributions to 'the work of critique', that is, to the historical and discursive analysis of asymmetrical relations of power and knowledge. I maintain that Foucault's most vital contribution in this respect is less that of a *theorist* than that of a *methodologist*. Foucault's analytics of power, that is to say, does not follow the route of 'grand theory'; his is not the project of writing power's ontology, of outlining its overall structure. In many ways, Foucault's is precisely a *de-theorizing* project that aims to resist final formularizations of power in favour of the attempt to generate solid analytic grounds from which we may fix aspects of its operational force and logic. In other words, we best benefit from Foucault's critical legacy – both as it applies to psychology and more generally – by examining and applying his 'analytics'. To this end, the book provides elucidations of three Foucauldian analytical frameworks: critical discursive critique, genealogy and heterotopology (the analytics of heterotopia), although, of course, a variety of Foucault's concepts – the notion of human technologies, the concepts of bio-power, apparatuses of security and governmentality – are important analytical tools in and of themselves. Not only do these approaches offer themselves as useful alternatives for researchers in the qualitative psychology tradition, they also offer very different lines of conceptualization, novel critical orientations to a variety of ostensibly psychological questions (such as issues of psychological deviancy and abnormality (Chapter 4), the notion of place-identity (Chapter 5), the social deployment of racist subjectivity). Ultimately, of course, Foucault's methods entail a position of critical reflexivity towards the knowledge-productions of the discipline within which one is working. In this respect, it should come as no surprise that what is frequently most valuable about Foucault for psychology – paradoxical as it sounds – is precisely his attempt to develop non-psychological, indeed, even *anti*-psychological modes of analysis and critique. In respect of this issue of critical reflexivity, I think it is worth pointing out that the very first chapter of this book (Foucault's historical re-contextualization of psychology) can also be read as a logical consequence of the methodology chapters that follow it, for no genuinely critical work can emerge from within psychology that does not scrutinize the disciplinary location from which it emerges.

I open the book by introducing Foucault's influential account of disciplinary power – or 'disciplinarity' as I refer to it – as a condition of possibility for the emergence of psychological individuality. Breaking from other introductory approaches to this material, I have moved away from the tendency to rely solely on Foucault's *Discipline and Punish*, refreshing many of these explanations with recourse to the recently published *Psychiatric Power*. Furthermore, while remaining faithful to the basic terms of Foucault's account – the critique of humanism; the notion of disciplinary technologies; the factors of surveillance, confession and normalization; the idea of the 'soul-effects' produced within disciplined bodies – I have also suggested that his analysis of power could be usefully advanced with a more developed category of 'the psychological'. To be sure, Foucault's account of disciplinarity helps emphasize the extent to which virtually all of 'the psychological' (as it is lived, practiced and rendered subject to knowledge) falls within the ambit of power. This is key to its critical utility – the fact that it forces us to reassess notions of a natural, universal psychological subjectivity. This notwithstanding, I have queried whether an implicitly psychological account of power – such as disciplinarity often seems – can in fact effectively dispense with all psychological modes of description and analysis. Just as the vocabulary of the psychological is often superseded by the terms of a Foucauldian analytics eager to play up the historical and political dimension of its practical concepts, so it is also the case that aspects of this vocabulary are, at certain crucial points, able to supersede Foucault's analytical frame.

Building on the historical grounds provided in the first chapter, Chapter 2 goes on to advance a series of methodological pragmatics for the analysis of power. Key injunctions here concern the attempt to 'desubstantialize' power, that is, to view relations of control, influence and subjectification not with reference to power as a structure, possession or repressive capability, but rather as a dynamic, relational, contingent assembly of forces working in both top-down and bottom-up directions. The idea of power as an 'unstructured formation' is presented, alongside a series of injunctions guiding the prospective analyst to grasp the technological specificity of a given relation of power and to suspend the assumption that the category of the individual comes before the constitutive role of 'power-knowledge'. Crucial here also are guidelines concerning the need to interrogate the epistemology of humanism, to think of power as intentional and strategic yet 'de-agented' and to understand how relations of resistance makes for a necessary precondition for the operation of power. The chapter ends with an evaluation of Foucault's 'desubstantialization' of power, along with a series of comments on its usefulness as a general set of methodological pragmatics.

I extend a concern with practical methodological issues in the third chapter, which examines that aspect of Foucault's conceptual and methodological work which has had the biggest impact on critical psychology. I have in mind here, of course, the analysis of discourse, which, to date, has come to represent a virtual growth industry in research psychology. Through a close reading of Foucault's crucial methodological statement of intent, namely his inaugural lecture at the Collège de France, 'The order of discourse' (1981), this chapter re-characterizes the concept of discourse from a firmly Foucauldian perspective. This exposition is contrasted with two prominent approaches to discourse analysis from within psychology, those of Parker (1992) and Potter and Wetherell (1987). Relative to these two methods, I argue, Foucault's conception of discourse is situated far more closely to the analysis of knowledge, materiality and power than it is to language. It is exactly the omission of these three dimensions of analysis that so undermines the epistemological strength, the explanatory power and the political abilities of both Parker's (1992) and Potter and Wetherell's (1987) approaches. The chapter ends by providing a series of Foucauldian methodological injunctions for the analysis of discourse, and by pointing to the necessity of grasping the fundamentals of genealogical analysis.

Chapter 4 explores how the procedures of a Nietzschean 'effective history' (genealogy) enables Foucault to accommodate and elaborate upon the analytical imperatives asserted in the foregoing chapter. Following the style of that chapter, I introduce a series of distinctively Foucauldian methodological injunctions, attempting to do so in a way that remains accessible without sacrificing any of the philosophical complexity at hand. Many of Foucault's comments on the strategic utilization of genealogy speak directly to an explicitly political project. Part of the work of this chapter is to speculate on how genealogy might enable the project of political criticism and to comment on how it might be put to use within the domain of psychology. Crucial here are a series of genealogical notions – the category of the 'event', the dissipation of the object, the rejection of the self-constituting subject and the reassessment of the 'relation to knowledge' – each of which represents a valuable line of critique apropos standard psychological objects of knowledge. I illustrate many of the methodological maxims introduced with reference to a series of examples drawn from a recent study on the historical formation of paedophilia within South Africa (Bowman, 2005; Hook and Bowman, 2007). These examples are in turn supported by a number of speculations on the historico-discursive production of abnormality derived from Foucault's (2003b) *Abnormal*; speculations, which I believe, exemplify many of the methodological injunctions of genealogy.

In hindsight of the commentaries on the methodological, philosophical and political issues raised in earlier chapters, Chapter 5 takes a somewhat different track. It offers an extended example of an applied empirical analysis – an analysis that proceeds on the basis of a relatively neglected Foucauldian framework – that of heterotopology (the analytics, in other words, of 'heterotopia'). Foucault's notion of heterotopia provides a means of conceptualizing 'differential', or 'other' social spaces. These are zones of social activity with prescribed functions and identities which are able to operate as spaces of alternate social ordering; heterotopia, in other words, are able to show up, critically reflect and subvert a society's commonplace norms and discursive values. Heterotopia are connected to a series of criteria – ritualized systems of opening and closing, a codified sense of social functionality, a distinctive ordering of time and the spatial realization of utopian aspirations – that Foucault applies as a set of steps for the analysis of spatio-discursive relations of power. The applied focus of this chapter is on a particular South African gated community, a site in which a particular formation of 'place-identity' – that of exclusion and privilege – is thrown into sharp perspective. The subsequent analysis identifies a particular discourse of privilege, a ' "rights" of entitlement' that gated-community inhabitants mobilize as means of justifying a series of exclusionary measures. This discourse and its associated modes of spatial ordering function as symptomatic indicators of far larger socio-historical structures of exclusion and privilege.

In Chapter 6, I have allowed myself more explanatory latitude than in previous chapters in terms of how I seek to apply a number of important Foucauldian conceptual motifs. My intent here is to develop the argument that a Foucauldian analytics needs to grapple with the role of certain psychological forces – in this case, *affect* – not merely as the outcome of power, but also as conduits, conductors, as its 'instrumentalizable' resources. Three lines of discussion come together here. First, continuing Foucault's re-conceptualization of power discussed in Chapters 1 and 2, I introduce the complimentary notions of governmentality, apparatuses, bio-power and technologies of subjectivity and self. These are crucial concepts: the notion of technologies of subjectivity and self provides a valuable means of thinking the interchange between structural forms of influence and ethical micro-practices of self; the concept of the apparatus helps us understand the diffused and indeterminate set of articulations which connect individualizing with totalizing means of power. Second, I discuss the issue of racism, both so as to point to the limits of a predominantly historico-discursive frame of analysis, and so as to motivate for the importance of an analytics of affect. Third, through a reconsideration of the model of technologies of subjectivity and self, and in conjunction with a series of contemporary examples of the governmental conduct of conduct, I present a tentative outline for how the analytics of governmentality might be advanced in such a way that takes seriously the *affective* dimension of such processes.

Foucault, Psychology and the Analytics of Power does not represent a working-through of a systematic or global position. The book combines both introductory and more advanced exploratory engagements with Foucault, both strict close-text commentaries and freer instances of applied analysis. This is a combination that has been aided by my decision to make use of discussion boxes, which allow me to present parallel contents which interestingly augment, question or exemplify the arguments of the main text. I am conscious that at times in the book I may appear to have adopted different argumentative positions depending on the particular objectives of the chapter in question. This is in part a function of combining didactic and critical speculative types of engagement with Foucault. It is also, no doubt, the result of exploring a *variety of perspectives* on what Foucault's genealogical work might mean to critical psychology, a 'body' of work, that should by no means be viewed as a closed system.

1
Disciplinarity and the Production of Psychological Individuality

[T]he individual is the result of... procedures which pin political power on the body. It is because the body has been 'subjectified,' that is to say, that the subject function has been fixed on it, because it has been psychologized and normalized, it is because of all of this that something like the individual appeared, about which one can speak, hold discourses, and attempt to found sciences.

(Foucault, 2006, p. 56)

Introducing disciplinarity

If we are to grasp the psychological from the perspective of a Foucauldian analytics, we will need to make recourse to a mode of history able to outline the emergence of psychological individuality as a nodal point of political and epistemic concerns in modernity. The particular history that we will need to trace – in following Foucault's lead – is that of a set of mechanisms and apparatuses that take the 'somatic singularity' of the body as their target and whose most significant effect is a series of investments, a 'core of virtualities', that we may refer to as the soul. What such a history will ultimately yield is the blueprint of a transferable technology that enables the production of individual, psychological subjects. What is required, in short, is an account not only of the workings of a disciplinary technology, and a review of the broader array of characteristic procedures, assumptions and strategies that characterize the more general domain of disciplinary power – which I refer to here as disciplinarity – but a description also of the privileged role of the psychological in this distinctive modern economy of power.

8

The first section of this chapter offers a historical backdrop to the advent of disciplinarity, and does so by discussing two pre-modern technologies of power: sovereign rule and the order of humanistic reform. The second section is devoted to outlining the core features of disciplinarity and with foregrounding the means through which such a mode of power enables the *production of psychological individuality*. While remaining faithful to the terms of Foucault's critique of the disciplinary practice and study of psychology, I have also suggested – perhaps paradoxically – that his analysis of power could be usefully advanced with a more developed category of 'the psychological'. I close by offering a series of critical speculations. Rather than repeating a set of standard critiques brought against Foucault's notion of disciplinary power, I have elected to query whether an implicitly psychological account of power can in fact effectively dispense with all psychological modes of description and analysis.

I

Power before discipline: The era of sovereignty

The paradigmatic example of punishment in the monarchical era of sovereignty is, for Foucault, the spectacle of the scaffold. This is a highly violent and demonstrative form of power, a type of physical retribution acted out on the body of the criminal and staged for the benefit of the public at large. In this early era of power, a breach of the sovereign's law was tantamount to an act of war. Such an infringement was to be understood as an act of aggression committed against the person of the king, whose body had (figuratively) been attacked in the action of the crime. Accordingly, the body of the criminal had to be attacked, tortured, often dismembered or mutilated, in a symbolic display of the sovereign's power.

As dramatic a deterrent as such spectacles proved to be, they were nevertheless limited in their efficacy. This was a discontinuous and performative type of power; each time the law was broken, a display of ritual atrocity had to be re-enacted. As spectacular and brutal as this mode of punishment was, its influence was incomplete; it did not saturate all possible spaces of illegality. The crimes that afforded the spectacle of ritual atrocity were typically of a more dramatic sort; a wide range of minor infractions – indeed, an entire spectrum of ongoing illegalities – were left unchecked. Such spectacles also made for a fundamentally unstable form of power; they risked the insurrection of the gathered masses who might (and often did) choose to sympathize with the punished criminals rather than with the presiding authorities. It is for these reasons that Foucault (2006) states that sovereignty requires not only the activation of the distinctive mark, but a 'cyclical game of ceremonies...the reiteration of a profound memory', namely that of the threat of violence which is always behind the relationship of sovereignty, for, after all 'the other side of sovereignty is...war' (p. 43).

Instability of the 'subject-function': Disjunctions of the body and power

One of the conclusions that Foucault draws from his historical observations of the era of sovereignty is that the 'pinning of the subject-function to a definitive body' takes place only in a contingent manner, in ceremonies, in those moments when the body is marked by insignia, by gestures, or in 'the violence with which sovereignty asserts its rights and forcible imposes them on...its subjects' (2006, p. 43). Subjects are thus only infrequently 'brought into power', and only by virtue of a discontinuous set of moments and actions. The 'subject-function' of the definitive fixing of bodies to power is both rare and less than guaranteed; the correspondence of 'somatic singularities' with activated relations of force cannot be assured. Part of the reason for this, claims Foucault, is that the relationship of sovereignty does not naturally apply to physical individuality but rather to multiplicities (families, communities), which lie above the level of somatic singularity, or, to fragmentary aspects of individuality presumably lying beneath this level of specification. There is hence a disabling disjuncture apparent within this mode of political control, a certain looseness in the matching up of bodies and power.

The effects of this disjunction – which, crucially, results in a lack of individualization – are reversed in the case of the sovereign. If, for Foucault, individualization is absent at the base of the population, it is most certainly present at its summit; there must, after all, be a single, individual point of arbitration and judgement atop this set of power-relations. The sovereign's body supplies this point of convergence. However, given the importance of this body – which holds together all the diverse and conflicting subsidiary relations within this pyramidal structure of sovereign authority – it cannot be allowed to decline within the failing physical attributes of an ageing king – it must rise above the level of somatic singularity. More than just this, the king's body is subject to multiplication; it is at least double – as in the case of a consolidating body politic, the idea of the population *as* the king's body.

These speculations lead Foucault to two conclusions. Firstly, although the relationship of sovereignty does connect political power with the body, such an attempt at co-ordination is marred by continuous disjunction – bodies and power are not coterminous entities in this era of power. Secondly, we are as such confronting a form of power without a broadly individualizing function, a political mode which outlines individuality only in the figure of the sovereign, and even then at the cost of paradoxical multiplication of the body. As such – and here a characteristically Foucauldian counter-intuition – 'We have bodies without individuality on one side, and individuality but a multiplication of bodies on the other' (2006, p. 46).

Bridges to disciplinarity: Humanizing power

The second order of pre-disciplinary power identified by Foucault is that of the humanist reformers, an era that begins at the end of the eighteenth century, with a series of protests against the inhumane excesses of the scaffold. Challenging the sovereign's absolute prerogative in matters of punishment, the humanist reformers advocated an art of manipulating representations, a 'curative' or restorative economy of punishment that was taken to be the means of the correct re-ordering of social life.

Punishment must now be an art of effects, a 'complex of signs' that 'reduce the desire that makes the crime attractive' (Foucault, 1977a, p. 106) and that creates an automatic association between crimes and the inevitable response of the law. In the first of a series of principles that anticipates disciplinarity, humanist reformers maintained that punishment could be justified only insofar as it plays a role in preventing the repetition of crimes; deterrence must be its paramount objective. Punishment, furthermore, must obey the maxims of moderation and the humane; calculated and measured punishments must be devised; analogical penalties must be adopted; crimes must come to be matched to didactic modes of punishment that undo the logic of the criminal act.

Several consequences of this transformation in the rationality of power are worth emphasizing. The spectacle of the destruction of the body of the criminal is now abolished as an indefensible excess of power. Crime is not to be understood as an assault on the person of the king, but as an attack on society *as a whole*. Justice, furthermore, is no longer an issue of revenge and the singular prerogative of the sovereign; the responsibility to punish consequently came to lie with the most appropriate representatives of the social body. Crucially, the standard of justice was now that of 'humanity', a joint humanity that all parties of the social contract were understood to share.

With humanistic reform, a type of quasi- or proto-psychological knowledge became a crucial component in exercising relations of punishment. This was true both of the demonstrative role of the punishment – which needed to suit the crime and the details of its intent – and of the pedagogic strategy adopted in the attempt to eradicate the roots of the crime. (I say 'quasi-' or 'proto-psychological' because the notion of psychology has as yet to receive the discursive and institutional weight that follows its establishment as a human science discipline). Proto-psychological concepts, issues of the criminal's will, their tendencies, dispositions, their recurring habits hence take on an increasing prominence. From this point, decisions regarding the penalty for a crime had to consider that which hitherto had not been considered: the individual defendant themselves, their intrinsic nature and way of life, their *attitude of mind*. '[P]sychological knowledge', notes Foucault 'take[s] over the role of casuistic jurisprudence' (1977a, p. 99). The intimation here is clear: one of the first instrumental appearances of 'psychological' knowledge occurs in a way that is intimately tied to the exercising of power.

Not only did the parallel classification of crimes and punishments now become a necessity – a guard against arbitrary sentencing – considerable attention was also paid to techniques of individualizing correction. This push towards individualization, this customizing of power so as to make the best correctional fit led to powerful collateral processes of objectification. Objectification, the generation of a particular problem-categories – as in the case of delinquents, perverts, homosexuals, hysterics, and so on – through which experts might know and predict the behaviours of deviant subjects, would become an crucial component of disciplinarity. The delinquent, to take one of Foucault's (1977a) examples, becomes a species to be studied and understood, an object to be *known*; the act of the crime something to be exhaustively coded and classified. For proper intervention to be made, as Dreyfus and Rabinow (1982) insist, the object (be it criminal or crime) needed to be fixed as an individual entity and *known in great detail*. It is thus in the realm of punishment that the first step towards a study of 'man', and 'his' behaviour and social environment is taken, and taken in the direction of a science of society that would treat 'men' as objects.

Knowledge – and for the most part a proto-psychological knowledge – thus came to operate as a crucial component of power. The complex reciprocity of these terms, the fact that power and knowledge came to be exercised in mutually reinforcing ways, stands as one of the cardinal features of disciplinary power. Foucault (1977a) couples these terms, and speaks of *power-knowledge,* thus emphasizing the fact of their dynamic co-investment. This practical inseparability results in new modes of control in which the growth of human science knowledge, the innovation of intricate disciplinary technologies and the production of the psychological subject all came to be linked. The epistemic and political coherence of the individual subject – a somatic singularity that comes increasingly to coincide with those effects of power projected upon them – takes on a new substantiality, a substantiality that in future years will prove impossible to refute.

Returning though to a focus on the era of humanist reform, it is no longer primarily the body, but souls or minds that increasingly come to be seen as the primary targets of correction, targets treated not through the means of pain, but through signs and representations. The scene is thus set for disciplinarity: emphases on humanization, individualization, objectification (in linked categories of deviant actions and deviant subjects) and, perhaps most vital of all, the quasi-psychological focus on problematic souls or minds, all pave the way for a revolution in the procedures and logic of punishment. I should emphasize here that for Foucault such humanizing initiatives served not so much to establish a more equitable system, but rather to create a better economy of the power to punish. Rather than punishing less, these initiatives punished better; power is rendered more effective, more constant, while at the same time its political and economic costs are diminished. Foucault's argument thus is that humanism, in all its guises, has 'enabled the insertion of power ever more deeply into the social body' (1977a, p. 82). This rationale of humanity would go on to prove indispensable to the spread of disciplinary procedures. Each of its discrete technologies would come to take this, the principle and value of the human, and of *the humane,* as their governing principle; it is from this formidable moral and philosophical basis that disciplinary practices would come to dispense a variety of curative, rehabilitative and punitive operations.

Discussion 1.1: The prime values of humanism

Given the prominence of humanism in what follows, and indeed, the vehemence of Foucault's critique thereof, it proves useful to sketch out a series of key ideas that inform this cluster of values. The most important assumption here is perhaps that of an essential distinctive individuality marking each human subject as a unique being. This is matched with a commitment to the idea that such individuals should themselves be the focus and principle of knowledge. Put differently, not only should such distinctive individuals prove to be primary subjects of the generation of knowledge, we should also endeavour to grapple with the world as it is understood and received by unique subjects. Along with such a belief in the epistemic and psychological primacy of the individual, we find attached a series of personal rights and prerogatives (the notion of 'human rights' springs immediately to mind as an example) automatically accorded to each subject. Core here also is the notion of consciousness, that is, a commitment to the substantive existence of a kind human interiority or psychology, a belief in the faculties of introspection and personal judgement and a prioritization of the 'freedoms of subjectivity' thus afforded. The notion of freedom makes for a third factor. Individual human liberty is treated as sacrosanct, as an inherent and universal value; hence the proliferation of invectives against forms of constraint or repression that are taken to impede intrinsic human goodness.

Foucault (1977f) argues that each of these basic commitments is linked to an inviolable principle. The notion of individuality becomes connected to the truism of Human Right, for example, just as the idea of consciousness comes to be attached to the rule of Human Truth, and the notion of freedom coupled to a sense of the goodness of Human Destiny. A variety of related ideals – justice, equality and community – play their part in this assemblage of values. Foucault's (1977f) point is not to suggest we eschew all such notions in preference rather of an antithetical set of values, but rather to question how each of these rationalities of the human come to operate as formidable routes, rationales and justifications for measures of power.

Moreover, claims Foucault, we see in such 'prime values' of humanism the promise of a kind of agency, be it that of human rights, the power of truth, or the prerogatives of liberty, despite that such relations of authority and control are centred elsewhere, in systems of power beyond the level of the subject. We have thus a series of 'pseudo-sovereignties' – in which psychological formulations, along the lines of notions of consciousness, play a key role – a series of apparent inviolable human prerogatives which appear to be centred upon the human subject but which generally operate at a different level of benefit and efficacy: that of modern disciplinary systems of power.

A structure and focus for an emerging sciences of 'man'

By the beginning of the nineteenth century, claims Foucault, one is able to trace the blueprint of a particular power-relation, that is, a structure of correction as exemplified in relations between criminals and those in a position to discipline them. We see in this blueprint a simultaneous arrangement of subjectification (i.e. the production of individualizing knowledges about singular subjects) and objectification, the pattern of which would come to be duplicated throughout the human science disciplines. Knowledge, as a modality of power, thus grew in two different directions at the same time, producing profiles of troublesome persons and related behaviours, while simultaneously refining the techniques of measurement, comparison and surveillance able to render such problematic individuals in ever more detail. This led to a circular relation: objectifying knowledge came to persuasively sanction prescriptions of expert intervention, which, in turn, intensified the procedures of individualization able to capture the problematic facets of deviant subjects.

The epistemic growth of the psychological is nurtured by a particular need – overcoming the failure of previous regimes to adequately co-ordinate somatic singularities with subjectifying effects of power. There is a pertinent role for psychological explanation here: joining such bodily singularities to individualizing types of knowing which tie this subject to a network of power-effects. To draw on an example of Foucault's, every criminal offence came to carry with it the legitimate suspicion of insanity or anomaly. Every sentence, more than being a legal decision that laid down punishment, came to bear with it 'an assessment of normality and a technical prescription for a possible normalization' (Foucault, 1977a, pp. 20–21). The point is not simply to suggest that there can be no psychology without disciplinarity, although this itself is a defensible claim. One should emphasize, in addition, that the prominence and accelerated growth of the discipline, the very fact that it has not been confined to the narrow parameters of a purely *academic* exercise, must be seen in the context of a new culture of power that massively prioritizes the docility of individual subjects.

What is signalled here is not only an explosion of conceptual sophistication in penal matters; there is also a flourishing in the industry of punishment. Parallel 'judges' multiplied around legal judgement; psychiatrists, criminologists and educationalists all came to play a part in informing such judgements. With the benefit of such expertise, legal judgements could now entail far more detailed prescriptions of corrective efficacy than was the case in mere sentencing. Not only did this mean that the assertion of guilt turned into a strange 'scientifico-juridical complex', it also led to an incredible expansion, that of 'a whole field of recent objects, a whole new system of truth...a mass of roles hitherto unknown in the exercise of human justice' (1977a, p. 23). The great 'corpus of knowledge, techniques, and "scientific" discourses' thus formed – here the real focus of *Discipline and Punish* – 'becomes entangled with the practice of power to punish' (p. 23).

What is of interest to Foucault is not only the switch of objects in punishment – a change from a primary focus on bodies or represent-ations to a prioritization of *the individuality* of offenders – neither is it simply the move from the logics of retribution or didactic moral insight to the privileging of a more holistic type of correction, modification, or rehabilitation. Foucault's interest also lies with the technological innovations – instruments and mechanisms of supervision, surveillance, calibration and modification – that accompany these shifts. It is in these ways, the bringing into view of a new object, the development of new types of intervention, innovations of technological means – all of which enabled a far more reliable and exacting correspondence of the somatic singularity with particular subject- and object-effects of power – that a new mode of psychological power-knowledge finds its feet. It is invaluable in

> inscribing offences in the field of objects susceptible of scientific knowledge ... [in] provid[ing] the mechanisms of legal punishment with a justifiable hold ... not only on offences, but on individuals; not only on what they do, but also on what they are, will be, may be.
>   (Foucault, 1977a, p. 18).

Discussion 1.2: The examination and psychologico-moral discourse

The examination is a mode of disciplinary scrutiny that Foucault studies in consid-erable detail. As Davidson (2003) remarks, 'The examination is that form of knowledge and power that gives rise to the "human sciences" '(p. xxiii). Why the examination represents such a crucial advance in the technology of power is that it functions as a measure of *potentiality*. The examination is not limited to the past, to the single deviant or criminal act that has already taken place, it is a measure of the subject's *future capability*, their prospective dangerousness to society. While legal punishment, strictly speaking, bears on an act, the broader array of punitive techniques needs to bring into focus the details of an entire life: the subject must be linked to their offence in a variety of ways, by reference to questions of instincts, drives, tendencies, their character and so on (Foucault, 2003b). The role of psychological knowledge is obviously crucial in this respect. An infraction is not to be understood simply in terms of prohibited relations between individuals, but with reference to 'the opening up of [the] domain ... of thought, its irregular and spontaneous flow ... its images, its memories, its perceptions ... impressions' (2003b, p. 189).

We have then, as Foucault (1977a, 2003b) is at pains to point out, a transfer in the point of application of punishment, from *the offence* defined by the law to *criminality* evaluated from the perspective of psychologico-moral discourse. Foucault speaks of a type of doubling here, referring to a whole series of psychological objectifications that it becomes possible to presuppose on the basis of the act itself – 'psychological immaturity', 'a poorly structured personality' and so on – objectifications which, in a tautological way, enable authorities of punishment to move from the singular act to a set of relatively stable traits, from an isolated instance of conduct to personality dispositions and inevitable tendencies, from the offence *to an entire way of being*. In this way, Foucault (2003b) remarks that the individual resembles his crime before he has committed it.

Initially psychological and legal discourses sit uncomfortably alongside one another; the disciplinary specificity of each is potentially compromised by this combination. Nevertheless, this juxtaposition, no matter how awkward, is ultimately functional – its inconsistencies must not be resolved. No one institutional intervention will do – if it is a case of merely psychological engagement with the 'individual to be corrected' then only therapeutic prescriptions will result; if it is exclusively a matter of legal intervention, then the authorities would be limited to the act itself in considering punishment. It is hence the corrective force of *the combination* of these two institutions that Foucault prioritizes. This collaboration ensures a far more extensive permeation of power through the problematic subject: not just their past but their future, not simply an isolated act but their entire life; indeed, the full ambit of their dangerous potentiality is thus all made accessible to legal consideration.

II

The advent of disciplinarity

The era of disciplinary power extended certain priorities of the reformist era – the rationale of humanism, the principles of objectifying and subjectifying knowledge and the proto-psychological notion of the soul – while definitively breaking with others. Perhaps most notably, whereas both the ritual of torture in sovereignty and the punitive demonstrations of the reformers had been ostentatious public spectacles, the new schema of punishment would require secrecy, and more than this, an autonomy of its own specialized means. In a reversal of the situation in sovereign power, where power itself was put on display and the masses were kept in the shadows, disciplinarity would be exercised through a kind of practical invisibility. Its mechanisms and rituals would remain out of sight even as it exposed its subjects to conditions of permanent surveillance, to saturating regimes of visibility. The need to glean a modicum of a quasi-psychological knowledge is a motivating factor in this regard – disciplinary systems strive to make surveillance an integral part of their schedules of production and control such that the individual subject can be precisely and comparatively observed. An additional factor is apparent here, namely subjects' consciousness of their own visibility; this is a type of self-awareness that makes such subjects – in a classic phrase of Foucault's – 'themselves assume responsibility for the constraints of power'(1977a, p. 187).

In an extension of an initiative of humanist reform, the era of disciplinarity ensures an increasing professionalization and fragmentation in the field of rehabilitative expertise. The rights of punishment and modification in disciplinary times are entrusted only to the most suitable authorities and specialists. Even though the disciplinary subject is more active than ever before – inscribing in themselves, as we shall see, 'a power relation in which they are the principle of their own subjection' (1977a, p. 203) – this internal functioning of power is matched and supported by the spread of a new kind of professional agent of power, the teacher, the doctor, the analyst and the counsellor. Such authorities of discipline – authorities that would come to require specialist training, competence in particular procedures of practice and proficiency in technical vernaculars – occupied a unique position between juridical authority and society. So, as in the case of the 'individual reclamation' of convicts, such authorities would exert a curative force, a 'concerted orthopaedy...isolated both from the social body and juridical power' (1977a, p. 130). What Foucault wishes to impress upon us is not simply that advancements in the treatment of deviance are accompanied by a parallel growth in the powers of disciplinary agents, he wants to emphasize how a whole new and autonomous domain of treatments, corrections and specializations is opened up: a zone of moral orthopaedic enterprises comes to be engendered in this way.

Technologies of discipline

Rather than the asymmetrical coupling of levy-expenditure in sovereignty – in which the sovereign, by divine right, imposes a levy on products, harvests and goods – there is no dualism in disciplinarity, no threat of war. The sovereign's fragmentary hold of power, conditioned promises of violence and the need of a continual reactivation of ceremonial affirmation cannot compete with the total hold of disciplinarity, which 'tends to be an exhaustive capture of the individual's body, actions, time and behaviour' (Foucault, 2006, p. 46). We have, in disciplinarity, not a periodic seizure of goods or services, but a continuous seizure of the body and of the soul. As Foucault makes clear in *Psychiatric Power*, the efficacy of the control exercised by the disciplinary agent is contingent on a basic requirement: their power must be a total power, undisturbed by any third party and able to entirely envelop its subject. Foucault (2006) provides examples of what such an autonomy of control might mean in institution of the asylum. Here it was necessary not only to cede the psychiatrist final authority in issues of treatment, but to completely divorce the patient from their usual familial and societal domain, delivering them thus into a domain of absolute order where the force of a controlled and intensified reality would become the principle of cure.

A given agency of disciplinary power would thus need to maintain 'its own functioning, its own rules, its own techniques, its own knowledge; it needed be able to fix its own norms and decide its own results' (Foucault, 1977a, p. 129). Furthermore, a relation of secrecy, particularly in relation to matters of technique, also proved to be an imperative. This is not just about a protected society of discourse, not just about procedures of initiation into particular domains of disciplinary practice; it is about consolidating the full force of a set of modificatory dynamics, which must be understood in combination and only appropriately applied within certain protocols of practice, within the regulated confines of a specialist discourse.

Discussion 1.3: An analytics of the psychotherapeutic: Auditory surveillance, subjectivizing talk

It benefits our discussion here to make recourse to a series of observations drawn from a study of the operation of power in psychodynamic psychotherapy (Hook, 2001, 2002). The study in question was not explicitly Foucauldian in design; it did not aim merely to apply or verify Foucault's concepts of power, nor did it adhere to a (historical) methodological frame derived from his work. Nevertheless, it may be taken as an example of a Foucauldian analytics inasmuch as it eschews existing theoretical explanations and seeks to grasp the minutia of a potentially productive form of power as implemented at a micro- (or face-to-face) level. Likewise, although the implicit focus was on how power flows from a psychotherapist to a patient, the analysis – aware of Foucault's injunction against exclusively repressive or top-down models of power – did not assume this to be the only possible direction of therapeutic power. Furthermore, by attempting to discern the instrumentality of psychotherapeutic power – that is, by isolating a set of regularly occurring tactics, mechanisms and skills of practice, each of which may be given as an example of therapeutic efficacy – the study was open to the idea that the psychotherapist's repertoire of interventions could be likened to a human technology. The methodological template for the study was drawn from a constructionist revision of Glaser and Strauss's (1967) grounded theory approach (Pidgeon, 1996; Pidgeon and Henwood, 1996). Some of the results of the study:

- The first category of psychotherapeutic power identified in the analysis, perhaps unexpectedly, was *listening*. Although apparently a passive and facilitative process, and while no doubt therapeutically operative, the results of the study suggested that therapeutic listening might be considered an exertive behaviour, indeed, *a purposeful and goal-directed form of action* performed by the therapist. The performance of therapeutic listening functioned as a form of inspection, a means of observing, *assessing, monitoring*; an *auditory surveillance* designed to elicit and sustain patient disclosure. Such performances seemed instrumental not only in eliciting compromising personal expositions, but in encouraging a confessional mode of exposition. Furthermore, like the doctor's gaze, that yields knowledge and prescriptions of intervention on the basis of visual analysis (an imposition of discourse through the act of perception), so the attentive ear of the psychotherapist brought with it a series of psychological knowledges and interpretations, an evaluative or diagnostic frame of intelligibility (the imposition of discourse through the act of listening).
- A second apparent category of psychotherapeutic power concerned the 'therapeutic talking' of patients. At its most basic, this therapeutic talk of patients was that of a personal narrative – self-attending, self-focused, often strongly problem-focused – of which the patient was both the author and the protagonist. In this way, such narratives were marked by a fundamental self-attention, a strong '*I*' foundation and pivot. A central component of these 'talkings' was thus the provision of a reflexive attitude, which, while often vague at first, soon grew in strength. This self-focus was in many ways the outcome, of the 'inactive intervention' of therapists, who, through explicit refutation of typical conversational structures, and through the strong prioritization of patient subjectivity, came to discretely promote and encourage this self-attending orientation. As therapy progressed, therapists 'slimmed down' their contributions to a bare minimum, enforced a guarded and tactical form of conversational detachment such that the therapeutic narrative came very close to resembling the therapeutic *monologue* of the self-monitoring patient. The placement of such a premium on the development of patient subjectivity and reflexivity was a strong feature of all analysed protocols. The patient's *self* increasingly became a level of awareness

and a surface of intervention that needed to be prioritized; it became the vessel through which therapists could repeatedly appeal to the patient's agency, to *their* own personal prerogative and responsibility, to change.

Disciplinary technologies hence advance, as Dreyfus and Rabinow (1982) affirm, by taking what were essentially *political* problems (problems of control), removing them from the domain of political discourse, recasting them in the neutral language of science and transforming them into *technical* problems for the sole attention of specialists and experts. The constructive role that power has played in the constitution of such problem domains is thus elided in the humanist attention to the refinement of various specialist technical domains of treatment. The aptness of the terminological choice of 'technology' needs to be emphasized, despite, as Rose (1991) points out, being a term not often associated with the human. We may thus understand 'human technologies' as discrete sets of practicable knowledge and expertise, as disciplinary arrays of technical skills and analytical procedures. Such technologies necessarily entail their own professional vocabularies – discrete languages of codification and control – along with their own regimes of treatment and analysis. They remain in the hands of select experts; they maintain a particular form of change or betterment as their stated objective; their implementation, as Foucault frequently emphasizes, brings about an increase in the productivity, the efficiency and the effectiveness of given relations of power.

The physicality of the soul

The physicality of the disciplinable body so neglected by humanist reformers returns in disciplinarity as power's first point of purchase, as *the* surface upon which discipline would focus its powers, at least, as Miller (1994) notes, in the earliest stages of its deployment. What is at stake here is not the destruction of the body as in sovereignty, but rather the analytical reconfiguration of the body's productive components – the body that is a point of concentration for a set of generative interventions – the body broken down, rearranged and then put to work. Foucault reiterates the vital importance of the body to disciplinarity when he asserts that 'the historical moment of the disciplines was born when an art of the human body was born' (1977a, p. 137).

This emphasis on physicality remains paramount; the material insistence of this form of power cannot be dissolved in a focus on representation, language or discourse. It is possible, in this respect, to read *Discipline and Punish* sub-textually, as Foucault taking issue with prevailing intellectual fashions at the time he was writing. Rather than the activities of variants of (post)structuralism – deconstructive, linguistic, semiotic modes of analysis which remain preoccupied with signification, meaning and textuality – he is insisting that we be aware of the complex relations between materially or bodily exercised regimes of power and the representational or discursive orders that spring from them. The growth and articulation of bodily implemented force-relations – ultimately the terminal forms of any regime of political control – must prove a focal point in the analysis of power.

A remarkable refinement of punitive measures follows on from this advance in power. Not only is it the case that penal intervention must operate in essentially corrective, orthopaedic or therapeutic modes, it is also the case that each corrective involvement is tantamount to an investment, which must yield a return, an increase in the subject's productivity. Each rehabilitative measure needs result in a proportional increase of obedience and productivity; docility *and* aptitude are always to be generated together.

The importance of the body as power's target must not, however, be viewed as total: power needs be traced upon the body *precisely in order to create a more lasting order of soul-effects*. A crucial factor in the renewed bodily focus of disciplinarity is found precisely in the imperative of fastening the 'somatic singularity' of distinguishable subjects to partic-ular subjectifying effects. As I have tried to emphasize in the epigraph of this chapter: 'It is because the body has been "subjectified"...that the subject function has been fixed on it, because it has been *psychologized* and *normalized*... [that] the individual appeared, about which one can speak, hold discourses, and attempt to found sciences' (Foucault, 2006, p. 56, my emphasis).

One can hence appreciate how a localizing, subjectifying function might be said to lie behind a variety of bodily procedures and oper-ations for Foucault, how his seemingly excessive preoccupation with the physicality of control must be linked to the formation of a series of related and contingent subject-positions and psychology-effects. The disciplinary body is the body fixed in regimes of time, space and prac-tice, the body as it is trained, educated, rehabilitated and healed. This is a surface of power that needs be viewed in conjunction with the correlate soul-effects that are thus established, a 'body-function' that must be grasped in the terms of the self-regulations, the norms, the expanding set of personalized lessons and self-knowledge – the psychology-effects in short – that it subsequently comes to emit, to recreate, to maintain and implement over itself – this is the body in discipline.

We must be careful to do justice to this double focus of disciplinarity, indeed, to the complexity of the relation between these two factors, neither of which can be collapsed into the other. The 'psychology-effects' of a soul are contingent on a certain positioning; there are no 'soul-effects' without the location of somatic singularities in space and time, in the absence, that is to say, of specific measures of productivity, or protocols of surveillance; programmes of disciplinary betterment require a physical locus of scrutiny. Similarly, power must have a soul, a series of lasting 'subject-effects', otherwise, interventions on the body are transient, impermanent and lasting only as long as their initial physical implementations. Something tantamount to a learning must take place here; these effects need to be inscribed, I would argue, in the form of *a psychological series*, that is, as an automated, self-implementing pattern or 'identity', as a regime of self-awareness and observation in which a series of physical procedures and attentions are taken up and *integrated* at a different level, at a level of power that cannot be reduced to isolated bodily attentions, to a mere physicality of practice.[1] Foucault's position is that the refined, technically elaborated return to the body in disciplinarity yields a 'surplus power'. This surplus power gives reality to the notion and indeed, *the experience* of the soul:

> It would be wrong to say that the soul is a illusion, or an ideological effect. On the contrary, it exists, it has a reality, it is produced permanently around, on, within the body by a functioning of a power that is exercised on those punished ... on those one supervises, trains and corrects ... This is the historical reality of this soul, which unlike the soul represented by Christian theology, is not born in sin and subject to punishment, but is born rather out of methods of punishment, supervision and constraint. This real, non-corporeal soul is not a substance; it is the element in which are articulated the effects of a certain type of power and the reference of a certain type of knowledge, the machinery by which the power relations give rise to a possible corpus of knowledge, and knowledge extends and reinforces the effects of this power.
>
> (1977a, p. 29)

The soul here is the reality-reference upon various concepts and domains of analysis have been constructed; notions of self, psyche, ego, personality, personal subjectivity and consciousness number amongst these constructions. Upon such a variously re-articulated 'soul' 'have been built scientific techniques and the discourses and moral claims of humanism' (1977a, p. 30). It is this soul – at once both a structure of reflexivity, an observant, regulative and judgemental relation to oneself, and an endlessly extended, varied product of psychological-knowledge production – which Foucault proclaims, in a reversal of Plato's formula, is now the prison of the body.

Discussion 1.4: Auto-therapeutic roles, voluntary confession and self-evaluation

A striking feature of the study of power in psychodynamic psychotherapy (Hook, 2001) was the degree to which its clients took on strongly proactive 'patient' roles and behaviours. Clients themselves were willing, at times, to impose direction and to offer explicit forms of self-evaluation, this was particularly surprising given the apparent lack of a more directive or didactic role on the part of the therapist.

An interesting correlate to the therapeutic objective of patient 'subjectivization' identified above (Discussion 1.3) was the development of an 'auto-therapeutic' narrative on the part of patients who appeared to take up both (patient and therapist) roles in their therapeutic talk. By taking on the speaking function of the therapist – a function determined not only by content, but by its structuring and enquiring qualities – clients started to conduct the facilitative, explorative and 'knowing self' therapeutic tasks in a relatively autonomous manner. The talk of patients in late stages of therapy was increasingly 'auto-therapeutic'; patients were not only able to adopt self-listening and self-assessing roles, but were also able to query and question themselves, to explore their own narratives, to attain new levels of self-realization. Patients were thus able to 'work upon themselves', to lead their own narrative with questions of a self-probing nature, even to provide self-assessments, self-recommendations and personal suggestions of reparative behaviour.

One of the most difficult factors to account for in the analysis of psychodynamic interchanges was the tendency of patients to willingly confess to wrongful or questionable actions or inclinations. The regularity of this phenomenon across protocols was unexpected, as was the seemingly *automatic* nature of 'confession-making'. Cross-case comparisons between published examples of psychodynamic dialogue suggested that such confessional forms of 'externalising conscience' were a characterizing feature of effective therapy. This near unfailing tendency of patients to disclose shameful or potentially deviant acts and then implicitly relate them to current norms of what might be considered normal/abnormal, deviant/ordinary, soon came to represent something of an explanatory crisis. Part of the frequency of this phenomenon seemed to lie in the fact that patients generally assumed that the therapeutic environment was an evaluative space, a place where their 'normality' would be assessed, even if only implicitly. Often this assumption accounted for patients' anxieties about entering psychotherapy, and therapists often expended a good deal of effort trying to persuade patients to the contrary. An early speculation on the part of the researcher was that the 'surveillance' of therapeutic listening, together with the patients' understandings and expectations of the role of the clinical environment, incurred within patients an implicit leaning towards normative values and standards.

It soon became apparent, in attempting to understand the 'normative evaluations' set in play by the context and operations of the psychotherapy, that it was necessary to look beyond the overt role of the therapist. The results of the analysis did not suggest that therapists forced or demanded confession of their patients, any more than they suggested that therapists were, in any obvious manner, guardians of normal or socio-politically dominant values. What became clear as the analysis proceeded was that the power of the therapist was apparent not only in the terms of what they actively *did*, but perhaps more importantly, in terms of what they managed to set in motion by *not doing*. In other words, as became a key hypothesis throughout the latter phases of analysis, the provision of a non-judgemental and non-moralizing attitude appeared to elicit far more private, far more 'confessional', secretive or 'well-guarded' material than an overtly evaluative attitude would have. The very suspension of normalizing or moralizing attitudes on the part of the psychotherapist appeared to induce such attitudes on the part of patients. What this seemed to imply was that certain therapeutic functions – for example, the location of self relative to a set of normative values – could be 'displaced functions' taken up by patients themselves precisely because such expected functions were not more explicitly implemented by the role of the therapists.

Despite the indirect or 'inactive' influence of therapists, the factor of patients' own initiative still proved crucial in understanding such self-evaluative procedures. One of the basic conclusions of the study was that *psychodynamic psychotherapy functioned to elicit, with impressive regularity and through non-directed or explicit means, a powerful impetus to normative self-evaluations on the part of patients.* The effectiveness of this process stemmed from the fact that it was the patient that ultimately took forward the implementing of such therapeutic initiatives, despite that such initiatives may initially have been induced as a function of the psychotherapeutic context. A second conclusion reached: *the process of locating self relative to social norms quickly became an automatic and self-implemented task for patients within psychodynamic treatment.*

Soul production

Never reducible to regimes of bodily treatment, disciplinary technologies dispense a thoroughly *moral* orthopaedics, a mode of treatment that has spread through an incredible range of institutions. The production of souls is, as one might put it, diffusely managed, not only through relations of supervision and constraint, but also through healings, treatments, medical interventions and the advice of experts. The logic of humanism is a crucial ally here; disciplinary power no longer operates through diminishing its subjects or extracting life. It is, by contrast, a force of betterment; it cultivates the productive capacity of individuals, it heals, it advances, it nurtures that which is most human. Furthermore, as McNay (1994) makes clear, the mechanisms of discipline are characterized by an extraordinary mobility; as a set of techniques rather than a solid institution, such technologies can be easily applied across a number of settings without being reduced to them. Employed by pre-existing authorities or apparatuses, used in conjunction with other modes of power without supplanting them, disciplinary techniques permit an endless variety of adaptations and customizations. This ease of incorporation has meant, historically, that their use has spread from prisons to other disciplinary sectors, to other administrations of control, other places of reform, rehabilitation and education. A diversity of souls is thus subject to varying applications of disciplinarity.

Foucault thus leaves little room for doubt regarding psychology's complicity in the procedures and agendas of disciplinarity. The parapsychological entity of the soul, whose design, deployment and management is central to disciplinary control, is both the subject- and object-effect of psychology. Psychology's subject, 'knowable man [sic] (soul, individuality, the self, consciousness, conduct…), is the object-effect of this analytic-investment, of this domination-observation' (Foucault, 1977a, p. 305). In disciplinarity then we have something like a constitutive condition, a historical surface of emergence, which also sets in place certain fundamental epistemic and discursive prerequisites, for the appearance and ongoing substantiation of psychological individuality. It lends a profound personal, scientific and political reality to this object-/subject-effect of individuality, and not only to it, but to a spiralling variety of psychological constructs and procedures predicated upon it (see Rose, 1991, 1996a for a more detailed discussion of the discursive explosion of psychological individuality). As Nikolas Rose (1991) indeed argues, psychological theories have proved indispensable in the birth and spread of the concept of the self, just as psychological methods have been at the forefront in the elaboration of the practices and techniques through which modern selves are understood, developed and remodelled.

Moral reflexive capacity: The psychological functioning of power?

It is worth pausing for a moment here to query Foucault's conceptualization of the 'soul-effects' of disciplinarity. The soul here is 'a trace of power', something possessed of a forceful reality, even if its underlying basis is little more than that of a reflexive loop, a folding whereby induced effects of power lend a functional reality to an internalized set of capacities. One might ask: Has Foucault selected the most appropriate analytic term in this respect? A secular audience might find this loose ontology of the soul somewhat puzzling within the frame of an ostensibly materialist analysis, especially given that a variety of less theologically loaded terms might prove better descriptors of this point of folding, this reflexive function of power within the subject.[2]

There are however a series of good reasons for the use of this term. For one, Foucault is able to emphasize that disciplinarity is not to be reduced to an 'anatomo-politics' (Deleuze's term, 1988) of bodily manipulations; his choice of term makes apparent that there is a surplus 'subject-effect' which results from the practicing of such measures. As intimated above, the reflexive (or, as we might put it, *psychologized*) subject, brought about through a disciplinary mode of subjectification, might be taken to be discipline's most impressive product. The term also has the benefit of joining a variety of contemporary moral orthopaedic measures ('tracings') to earlier attempts within the apparatuses of Christianity to establish a regime of moral authority tantamount to a governing of souls (as Foucault (2003b) discusses in *Abnormal*). Consequently, this concept is able to link problems of sinfulness with those of deviance and abnormality, a regime of spiritual ordering with a regime of normal conduct.

Then again, surely there are a variety of terms that may more sharply evoke something of this productive moral reflexive capacity, this 'I-relation' as it is posed in terms of normalizing disciplinary power? Might there not be terms derived from theoretical psychology that could compliment and extend Foucault's conceptualization? One such term, suggested by Judith Butler, is the psychoanalytic notion of the ego-ideal. In the psyche, she points out, the subject's ideal corresponds to the ego-ideal; this is the benchmark by which the ego is measured by the superego, the 'position' of the subject within the symbolic realm, 'the norm that installs the subject within language and hence within available schemes of cultural intelligibility' (1997, p. 86). Foucault's 'soul' would thus seem to have much in common with this ego-ideal, especially in reference to its evaluative, self-regulatory dimension. In the light of this comparison, we may ask of Foucault whether his notion of the 'soul' – so carefully distinguished from the subject of Christian theology, so warily de-psychologized – is not exactly a metaphor for the psychological functioning of power?

The charge that might be taken up against Foucault here is that he uses a deliberately non-psychological term to describe what is, to all intents and purposes, a *psychological* process – that operation whereby effects of power are enfolded into the subject, subjectified along the lines of reflexive identification. Van Zyl (1990) puts this bluntly: the novelty of Foucault's account, she claims, is to demonstrate that modern power is essentially psychological in form. We are seemingly presented here with a prime example of a political process taking a psychological route. Put differently, is this not a case of the 'subject-function' working within the dynamics of recognition and self-awareness, operating precisely on the basis of a consciousness of how one appears to the others of power? More to the point, is this not an overtly political process whose complex mechanisms might be best mapped and traced with recourse to psychological concepts?

Despite the descriptive utility of a psychological lexicon, these are precisely the terms that Foucault cannot make reference to. Not only would they flatten the historical range of his analysis – committing to a psychological vocabulary inevitably means the projection of contemporary systems of knowledge onto the past – such a frame of reference would also, presumably, align Foucault to a meta-psychology, a view of consciousness, which brings a variety of humanist concepts and epistemological assumptions in its wake. More obviously, this would require the utilization of a conceptual repertoire drawn from exactly the style of thinking and the mode of power that he is attempting to historicize and to critique. We might take this as a case in point of the ability of individualizing psychological humanism to over-ride other factors of explanation. This is an apolitical and anti-historicist discourse, a language of comprehension in which the factors of political influence and the manifold constructions and subjectifications of disciplinarity are easily naturalized and given permanent residence, as one might put it, within the universal structures of psychological individuality.

Discussion 1.5: Internal routings: A different analytics of power

Despite that one may fully concur with Foucault's choice to avoid descriptive reference to psychological discourse, it does seem difficult to deny that power is internalized in disciplinarity, that it is lent something akin to a 'psychological' dimension and mode of operation. A degree of strategic reference to the language of 'the psychological' might thus profit the analysis of power. There are at least two routes that one might take in this respect, depending on the degree to which one is willing to risk reifying a series of psychological constructs. One might opt to perform a careful tracking of how psychological concepts produce particularized souls, aiming thus to link the jargon and methods of particular schools of psychology to the emergence of different selves and distinctive technologies of betterment (as is the case in the work of Rose 1991, 1996a). Maintaining the genealogist's distance from the concepts that are being re-historicized, there can, from the standpoint of this approach, be no descriptive recourse to psychological language.

On the other hand, one might take the route of the examination of 'the psychic life of power' in Judith Butler's (1997) phrase, a perspective willing to grant the fact of the disciplinary production of individuality, a perspective that insists that subjectification precedes psychological subjectivity. I should be emphatic here: this is an approach which refutes the ascendancy of psychologistic modes of explanation that presume an individual psychological subject *existing prior to* the constitutive forces of political, material and bodily factors. Nevertheless such an approach is still eager to query the vicissitudes of an internalized power, to press ahead with questions concerning the psychic mechanisms of *subjectivization*, mechanisms that are perhaps not adequately apprehended without a strategic reference to psychoanalytic discourse in particular.

Properties of the soul

What are the principles of disciplinarity made possible by virtue of the soul-effects it is able to produce? Perhaps the easiest of these to anticipate is the principle of *potentiality*, of *pre-emptive intervention*. Unlike the interventions of sovereignty which are intermittent, violent and which are typically obliged to take the form of *response*, disciplinary power has 'an inherent tendency to intervene at the same level as what is happening, at the point where the virtual is becoming real' (Foucault, 2006, p. 51). In other words, disciplinary interventions are, ideally, pre-emptive, occurring prior to the translation of intention into act. The soul is the explanatory vehicle that can best enable the necessary order of predictions; the soul moreover, and the chain of associated psychological terms through which it must now be understood, is precisely the point at which the virtual in the subject can be apprehended before it is realized. The 'psychological' is thus a privileged domain of intervention: 'Disciplinary power must intervene somehow... before the body, the action, or the discourse, at the level of what is potential, disposition, will, at the level of the soul' (p. 52).

A second principle of disciplinarity stemming from its ability to produce and affect souls is the principle of *differential individualization*. Here the double focus of disciplinarity emphasized until now – of bodily intervention and the linked generation of related types of subjecthood – needs to be complimented by a third pole, an epistemological one. It is likewise important here to link surveillance and knowledge technologies, to make clear that the disciplinary state of permanent surveillance that Foucault so frequently reiterates must not be reduced merely to a condition of ongoing visibility. Indeed, what is implied here is not simply an optical regime of control, but the imperative to produce *maximal and penetrating knowledges about the subject*. For Foucault then, individuality was introduced into the field of knowledge just as power fixed individuality in the field of observation. The drive to surveillance 'proceeds towards a centralized individuation' whose main support and instrument is documentation 'and a continuous punitive action on potential behaviour that behind the body itself, projects something like a psyche' (2006, p. 52). Disciplinary mechanisms are able, in other words, via extractions, productions of knowledge, to produce a kind of singularity of the individual. This individualizing capacity, crucially, works differentially; rather than bending its subjects into a single uniform mass, disciplinarity cultivates differences, it separates and distinguishes, it makes unique.

The endless generation of knowledge upon which the progressive individualization of disciplinarity depends is itself reliant on continuous assessment, on the accumulated details of personal histories, the 'volunteered' expositions of confessions. Hence the time devoted in Foucault's genealogical analyses to the 'fixing of the individual in writing', to the testing, measuring and examining of subjects, to the comparative analytical scrutiny that makes the many dimensions of individuality possible. This generative aspect cannot be overestimated: it is this productive influence, the precise observation, calibration and comparison of disciplinary activity, this isolation 'to the point of necessary single units' that succeeds in training 'the confused, useless, moving multitude of individual elements' (1977a, p. 170). It is the combined efforts of such technologies which, Foucault claims, forms modern individuals who are simultaneously the outcomes of disciplinary knowledge and its recursive 'instrument-effects'.

To be sure, the monitoring, recording and surveillance technologies of such individualization procedures must enable a psychological 'thickening' of the subject. They must ensure an expanding basis of subjectification, that is, a broadening and deepening of something akin to a 'psychological core' of subjectivity that will allow for potentially endless elaboration. Foucault has in mind here not only the generation of scores and rankings (intelligence quotients, diagnoses of pathology, assessments of personality, aptitude), or just the future and historical orientation of such enquiries (the enabling of predictions, the re-visitation of personal histories). He is alluding also to a proliferating set of accounts, references and assessments which means that the psychological individuality produced is both potentially endless (it always permits further re-articulation) and endlessly distinctive (disciplinary individuals must be unique, always discernable from one another). Paradoxically then, an advance in the technological apparatuses of individualization guarantees a proportionate increase in the complexity of human psychology; the greater the sophistication of such instruments, the more intricate the psychology of analysed individuals. Disciplinary methods of knowing the human psyche thus relate to it – to borrow from Butchart (1998) – 'not as a means of discovery against an object waiting to be known, but as a productive power towards an object that is also its effect' (p. ix).

It is important, I think, to emphasize that we are not concerned here merely with the *discursive* production of individual difference, or simply with the marking of somatic singularities into separable units of control. We are concerned also with the fact that these processes lend an unprecedented depth and dimension to subjectivity. These comments help me in drawing an important distinction – one deserving of more attention in Foucault – between subjectification and subjectivization. In terms of the former, I have in mind – as discussed above – the promotion and elaboration of a thoroughly individualizing set of knowledges about the singular subject who is effectively normalized and psychologized as a result. The knock-on effect of such practices, the feeding back of such knowledges to a subject who comes to apply such notions, to understand and experience themselves in the terms of subjectification, is what I understand as *subjectivization*. This, in short, is the difference between being accorded a subject-position, and what it might mean to take on, to assume or personalize, such a subject-position.[3]

Individualization, in all of the capacities discussed above – as a function of subjectification and subjectivization alike – remains for Foucault a contingent phenomenon, an after-effect of the functioning of modern disciplinary power. He is insistent in this respect: 'we cannot say that the individual pre-exists the subject-function, the projection of a psyche, or the normalising agency... [I]t is only insofar as the somatic singularity became the bearer of the subject-function through disciplinary mechanisms that the individual appeared within a political system' (2006, p. 56).

There is a third important principle made possible by the fact that disciplinarity takes the soul as its prime object-effect. This is the ideal of the *saturating influence* of disciplinary technologies. The maxim of disciplinarity that one might devise in this respect is that of the 'exhaustive capture' (Foucault's term) of the body, actions and time of subjects. This ideal overlaps with another: the hope that disciplinary interventions might become self-perpetuating. The operation of discipline must look forward, as Foucault puts it, to the time when only virtual supervision and instruction will be necessary, to the moment when discipline *keeps going by itself,* when its acquired skills become self-implementing, automatic, indeed autonomous functions of the subject. This, incidentally, is one of the reasons that Foucault is often reticent to limit the focus of his analyses to the obvious agents of discipline; if disciplinary interventions are designed such that ultimately they can work independently then 'the person in charge... its director, is not so much an individual as a function that is exercised' (2006, p. 55). In short then, the best means of guaranteeing the degree of total influence that disciplinary technologies aim at is if they become self-implementing systems, functions of a subject's reflexive relation to self.

These adjoined principles of self-perpetuating activation and endless, complete influence make for an overwhelming priority of disciplinarity power. All of its mechanisms aim to ensure that subjects adopt certain fundamentally reflexive, self-monitoring and self-assessing relations to *themselves.* This self-observing, self-policing quality is famously exemplified by Foucault in the figure of the Panopticon: a watchtower structure at the centre of a prison that grants warders a permanent visibility over the inmates, despite that the prisoners themselves cannot see if they are being watched; such a structure assures that the prisoners know at all times that they *may* be under surveillance. Prisoners, or 'souls' more generally, thus come to operate as if under constant surveillance, taking on the role of controlling observer upon themselves. Power-relations are thus implemented and reproduced from an internal position. Subjects can thus be said to 'inscribe in themselves a power relation in which *they* are the principle of their own subjection' (Foucault, 1977a, p. 203).

As argued above, disciplinary technology cannot be reduced to a set of corporeal measures, to a mere materiality of power. Disciplinarity is, as Foucault repeatedly emphasizes, more flexible, more profound and more permanent in effect than earlier technologies of power. This, I would argue, is partly due to the fact that such modalities of power entail, as a fundamental condition of possibility, something tantamount to a series of psychological operations – the 'soul-effects' of power, in Foucault's terms, as detailed above – operations, which I would suggest are not adequately understood merely as *after-effects* of power. Importantly, what is illustrated by the example of the Panopticon is not just a relation of self- consciousness, or a relation of continuous self-awareness, what is also implied is a complex relation of virtuality to action, of the present to the future, a relation, in other words, of self to potentiality.[4] What I am trying to suggest here is that in each of these relations we are dealing with a relatively complex process; in each case we are faced with a form of repetition and learning, indeed, with a type of *mediation* that cannot be completely explained by structural factors alone.[5] The psychological component to disciplinarity is an issue I will return to.

Discussion 1.6: Producing problems: The co-construction of therapeutic meanings and affects

Returning to the study of psychotherapeutic power, a crucial category of the analysis proved to be the role of the therapist in directing and encouraging client verbalization. Therapeutic talking was guided and facilitated by therapists in a number of ways; producing an impetus to disclosure proved a clear priority of psychodynamic clinical technique. A variety of minimal contributions on the part of therapists – encouraging gestures, supportive expressions, affirmative sighs and vocalizations – facilitated the flow and direction of the emerging clinical narrative. Therapists' use of tactical questioning was perhaps the most prominent of such mechanisms, although a variety of associated techniques, prompting, redirecting, reflecting and 'echoing sentiments' were also a part of a clear clinical directive – that of locating a substantive 'problem focus' for the therapy. The use of an unbroken sequence of related questions, the building-up of a 'momentum of enquiry' was particularly useful in this respect, in probing for evidence of emotional disturbance, dysfunctional traits or indications of underlying psycho-pathology, as in the following example:

Th. Are you completely satisfied with your present life and adjustment?
Pt. Yes . . .
Pt. No.
Th. Your mother thinks you ought to get treatment. I wonder why?
Pt. I don't know.
Th. Maybe you're angry that she sent you here if you don't need treatment.?

Pt. I'm not angry.

Th. Mmm. *(pause)* But there must be some area in which you aren't completely happy.

Pt. Well... *(pause)*

Th. Are you satisfied with the way everything is going in every area of your life?

Pt. *(pause)* No, not exactly.

Th. Mm hmmm. *(pause)*

Pt. It's that I don't go out much, not much, I don't go out with boys... (Wolberg, 1977, p. 463).

Questioning techniques of this sort added significantly to the ability of therapy to *construct* rather than merely *discover* the patient's presenting problems. Indirect patterns of enquiry proved in this respect to be commonplace in unearthing emotional disturbances and in consolidating a 'problem focus'. In probing for aetiological and diagnostic information, therapists very seldom asked outright or blunt questions, but approached the characterization of problem areas more obliquely, picking up on certain trends and tendencies already mentioned by the patient. Various other forms of indirection, such as juxtaposing placid and provocative enquiries or obvious with investigative questions, were also apparent. In this respect, the researcher found it difficult to determine whether psychotherapy was a probing process of discovery, or, a 'calling into being' of certain working problems. Two conclusions evolved out of of the study: (1) psychodynamic therapeutic dialogue is notably 'problem-centric', it must, as a condition of its own ongoing viability, establish a substantive problem area, a strong working focus for the therapy, (2) psychodynamic therapists have at their disposal a variety of questioning tactics and rhetorical manoeuvres, which, taken in conjunction with their ability to reconstruct patients' own accounts of certain events, provides them with a broad constructive latitude within the therapy.

Certainly a fundamental factor in the therapists' warrant to make 'problem attributions' was the ambiguity and instability of reconstructed emotions. The general murkiness of emotions, and the ease with which they are distorted, meant that emotional constructions featured prominently in therapists' attempts to probe for, and then solidify, psychological problems within patients. A series of related tactics were identified in this respect, most prominent of which were the identification of ostensibly latent emotions and the amplification of emotional descriptions. Whether by offering a pinpointing emotional term that carried a powerful resonance, or by the introduction of a *new* term with a different weighting of meaning altogether, therapists appeared to play an active role in co-constructing the meaning of the therapeutic narrative. A brief example illustrates such an emotional attribution and its role in the construction of a larger presenting problem:

Pt. Dr... sent me here for these headaches. He thinks it might be mental. I don't think it was necessary for me to come.

Th. Do you believe it's mental?

Pt. Good Lord, No! I think I need something that will ease this pain, I've been told a million different things of what's wrong.

Th. Perhaps you are right. It may be entirely physical. What examinations have you had?

Pt. *(Patient details the consultations he has had, maintaining his position that his problem is physiological).*

Th. Then it perhaps made you angry to come here?

Pt. I was angry. Not now though. Do you think you can help this headache?

Th. I'm not sure; but if you tell me about the trouble from the beginning, I might be able to help you with any emotional factors that can stir up a headache.

Pt. How can that do it? I know I have been emotional about it (Wolberg, 1977, p. 398).

Noteworthy here is the way in which the therapist has asserted an emotional problem, if not as the fundamental complaint, then as undeniably attached to the presenting complaint. An additional conclusion of the research : psychodynamic therapists maintain a *powerful latitude in identifying the strength and appropriateness of feelings within patients; this latitude of emotional attributions plays a crucial part in ascertaining – indeed, in constructing – a working problem focus for the therapy.*

Confessional subjects

Despite the emphasis in *Discipline and Punish* on the optics of power, one should bear in mind that not all information-gathering instruments of disciplinarity take on an exclusively visual form. Elsewhere Foucault (1978a, 2003b) focuses more on verbal modes of assessment, indeed, on that longstanding mechanism of power whereby subjects are induced to speak the secret of their guilt, to make apparent those sins, fantasies and hidden pleasures that disciplinary agents would not otherwise be able to access. The confessional, in short, must be seen as a crucial disciplinary instrument. As Butchart advances, this is a technique of intimate surveillance 'through which the most confidential ideas and private secrets ... are amplified to audibility and lifted into socio-medical spaces as devices of disciplinary subjectification' (1997, p. 107). Butchart views psychology and its associated 'culture of disclosure' as playing a particularly important role here: departing from the predominant point of access in medical technologies – the gaze, the visual inspection of the sick body – psychology came to prioritize a disciplinary technology of *listening*.

Foucault's historical engagements with confessional procedures are not limited to the era of disciplinary modernity. He makes it clear – that voluntary confessing requires the participation of a soliciting agent who is always more than a silent interlocutor. Despite a range of differing historical utilizations, Foucault (1987) isolates a basic logic underlying the mechanism of confession: the more one speaks, the freer one will be. The impetus to confess is hence always wrapped up in goals of salvation, liberation and well-being.

It is worth emphasizing that confessional processes do not simply extend or translate the visual tactics of surveillance into an auditory form. There is an additional factor at work here; the reflexivity involved in this type of self-exposition involves an extended turning of self into discourse, a kind of narrative subjectivization not necessarily present in the dynamics of Panoptic surveillance. This is a mode of power in which the speaking subject is also the subject of their own speaking. (The ambiguities of this term serves us well here: the speaking subject is both *subject to* their own speaking and the *subject of* what is spoken about, in addition to being that subject *that is speaking* – a reflexive looping of self into discourse that epitomizes the subjectivization discussed above.) Rose (1996a) helpfully expands on this point: the therapeutic perform-ance of depicting one's self in speech, the truthful speaking of who one is and what one does, is, at the same time, an identifying and a subjec-tifying act. It both constructs a self in terms of given norms of identity, and it scaffolds this self within an array of authoritative constructs that it will need make recourse to in order to attain insight, understandings of the self. Twin processes of subjectification and subjectivization are thus in evidence. In the technical form of therapeutic processes, says Rose (1996a), the confessing subject is identified: 'The "I" that speaks is to be ... identical with the "I" whose feelings, wishes, anxieties, and fears are articulated' (p. 96). Here then, the folding of disciplinary subjects locked into reflexive patterns of self-production and self-awareness, is the process of subjectivization. Of course, in the very act of becoming the subject of one's own narrative, one becomes 'attached to the work of constructing an identity'; by being affiliated to an identity project one is 'bound to the language and norms of psychological expertise' (Rose, p. 96), a positioning I understand as subjectification.

Not only do procedures of confession extend professionally prescribed categories and projects of identity, not only are they actively subjectiv-izing, but they also consolidate and extend the authority of experts. As

Foucault (1978a) insists, it is increasingly only through the mediation of expert interpreters – doctors, psychologists, psychiatrists and counsellors – that the individual can properly know the truth of their own internal nature.

Normalization and the generation of deviance

Having emphasized the generalizability of disciplinary technologies, along with the fact of the 'psychological depth' that they are able to generate, it seems important now to ask what overarching objective might unite all these diverse systems of discipline. What is it that all moral orthopaedic projects lean towards; what might be the ultimate goal of a culture of disciplinarity? For Foucault, all interventions of this sort are taken to share the same basic objective: normalization, that is, the generation of productive, docile self-regulatory souls and the progressive elimination of social and psychological irregularities. It helps here to make a clarification: what is produced in the corrective attentions of disciplinarity is not only the singular differentiation of individual subjects, but also a broad comparative domain – a mass of scores, indicators and averages – which forms the backdrop against which individualization becomes possible. Put differently, individualization takes place in relation to the production of populations – the individual and the population are for Foucault coterminous inventions – it is beneath the production of a disciplined population (be it one of learning, labour, psychological wellness, obedience) that one finds such effects of individualizing fragmentation. What I have referred to as progressive individualization necessarily involves recourse to a set of classifications, to hierarchical arrangements, categorizations of ability, skill and deficiency: an 'accumulation of documents ... the organization of comparative fields' makes it possible 'to classify ... categories, determine averages, fix norms' (Foucault, 1977a, p. 190).

Comparisons of this sort, hierarchies of performance and ability – never merely taxonomical, always arranged according to the valued productivities of a given society – quickly become a preoccupation of modern disciplinary culture. The fact of such a comparative basis, epitomized for Foucault in sets of *norms*, helped to unify the operations of disciplinary power, enabling a kind of 'normalizing judgement' to spread throughout society. Importantly, a *norm* is not to be understood as the mid-point of a binary division of pass/fail, but rather as a point on a graduated scale. Not only do we have an average then rather than a steadfast rule – an average which gives us the zero-degree of conformity, the minimum score beneath which everything is punishable – we have also a quantitative hierarchization of the 'nature' of individuals, a 'value-giving' measure 'of individuals themselves ... their potentialities' (1977a, p. 181). This is a type of evaluation which ensures that attributions of abnormality are not only socially significant and forceful, but essential-izing also, inseparably tied to what individuals *are*.

It is the nature of the norm that every aspect of 'the human' can be assigned a value in relation to an average position. This means that not only a far greater variety of human qualities can now be assessed – not all human capacities are easily accorded a 'right'/'wrong' judge-ment; all may be accorded a description relative to a norm – it also means that a wider system of gradation is enabled than is the case in crude binary distinctions. This leads to a downward saturation of disciplinary values, a spectrum of penalization as one might put it, an 'infra-penalty' wherever more capillary aspects of social and psychological life become potentially punishable. Foucault (1977a) is unequi-vocal: the slightest deviances from a norm are now punishable; every quality, every facet of human life is now locked into a perpetual rela-tion to the standard of the norm. Why this is such a boost to the culture of disciplinarity is that a mass of behaviours previously diffi-cult to isolate and punish – time-wasting, low rates of productivity, minor disobediences of dress, speech and posture – now became highly visible and punishable. Disciplinary mechanisms thus could be said to secrete 'a "penalty of the norm", which is irreducible in its prin-ciples and functioning to the traditional penality of the law' (1977a, p. 183).

In speaking of normalization then we are not merely concerned with the homogenizing effects of certain standards of conformity, or the moralizing implication of the hierarchical judgement of subjects *them-selves*, we are concerned also with a set of exclusionary principles, with the production of deviance. This stands to reason: the normalizing assessments of disciplinarity permit not only for degrees of upward achievement, they also make possible a set of roles and categories of under-performance. There were no deserters, observes Foucault (2006), prior to the historical emergence of disciplined armies. Similarly, the designation of the 'feeble-minded' only appears once a system of school discipline is implemented. Rather than viewing disciplinary institutions as the result of various problematic individuals within society who need to be cared for and protected, such individuals should rather be seen as the outcome of the installation of disciplinary systems. Disciplinarity hence may be said to engender its own deviance, thereby enabling and justifying its own recovery systems. There is a kind of reverse logic at work here: technologies of normalization are themselves integral to the systematic classification and control of anomalies within a given social body. It is true thus to say that normalizing power succeeds all the more for its shortcoming. The real goal of rehabilitative and punitive endeavours is thus not the complete elimination of deviances and transgressions, but rather the tactical use, the strategic deployment of such problems as a means of justification for ever greater schedules of control and surveillance.

Discussion 1.7: Family as switch-point between disciplinarity and sovereignty

Although the 'psy-disciplines' clearly play a key role in the schema of disciplinary power, we need to understand their role in relation to an additional factor, the familial domain. By making reference to the structures of family power, Foucault is able to offer an account of what he terms the 'Psy-function'. Doing so proves crucial, it enables Foucault to speak of how certain measures of sovereign power *persist* within disciplinary eras – something for which he is often criticized for neglecting in his alleged overgeneralization of the model of disciplinarity (McNay, 1994).

The operation of power within the family, he insists, resembles more closely the shape of sovereignty than that of disciplinarity, a fact which is particularly true of how individualization works within family structures. As opposed to the anonymity of power and an ascending order of individualization, the patriarchal family exhibits a kind of 'maximum individualization' on the part of the father, whom, as a bearer of certain prerogatives and familial rights, returns us to the pattern of sovereign authority. This is not to suggest that the family is an outmoded 'diagram' of power and that its particular arrangements will simply be assimilated by disciplinary measures. It neither suggests that supervision and surveillance or related disciplinary mechanisms cannot be applied here; it is not the case that the micro-sovereignty of the family works against disciplinarity. Quite to the contrary, this non-disciplinary unit makes an invaluable contribution to the viability of disciplinary systems. It is precisely because arrangements and structures of family power cannot be wholly assimilated into disciplinarity, precisely this 'standing outside' which means that they can ensure the system's solidity.

Families, Foucault (2006) suggests, are instrumental in allocating appropriate disciplinary locations to subjects; registration in disciplinary institutions is largely the function of the family's system of commitments, obligations and responsibilities. There is a degree of reciprocation here: family structures are required to take up the discards of disciplinary interventions; disciplinary institutions are called upon to fulfil neglected familial responsibilities – types of nurturance, moral care and guidance – when the family unit has collapsed. As a result, Foucault treats the family as a relay between disciplinary sites; it is a point of transfer that connects the school and the military, the military and the workforce, an intersection between educational and clinical locations. When individuals are not adequately bettered by a given disciplinary system, they need to be redirected; the family is the non-disciplinary switch-point that makes such redirection of interventions possible.

Foucault maintains that it is precisely because arrangements and structures of family power cannot be wholly assimilated into disciplinarity that they can ensure the system's solidity. The heterogeneity between these two domains makes for a functional complimentarity of forces: the only way disciplinary mechanisms are able to 'get a grip with maximum intensity and effectiveness' on individuals is if 'this cell of sovereignty constituted by the family' works alongside them (2006, p. 84). This exchange enables power not only because it disrupts the predictability of monotonous disciplinary mechanisms, but also makes possible a series of novel and spontaneous effects like the emergence of the 'Psy-function'. Foucault has in mind here those aspects of the psy-disciplines which make their appearance precisely as disciplinary substitutes for the family. The 'Psy-function' must thus be understood as the quasi-familial mode of disciplinarity, a refamiliarization of deviant individuals.

The new order of individualization

What Foucault's genealogical history of punishment enables us to do is to link the disciplinary sites of the school, the clinic, the consulting room back to far starker disciplinary contexts: the prison, the factory floor, the military base. The normalizing objectives of the human science disciplines – whether we have in mind here psychology, criminology, social work, pedagogy or psychiatry – have no doubt taken on far more refined, far more sophisticated and distinctive technological means, but at basis they share the same recuperative, rehabilitative or corrective objectives as these austere disciplinary institutions. The fundamental task of all disciplinary interventions is to rehabilitate subject-positions that have failed, to (re)institute normalizing souls that entail a fundamental structure of observant, reflexive and judgemental relations to self; hence, Foucault's (1977a) reference to psychologists as 'servants of moral orthopaedics'.

As Dreyfus and Rabinow (1982) insist, it is in this attempt to eliminate behavioural social and psychological deviances of all sort that various disciplinary technologies have broken fundamentally with neither the aim nor the methods of the prison. Furthermore, as long as the human sciences continue the search for deep human truths – an order of meaning they claim to have privileged access to – and so long as they insist that the truths they uncover lie outside the sphere of power, 'these sciences remain vital strategies of disciplinary power, despite the privileged externality they would pretend' (1982, p. 181).

The disciplinary institutions that Foucault mentions are not, of course, one and the same; there are evident differences of practice and crucial analytical distinctions separating the asylum from the barracks, the classroom from the hospital. Foucault's point is not that these zones of moral orthopaedic intervention are simply homogenous; it is rather the case that in the carceral network of the disciplinary city, these institutions work together. Many of the newer disciplinary modalities may be said to do something tantamount to the work of prisons, albeit in a preventative capacity:

> In the subtle gradation of the apparatuses of discipline....the prison does not at all represent the unleashing of a different kind of power... [b]etween the latest institution of 'rehabilitation', where one is taken to avoid prison, and the prison....the difference is (and must be) scarcely perceptible... Prison continues, on those who are entrusted to it, a work begun elsewhere, which the whole of society pursues on each individual through innumerable mechanisms of discipline.
>
> (1977a, pp. 302–303)

All of the human sciences and their associated practices emerged first from disciplinary institutions, from the context of relations of power through practices of exclusion, surveillance, objectification and confinement, and are as such, according to Foucault (1977a), rightly called 'disciplines'. From such institutional bases they have grown to new levels of refinement and specialization, attaining their own rules of evidence, modes of recruitment and exclusion, refined their own particular practices, their own unique languages of control and have done so within the template of a general disciplinary technology. The psychological, pedagogical, sociological and criminological disciplines continue to contribute to the innovation and extension of new techniques of power. Institutions like the asylum, the school, the clinic and the therapeutic arena have functioned, and still do – to paraphrase Best and Kellner (1991) – as laboratories for experimentation with correctional techniques and the acquisition of knowledge for social control. These institutions are the places where individuals – with increasingly detailed case-studies and personal histories – are simultaneously the level of observation and intervention, the font of ever further knowledge production, and the raw materials of a continually expanding and continually refined systems of diagnosis and categorization.

As discussed earlier, individualization was once apparent only where the rights of sovereignty were exercised, only as one approached the spectacular apex of a pyramidal hierarchy of power. This was an ascending order of individualization, a mode of individualization which remained 'below the threshold of description' for the vast majority. In disciplinary eras, individualization is, in Foucault's terms, compulsory and descending; all subjects are caught in its regimes of visibility and normalization. Those on whom power is most concentrated are the most individualized, while power itself tends to anonymity. Individualization, perhaps the strongest instrument-effect of these goals, is hence characterized – paraphrasing Foucault (1977a) – by an inversion of invisibility into an intensive gaze of power, a gaze, furthermore, that subjects often come to bear upon themselves. Turning this insight to the 'psycho' sciences, Foucault contends

> All the sciences, analyses or practices employing the root 'psycho-' have their origin in this historical reversal of the procedures of individualization. The moment that saw the transition of historico-ritual mechanisms for the formation of individuality to the scientifico-disciplinary mechanisms, when the normal took over from the ancestral and measurement from status... that [was the] moment when a new technology of power... [came to be] implemented.
>
> (Foucault, 1977a, p. 193)

It is at this moment that power and knowledge become inseparably intertwined; it is here that the vast proliferation of knowledge on individuals and populations coincides with the continuous flourishing of new areas of research *and* the concurrent refinement of disciplinary techniques for observing and transforming subjects. So, to reiterate, for Foucault (1977a), it has only been through the variously articulated marriages of observation and technique, of investigation and intervention, knowledge and method, that the 'man' – that is, the distinctive psychological individual – of modern humanism, the subject/object of social science was born in the first place. Subsequently, one might assert that this psychological individual is inseparable from the forces of disciplinary technology that come to have an increasing bearing upon their nature, on what they most essentially are, will, may be or eventually become.

Discussion 1.8: Crossings of family and discipline: The 'Psy-function'

The Psy-function performs a disciplining role on those who could not be otherwise disciplined. As a result it soon achieves a place at the top order of disciplinary mechanisms; it becomes, indeed, something akin to a supra-disciplinary element which would be relied upon when other disciplinary measures fail:

> The Psy-function became both the discourse and the control of all the disciplinary systems. The Psy-function was . . . the establishment of all other schemas for the individualization, normalization, and subjection of individuals within disciplinary systems.
>
> (Foucault, 2006, p. 86)

The psy-disciplines have a privileged role to play here, their applied and clinical forms of treatment make them an exemplary case of para-familial disciplinarity. Indeed, psychology, inasmuch as it may be thought of as representative of the Psy-function, could be said to be the master component within the operations of disciplinary culture, a fact which tells us something about the authority and popularity of psychological discourse and expertise today. This alerts us to the importance of a Foucauldian analytics for how we think 'the psychological'. Moreover, it signals the role of this mode of power-knowledge in investigations of even the broadest structures and dynamics of social power. Foucault is emphatic in this respect:

> psychological discourse, the psychological institution, and psychological man [*sic*] are connected up *to this* [Psy] *function*. Psychology as institution, as body of the individual, and as discourse will endlessly control the disciplinary apparatuses on the one hand, and, on the other, refer back to familial sovereignty as the authority of truth.
>
> (Foucault, 2006, p. 87, emphasis added)

Hence for Foucault the importance of interrogations of the psychology of work, of psycho-pedagogy, psycho-criminology and the discourse of psychopathology as applied in clinical and penal institutions. We have here an enquiring sensibility, a predicative, explanatory and interventionist set of discourses – which is to say nothing of their diagnostic and prognostic components – always interwoven with their own dynamics of practice, with regimes of subjectivization (i.e. the 'identity-function' of such discourses).

If we are to adequately understand this game of cross-reference between sovereignty and disciplinarity we need to appreciate more than the *familial content* of much psychological discourse. The potency of the Psy-function is not simply about the prevalence of 'family discourse' as a favoured trope within clinical settings. The potency of the Psy-function is about how an aspect of familial sovereignty may be introduced into disciplinarity, and about how aspects of disciplinarity are introduced into a 'familial' environment. In the case of the former, we might provide the example of the clinical authority of psychotherapists, their prerogative to set boundaries and the rules of intervention; in the case of the latter, we might give thought to how effects of discipline are pursued within the setting of a significant emotional bond, the fact of transference dynamics explored to corrective ends. Foucault makes a series of passing remarks in this respect, eluding to 'the investment of the family function in the clinic [as] . . . the effective agency of the cure', as well as to the 'activation of canonical types of family feelings' (2006, p. 113), and to the pseudo-familial organization of the therapeutic domain.

While it is true that the particular modality of power that Foucault is driving at here probably receives its definitive treatment in the notion of the pastorate (see Chapter 6), it may help to provide a brief illustration in the form of the 'contrabond'. The contrabond, as discussed by Van Zyl (2003), stands in contrast both to the legalistic binding of formal, *contractual relations*, and to the affective commitments that underwrite the sentimental attachments of *bonds*. A contrabond – as evidenced in relations between teachers and students, doctors and patients and therapists and clients – represents something of a compromise-formation between these incompatible types of relation, an awkward balancing of facets of both. This mode of relation means that it is acceptable to provide emotional guidance and to feel real bonds of attachment within the frame of a professional relationship. It also means, of course, that instances may occur when the agent of discipline is obliged to compromise this affective bond by higher order contractual requirements (the rule of confidentiality can be broken, for example, if a crime could be prevented). Such formalized affective relations provide an elementary example of the Psy-function; this is an example which illustrates the inter-penetration of disciplinarity and sovereignty, and which also emphasizes the extension of certain professional psychological instruments (or modes of relating) into diverse types of disciplinary life.

III

The elision of the psychological

In what has gone above, I have called attention to Foucault's conceptualization of the 'souls' of disciplinary power and intimated that tactical reference to a variety of psychological concepts may usefully aid us in tracking the operations of power. I also suggested that the disciplinary folding of subjects – the induction of powerful subjectifying relations of self-reflexivity and self-scrutiny – was not the outcome exclusively of structural factors. My position was that the effects of 'panopticism' – continual self-surveillance, linkings of self to potentiality, the relation of one's present situation to the possibility future action, and indeed, the learning of certain self-implementing patterns of behaviours – assumed a degree of psychological complexity, and more than this, an order of psychological mediation not fully accounted for by reference to ingenious material, spatial, bodily technologies and arrangements of power.

It is not the case, I would argue, that disciplinary power is the exclusive principle, the over-riding factor, in the production of psychological individuality; it cannot completely account for the 'individuality effects' of sharply distinguished subjects. Nor is it the case that disciplinary power alone is able to induce the set of psychological reality-effects suggested by Foucault (the need, for example, to establish a reference point of reflexivity, to consolidate an individual 'identity' designating one's action and location relative to power or to assume a consciousness of the norm, of what about the self needs to be improved upon). What also needs to be considered here is the possibility that disciplinary power involves a number of *psychological prerequisites* for the achievement of disciplinary effects; such preconditions may stand as absolute preconditions that need to be attained if this particular power of 'mind over mind' is to be at all possible.

One might, in this respect, make recourse to the materialist, constructivist psychology of Lev Vygotsky. This is a psychology which is highly sensitive to the determining role of material, structural, socio-historical and cultural factors; such factors are taken to influence not only the contents, but also the historically specific structures of mental processing (Rieber and Robinson, 2004; Vygotsky, 1978; Wertsch, 1985). Vygotskian psychology places particular emphasis on a series of 'higher mental functions', which it understands as the unique capacity of human cognition. Focussed attention and deliberate symbolic memory make for two cases in point, two examples of an order of cognition that Vygotsky opposes to the reactive attention and associative memory evidenced in lower mental functioning. Symbolic rather than purely motor-sensory thought makes for the crucial distinction here. Turning our attentions for the moment to Vygotsky's developmental account: by assuming the 'psychological tools' of language and other related symbolic, numerical and mnemonic skills – all of which are, importantly, culturally mediated – means that the child makes massive strides in learning, in the ability to take on a reflexive relation to one's own history and prospective future. Similarly crucial is the fact of a consolidated 'I' function which allows for a set of *culturally mediated* rather than predominantly instinctual responses to environmental stimuli. The lower mental functioning of animals is understood as lacking the same degree of self-consciousness, the same ability to learn, to internalize cultural and symbolic instruments, to assimilate and respond to the standards and norms of a given society.

Although I am unable to discuss here in any detail the further differences and prospective overlaps between Foucault and Vygotsky – a point of intersection which may represent one of the most promising means of extending Foucault into psychology, and psychology into Foucault – my point with this brief allusion to Vygotsky is clear. Higher mental functioning is what ensures that human subjects can be disciplined in a symbolic and self-automating manner; indeed, this is what ensures that humans can be disciplined at a qualitatively different level (entailing developed properties of self-reflexivity and mediation) than animals.[6] The psychological apparatus constituted by this set of higher mental functions presumably thus counts as something of a condition of possibility for panopticism to function.

Here we might link to an argument Judith Butler advances apropos the body in Foucault. On occasion, she notes, Foucault wants to refute the possibility of a body that is not produced through power-relations, yet 'sometimes his explanations require a body to maintain a materiality ontologically distinct from the power relations that take it as a site of investment' (1997, pp. 89–90). This is a problem which also seems to apply to the production of psychological subjectivity in Foucault. The fact of the latter's production through the activation of power begs the question of what factor of the subject, what capacity or faculty first does the receiving; what is it, we might ask, that manages the integration of an awareness of power *into a reflexive turn* which becomes subject-instituting? So the question that Butler asks of the body in Foucault – does it require 'a materiality ontologically distinct from the power relations that take it as a site of investment' – we might adapt and ask of Foucault's treatment of psychological subjectivity.[7] Does Foucault's understanding require a mode of psychological operation that is ontologically distinct from the humanist, individualizing and subjectivizing psychology he takes issue with? If so, does this not weaken his claims about the formation of individualizing psychological subjectivity? If this is the case, if Foucault's argument is obliged, at points, to assume an implicitly psychological type of explanation, then it seems he lets through the back-door aspects of the individual psychological subjectivity his account of disciplinarity appears to account for.

What of the psychological exceeds the soul?

Surely there is a possibility – by virtue of the complexity of the psychological operations mentioned above – that power is differently received by subjects, that it is differentially assimilated and relayed? Despite Foucault's argument about the differential production of individuality, it would seem that not all subjects are inducted as self-monitoring individuals in precisely the same way. There must be some variation in the induction of reflexivity; how else do we understand relations of resistance as arising in some subjects rather than others? Is it not the case then that we need make allowance for variation in how power is initially *affected*, and surely such variation can be explained not merely as an outcome of a productive power, but as, at least in part, a result of a differential 'uptake', a differential response *in subjects* to its effecting aims? If we overlook this factor, we surely overlook also the possibility of meaningful resistance. Peter Dews offers apposite critique in this respect. Foucault, he says, offers a haunting evocation of the solitude and powerlessness of the individual in contemporary society. However,

> his peremptory equation of subjectification and subjection erases the distinction between the enforcement of compliance with a determinate set of norms, and the formation of a reflexive consciousness which may subsequently be directed in a critical manner against the existing system of norms.
>
> (Dews, 1984, p. 95)

Although articulated in very different theoretical terms, Butler (1997) expresses a similar concern. She draws attention to the psychoanalytic distinction between subject and psyche. Whatever resists the normative demand by which subjects are instituted, she argues – we have discussed above the ego-ideal as the ideal against which the ego is measured – necessarily remains unconscious. For this reason, the psyche, which includes the unconscious, must be seen as very different from the subject:

> the psyche is precisely what exceeds the imprisoning effects of the discursive demand to inhabit a coherent identity... the psyche is what resists the regularization that Foucault ascribes to normalizing discourses.
>
> (p. 86)

Essentially then, as Butler puts it, the psyche is what exceeds and confounds the injunctions of normalization. Foucault thus appears to have reduced the notion of the psyche to the operations of an externally framing and normalizing ideal. Foucault again seems to miss something here; once more there is something to psychological subjectivity – understood in broad meta-theoretical terms – that exceeds his account. Furthermore, to quote Butler (1997) once again:

> Does the reduction of the psychoanalytically rich notion of the psyche to that of the imprisoning soul eliminate the possibility of resistance to normalization and to subject formation, a resistance that emerges precisely from the incommensurability between the psyche and the subject...?
>
> (p. 87)

Dews' (1984) problem is thus recast: if Foucault understands all of the psyche as an imprisoning effect in the service of normalization, then how might one account for resistance to normalization?[8]

A vacuum of psychological individuality?

This talk of resistance and individualization raises a related issue: the fact that power can be differentially assimilated and relayed seems to imply that there is a modicum of individual difference – and indeed, a modicum of psychological activity – that pre-exists power and is not wholly produced by it. To take this question up in a different way, if there is no significant psychological individuality *prior to* that affected by power, then surely all subjects would react in a largely similar way to the implementation of its effects? Or, in the terms of a related issue: if the various factors of differing life experience – to slip for a moment into psychological discourse – are not enough to produce meaningful individual psychological differences between subjects, then why should the factors of disciplinary power be sufficient?

The Foucauldian response here is of course to insist that it is precisely through the productions of discipline that individual differences become historically apparent and operational; it is not so much a case of the *differential assimilation* of power as of the differentiation *produced by* power. Furthermore, to continue a Foucauldian retort, the above questions make a category error: they confuse the *practical implementation and conceptualization of a political type of psychological individualization* with *the experiencings, the 'lived psychologization' of subjects on the other.* The former makes for an appropriate Foucauldian problematic; the latter does not. (One might in fact view this as a failure to properly distinguish between processes of *subjectification* and *subjectivization*.) A distinction of this sort, to continue, would seemingly account for the fact that a degree of psychological difference appears to *precede* the fact of its disciplinary activation, when in fact the latter is the historical condition of possibility for the former.[9]

As useful as such retorts are, they beg a series of further questions. First, if we understand Foucault's notions of disciplinary individualization and psychologization in a total way – thus not buying into the distinction between different orders of individualization posed above – then are we not led to presume a degree of 'psychological' homogenization prior to power? In other words, does Foucault's argument about the diverse and differential production of psychological individualism not oblige him to presume that subjects were undifferentiated and unindividualized before its effects, and not simply conceptually, but practically also? Not just the case then that no 'psychological' differences had been rendered in the terms of human science knowledge as political categories, but that none existed at all, even within the relatively non-conceptual terms of everyday interaction or experience. This implies that 'pre-individualized individuals' – if the term is to be excused – were tantamount to automatons, devoid of any significant psychological life, wholly undifferentiated in psychological functioning. This, clearly, is a difficult position to defend. It is easier, surely, to concede that there is some prior differentiation between subjects – of experiencings or 'lived psychologization' as opposed to the conceptual, political and historical category of 'psychological individualism' that Foucault has in mind. This though would seem to be exactly the kind of distinction that Foucault cannot make inasmuch as it leaves in place a kind of 'natural' psychology prior to or outside of those disciplinary systems, which Foucault claims effectively brings them into being. Drawing such a distinction seems to rely on a prior separation between the political and the subjective, a fact which would mean that Foucault ends up relying on a kind of residual psychologism.

Butler's problem with Foucault – the idea that productive power both *wholly produces* its objects and yet sometimes occupies a position ontologically distinct from its powers of production – manifests also as an epistemological concern. What, we might ask, is it that underwrites certain constructions, which makes them effective and possible? So, assuming that power *is* able to produce difference and individualization – politically, conceptually, practically or otherwise – out of an undifferentiated mass, then what is its principle of 'differential implementation'; on what basis are some individuals brought into a heightened relations of disciplinary surveillance and inspection rather than others? Not all subjects can be equally constructed as savants, as delinquents, as prodigies, surely? Put differently, what is it that 'allows' the subject to be constructed in some ways and not others? What is it that initially grabs power's attention; what is the 'reality-reference' that allows the productive energies of disciplinarity some verifiable basis upon which to construct a significant subject-category of power-knowledge? The 'somatic singularity' that comes before the constructions of disciplinarity is not, presumably, simply hollow?

Ardent Foucauldians might object at this point that we have not as yet stepped outside of the discourse of individualizing psychological humanism to appreciate the point at hand. These subject-objects of power, the savant, the imbecile, the delinquent, the pervert and so on do not exist outside the parameters of disciplinary knowledge, or beyond its network of technologies, institutions and interventions. The existence of such subject-categories as robust categories is, after all, precisely testimony to the productive force of such disciplinary apparatuses. This is a crucial point: it directs our attention to the energies of consolidation and amplification whereby particular object- and subject-categories are continuously reiterated, made practicable, formed into robust categories of expertise and treatment. However, we may concede as much while still objecting that this argument begs the question: what was it that power latched onto, its initial point of interest, the subsequent target of its productive energies? The paradox of this situation is that surely some quality, some degree of *differentiability* is a precondition for disciplinary/discursive productions of difference.[10] Or to develop a parallel argument: surely some degree of psychological operation must be a precondition for the disciplinary functioning (or panopticism) that is said to produce aspects of psychological individualism (consciousness of self before power and so on). The instantaneous subjectivization of panopticism surely begs the question of the platforms in place, the psychological operations and structures that guarantee that aims of power are adequately assimilated? If this is the case, if there is a minimal degree of psychological functioning in place, then Foucault leaves open the possibility for a type of individual difference that disciplinarity *builds upon*, animates and extends, rather than producing from the ground up in a total or originating manner.[11]

Discussion 1.9: Problems in construction

This is a recurring problem for many constructionist types of analysis (particularly those maintaining a narrow definition of the discursive): if a mode of socio-historical construction has 'brought into being' certain significant political difference where previously none had existed, or to alter the terms somewhat, if certain objects have been effectively invented where nothing previously existed in their place, then what was the anchoring-point that makes such differentiations, such inventions viable? My point, rather than to discredit constructionist approaches, is to suggest that at moments like this it is often helpful to draw on an additional mode of explanation, so that we may be able to make reference to the logic of capital, histories of imperialist conflict, the tenacity of affective structures – to offer a very unFoucauldian set of examples – to explain why certain constructed social distinctions have been so historically potent, and have taken on the tenacity, the recalcitrance, the 'essentiality' that they have. One is hence better placed to understand what motivates such distinctions, what brings them into visibility in the first place.

There is also a second consideration here, an awareness of the limitations of attempting to apply constructionist accounts as total explanations. There may be aspects of the object of analysis that seemingly exceed a historical, political, discursive frame of analysis; as I have argued above, not all facets of psychological functioning can be explained as after-effects of the implementation of discipline. Importantly, none of this is to suggest that constructionist critiques necessarily make reference to a mode of realism – this would seem anathema to Foucauldian approaches, especially where the realism in question is linked to the epistemology of humanism. The point of my argument is to suggest that constructionist accounts often work best in conjunctions of the sort I have hinted at above, such that discursive constructions of a given subject-category are cross-referenced with a different order of explanation (say that of physical/bodily practices, material arrangements and historical contingency, as in the case of Foucault's genealogies). It is also, furthermore, to suggest that constructionist accounts may require the supplementation of a different order of explanation, that certain strategic articulations with other types of theory may advance the project of critique. These are important issues, I think, because discursive constructionist accounts do sometimes risk becoming overly self-referential in the answers they provide, implicitly treating their own opening assumptions – that is the constructed nature of the world – as also the essential 'whys' and 'hows' of power, without adequate attention to additional possible explanatory terms. A somewhat similar type of problem sometimes threatens to emerge in Foucault, where disciplinarity some-times seems its own sufficient or self-evident principle of motivation. A question to pose to Foucault: Is enough attention always paid to those mechanisms, instru-ments and modes of power that are themselves not strictly disciplinary but that profit from and impel the functioning of disciplinary power?

The Foucauldian response to the issue, the 'anchoring-point' that precedes a given construction and that seemingly makes it viable is simply to argue that *nothing* needs exist before the problematizing ener-gies of disciplinarity; such energies are capable of generating an issue, a deviance, a lack of health in the very act of 'discovering' it. Here, again, the Foucauldian retort would be to guard against the impulse to locate a realist set of objects or attributes that exist somehow outside the domain of the discursive; the warning, once again, would be to emphasize the remarkable generativity of disciplinary power. As prudent as such a cautioning may prove in respect of the analysis of power – this is a methodological point I take up in more detail in the following chapter – it remains a somewhat unsatisfactory response in relation to present concerns, especially so if it means we are obliged to accept that there is something tantamount to a vacuum at the site of the individual psychological subject prior to the activation of disciplinary methods.

Surely there is a middle road here? Can we not accept that modern psychological individuals are produced in considerable conceptual and practicable 'psychological' detail, without accepting that there was something tantamount to a psychological void – an absence of opera-tions of mediation, reflexivity or conscience – existing before the imple-mentation of a disciplinary subjectivization. Perhaps the project then is not so much the investigation of an absolute zero-point or the origin, in particular disciplinary apparatuses, of the self, the psyche, the soul, but rather to mount an investigation of how various heightened forms of psychological life – which do appear genuinely unprecedented – are activated, animated and pressed into the service of varying goals of power. Moreover, might such 'activations' be linked, via various histor-ical technologies of control, to roughly equivalent 'psychological' formations in other eras of power? And might such linkages lessen what is taken to be so distinctive of disciplinary modernity, which perhaps does not own the soul-function of 'psychological individuality' in quite such exclusive terms as Foucault seems to imply?

'Psychological formations'

A last defence of Foucault, it seems, is called for at this point, a defence which requires us to return to and insist upon a basic distinction introduced above, which clarifies the ambit and focus of a properly Foucauldian or genealogical critique. In speaking of 'the psychological' we need to differentiate between psychology as *a discipline*, an institutionalized system of power and knowledge – indeed, as an entire discursive network of functional constructs – and psychology as *a set of human capa*cities.[12] Or, differently put, we need to discern between psychology as *the means through which the subjectivity of modern individuals is formed* (the higher mental functions of basic cognitive operations, the awareness of self relative to the ideals of normalizing disciplinarity, types of learning that internalize effects of power and so on), and *the formidable cultural and historical apparatus of 'the psychological'* through which a whole series of related concepts, modes of practice and formations of experience unfold.

This is a potentially crucial distinction between two adjoined ontologies of 'the psychological'; it is on this basis that one can assert that Foucault is not arguing for a complete absence of psychological life prior to the advent of disciplinary power. So, on the one hand, the defence of Foucault against many of the argument offered above relies on such a distinction. However, before assuming that these two adjoined ontologies of 'the psychological' are easily or necessarily separable we need to turn back to Foucault's descriptions of disciplinary effects. We should be clear here that – for this is perhaps Foucault's most strident critique of psychology – the historical constructions of the disciplinary psy-industries include the reality-effects of disciplinary subjectivization, that is, the effective activation of certain psychological properties in, for example, everyday modes of self-reflection and self-evaluation. Such productions possess an actively psychologizing force; they may be said to lead to certain 'psychological formations' of which 'identity' itself may be considered an example.[13]

There is something compelling about this description: in effect it breaks down the subjectivization/subjectification distinction – all subjectivization here *is subjectification* – insisting that all 'natural' psychology (psychology as human capacity, as the stuff of subjectivity) must be seen in the light of the disciplinary instrumentalization from which it can never be completely separated. In retrospect, is it not exactly this distinction that the theory of disciplinarity calls into question – to refer to such a difference is to pose a false dichotomy, a humanist abstraction, a myth – that it attacks and collapses? This point of collapse lies at the heart of what in Foucault is most useful to a reassessment of psychology; it is precisely this which causes us to distrust innocent appeals to interiority. This, I would argue, is where Foucault offers his most radical critique of psychology: in problematizing the routine application of a series of untroubled 'soul' concepts which are deployed in the absence of any interrogation of how their utilization may extend technologies of control and governmentality to which they may not seem to be obviously linked.

So although there are moments where Foucault's argument is implicitly obliged to make the distinction in question – for example, in escaping the contention that a psychological vacuum exists prior to disciplinarization – there are also moments when such a distinction is rendered untenable. Another exemplification of Butler's problem: two different and opposed ontologies must be set side-by-side if this type of explanation is to work. On the one hand the psyche is understood as simply *produced by* disciplinary discourses and institutions. On the other hand, Foucault requires a forerunner of sorts – a 'proto-psychological' reference point – which we might equally understand as the psyche – upon which power can be applied.

Discussion 1.10: The 'subject-function' of the soul: Unprecedented entity or recurring historical object?

The account offered in *Discipline and Punish* wants to insist on the absolute historicity of the soul, indeed, even more so, on the historical contingency of the notions of 'the psyche', 'the self', and so on. Foucault has in mind here the 'core of virtualities', that is, the subject-function as it comes to be fastened to the 'somatic singularity' of individuals, the psyche – or indeed, 'body-psyche' – as it comes to be produced as an extension of techniques of political power (Foucault, 2006).

Foucault is most certainly right to insist on the absolute historical contingency of particular configurations of power-knowledge in this respect. It is vital to point out the specificity of the objects and subjective 'reality-effects' induced by the practice of psychoanalysis, as opposed to those induced by earlier governments of souls within the apparatuses of Christianity (2003b), and these in turn from the technologies of self entailed by Senecan self-examination or Oriental modes of contemplation and self-obedience (Foucault, 1988a). However, do these diverse historical moments not all share, even at the most rudimentary level, a similar axis of implementation? Is there a methodological inconsistency here, a disparity between the rule of absolute historicization and a kind of historical regularity? In Foucault's later works, particularly in his conceptualization of technologies of the self, we evidence this tension, the regular historical reoccurrence of something like a soul, accorded a set of distinctive yet similar mechanisms in each case. Here we have a sense – contrary to Foucault's strong historicizing instincts – of a model of political operations, indeed, of a general temple of how then 'body-psyche' is fastened to power, reappearing (albeit with differences) in different historical eras (see also Foucault, 2003b).

Is a kind of historical regularity thus being smuggled into an ostensibly radical historical analysis? It seems puzzling that this vehicle – disciplinary self-examination, awareness of self apropos the rules of power and the soul-function of power – is such a constant historical figure. If disciplinarity is as much of a revolutionary advance in the history, power as Foucault implies, then surely we would expect less degree of this historical regularity, and, indeed, more evidence of those eras of power evidencing no 'soul function' whatsoever?

As I will discuss in later sections of this book, the body, in spite of many reinventions, and in spite of dramatic transformations in the historical apparatuses of control, remains a point of constant fascination for Foucault, indeed, a priority for genealogical analysis. In returning to this contingent object of the body, this construction – never to be approached as a universal category – the objective is not to extract the body from the flux of historical transformations and eventualities, but rather to trace its different operationalizations by diverse modes of power which, after all, need to return to the body as an irreducible anchoring-point of political effects. Can we not then ask whether something akin to the 'subject-function' of the soul must not also, necessarily, be a returning focus of analysis; moreover, whether this operation of the folding of the soul as induced by techniques of power – what we might refer to as the psychological functioning of power – attains a similar degree of historical reoccurrence to that of the body? Just as the body provides an indispensable set of reference points for power (singular physicality in space and time), so the soul, surely, provides a vital set of subject-functions (automated, self-reflexive, self-knowing, self-disciplining functions fastening the body-psyche to power)? This would give us grounds not to overturn the Foucauldian schema of disciplinarity, but to question the degree to which it functions as a wholly unprecedented paradigm of power.[14]

Is it enough, given the historical regularity evidenced by the body, to merely historicize it? Furthermore, given the historical reoccurrence of the soul function – which, like the body seems resistant to the rule of absolute historicization – is it enough for us to rely in this respect upon a predominantly historicizing sort of criticism? If various 'psychological' relations, mechanisms and modes of reflexivity are not simply exhausted by this mode of critique, if they persist and reoccur in varying forms beyond the horizon of this type of enquiry, then surely we need engage with them in another way also, in the terms, for example, of a psychological language of analysis? To pose a related question: perhaps the critical use of psychological concepts should not be limited to an exercise in historical contextualization. Perhaps there is more to be done with these concepts than simply consigning them to a position along a familiar trajectory of power-knowledge; indeed, might they not enable a new mode of scrutiny to various historicized psychological relations of power?

Delimiting critique

We are thus able to point to what Foucault cannot speak about, but must nevertheless presume, namely the psychological functionality of the subject that potentially exists before the implementation of disciplinary power. The concern voiced above returns: what – speaking psychologically for the moment – might be the mechanisms that ensure that disciplinary procedures 'catch', what are the predominant factors that enable them to become self-activating or, alternatively, what psychological qualities play a role in barring their hold, in disrupting their functioning? Butler gives this line of questioning a psychoanalytic inflection: how is it that disciplinary apparatuses that attempt to produce and totalize identity become an abiding object of passionate attachment in subjects? Or in a variation of Mladen Dolar's (1999) argument (discussed below): what psychological effects of the positioning of the human subject in a cultural-symbolic milieu enable Foucault's system of panoptic awareness to 'take', to assume such a potent imaginative and unconscious dimension? In his unwillingness to discuss an extra-disciplinary dimension to psychological life, indeed, in his implicit refusal of such a dimension, Foucault unnecessarily delimits possibilities for critique.

My point in bringing together the various arguments gathered above – some of which take aim less at Foucault himself than at positions that may be derived from his work – is simply this: it would seem that there is a more complex order of human psychological functioning than the Foucauldian schema of disciplinary power will allow for. This, surely, is an order of functioning that we cannot ignore; indeed, we must engage it if we are to further an understanding of the internalized workings of power, of subjectivization in all its complexity.

Inasmuch as the subject is an epistemological entity and a political object, and, in addition, the target of subjectifying political forces[15] – then Foucault's argument about the disciplinary invention and production of individuals is hard to refute, indeed, dangerous to ignore. My response to such an argument – while not wishing at all to diminish the impact of the claims thus made – is that this is not all there is to subjects, to subjectivization or, indeed, to psychological individuality. It is not, to my mind, the case that power fully exceeds or exhausts that which is circumscribed within the area of the subject. To offer such a retort to Foucault is not necessarily to provide a foothold for humanism, nor is it to pose that the domain of subjectivity represents an 'outside' of power. (Individual psychological functioning may indeed be inseparably linked to power, may never in fact be free of its influence and conditioning *without being in effect reducible to it*.) To offer such a retort is not to make the case for a heroic form of individualism, or to assert an agency of creative subjects able to make themselves in the terms of their own choosing. Furthermore, the attempt to make descriptive recourse to a psychological lexicon – and, indeed, the querying of a domain of psychological functions not reducible to disciplinarity – is not necessarily to slip into the language and epistemology of humanism.

The possibility that is thus opened up is that certain of the terms and concepts of the 'psy-disciplines' – and the anti-humanism of much psychoanalysis makes it one of the best candidates in this respect – provides us with a set of descriptive tools which might bring certain facets of subjectivization into greater critical visibility. Here it is tempting to suggest that one read Fanon's *Black Skin, White Masks* against Foucault's *Discipline and Punish*. Although Fanon (1986) is strongly vigilant regards the tacit political dimension of much psychological discourse – aware indeed of its potential in the colonial world as a means of racist subjectification (Bulhan, 1985) – he is willing nevertheless to make strategic use of psychoanalytic terms in order to build a 'psychopolitical' critique of white racism (Hook, 2005a). Clearly these texts represent two very different intellectual projects, but the question posed by the juxtaposition stands: what critical opportunities are made possible for reading the mechanics of subjectification, subjectivization and indeed of resistance by means of recourse to fragments of psychological discourse? Is it possible, following Fanon, that certain psychological concepts may be extracted from a depoliticizing context and put to the work of political critique, while other facets of the discipline need be shown up, their formative and constructive powers, their role in disciplinarily exposed?

Discussion 1.11: Power and the Other

Dolar (1999) offers a sympathetic critique of Foucault via the Lacanian notion of the Other. The Other, he notes, 'is the hypothetical authority that upholds the structure and supposed addressee of any act of speech, beyond interlocution or intersubjectivity, the third in any dialogue' (p. 87). The Other emerges whenever a subject is confronted with the symbolic structure, it is a point of appeal, a point of intelligibility beyond the subjective interpretative frames of each communicator, that ultimately makes language and symbolic exchange work. In slightly more accessible terms: we may understand the Other as the sum total of the symbolic domain, that is, the entirety of symbolic processes, language, laws and social structure, as it is particularized for each subject (Evans, 1996). The Other hence supplies the reference points, the co-ordinates for how we are situated in the matrix of social relations of which we are a part.

For Lacanian psychoanalysis, the assumption is that the Other is always already there and that it plays as crucial role in accounting for certain mechanisms of power, certainly inasmuch as it sets in place a certain structure of reflexivity (*How am I seen by the Other? What does the Other want from me? What are the social values it holds most dear?*). As Dolar (1999) puts it: that the Other emerges at all, the supposition that such a point of appeal 'makes sense', or that *there is even sense to be made*, that there is knowledge, a Truth that the Other knows – this is the kernel of both power and knowledge.

Foucault, it is safe to assume, would not accept such an assumption. Not only does the notion of the Other re-centre a kind of final authority, exactly the figure of sovereignty that he wishes to escape from – who after all is the Other but *the* figure of symbolic law, the point of appeal and truth? – it also begs the question: if there is a set of effects stemming from 'the Other', then where does 'the Other' itself come from, surely it must itself be explained as an effect of sorts, something produced by relations of power, for it cannot, surely, be seen as a 'transcendental structure', as an automatic dimension of human existence.

Dolar questions whether Foucault's work at points does effectively rely, even if rather covertly, on something akin to such a notion of the Other, 'not just as an effect produced by the mechanisms, but as something that itself produces effects' (p. 87). In *Discipline and Punish*, he claims, Foucault makes assumptions that cannot be covered by his methodological injunctions; furthermore, it seems certain assumptions about the structure of subjectivity are at work in the model of disciplinary power which appear to run counter to the notion of subject as only effect (outcome) of power. Dolar points particularly to the discrepancy between Foucault's methodological proclamations (regards specificity of instruments and locations of power) and the generalizability of the results of his analysis of disciplinary power. Despite that there may well be a diversity of procedures and tactics in the disciplinary domain, the diagram of the Panopticon – which Foucault often treats as paradigmatic of modern power – easily unites these facets into a common pattern. It is astonishing, ventures Dolar

> that the multiplicity of dispersed and heterogenous micro-relations converges into one single image of power which is entirely imbued with the figure of the Other... doesn't Foucault's strategy of dispersed micro-relations eventually converge in a much more massive presence of the Other than psychoanalysis would ever dream of?
>
> (1999, p. 88)

Of course, Dolar is by no means suggesting that we reject the importance of Foucault's analytics of power, just as he is not suggesting we do away with Foucault's theorizing of modern disciplinary power. What he is arguing – and why his critique is of importance to those of us wishing to explore the promise of Foucauldian analytics vis-à-vis ostensibly 'psychological' dimensions of power – is that we undercut the efficacy of our own analyses if we do not take seriously the possibility of something like the Other, as a point of appeal and authority able to anchor subjects in the social-symbolic matrix of relations without itself being reduced to a secondary effect of power. As he puts it, 'without the Other, there is no 'effect' of power nor the 'psychic economy' that makes it possible... Power works only if and as long as we assume the Other' (p. 92).

Conclusion

In the course of *Psychiatric Power*, Foucault provides a concise description of individualizing disciplinarily, a description which I think provides a synopsis of much of the foregoing chapter:

> Disciplinary power is individualizing because it fastens the subject-function to the somatic singularity by means of a system of supervision-writing, or by a system of pangraphic panopticism, which behind the somatic singularity projects, as its extension or its beginning, a core of virtualities, a psyche, and which further establishes the norm as the principle of division and normalization, as the universal prescription for all individuals constituted in this way.
>
> (Foucault, 2006, p. 55)

As I hope is apparent, my intention is by no means to dismiss Foucault's arguments in relation to the dynamics, instruments and productive efficacy of disciplinary technologies. The Foucauldian argument concerning the disciplinary production of psychological individuality is crucial, it helps emphasize the extent to which virtually all of the psychological (as it is lived, practiced and rendered subject to knowledge) falls within the ambit of power. Certain rudimentary psychological operations may have been greatly extended and elaborated in this way, been given a particular historical nature, a pressing political dimension so distinctive that they may appear to have been given an 'inaugural existence', at this distinctive point of disciplinary modernity. This does not mean however that the fullest range of such prospective 'psy-functions' are reducible to such an origin, or that we cannot tentatively compare different versions of similar subject-functions in different historical eras (i.e. varying and complex modes of self-mediation, reflexivity and self-prediction). Nor does this necessarily mean that a suitable analysis of these psychological operations – as *psychological operations* – would not further our understanding of the tenacity and efficacy of disciplinary production.

If a double ontology is what is required here – which, in effect, is what I am arguing – then is one complimentary 'ontology' to the work of genealogical discursive critique not, paradoxically, a provisional reference to 'the psychological'? This need not capsize the Foucauldian endeavour; indeed one might argue that the possibility of such an unlikely collaboration depends upon the mode of critical psychological discourse one makes reference to. We know that for Foucault psychoanalysis escapes many of the trappings of humanism even while its clinical forms often succumb to a mode of normalizing disciplinarity (although this is perhaps less true of Lacanian applications (see for example the accounts of Fink, 1995; Parker, 2004)). We also know that constructivist types of psychology do not over-ride considerations of historical and cultural specificity with an emphasis on a set of universal psychological structures of the individual which necessarily transcend time and place (see Kozulin, 1990).

Might it be the case that facets of such non-humanistic modes of psychological analysis could be tactically employed, not in an unconditional or totalizing but rather in an *exploratory* manner, so as to suggest novel possibilities for critique? Select psychological notions might serve as 'scaffold concepts', that is, as a means of spurring a new collaborative analytics, the generation of novel sets of critical tools, even if these concepts would subsequently need be re-theorized, taken apart, such that the systems of thought – of which they are components – are themselves subject to historical scrutiny of genealogy.

Just as the vocabulary of the psychological is often superseded by the terms of a Foucauldian analytics eager to play up the historical and political dimension of its practical concepts and how they are deployed in the world of power, so it is also the case that aspects of this vocabulary are able at points to supersede Foucault's analytical frame. This is by no means to dismiss the critical utility of Foucault, which is of paramount importance to a rethinking of the structures of a neutral, universal psychological subjectivity, which, as his work makes us aware, can never be fully divorced from the realm of power. What the above conclusion does point us towards is the rather paradoxical possibility that certain rudimentary psychological concepts – and perhaps Vygotsky's strongly socio-cultural brand of constructivist psychology provides us with the safest ground here – might enable us to fill in the blanks in an exegesis and contestation of a psychological form of power – referring here to the effects of disciplinarily – one of whose most prominent and effective components is the discourse and practice of the discipline of psychology itself.

2
'Desubstantializing' Power: Methodological Injunctions for Analysis

> ...power is not an institution, a structure, or a certain force with which certain people are endowed; it is the name given to a complex strategic relation in a given society.
>
> (Foucault, cited in Gordon, 1980, p. 236)

'De-theorizing' power

This chapter hopes to provisionally 'de-theorize' power, to suspend a variety of suppositions that routinely come into play when power is discussed. Foucault's work is invaluable in this respect inasmuch as it explodes a series of prior presumptions and possible misconceptions regards the nature and functioning of modern power. This is a crucial task: a complacent reliance on stereotypical notions of power may work to mask the complexity of contemporary productions of power, desensitizing us to the mechanizations and manoeuvrings of relations of force which are not only thoroughly complex, but also heteromorphous and adaptive.

The task of 'de-theorizing' power can never be completely successful; even in interrogating a series of traditional notions of power we are of course implicitly involved in a project of re-theorizing power. One might say that this is the objective of the chapter that precedes this discussion in so far as it focuses on Foucault's substantive historical works and offers depictions of modern power tailored to a set of genealogical observations. Then again many would find this an odd use of the idea of a 'theorization' given that such analyses cannot easily be extrapolated out of the bounds of their specific contexts of examination. This helps to make the fundamental point: Foucault's writings on power *should not be read as a form of global theory*. Although Foucault obviously wrote extensively on power, his work never amounts to a context-free, ahistorical or structural schema. On the contrary, genealogies prioritize contingency, discontinuity and singularity of events; they are not models designed for general explanatory application.

As such the discussion of Foucault's ideas presented here should be read as an attempt to uproot a variety of misleading preconceptions and as a way of 'desubstantialising' power (Gordon's (1980) term), rather than as a means of surreptitiously asserting a grand theory. My aim here is to introduce a series of speculative hypotheses regards attempts to apprehend and scrutinize power. By the end of the chapter, I will have offered a series of practical methodological guidelines for how we might suspend a variety of unhelpful stereotypes of power. I supply these guidelines as a means of sharpening our analyses and with the hope of enabling innovative kinds of critical research focused at the level of the 'micro-political'. Like all the chapters in this book, this chapter bases itself on a close reading of the most relevant section of Foucault's work to the question at hand. Whereas in Chapter 1 I traced the arguments of *Discipline and Punish* here I attend to many of Foucault's 'de-formulations' of power in the collection of interviews and writings, *Power/Knowledge*.

Micro-political analysis

A first priority lies with distinguishing the particular area of focus that Foucault privileges in many of his genealogical analyses; doing so also helps give a sense of what is distinctive about Foucault's approach to the analysis of power. Foucault is typically concerned with pinning down the discrete procedural logic of power as it is manifest at a micro-political level. Differing from those broader-based approaches which view power within the rubrics of signification or economic production and which have instruments of analysis already available to them – as in the case of semiotics and the discipline of economics – the study of the micro-political can rely on no pre-existing tools of analysis. If we are to develop an adequate micro-political frame of analysis able to trace what Foucault sometimes refers to as the 'microphysics' of power, that is, a frame capable of grasping the very finest capillary levels of the articulation of power, then it becomes absolutely necessary to break from broader structural models that understand power in large-scale and typically repressive, juridical, economic and ideological terms. A new theory is not what is needed here, even less, warns Foucault (1982), a new objectification. The way ahead is rather to offer a series of critical, speculative hypotheses – to be developed in tandem with a linked set of methodological pragmatics – that will loosen the rigidity of prior understandings and necessitate the constant checking of grids of analysis.

Outmoded conceptualizations

Oversubscription to generalized theorizations of power means that we run the risk of delivering limited, if not wholly redundant, types of analysis. Foucault's imperative is to avoid caricatures of power, warning that the functioning of power may be more sophisticated, multidimensional and productive than we may have previously assumed; there is no transhistorical schema of power that might fit all arrangements of domination.

The analysis of power, for Foucault (1980b), has for too long been dominated by the question of juridical power and its warrants, first, and by a concern with relations of production and class domination, secondly. Such modes of explanation have very little to offer the critique of local institutions of power, such as that of 'psychiatric internment…mental normalization, or of the therapeutic interaction' (1980b, p. 116). In opposition to sociological, structural or economic analyses, Foucault advances the need to engage the elementary specifics of how power is exercised at the *precise and localized individual levels of particular institutional interfaces*; he prioritizes as such the specifics of how power is 'interacted' between subjects and institutions.

Foucault is more precise in his critique. In the case of classic juridical theory, power is taken to be a right, which one is able to possess like a commodity; it is something which each individual *holds*, it is something of which they can be deprived in a complete or total way. In the second case, power is conceived primarily in terms of the role it plays in the maintenance of relations of production and class domination. But is it really the case, asks Foucault – and this is part and parcel of his wider critique of Marxist forms of thought – that the essential aid and purpose of power functions only as commodity, that 'it is exclusively something that someone can possess, acquire, cede through force of contract?' (1980a, p. 89). If power seems almost invariably to exist in a relational form – as I will move to discuss shortly – then it is perhaps an error to think of power solely in terms of a quantity or possession that can exist in all or nothing terms, in absolute categories of total control or complete subordination. Here it is worth citing Lazzarato's (2002) pithy formulation of Foucault's difficulties with Marxism: 'Foucault faulted Marx and political economy with reducing the relations between forces to relations between capital and labor, with making these binary and symmetric relations the source of all social dynamics and every power relation' (p. 102).

One should bear in mind that Foucault's comments emerged in an intellectual climate in which Marxism presented itself as an unavoidable register of critique; his attempt here – at least in part – is to avoid this orthodoxy and offer something new. Today we may be a little less eager to dispense with these analytical terms of possession, contractual exchange and so on, even though their utilization risks importing a series of analytical presumptions. Given the complexity, the *overdetermined* nature of relations of power and wary of the fact that the micropolitical may not always be easily isolated from the macro-political, we should perhaps opt to use as many complementary analytical perspectives as might aid us. We should be attentive to Foucault's point though, which is about more than challenging fashionable trends of thought and the characteristic blind spots they introduce into the analytical domain. As soon as a 'school' of social critique itself becomes a viable body of knowledge, a systematized vehicle of thought, then the discursive ensemble in question will already be producing power-effects of its own. For Foucault, any regularized scrutiny of an object – even if this object is power itself – requires that a critical sensibility be turned upon those institutional settings and procedures that bring this object into critical visibility in the first place. This is a point I will take up in Chapter 4's elaboration of genealogical method. Suffice for now to say that Foucault seems suspicious of the 'conventionalising of thought' introduced by the formalization of any given system of criticism; such a formalization brings with it not only a series of reductions (such as those of class domination) but also a set of characteristic preoccupations (such as issues of political sovereignty) which detract one's analysis from the sustained consideration of the minutia of power's everyday operation.

Anticipating complexity

The first of the pragmatic postulates that we may draw from Foucault as a means of sensitizing our analyses of power is this: First, rather than power being primarily the maintenance and reproduction of economic relations, it may in fact be, above all, *a relation of force*, manoeuvring in multiple and often less than predictable ways. Second, rather than being held, possessed, exchanged, given – existing as a potentially static entity – power may find form only as something that is *exercised*. Power exists possibly only in action, enacted in frequently indeterminate, 'incompleted' yet over-determined relations of force. Foucault is unwilling to shy away from the complexity of power; this unwillingness requires the vigilance of an ongoing suspension of typical suppositions of the 'how', 'why' and 'what' in particular relations of power. It also requires a constant refreshing of analytical categories through which power might be brought into critical visibility and, further yet, the possibility of methodological eclecticism: a heterogeneity of critical methods and approaches able to match the heterogeneity of power-relations themselves. A clear priority thus lies with devising a set of analytical tools that are not marked with strong theoretical allegiances. What is needed are pluralized analyses, conducted without the requirements of an overarching theoretical 'fit'.

It is useful in this respect to refer to Foucault's description (1980b) of the elementary requirements of a basic analytics of power. A critical project of this sort needs both to 'provide a definition of the specific domain formed by relations of power...and to determine the instruments that will make possible such a critical analysis' (Foucault, 1978a, p. 82). Foucault's position is thus that each site-specific analysis of power needs, to some degree, to start anew. Attention should be paid to setting the parameters of the selected domain, to giving it a name and then to attending to the particular vicissitudes and relations of force and authority that best characterize it. Moreover, each analytical project may require an idiosyncratic set of tools best suited to making visible the power-effects of its particular site. This puts us in a rather novel situation, relative at least to the application of standard methodological procedures, one in which the researcher is charged with the task of devising new concepts, new tools, new routes of observation and analysis that might best enable a politically operative analysis of power. The methodological injunctions provided in this chapter will hopefully go someway to achieve this goal.

Foucault is particularly vocal about the implications of considering power as reducible to law and, on a related note, about the dangers of underwriting a 'schema of power' considered to be homogenous for every level and domain. Reduction of power to law means that power is 'what says no' and 'can never be thought of in any other than the negative terms of refusal, limitation, obstruction and censorship' (Foucault, 1980c, p. 139). A crude form of approximation comes to predominate here: the idea that power is essentially nothing more or less than prohibition itself. However, if power is taken as analogous to rule-making and rule-enforcement, to binary systems of the allowed and the forbidden, then suddenly a variety of more ambiguous modes of social influence and control fall out of the analytical frame. Here, by way of contrast, we might consider the example of the loving influence of certain moral orthopaedic interventions, the progress in the productive capabilities of cared-for individuals in medico-therapeutic settings. Such forms of power are surely not to be explained away through a politics of censure, prohibition and punishment? These are not simply relations of obedience and enforcement, but belong to a far more generative and flexible regime of health and betterment. The schema of power as 'that which says no' results in an image of power as monotonous in its tactics, poor in its resources and locked into ineffective patterns of repetition (Foucault, 1980b); we should, by contrast, look to what is inventive and generative in relations of power, aware that many such relations resist simple formalization.

The model of repression

These concerns with caricaturing depictions of power are reiterated in Foucault's opposition to what he dubs the 'repressive hypothesis'. A solely repressive understanding of power does not serve us well; it echoes the juridical conception by conflating an apparent operation of power with the force of prohibition. Even if it is the case that certain manifestations of power do take on negative or repressive modes – historically this seems difficult to dispute, as Edward Said (1983) advances against Foucault's tendency to underestimate repressive mechanisms – this is no reason for contemporary analyses to focus exclusively on relations of reduction, exclusion, depletion, only on power's faculties of constraint. Our analytic engagements should remain receptive to generative instances in the production of knowledge and practice, attuned to its many constructions, its outcomes of innovation and invention. Repressive models of power seem unable to explain the generativity and adaptability of modern power, the fact of its ability to produce both knowledge and pleasure alike:

> What makes power hold good, what makes it accepted, is simply the fact that it doesn't only weigh on us as a force that says no, but that it traverses and produces things, it induces pleasure, forms knowledge, produces discourse. It needs be considered as a productive network.... more than as a negative instance whose function is repression.
>
> (Foucault, 1980b, p. 119)

This is about more than the misrecognition of power's predominant modes of operation, it is a warning that in adhering to repressive notions of power we unwittingly perform the task of masking modern power's preferred mode of operation. Put differently, the repressive hypothesis enjoins us to speak out against negative procedures of power without an awareness of how doing so may prove to be complicit in obscuring, *even producing*, various of its more positive effects. Humanist critiques of psychotherapy seem to be an obvious case in point. The vigour of such reproaches of behaviourist modalities of treatment – as mechanistic and failing to grasp the true individuality of the unique person – is itself part and parcel of the production of a particular discursive object – the 'self-sovereign' individual human subject – which itself needs to be grasped as an object-effect of power.

This line of argument poses a significant problem for those modes of critique that operate on the basis of liberationist expressions. Such liberationist objectives may themselves be invested with power, or diverted by it, certainly inasmuch as they may ultimately take the route of subjectivizing discourses which rely upon a set of questionable normative understandings that come to be distributed across society. Then again we might suggest that there is much to be gained in the 'normative distribution' of a given set of ethical standards across society (an ethics of sexual conduct for example, as befitting an awareness of sexual harassment). Foucault, by contrast, has pronounced concerns – in this respect much like Nietzsche – about what it means for certain notions to become normalized, to enter the world of human knowledge and practice not merely as *operational constructs* but as *universal 'truths of being'*. Along with Foucault one might argue here that to downplay concerns of normalization is to underestimate the power of discourse, to neglect the forcefulness of those circuits of discourse–knowledge–practice which overly homogenize certain facts of human life (the heterosexist regulation of sexual practice makes for a good example) and that aim to regularize and moralize sociality and to subsequently eliminate all deviances from social life.

Limiting the critique of humanism

The above argument works better for some examples rather than for others. The pleasures of sexual interaction between consenting adults may well benefit from a loosening of restrictive norms, from an exploration of deviance. The same might well be said of the rigid conventions of traditional gender categorization. What though about an ethics of anti-racism? Surely the normative distribution of such a set of ethical standards is something one cannot fail to support. Foucault may well withdraw his support here, not on the basis that he exhibited a tolerance for racism – his disdain for racism and anti-Semitism was well documented (Eribon, 1991; Macey, 1994) – but on the basis that he opposed the transformation of ethical standards into blunt, universal moral categories. A Foucauldian response here might be to suggest that there are many viable tactics for an anti-racist politics that do not reduce racism to a problem of normalized moral rules; this would seem particularly the case if such a normalization resulted in the implicit reification of racial categorizations. One might agree with Foucault to a degree here – one would hope that anti-racism is more than a set of codes of conduct and representation that people abide to out of a sense of what is normative – without necessarily agreeing that the normalization of values is always to be avoided.

Another issue presents itself here, in view of Foucault's implicit critique of liberationist sentiments. Surely there are certain provisional gains to be made by a kind of *strategic humanism* utilized in specific and provisional ways at precise historical moments. It would seem so, as in the political urgency of the call of Black Consciousness in apartheid South Africa. Even in such circumstances, however, it would seem an imperative to underscore the qualification of *strategic* in the progressive utilization of humanism, for the insidious values that occupy this site have more than once been shown up as less than inclusive, less than truly democratic or egalitarian, as a variety of post-colonial critics have argued (see Gandhi (1998) for a useful overview). Having said this, renewed enthusiasm for contingent and variant forms of humanism have proved telling in the domain of critical race and post-colonial studies of late (Gilroy, 2000, 2004; Said, 2003), signalling the fact that this is an avenue of politics we cannot simply ignore.

It is worth noting that as a political activist Foucault did take seriously anti-repressive and humanitarian arguments. This is true in both the case of his support of persecuted Soviet dissidents in 1976 and, also, as Macey (2004) makes clear, in the recourse Foucault makes to a language of universal human rights and justice when denouncing Franco's regime. So while this means that there is often an important discontinuity between Foucault's work and his politics – and, indeed, a degree of flexibility in how certain political projects should be advanced – this should not detract from the importance of what Foucault is advancing. The classic Foucauldian argument of the late 1970s is exactly to advance that those sacrosanct realms of truth, knowledge and individual subjectivity are not external to power or anathema to its functioning, but are instead internal to it, intrinsic components, necessary to its operation. Here then a further methodological pragmatic (and this is perhaps the best way to take Foucault's argument forward as a methodological caution rather than a hard-and-fast rule): adopt a wariness towards any presumption that such humanistic categories (the singular integrity of the autonomous subject, the truths of subjectivity or individual uniqueness) are necessarily outside of the bounds of power, antithetical to its effects. The point here is to examine how such privileged notions may come to be utilized as rationales for particular implementations of force, as justifications for power that are particularly difficult to argue against.

That conditional forms of humanism may advance progressive political causes in certain socio-historical conditions is a difficult point to refute, particularly in contexts where racist objectification and abject dehumanization are rife. Here it helps to distinguish between the project of practical activist politics and the attempt to develop a sharpened critical sensibility regards the more counter-intuitive workings of power. This chapter is obviously focused on the latter. It is in this spirit that it advances Foucault's warning that humanism remains a dangerous currency *for any adequate critique of distinctively modern relations of power.* Having said this, it remains important to signal a possible limitation to the analytical injunctions lifted from Foucault's work on the operation and sensibilities of modern European power. Clearly the anti-humanism of such injunctions does not make for the best analytical fit regards the scrutiny and critique of certain racist colonial regimes of power in which the horizon of a commonly shared and mutually respected 'humanity' cannot as yet be assumed.

These critical speculations lead to a cautioning. As noted above, Foucault treats humanism as *the* discourse of the rationalization of power in late modernity. What this seems to imply – particularly given Foucault's prognosis in *The Order of Things* that the epistemic allure of the human will pass – is that other discourses may come to play this rationalizing role in the future. If this is the case, then we should be wary of fixating our critique on the subject of humanism alone. Of course to underestimate the hegemonic hold of such a discourse would be a crucial error, despite the case made above for certain strategic types of humanism. Humanism is not simply another discourse in modernity; given the configuration of knowledge, truth and power that characterizes the current Western episteme, humanism is not something that one can simply step outside of. Then again it would seem important that we avoid conflating the critique of humanism with an adequate analysis of power, a conceivable misreading of Foucault's intentions in his analyses at the time of *Discipline and Punish*. If a division between the hegemony of humanism and the operation of certain modalities of power can be made – and it seems questionable at this epistemic juncture whether it can – then it may be the case that conditional forms of humanism may be put to incisive political use, provided one is thoroughly versed in how effectively humanism rationalizes power.

Discussion 2.1: Foucault and liberationist psychology

Butchart (1997) takes issue with those applications of Foucault's work within psychology that attempt to adapt it to a liberationist framework. In such cases, his work is typically pressed into precisely the liberal-humanist and Marxist analyses that Foucault himself was so concerned to dispel. If we sufficiently grasp Foucault, argues Butchart (1997, 1998), we realize that what we understand as human subjectivity is not the origin of power, nor the source of any answers, *but instead the end result and effect of its forces*:

> What makes the psyche conceivable as the origin of thought and locus of personal identity...? The Foucauldian answer...is that...such entities exist only in so far as they are fabricated and sustained by the socio-medical sciences as objects of positive knowledge...without psychology to produce the subject there would be no notion of subjectivity...the socio-medical sciences do not find but invent the objects of their investigation, and therefore instead of being appendages to power the socio-medical sciences are in fact *its very essence*.
>
> (Butchart, 1997, p. 102, emphasis added)

Given that power is intrinsically a part of such disciplinary procedures, Foucault sees little potential of meaningful escape from power *within* such forms of knowing and acting. In Foucault's account, even the terms of the most progressive or liberationist psychology are inevitably going to re-inscribe procedures of subjectification and objectification that ultimately link to greater programmes of power. Notions of freedom, empowerment and liberalism are hence always double-edged, for they are 'at once enhancing and at the same time a concealing veil under which an ever more finely tuned machinery of surveillance installs itself within and around everyone' (1997, p. 107). Even a political movement like Black Consciousness, whilst offering to liberate Africans from internalized oppression, still manufactured 'a new and essentialist African personality...wherein each African was his own overseer, exercising surveillance over and against himself [*sic*]'.

Participatory and action research initiatives within psychology are subject to the same type of critique:

These...novel analytical techniques [whilst] inviting people to empower themselves through the verbal confession of their thoughts, feelings and emotions, fashion subjectivity itself as an object and relay through which power is articulated in an ever more anonymous and insidious format

(1997, p. 104)

One way of responding to these comments is to suggest that it is often necessary to carefully distinguish the aims of a given political or activist project. If the project is to try and escape from insidious modes of subjectivity through which we produce and police ourselves in line with moral orthopaedic norms, then a programme of political awareness like Black Consciousness is less than appropriate. If, on the other hand, we are concerned with combating a different order of power, such as that of the insidious effects of an institutionalized racism, then a strategy like Black Consciousness does seem a well-suited form of resistance, certainly inasmuch as it offers the tactical possibility for alternative positionings, imaginings, modes of reflection, re-contextualization and contestation that may not otherwise have been possible.

Assumptions of externality

Many traditional ideological conceptualizations of power share the assumption of the repressive account that there is a vital truth of sorts – a kind of antidote to power – that exists beyond the domain of power's jurisdiction. An external truth of this sort is, for Foucault, more than a critical analyst of power can risk assuming, particularly given that the workings of discourse can be said to exert a determining relationship on what counts as 'truth'. The question of discourse as a vital component in the successful functioning of power is crucial here; modern power is only effective to the degree to which it succeeds in blending its operative forms with various 'languages' of truth, knowledge, utilitarianism and freedom (this is discussed further in Chapter 3). It is for this reason – to reiterate aspects of the above discussion of humanism – that Foucault advances a pronounced methodological suspicion towards those humanistic rationales promising greater liberty, health, well- being and so on. Rather than take these accounts at face value, one should treat such alibis as the rationales by which power makes itself acceptable, the codes by which it prescribes what we conceive of it. As Hook, Harris and Landsman (1999) assert, it is just the ability of power to so progress us, to deliver us from ignorance, sickness and disorder, just its promises of enlightenment, justice and welfare that endears the continuation of its practices to us. What this assertion makes clear is that any analysis of power should engage with the primary representations of the field with which it is concerned. That is, we should grapple with what we might call the public ideals – the commonly understood objectives and imperatives – of the relation of power in question (be it of therapeutic change, military discipline, medical betterment, etc.). Such a *discursive scrutiny* of power's various rationalizations and humanisms will prove essential.

Foucault extends his critique of ideological notions of power by advancing that they presume 'the order of the subject'. The category of the subject, like 'truth' itself, cannot be assumed to 'come before' to exist in a state external to (or antagonistic towards) a given network of power-relations. As Foucault warns in *The History of Sexuality* (1978a), the sexual or psychological category of the subject cannot be assumed to pre-exist the relations of power 'that may have functioned to establish it as a possible object of intervention' (p. 98).

While individuals are at all times locked into the dynamics of multiple relations of power and resistance – so much so that this can be considered a permanent condition of modern existence – we must, nevertheless, avoid the mistake of idealizing the capacity of individual human agency. This is not to adopt a fatalistic position, to conclude that any form of individualized resistance is wasted effort or that human agency is a non-operative category. Any reading of Foucault that leads us in this direction is wide of the mark. The point is not to dismiss all possibilities of contestation and argumentation, but to question the degree to which we prioritize subjectivity and human individualism as a means of doing so. Subjectivity for Foucault, as discussed in the previous chapter, is something like a reflexive loop – a fold, in Deleuze's (1988) useful formulation – in which certain principles and values of power are re-inscribed, redistributed at an ostensibly 'internal' level. Gordon (1980) puts this well in his rejection of the subject–object polarization that often takes precedence in the analysis of power: such a polarization comes to privilege subjectivity as *the* form of moral autonomy. We should suspend the assumption that domination falsifies the essence of human subjectivity, asserting instead an awareness that 'power regularly promotes and utilizes a "true" knowledge of subjects...[that it] constitutes the very field of that truth' (p. 239).

At his most anti-humanistic, Foucault (1980b) warns that one needs to 'dispense with a level of focus upon the individual, constituent subject, and instead arrive at an analysis which can account for the *constitution of the subject*, as [s/he] appears within the framework of current power relations' (p. 117, my emphasis). This perhaps appears an extreme cautioning, one better suited to genealogical projects that are equipped with an adequate depth of historical perspective and with an alternative set of analytical categories such that the analysis may proceed in the absence of the subject. This is exactly the challenge Foucault sets us – incongruous as it may appear to those of us accustomed to offering psychological accounts of events – a doing away with psychological types of explanation in favour of the less subject-orientated descriptions of discourse, the event, history, apparatus and so on. (I extend this argument and offer a more developed description of these concepts in the chapters that follow.) The cautioning that follows from this argument is that many natural or essential or human qualities observed within the domain of power *already are* the effects of a power-relationship. A further analytical precaution arises here: be wary of certain commonplaces of causation that rely upon subject–object polarizations; much of what we may assume to be exempt from power may be more its produced effect than an exception to its influence.

Instrumented domains

Foucault's analytical couplet of 'power-knowledge' – already discussed in Chapter 1 – goes some way towards combating the tendency to absolve knowledge from the analysis of relations of force. It is worth reiterating Foucault's (1977a) warning that the exercise of power inevitably results in knowledge and that the applications of knowledge inevitably produce effects of power. A series of methodological injunctions flow from this assertion: (1) an awareness of the circularity of this productive relationship, (2) an analytical vigilance vis-à-vis the fact that power cannot, in effect, be exercised *in the absence of relations of knowledge* and (3) a corresponding awareness that the activation of *relations of knowledge* cannot but engender effects of power.

The mutually reinforcing relationship of power-to-knowledge and knowledge-to-power works to establish complex sets of institutional mechanisms and procedures. It is the day-to-day functioning of these apparatuses – possessed as they are of highly specific procedural techniques and specialist instrumentations – that should become prime targets of analysis. In making such a claim, Foucault provides us with a means both of concretizing and of sharpening our analyses of power. He is directing our attentions to the instrumental minutia and their corresponding principles of articulation that ultimately enable localized institutional operations of power to link generalized strategies and tactics to highly individual outcomes. If we are to grasp the procedural logic at work in such situated relations of power, indeed, if we are to develop appropriate micro-political grids of analysis, then rigorous observations of such institutional mechanizations will prove invaluable. Foucault's genealogical analyses are full of observations of such instrumentalizations. *Discipline and Punish* presents a rich tapestry of such examples: modes of registration and calibration, techniques of surveillance and confession, procedures of comparison and individualization illustrate the text throughout. The same is true of *Abnormal* and *Psychiatric Power*: from careful descriptions of the architectural arrangement of asylums (thought to be coextensive with the body of the psychiatrist), to discussions of the furniture most appropriate to eliciting confessions, Foucault seems intent on providing us with as exhaustive as possible inventories of the mechanisms and protocols of power.

We have thus a material subject-matter with which to ground our examinations of institutional power. If we then work upwards, from the scrutiny of such discrete minutia of power to something approaching its general rationality, then we are gradually able to identify the principles of coordination through which the joint articulation of its various component procedures makes sense. This seems quite the reverse of a theoretical project that applies broad sociological or socio-economic principles to a particular domain of analysis; it is the meticulous collection of a diverse array of artefacts, documents and records that eventually yields a series of logics of control. A further methodological injunction then: the strategies, protocols, objectives and rationales of a given plane of intervention, like the specific procedural technologies and apparatuses of a given sphere of knowledge production, serve as the nodal points of one's analysis. Furthermore, a principle of 'theoretical estrangement': rather than attempting to match and apply large structural/theoretical explanations to the data of our analysis of power, proceed instead by continually grounding one's analysis, by collecting a variety of observations and proofs of its micro-processes and doing so as a means of attempting to understand elements of its broader rationality.

Foucault's project is again to be differentiated, here, from that of a grand schema of power; a Foucauldian analytics is concerned with power at its lowest levels, at its extremities, 'at those points where it becomes capillary, in its local and regional forms and institutions' (Foucault, 1980a, p. 96). The micro-political level of analysis starts by grappling with 'infinitesimal mechanisms' of power and by climbing upwards from these smallest of implementations to offer an ascending order of analysis.

Spotlight 2.1: Foucauldian methodological injunctions for the analysis of relations of power

- Keep at bay the conventionalizing force of theoretical models, particularly so in the case of structural or socio-economic accounts that compromise one's ability to grasp what is most specific about discrete micro-political spheres. Be wary of assumptions of power as all-or-nothing possession (or unvarying structure of *dispossession*), of understanding power only within the terms of law/prohibition/interdiction.

- Rather than attempting to fix power as a static set of entities, as substance or as a function of objects, remain open to the possibility that power may only become effective once it is exercised, enacted or interacted in indeterminate, 'incompleted' yet overdetermined relations of force.

- Beware of routinely applying a single formula of power; treat with suspicion any general schemas in which power is considered to be homogenous at every level and domain; remain receptive to the possibilities of eclectic forms of analysis.

- Remain suspicious of the logic of repression as the basic principle of power. Treat relations of power as less than necessarily repetitive or formulaic; regard them as potentially adaptive and generative, as inventive, innovative and *productive*.

- Be prepared to interrogate the 'epistemology of humanism' as it occurs in various instances of analysis; representations of this sort often obscure the procedures and rationality of power. Develop a methodological suspicion towards rationales of this sort, not so as to impede progressive forms of politics and activism, but as a means of questioning how such imperatives might extend relations of authority and control.

- An analysis of power should be able to engage *on a discursive level* with the representations of the field of its analysis. Accordingly prioritize the scrutiny of those 'public ideals', those commonly understood motivations, objectives and imperatives that feature most prominently in depictions of the field of power in question. Treat as especially important those objects and notions that are typically assumed to exist outside the sphere of power, that are thought of as exceptions to power's jurisdiction of influence.

- Be vigilant of the productive circularity of knowledge-to-power and power-to-knowledge relations; where a relation of power is in place, be sure to examine associated relations of knowledge (be aware of the order of objects it constitutes); proceed on the assumption that operations of knowledge cannot but effect relations of power and that power engenders its own brand of knowledge.
- Attempt to grasp the 'technological specificity' of the particular site of power that one is studying; how is it set apart from the broader field of power-relations? What are the procedures, the institutional minutia, the precise mechanizations, the concrete and specific machineries of this particular site of power?
- Avoid the temptation to apply broad structural/theoretical meta-narratives to the data of one's analysis, preferring instead to ground one's analysis on the basis of documentations and observations of its various micro-processes and practices.
- Look for elements of *process* and *activity* rather than for those of *structure* or *substance*; power should be analysed as *a relational force* that circulates and functions always in the form of a chain.
- Do not presume 'the individual' as a pre-given factor in one's analysis; rather trace its development within a given domain; question how versions of individuality may exist as object-effects produced by this particular set of relations of power.

Unstructured formations

I intimated above that power is best grasped in *exercised, practiced* and *interacted* forms. The reason behind this injunction has much to do with the attempt to 'de-structure' power and hence to anticipate something of its heteromorphous quality. One of the most persistent problems attached to the analysis of power is the 'ontological compulsion' evidenced in so many forms of critique, the tendency, in other words, to put a determinate face, name or structure to a diverse collection of effects. That power is often affected in discontinuous ways, that it may be realized in unstructured formations, clearly poses problems for conceptualizations of this sort. Foucault, by contrast, asks us to grasp power in the form of an irregular and incommensurate series of components that need never quite constitute a cohesive unit. Power may exist in scattered circuits of activation that are able to conduct the flow of relations of force and docility despite that none of their components can be said to be representative of its functioning as a whole.

In calling attention away from the substantive (*le'pouvoir*) sense of power – as is conveyed by the use of the definitive article – Foucault underlines that relations of power never need coalesce into a clearly decipherable network, a fixed collection of commodities, a rigid constellation of positions or the ordered control of a set of institutions. Such attempts to name and place power, to grant it a final position of location or point of emanation, is to offer a reductive analysis unable, as Foucault puts it, 'to take into account the considerable amount of phenomena at work in its functioning' (Foucault, 1980e, p. 198). Given the prospect that power may not be a fixed quantity or a regular arrangement of physical force, but rather something more akin to 'a stream of energy flowing through each living organism and society in a formless flux' (Miller, 1994, p. 15), the problem facing us is not so much to sketch the profile of a power that must have a fixed form or substance, but *to identify its diverse operational modes*. The imperative is to rethink power in formations of practice rather than in singular manifestations of substance, to gear our analyses towards apprehending power more as a *verb* (a doing) than as a noun.

Furthermore, as Foucault insists, one can never locate all the effects and mechanisms of power on a single stratum of actions. '[T]here is a whole order of levels of different types of events differing in amplitude, chronological breadth, and capacity to produce effects', the functioning of power may thus occur with recourse to different 'networks and levels...along which they belong and engender one another' (Foucault, 1980b, p. 114). The plurality and complexity of the multiple and overlapping fields of control that Foucault has in mind here exhibit no necessary isomorphism.

'Relationality'

Power, furthermore, should be viewed within the analytical parameters of a 'dynamic relation', a force in flux that no one owns and that can be 'exercised from innumerable points in the interplay of non-egalitarian and mobile relations' (Foucault, 1977a, p. 26). We should thus replace the analytical category of power-as-property with that of power-as-strategy and supersede the notion of power *as appropriation* with the idea of power *as disposition*. The field of power-relations makes for uneven territory. A constant set of tensions and fractured alliances, of flexible and adaptive manoeuvres, its endless dynamic of forces and resistances cannot be reduced to the concise formulations of single or binary logics of force. What this means is that individuals do not 'control' power, certainly not in any singular or exclusive sense. Nor are they merely its anonymous points of application. Individuals are instead the conduits and by-products, the 'object-effects' of power, its most creative points of instrumentalization. (I elaborate upon this in Chapter 6's discussion of technologies of subjectivity/self.) A necessary aspect of our analytical efforts is hence to capture the 'reactivated' element of individualized power, to engage with the fact that power is both transmitted *by* and *through* those subjects it comes to invest.

Part of the analytical complexity Foucault is grasping at here is the idea that the 'circuitry of power' he investigates is never simply unidirectional but is rather (at least) bi-directional; it entails simultaneous relations of being *subject to* and *subject of* particular relations of force. One might put this differently: the subject for Foucault is a point both of the consolidation of existing relations of force and for performative extension of various of its effects. This conceptualization gives reason to voice concern; if we accept Foucault's insistence that power is a *dynamic and interactional force*, then we need to also accept the possibility that those subjected to power may also, paradoxically, play a significant role in the functioning of that power which acts upon them. This is not an element of Foucault's analytics we can shy away from, despite that it may seem to lead us into difficult ethical territory, particularly so when we are dealing with radical asymmetries in power. Foucault (1977a), however, remains adamant: all power-relations, no matter how unequal and/or hierarchical, can be promulgated on both sides from above and below. All power-relations, furthermore, may be treated as constraining on both sides.

Again here it seems useful to draw a distinction between an ethical project aiming to formulate a practical politics of intervention and an analytical project that hopes to map as extensively as possible the diverse aspects of a particular sphere of power. While in many instances it seems ethically indefensible to scrutinize those who have suffered the worst-effects of radical imbalances of power – and as an ostensibly critical form of engagement, Foucault's analytics of power is certainly answerable to such attacks – it is worthwhile considering a few points in Foucault's defence. His analytics of power is in no way a moral undertaking. Nor is it an approach that accepts the notion of individual agency as an adequate category of explanation, a point that cannot be overemphasized. As such, any attempt to assign a form of moral culpability to those who have suffered the effects of power, like any attempt to apportion individual blame for the agency of power, cannot be considered part of a Foucauldian analytics. As will become apparent as we continue, this way of dividing up the analytical field – those without power who are *acted upon*, as opposed to that array of the powerful who *do the acting* – replicates aspects of the object/subject polarization that Foucault is intent on avoiding. Of course, that a Foucauldian analytics avoids the rhetoric of blame, that it dispenses with a singling out of individual agents and ultimately treats the objectives of moral philosophy with extreme prejudice may, admittedly, remain problems for those committed to more immediately ethical programmes of political intervention. We should not, however, lose sight of Foucault's overarching agenda here: that of grasping the reciprocation of passive and active positions in the conduction of power, of tracing the joint productions of 'top-down' and 'bottom-up' flows of power.

How though might we go about apprehending this 'relationality', how might we analyse it in dialogical and participative rather than monological or unanswered forms, in the interaction of relations of response, interaction and resistance? Another focus of analytical attention is suggested here: given the diversity and plurality of the types of power Foucault analyses, what basic analytic category – if any – might we rely on, what regular form can we look for to isolate such effects of power, given this evident emphasis on relationality? Foucault's caution against assuming an 'externality' of power is again pertinent here: rather than existing beyond the bounds of other types of relationships, power-relations may well be *interwoven within them*, playing at once 'a conditioning and conditioned role' (1980c, p. 142). If we take this idea of the relational form of power seriously, we have something of an answer to the apparent ubiquity and unavoidability of power. It is because of power's relational form – because it is an internal dimension of all forms of relationship – that it is able

> to sink to the depths of society without being localized [exclusively] in the relations between the state and its citizens or between different classes or groups, being taken up instead by the idiosyncratic shapes of local procedures of control and domination.
>
> (Foucault, 1977a, p. 26)

Hence the need to look to relationships, between subjects, between subjects and institutions, between outcomes and intentions; look here, not obviously for psychological factors, but for distinctive – if not complex – arrangements of power. The relation, one might say, is Foucault's favoured analytical term when it comes to the identification and scrutiny of power.

'De-agented' power

Having attempted to remove the terms of humanism and the notion of structure from his analysis of power, Foucault now targets the notion of 'agent'. There is something of de-psychologizing impetus at work here. Foucault suggests that we refrain from questioning the objectives and intentions of those exercising power. Power, he maintains, is reducible neither to the actions nor the intentions of its putative agents. We should not attempt to glimpse inside the 'mind' of power, to understand it from 'inside out'. To do so risks psychologizing power into a series of mental or unconscious dynamics such that power is understood reductively as a function of greed, ambition, madness, arrogance and so on. Such an anthropomorphization of power is to be rejected, not only because it detracts attention from the fact of material arrangements of force, but because it slips easily into a moral discourse of what is right and wrong in a human aetiology of power. Foucault rejects such personifications of power unreservedly; imbuing power with a psychological presence lends to it exactly those qualities and formulas of the human that he wishes to escape.

Rather than speculating about the ostensibly psychological dimensions of power – which is not to rule out issues of strategic arrangement – we need to study power 'in its external visage', where its intention, if it has one, 'is completely invested in its real and effective practices' (Foucault, 1980a, p. 97). Although Foucault has prioritized the relational form of power, as discussed above, it is important to guard that this analytic focus does not result in the polarization of subject – object, worse yet, that it does not polarize 'power' and 'subject' – or powerful and the powerless – as separate categories. To be clear, the methodological injunction to trace relational forms hopes precisely to avoid the rigid demarcation of the categories of 'power' and 'subject'. I can put this differently: the attempt to comprehend the relationality of power should result in an understanding of a dynamic functioning which is greater than the sum total of its parts. This helps us grasp what Foucault is getting to when he directs our analytical attention to those points where power is in direct and immediate engagement with its objects, its targets and its field of application; at such moments these divisions (power versus its subjects/objects, power as opposed to its domain of expertise) are difficult to maintain. This is not to say that such distinctions are never (cautiously) to be drawn, nor is it to demand that such divisions be automatically collapsed. It is often analytically useful to make provisional distinctions of just such a sort, especially when it comes to thinking of opportunities for resistance. The point rather is to emphasize that at its moments of optimal functioning, the flow of power – like an electrical charge running through a circuit – cannot be divided up into stand-alone parts and is better traced as a *pattern* than as a list of components.

We then understand better why Foucault warns that the functioning of power is not simply reducible to a sovereign figure, that 'an agent of this sort would be only a terminal form referred to by power, rather than its general means of functioning' (Foucault, 1980a, p. 92). Similarly, in reference to disciplinary relations between expert and subject, Foucault suggests that we avoid asking simply who has the right to know and who is forced to remain ignorant, seeking 'rather the *pattern of modifications* which the relationships of force imply by the very nature of their process' (Foucault, 1980a, p. 99, my emphasis). Questions of power's distribution and of its appropriations of knowledge should not be put to putative agents of power. Foucault's suggestion rather is that we focus on what he terms the *matrices of transformation* that qualify and condition such processes. Not only does Foucault here avoid splitting power into atomized components, but he directs our analytical attentions to *that which is changed*, that is, to what is effected, altered, made different, indeed, *enabled* because of the presence of operations of power. Reiterating this point, he enjoins us to focus on how things *work* at the level of ongoing subjugation, on the continuous and uninterrupted processes that *change* the gestures, behaviours and self-relations of subjects.

The intentionality of power

A paradox emerges here: although power-relations are non-subjective and they are not thought to be fundamentally 'agented', they remain nonetheless *intentional* for Foucault. The fact that power-relations are intelligible at all, he claims, is because they are so thoroughly saturated with calculation:

> [t]here is no power that is extended without a series of aims and objectives... the rationality of power is characterized by tactics that are often quite explicit at the restricted level where they are inscribed... tactics which, becoming connected to one another, attracting and propagating one another... end by forming comprehensive systems.
>
> (Foucault, 1980a, p. 95)

Often the logic within the operation of power is quite clear, just as its aims are often easily identifiable, despite that there is no one there to have formulated them. Here then is one of Foucault's most provocative assertions regarding the nature of power, that its implementation can be viewed as intentional and strategic while *lacking a fundamental or singular agent or strategist*. This contention seems difficult to grasp, yet despite the riddle thus posed – what analogue for power would explain how it is able to exhibit strategy without a strategist? – it makes for a vital pragmatic in identifying the presence of power-relations and in tracing their overall patterns of efficacy.

One might suggest that the value of Foucault's comments in this respect reside more in their analytical utility than in their logical coherence. This logical impossibility – that there is strategy without a strategist – finds an interesting parallel in psychoanalytic thought, particularly in the case of symptomatic actions which display an intention of sorts despite that one can isolate no one conscious, rational agent of intention. There, as here, the objective is not to locate the 'person' behind the symptom – we know 'who' this is in psychoanalytic theory, it is the 'who' of the unconscious – but rather to apprehend the pattern of 'rationality' at work here. This of course is not to suggest an 'unconscious' of power, nor is it to reduce an analytics of power to an exercise in signification (to symptomatic types of reading); it is rather to point to the value of a model that is able to accommodate overdetermination in its understanding of effects of power. To take up in a slightly different way, sometimes designating a single strategist results in a cutting up, a limiting of chains of intentionality and strategy that are perhaps only coherent once articulated over complex enough matrices of transformation. Importantly, Foucault has not totally impoverished the categories of agency and individual intent. He provides a useful qualification in this respect: it is not the case that those in a position of power *do not know what they do*. Frequently, he says, they do know *why* they do what they do; what they do not know is what they do *does* (Foucault, cited in Dreyfus and Rabinow, 1982, p. 187). In other words, there is an awareness of action, a rudimentary sense of effect, a limited appreciation even of rationale and motive that can, in many instances, be located in an agent of sorts – although there is not *an awareness of the overarching rationality, the broader consequences of power of which their actions are part.*

There is a logic to the practices of power, a push towards a strategic objectives; this is the 'sensibility' of power that the analyst should seek to understand. Unless we make use of patterns of elaborated and circuitous intention – patterns not devised from beginning to end by any singular agent – we will remain unable to discern the operations of power over discontinuous or disconnected modes of action and influence. It is these dispersed and dispositional practices of power, in their relatively 'de-agented', 'de-subjected' and yet strategic material reality that must, for Foucault, form the over-riding focus of the analysis of power. To underline the point, the objective in speaking of 'strategy' and 'intention' vis-à-vis the operations of power is not to trace a route to its primal origin, to isolate a definitive agent or cause: it is rather to understand the workability of this particular instance of power, to grasp its lines of efficacy, to fathom something of the contingencies and conjunctions that have made it possible.

Resistance as condition of possibility

The 'relationality' of power emphasized earlier clearly implies qualities of interaction, dynamism and dialogical interchange, all of which, by virtue of their very bi-directionality, permit opportunities for response, for contestation, for answering back. The possibility for resistance is thus an elementary condition, for Foucault, of every conceivable relation of power. He is categorical in this respect: power-relations remain ever fraught with resistance; there is always a strategic possibility for loosening the hold of a given relation of control. More than this, Foucault (1982) also maintains that resistance is a *necessary precondition* for the operation of relations of power: there can be no power without resistance. In a strictly logical sense this must be so, he insists, resistance must be a precondition for power: without such forms of contestation and struggle there would be only complete domination, subservience and obedience.

A question arises at this point: if no dissent emerges as a result of a given arrangement of social ordering, do we even register the presence of a relation of power? We can develop this question in two ways. The first is to speculate whether, in the *absence* of resistance, prevailing relations of power come to be so naturalized, so thoroughly integrated into the normal order of things that they remain totally undetected, mutely accepted as necessary constituent features of society. If this is the case then one imperative for a project of critique is precisely to bring into critical visibility that which seems beyond reasonable scrutiny, to draw the seemingly apolitical factors of human existence increasingly into the frame of political examination. Here one might suggest that Foucault's inventive de-substantializing of power is already a mode of resistance inasmuch as it brings into critical visibility a series of relations of power – of human science knowledge, of the truths of humanism – which may not otherwise have been identified as modes of power.

There is also another more critical way of responding to the above question. Granted it may well be the case that in the absence of resistance, no relation of power is registered. Might it not also be the case that in the absence of any resistance *no relation of power exists at all*? A dangerous implication can thus be read out of Foucault's formulations on the interdependence of power and resistance: unless there is some relation of resistance – a relation which presumably also means some stake of interest – the relation thus constituted is not one of power, but of agreement. The obvious rejoinder here is that power may be present despite a lack of any apparent resistance or of an immediately identifiable stake of interest. To put it another way, although instances of resistance virtually characterize all interventions of power, we should not necessarily accept that *the absence of resistance signals a relationship of agreement or equality*. A slight addition then to Foucault's thoughts on power and resistance: the factor of resistance which is seen as power's precondition may not always be obvious, overtly present; in such cases it may benefit us to consider what previous relations of resistance have existed or what future relations of resistance are imaginable, conceivable.

Power and the potentiality of resistance are hence thought to be coterminous. This, given Foucault's notion of power as heteromorphous and adaptive, as exhibiting strategy and resourcefulness, would have to be the case: what else would drive the constant variation, the diversity of tactics, indeed, the very plurality of power's forms, other than the need to surpass hurdles to its measures of control? Perhaps where we had expected to find a single agent, a strategist, a wily deviser of programmes of power, we should instead look to the role of relations of resistance, sometimes spontaneous, indeed sometimes 'strategic', relations which in many cases would seem to require no more of a sovereign agent of intention and strategy that power itself does. Perhaps it is this factor of resistance or, more directly, the *priority of finding alternative routes of access* to such obstacles that lends power the appearance of forethought, of strategy and intentionality. Like an electrical current able to find a path of conduction despite multiple impediments, power may be said to hold an apparent objective, to exhibit an 'intentionality', without possessing the embodiment of a given social actor, without requiring the role of an agentic subject. While the fact of the strategy evidenced in the overcoming of relations of resistance may lead us to 'personify' power, we must nevertheless hold in abeyance the urge to identify a singular-conscious-thinking agent. As a methodological pragmatic, it helps to question the strategy, the intentions, the choices apparently manifest in operations of power, even though none of these categories can be understood in a human capacity as necessarily correlated to a strategist, to a subject of intentionality.

Foucault's qualifications as to the necessary role of resistance in power lead to a methodological cautioning: don't treat power as *complete control*, as *absolute subservience* – we are better placed to understand the vicissitudes of power when we observe how it is always accompanied and conditioned by that which resists its authority. If, as Dreyfus and Rabinow (1982) argue, it is only through the articulation of points of resistance that power can spread through the social field, then it follows that the identification of such resistances will provide the analyst with an alternative channel of access to the workings of power and the gaps in its efficacy.

A further guideline for analysis then: resistance makes for a particularly crucial focus in the analysis of power. One should attempt to isolate those points where power is most effectively challenged, scrutinizing its most strained attempts at control. Doing so provides a vantage point not only on the operations and weaknesses of system of power, but also on its ongoing tactical adaptations and developments. For each point of power we should be able to locate a corollary of resistance – even if only imaginable, conceivable – for the route of power, its form, is given shape and force precisely in view of how it attempts to surpass, to overcome resistance.

Discussion 2.2: Insurrections of the body

In grappling with some of the conceptual difficulties arising in Foucault's understanding of resistance, it helps to provide a series of practical examples. In his analysis of nineteenth-century psychiatry, Foucault (2006) argues that the power of the psychiatrist was not that of 'monopolizing the truth of what was and was not madness' (p. 132). Rather than considering what the mad person said from the standpoint of truth, instead of placing the question of the truth of madness at the heart of the relationship with the mad person, the psychiatrist came to take on the role of the 'master of reality'. Their task was to 'ensure that reality has the supplement of power necessary for it to impose itself on madness... [the psychiatrist] must remove from madness its power to avoid reality' (Foucault, 2006, p. 132). This is not to say that scientific discourses of truth were not an issue at all – the role of diagnostic categories and of anatomical–pathological knowledge was certainly growing in importance – however, psychiatric power only posed the question of truth 'within itself', as Foucault puts it, and as a secondary consideration relative to the primary objective of imposing reality on the mad.

Given this context, the greatest problem of nineteenth-century psychiatry was not that of the accuracy of concepts or the scientific facts of illness – these truths did not need to be openly debated – its over-riding problem was that of *simulation*. Simulation here is not understood as an act of pretence by which someone who is not mad affects that he or she is; such acts, insists Foucault, do not really put psychiatric authority into question. The simulation he has in mind is 'the historical problem of psychiatry in the nineteenth century', namely 'simulation internal to madness...[the] simulation that madness exercises with regard to itself, the way in which hysteria simulates hysteria' (2006, p. 135).

So if it was the case that psychiatry was unwilling to pose the problem of truth with those who were mad – on the basis that this truth was its sole prerogative, an internal question, its own exclusive terms of knowledge – then the 'response' of madness, inasmuch as madness was to resist the powers of psychiatry, was to 'install' a kind of falsehood. This is clearly not a case of outright deception, of simulation in the obvious sense of pretence. Rather we have the situation, brought about by psychiatric power itself, in which the clarity and definitiveness of the epistemology of psychiatry has been relegated to a secondary position relative to practices of heightening reality; the 'response' of madness, the resistance thus posed, is a renewed 'commitment' to falsehood which makes such engagements harder to manage. The more psychiatry refuses questions of truth, the more madness responds with falsehood, changing thus the footing, the terms of this relationship, in a way that undermines psychiatric authority: 'The untruthfulness of simulation, madness simulating madness, was the anti-power of the mad confronted with psychiatric power' (p. 136).

The problem of simulation thus flows from psychiatry itself; it stems from an internal confusion, an inability to sort out and distinguish various groupings of madness on the basis of its own insulated truths. These 'truths' were not amenable to external verification or critique and were hence unable to adequately grapple with the falsehoods of madness. It is this set of internal shortcomings that madness is able to exploit as a mode of resistance, without explicitly intending to and without a delineated programme of dissidence; this set of shortcomings becomes principle of psychiatry's inefficiency and incoherence.

It is in this way that Foucault understands hysteria, the 'typical asylum syndrome', not as a pathological phenomenon, but 'as a process by which patients tried to evade psychiatric power' (p. 137). Importantly he factors into his account of simulation the role of a series of intermediaries (warders, asylum doctors and various medical subordinates) who move between psychiatrists and patients. We then have not only contact between patients, but also a series of complicities (sometimes spontaneous and involuntary, sometimes explicit) between asylum personnel and inmates. Simulation should thus be understood not only as in part a function of these relationships, but also as a breakdown in how systems of recognition and intervention were passed between psychiatrists and their subordinates. There is then a kind of confusing reverberation between the symptoms and bodily responses of patients and the categorical 'knowings' of an exploratory system of power-knowledge that forcibly asserts an order of reality while still somewhat uncertain of its own categories of truth.

We see here some of what is most distinctive and counter-intuitive about Foucault's formulation of resistance; we are able to isolate a kind of intentionality (i.e. the 'response' of madness, its 'commitment' to falsehood) despite that there is no one single architect or plan of action; there are 'agents', the mad persons, who are able to spontaneously effect such resistances without anticipating the full future consequences of their actions, without being fully appraised of a precise set of tactics; resistance flows from power itself, as an internal element of its own inadequacy.

Foucault follows a similar line of analysis in his discussion in *Abnormal* (2003b) of the religious and medical problematic of convulsion in the sixteenth century. The difficulty of governing the flesh, he suggests, was to 'enter into' the body, to subject it as thoroughly as possible to the probes, categories and questions of a Christian discourse eager to examine it for any taint or sinfulness. The more exhaustive such procedures become in their attempts to unearth evidence of sinfulness, the more total their mappings and examinations of the body – Foucault is preparing the ground here for an engagement with the pre-history of medicine – the more they risk incurring types of bodily withdrawal, evasion, flight and 'counter-power'.

Convulsions and possessions did not thus appear because of a belief in the devil; if we are to understand how and why these and related phenomena occur – such as that of witchcraft, which likewise evidences a series of bodily effects and resistances – we need to undertake 'a history of the relations between the body and the mechanisms of power that invest it' (Foucault, 2003b, p. 214). In the case of both witchcraft and possession, we have 'the effect, point of reversal, and center of resistance to . . . Christianization and its instruments' (p. 214). The 'resistance-effect' of witchcraft is the point of reversal that arises in response to the apparatuses of the inquisition; possession is the resistance-effect engendered by Christianity's techniques of the confessional and spiritual direction. It is in this way that the convulsive flesh 'appears as the endpoint, the abutment of the new investment of the body established by government of souls . . . It is the body that opposes silence or the scream to the rule of complete discourse, the body that counters the rule of obedient direction with intense shocks of involuntary revolt' (p. 213).

Different formulations of resistance

The above discussion gives rise to a question: Is resistance for Foucault a commensurate form, power itself, but of an opposing variety, such that power-resistance relations are essentially a confrontation of power-to-power? This interpretation seems in line with Foucault's notion of multiple relations of opposing force, with the model proposed in *Society Must Be Defended* of the social field as an unbalanced, unstable array of force-relations continually at war with itself. Here one might question whether resistance is in fact being conflated with 'counter-power', whether this order of resistance is not simply an opposing force of an equivalent type to power itself. The charge thus is that resistance has not been properly theorized; opposing vectors of power have simply been labelled 'resistance'. What is power and what is resistance here then becomes a matter of perspective, a matter of where one's interests lie.

In contrast to such a view, might it not be preferable to understand resistance as that which *impedes* the flow of power? Resistance then might best be grasped at those points where power stumbles, at those moments of inefficacy where its conductions break down into disarray, at those lapses and gaps in its regime of control. Not simply another form of power then, resistance is power's failure to assert its complete jurisdiction. Such a view allows us to maintain the argument that resistance is an internal property of power – a condition of operation that remains inherent to power itself – whilst still keeping the space open for resistance as something other than simply *another category of power*. In some ways, an explanation of this sort seems a conceptual necessity: in the case of resistance as merely counter-power we have effectively only power, and resistance seems not to represent a separate category of analysis and action at all. Then again, this explanation is not without its difficulties: if resistance emerges only as an internal property or production of power – as one of power's constitutive and constituted components – then power would again be the dominant category of analysis, and we would seem again to run the risk of losing resistance as a meaningful category of analysis. This need not be true, however: that resistance may spring from the exercising of relations of power – appearing thus as something of an internal property – does not mean that it will be wholly determined or exhausted by power. In Foucault's own terms, 'resistance to power does not have to come from elsewhere to be real, nor is it ... frustrated through being the compatriot of power ... [i]t exists all the more by being in the same place as power' (1980c, p. 142).

Conditions of resistance set in play by circumstances of power can certainly challenge relations of authority, subverting apparatuses of control and calling certain modes of knowledge and truth into question; Foucault provides a series of examples of this, in the bodily resistances of convulsion and possession (2003b) of simulation and hysteria (2006) (see Discussion 2.2). Although it is important to signal the distinction made above – between resistance merely as a different power and resistance as power's undoing – Foucault does not appear to commit wholly to either conceptualization at the expense of the other (indeed, 'resistance is multiple' (1980c, p. 142)). Methodologically this means we should be prepared to trace resistance in either 'medium', if not, indeed in *both*, perhaps even simultaneously. Nevertheless it is worth highlighting what I take to be a risk of the first position, namely a type of political fatalism. From arguing that resistance is power, to the idea that power is inescapable but through rival relations of force (the belief, in other words, that generating relations of control is the only means of avoiding subjection), here we are left with little more than a spiral of power; worse yet a spiral to which we are contributing in a proactive capacity. Such a view of power can lead to the rather bleak conclusion that all we can try and do – given the intransigence and insistence of prevailing forms of power – is to ensure that power does not become overly fixed, an at best paradoxical response which can be read as the reverse of critique, certainly so inasmuch as to prevent stasis or 'fixity' in power, would seem another way of facilitating the expansion and evolution of a given order of power-relations.

Discussion 2.3: An undeveloped analytics of resistance

Foucault's description of resistance is perhaps the aspect of his analytics of power most often singled out for criticism. He is held accountable for not better theorizing resistance, for not prioritizing the prospective elements of its logic and success to the same degree he does those of power. There is some truth in such complaints: resistance never receives the same degree of attention in Foucault as does power; it remains a relative minor term in his analytics. Here then is another shortcoming in Foucault's analytics as a template for political action. Simons (1995), for example, complains that Foucault's optimistic assertions about the possibilities of resistance are unconvincing in comparison with his portrayals of domination. This is not simply a case of the under-theorization of resistance, it is also a question of Foucault's alleged overestimation of the success of panoptical/disciplinary apparatuses (McNay, 1992), an exaggeration which means that he pays less than sufficient attention to the elements of resistance evident in the 'fragmentation and inconsistencies of contemporary modes of government and subjection' (Simons, 1995, p. 83).

In this respect, we might follow Taylor (1984) – and here the Black Conscious example offered earlier makes for a useful case in point – in asking what possibilities for resistance are supplied by humanist modes of thought. Taylor contends that Foucault's assessment of humanism is one-sided; the lack of balance in this critique is reflected in the inadequacies of Foucault's conceptualization of resistance. Simons (1995) extends this, arguing that Foucault failed to elaborate on the capacities for resistance endowed by the very mechanisms of humanist subjection. Now while this is no doubt true – the very successes of disciplinary operations can in certain instances give rise to certain technologies of resistance – one can appreciate Foucault's reticence here inasmuch as he is wary of linking resistance to the actions and responses of individual human agents. For Foucault this is not the right level at which to approach the analysis of resistance; it is not, as one might put it, the right analytical form.

There is also the issue of a seemingly naïve romanticization of resistance, perhaps most starkly evidenced in Foucault's writings on the Iranian revolution, in which he identifies a 'spiritual politics', a 'groundswell with no vanguard and no party', indeed, a 'mass anti-systemic singularity' (Afary and Anderson, 2005), something akin to a primal capacity for resistance (Toscano, 2005). Foucault discerns within this particular political field a spiritualization of resistance ostensibly capable of uniting all levels of society (Afary and Anderson, 2005). However, such a pure expression of general will against the 'modernisation-corruption-despotism' series failed, as Macey (2004) notes, to anticipate the fundamentalist theocracy of the Khomeini government that would soon follow. Part of the problem here – leaving aside for the moment the fact of the mismatch between the instruments of micro-political analysis and a clearly macro-political situation – is that of attempting to conceptualize resistance with a wholly inadequate set of conceptual resources. This is evident in Toscano's (2005) criticism: Foucault's dispensing with notions of political revolution, social contradictions, class struggle, a political vanguard, along with the analytical opportunities these notions afford, leaves him ill-equipped to sketch a useful image of resistance. My point here is not to endorse a return to Marxist forms of critique, but to highlight the dangers of offering or overly optimistic analytics of resistance in the absence of an adequately developed repertoire of concepts and methodological tools.

Evaluating Foucault's analytics

There is no doubt that Foucault has pioneered a novel sensibility of power, one that is impressive in its fluency to recognize modern power in its ubiquity, multidimensionality and flexibility. This is often quite overt in Foucault's terms of description; consider, for example, the following passage from the first volume of *The History of Sexuality*:

> power [is omnipresent] not because it has the privilege of consolidating everything under its invincible unity, but because it is produced from one moment to the next, at every point, or rather in every relation from one point to another. Power is everywhere; not because it embraces everything, but because it comes from everywhere.
>
> (1978a, p. 93)

In passages like this, one cannot help but wonder what the costs of such a conceptualization are relative to a formal system of analysis that requires a set of well-defined instruments of measurement and comparison. To put this somewhat differently: how, as social scientists, can we speak of power with any surety, with any epistemological rigor, if it remains so devoid of definitive form? Or, differently again, in the terms offered by Eagleton (1991), we may well agree that power is everywhere, while wanting for practical purposes to distinguish between more or less central instances of it.

Do we have here a concept without bounds, something like a common denominator of all sociality, morphing from one dimension of human or social life to another without limit? A related issue: given power is integral to any conceivable social relation, will we always be able to adequately distinguish power from that which it comes to possess? How then might we hope to limit this concept and hence prevent 'over-reading' power in all the diversity of its flexible, omnipresent and de-substantialized forms? Perhaps even more pressing: how are we ultimately to discriminate power from non-power; what in Foucault is power's principle of *falsifiability*?

Defying delimitation

The heteromorphous breadth that Foucault imparts to our understandings of power-relations seems necessarily to limit our ability to talk about power in a definitive or disciplined way. In de-individualizing, de-agenting, de-structuring power, in forcing it to resume its integral connections to the production of knowledge, humanism and truth, Foucault has created an increasingly spectral image of power that stretches everywhere, permeating all of social life in a seemingly unremitting and inescapable manner. This prodigious diversity of forms, this apparent ability to possess all order of relationships, all types of strategy makes it so omnipresent, so virtually *everywhere and everything* that it risks becoming nothing at all.

Then again in voicing a series of scattered methodological precautions regards the analysis of power, Foucault may seem to have the licence to make a variety of disparate or even inconsistent claims regards the potential functioning of power. His attempt, after all, is precisely to desubstantialize power; surely thus we should grant him the latitude to throw his net of conceptualization as wide and as open as possible. Given that the methodological injunctions foregrounded here are detached from the substantive historical writings from within which they first emerged, they no doubt appear 'spectral', hopelessly diverse, at times perhaps contradictory. I should emphasize here that Foucault's analytics are best evaluated in the context of their actual application. Certain of the above problems (the over-inclusiveness of power, seeing power everywhere and in everything) seem to stem from offering a general analytics derived from Foucault when his own analyses are always thoroughly immersed in the contextual and empirical particularity of a precise domain of interchange. Lending specificity to one's analysis, as always for Foucault, might be taken as one means of narrowing, refining the particular account of power one is attempting to devise. Likewise the best means of limiting one's formulations of power is with recourse to actual grounded historical examples taken from the specific field of analysis (hence the priority placed on being as clear and concise as possible in the delineation of one's subject domain). This is perhaps the best way of developing a set of possible 'falsifiables'; it is with ongoing reference to practical examples of its distinctive functioning that one can assert a series of 'nots' regards how this instance of power works and which hypotheses and conceptualizations should be ruled out.

However, although we may grant Foucault some latitude *re* the inconsistency and diversity of his formulations, and although there may be some empirical basis to develop the most rudimentary distinctions between how power *is* and *is not* working at particular sites, a more general problem remains. Here it helps to trace Dolar's (1999) précis of Foucault's analytic formulations. Power, for Foucault, is not a place, a definable location or a locus in the social; irreducible to either violence or law, power 'is not an epiphenomena or a superstructure whose basis is somewhere else' (Dolar, 1999, p. 81), that is, power cannot be reduced to something more fundamental lying behind it. There is, furthermore, no hidden depth of power, it can be said to possess no 'natural' or transcendent origin; power does not form a totality, it does not totalize the social; furthermore there is no outside of power, no exteriority, no essence, but then again no interiority. This is what Dolar (1999) has in mind when he suggests that Foucault has a 'negative theory of power', that his conceptualization works on the basis of a series of constant negations. Valuable as this can be as a means of extending our analytical and observational *nous*, it also means that Foucault's notion of power defies delimitation; moreover such a non-totalizable notion of power runs the risk of becoming effectively 'non-conceptualizable', that is, power for Foucault 'emerges in a paradoxical status of a non-concept' (pp. 81–82). Again this might be seen as part and parcel of the benefit of Foucault's thoroughly de-essentialized and unorthodox approach to power. The side-effect of this approach, however, as Dolar notes, is that Foucault is required to constantly multiply the attributes of power – crediting it with the faculties of proliferation, multiplicity, dispersion, prolixity, enhancement, diversification, production, heterogeneity and so on. The concept of power thus becomes a supra-concept.

A solipsism of power?

In this vein, one might query whether in Foucault's genealogical writings power becomes an encompassing category, something akin to a *first principle of explanation*, or more severely yet, *the prime concept* that his analytics of social and discursive systems cannot do without. It certainly seems the case that Foucault is wearing his Nietzschean allegiances clearly on his sleeve in his later writings: a great deal of his genealogical work is predicated, even if rather implicitly, on adherence to Nietzsche's 'will to power' as *the* imperative of all sociality and history. Perhaps this is a problem that Foucault shares with much of the totalizing theory that he opposes: the privileging of a basic concept (be it the unconscious, the notion of class struggle or, in this case, the constant presence and adaptability of power), a concept that ultimately must take on an essential (if not itself essentialized) explanatory role.

Another question: Does Foucault effectively risk a 'solipsism of power' in his studies of this period? Is power evoked to explain too much (the fact of individuality, the functioning of subjectivity and the discourse of humanism) when other dimensions of explanation might offer a more multi-faceted and nuanced account? Should psychological discourse, for example, be completely jettisoned, for the reason that it replicates many of the trappings of disciplinary individualizing humanism, despite that it may offer us some explanatory purchase on the social asymmetries of racism, homophobia, sexism and so on? What, one might ask, is left if this component (the notion of power) is removed from Foucault's vocabulary of concepts; what other concepts, indeed, what *methods* remain viable in the absence of this construct? (Thinking here in particular of the critical practices of discourse analysis, genealogy, heterotopology, to what degree do these modes of examination remain feasible if we are not able to rely on the presence of *power?*)

This, of course, is to offer a somewhat reductive reading of Foucault, but it pays to play devil's advocate here, so as to point out prospective limitations in flat-footed applications of Foucault's analytics. In response to a critique of Foucault's analytics one best responds perhaps by reiterating certain of the above methodological injunctions: make use of the tactic of constant reference to actual examples from 'grounds of practice'; putting one's developing account of power in a constant relationship with a wide set of empirical and historical data should prove a constant requirement of one's analysis. Taking up again the issue of over-inclusiveness: as regards the tendency to view power as a factor of complete omnipresence and in relation to the supra-conceptualization of power into an unbounded set of attributes and abilities, one is left to recommend the imperative of differentiation and, additionally, a far more sustained attention to relations of resistance. It stands to reason – despite the cautioning that power and resistance are coterminous – that if we wish to limit the all-pervasiveness of power (its ability to be all things at all times) and the lack of distinction between different modes, we should look increasingly to the roles of contestation, struggle and refutation as precisely moments when power is not complete or all-pervading.

Spotlight 2.2: Foucauldian methodological pragmatics for the analysis of relations of power

- In order to focus one's analysis, identify and delimit a 'general matrix of force relations' existing at a given time and location, that is, be as specific and clear as possible in the delineation of one's subject domain.
- Prioritize the identification of diverse operational modes of power; explore the possibilities of power-as-strategy and power-as-disposition at the cost of ideas of power-as-property or power-as-appropriation; think power in *formations of practice* rather than *manifestations of structure*. Remain aware that power may exist in an irregular and incommensurate series of components – in scattered circuits of activation – that need never constitute a complete whole.

- Factor in the role of subjects, not as sole agents or controllers, but as the conduits and by-products, the object-effects of power, as points of both the consolidation of existing relations of force and for the further performative extension of its effects.
- Do not fix the flow of power in a single direction; look for bi-directionality; attempt to grasp the reciprocation of passive and active positions in the conduction of power, trace the joint productions of 'top-down' and 'bottom-up' flows.
- 'Zero in' on relations between subjects in contextualized settings (of specific institutions, particular environments or social spaces); whenever there is a relation between subjects or between subjects and institutions or between effects and strategic intentions, try to discern a distinctive pattern or balancing of power. Treat the relation as a favoured analytical category.
- Avoid mutually exclusive divisions between power and its subjects/objects, between the absolutely empowered and the completely powerless, between power and its field of application. Remain aware that at its optimal functioning the flow of power cannot simply be divided into a list of component parts but must instead be approached as a pattern, a relational form always bigger in its effects than the sum total of its parts.
- Attempt to establish matrices of transformation, patterns of modification; one is sensitized to operations of power by becoming attuned to transformative effects, by focussing on those processes that change the behaviours and self-relations of subjects.
- Do not stop at descriptions of the motives and rationales of apparent 'agents' of power; there is a larger intelligibility to relations of power, a push towards strategic objectives that exceeds the limited intentions that may be attributed to any one given strategist.
- Identify the conditions of the 'workability' of the operation of power in question; attempt to isolate its lines of efficacy along with the unexpected contingencies and conjunctions that have made it possible.
- Look for relations of resistance: for each point of power there is a conceivable corollary of resistance. Isolate those points where power is most effectively challenged; doing so provides a valuable perspective on the operations and weaknesses of a system of power and hence also on its ongoing tactical adaptations and developments.
- Resistance may be apparent as either a counter-power (an opposing force of an equivalent form to power itself) or as power's undoing (the gaps, the lapses in its efficacy); be prepared to trace resistance in both

forms, aware that both aspects of resistance may be simultaneously apparent.

- Make use of the tactic of constant reference to actual examples from 'grounds of practice'; putting one's developing account of power in constant relationship with a wide set of empirical and historical data should prove a constant requirement of one's analysis.

Conclusion

Having turned his back on both generalized schemas of power and the domain of the macro-political, Foucault prefers to focus his analytic attentions on the micro-political. The prioritization he places on ascending, peripheral and often paradoxical operations of power makes for an innovative means of critical engagement; his refutation of a variety of caricatures of what power is and how it functions clears the way for new forms of analysis. His rejection of the primacy of previous categories of analysis, such as the notions of agent, structure and repression – such as his refutation of purely economic and judicial models – likewise opens up a series of inventive possibilities for rethinking the functionality of power. This is true also, of course, of his scepticism towards a series of values traditionally assumed to be intrinsically opposed to the practice of power; the properties of humanism, of knowledge, 'truth' and individuality are no longer to be accepted at face value.

It is important, I think, to emphasize that the injunctions offered above are neither absolute nor prescriptive; rather than definitive declarations of what power is, they should be treated as methodological warnings of what power *may not be*. They are suspicions designed to sharpen an innovative and penetrating analysis of power-relations (this despite the fact that Foucault's arguments often taken on a declarative force in their attempt to disabuse us of the more routine formulas of power!). When all is said and done, Foucault leaves us with neither a general theory nor a rigid template for analysis. The analytical imperative he poses, in contrast to both of these objectives, is that of undertaking 'pluralized and discontinuous analyses of power across a range of various fields' (1990, p. 59). The open definition with which he leaves us to pursue our own analytics of power is that of a 'general matrix of force relations', existing at a given time and location, best identified and scrutinized with reference to a web of unequal relations (2003a).

One of the key points of critique brought to the fore in this chapter was the issue of over-inclusiveness, that is, a lack of exclusion or definitiveness in what counts as power. Chapter 6, which examines much of Foucault's writing on macro-political power, introduces a more considered differentiation of types of power. This is partly enabled by Foucault's willingness to accommodate negative relations in his late descriptions of the 'sovereignty-discipline-government complex'.

Discussion 2.4: Does the subject deserve a distinctive ontology?

Alain Badiou, a contemporary and colleague of Foucault's, argues that there is a crucial problem with much of the philosophy of Foucault's generation: there is no distinction between the general field of ontology and a theory of the subject. This criticism obviously takes different forms according to the school of thought – Lacanian psychoanalysis, post-structuralism, analytic philosophy – that Badiou has in his sights. In the terms of Foucault's work, one might state the problem as follows: there has been a merger of the subject with a general ontology of discourse, power and historical events such that there is no longer anything self-defining, distinctive about the subject itself: the subject typically seems wholly determined, wholly produced by just such forces. Thus if we are not to rely on any distinctive ontology or theory of the subject that exceeds the explanations of power/discourse/history, then how might we account for the different level of effects that power has on subjects who are differentially produced? More pertinently yet, to follow the lead of Badiou's commentators Feltham and Clemens (2003): how can one subject be differentiated from another without recourse to some sort of definable identity?

An initial Foucauldian response might be to argue that if individuals are indeed differentiated, then this is already an effect of normalizing power that precisely compares, contrasts and hierarchizes individuals; there are indeed individual differences, but these are precisely recognized within a horizon of power. Moreover that we may have some leeway in how we respond to the task of self-formulation in particular discursive settings, to take this as an example, says less about the transcendent properties of the human subject and more about the complexity and variability of the discursive networks within which we are located.

This may well be true, but there is nevertheless something unsatisfactory about this response, not the least of which is that it brings us very close to a 'blank slate' theory of the subject. Might we not accept the full significance of Foucault's important arguments concerning the differentiation and production of individuals and not still suggest that the 'subjectivity' of such individuals is not wholly accounted for by power, discourse and historical circumstances? Is the subject not deserving of a distinctive ontology, a type of explanation that makes allowance for a locus of features that are more than the simple outcome of various operations of power? Might we not begin to question what it is about that distinctive vector of forces united in those 'somatic singularities' (Foucault, 2006) that exist prior and perhaps even *as preconditions of* the effective operation of disciplinary power? Might it not be the case that we get a better sense of how power works – here we return to Dolar's (1999) argument from the previous chapter – if we understand something of the complex and *reciprocal* relation between contemporary relations of force and certain 'powers of subjectivity' that respond to, assimilate and extend such effects? Might a separate theory of the subject not ultimately advance the sophistication and indeed the overall political cause of an advanced analytics of power?

There is another problem here: the issues of agency. We know that for Foucault power makes individuals and, furthermore, that power may be said to produce resistance. The resulting problem, in terms of Badiou's philosophy, lies in accounting for the source of resistance:

> If the subject – right down to its most intimate desires, actions and thoughts – is constituted by power, then how can it be the source of independent resistance? For such a point of agency to exist, Foucault needs some space which has not been completely constituted by power, or a complex doctrine on the relationship between resistance and independence.
>
> (Feltham and Clemens, 2003, p. 4)

Although these comments emphasize what I take to be a significant critique of Foucault – the lack of any distinctive theory of the subject not loosely predicated on primary conceptualizations of power, discourse and history – they do seem to misread Foucault's notion of resistance in at least two ways. As I have attempted to explain with reference to Foucault's discussions of convulsion, simulation and hysteria (see Discussion 2.2), resistance, even in some of its most effective and belligerent forms, need not necessarily be independent of power. Moreover why should resistance be sourced in the subject? Granted this may mean that Foucault has no adequate theory of individual human agency; then again perhaps this is not where we should seek to locate agency.

3
Discourse, Knowledge, Materiality, History: Foucault and Discourse Analysis

> ...in any society there are manifold relations of power which permeate, characterise and constitute the social body, and these relations of power cannot themselves be established, consolidated nor implemented without the production, accumulation, circulation and functioning of a discourse. There can be no possible exercise of power without a certain economy of discourses of truth which operates through and on the basis of this association.
>
> (Foucault, 1980a, p. 93)

Discourse analysis and psychology

There can be little doubt that discourse analysis has come to represent something of a growth industry in critical and qualitative forms of psychology. Together with a proliferation of various models for the analysis of discourse (Bannister, 1995; Fairclough, 1995; Parker, 1992; Potter and Wetherell, 1987), there has been a veritable explosion of discourse analytic work. This nearly unfettered expansion of discourse analytic work has led, one might suppose, almost inevitably to a variety of misapplications of the work of Michel Foucault, whose name is often attached, practically as a matter of course, to varieties of discourse analysis. It thus seems important to return to Foucault, to clearly define and qualify his understanding of the notion of discourse, and to do so as a means of offering a degree of preciseness to a term which often appears to be both overused and under-defined. I am not suggesting that all instances of discourse analysis misapply Foucault's work; after all, certain such models of analysis base themselves on an entirely different set of conceptual resources (as in the example of Potter and Wetherell, 1987).

100

Nevertheless I would argue that a return to Foucault's delineation of the concept remains vital, if for no other reason than to sharpen the critical potential of such analyses, and to avoid a series of characteristic lapses of critical judgement. Rather than taking issue with discourse analysis *per se* then, my objective here will be to re-characterize a Foucauldian perspective on what discourse is and on what a sound critical discursive analytic methodology should entail. These objectives will be achieved through a close reading of Foucault's inaugural lecture at the Collège de France: *The Order of Discourse*. Furthermore, this discussion will, where appropriate, be illustrated (or contrasted) with reference to two prominent approaches to discourse analysis in psychology, namely those of Parker (1992) and Potter and Wetherell (1987).[1]

Processes of formation and constraint

In a succinct introduction to *The Order of Discourse* Young (1981) notes that the central focus in Foucault's paper is on the rules, systems and procedures that constitute, and are constituted by, our 'will to knowledge'. These rules, systems and procedures comprise a discrete realm of discursive practices, the 'order of discourse', a conceptual terrain in which knowledge is formed and produced. As Young specifies, what is analysed here is not simply that which was thought or said *per se*, 'but all the discursive rules and categories that were a priori, assumed as a constituent part of discourse and therefore of knowledge' (1981, p. 48). In this way, the effects of discursive practices is to make it virtually impossible to think outside of them; to be outside of them is, by definition, to be mad, to be beyond comprehension and therefore reason.[2]

Discursive rules are hence strongly linked to the exercise of power: discourse itself is both constituted by, and ensures the reproduction of, the social system, through forms of selection, exclusion and domination (Young, 1981). As Foucault asserts near the beginning of the paper:

> in every society the production of discourse is at once controlled, selected, organised and redistributed according to a certain number of procedures, whose role it is to avert its powers and dangers, to cope with its chance events, to evade its ponderous, awesome materiality.
>
> (1981a, p. 52)

It is exactly these attempts to master and domesticate such a formidable materiality that constitutes the order of discourse. From the outset

then, Foucault is involved in a concerted attempt to restore materiality and power to what, in the Anglo-American tradition, has remained
the largely linguistic concept of discourse. It is equally clear that he
wants to centre the analysis of discourse *within* the field of political
critique. These concerns with not underestimating the broader political and material functioning of discourse lead also to his emphasis of
the fact that discourse is both which constrains *and enables* writing,
speaking and thinking. What he terms 'discursive practices' work
both in inhibiting and productive ways, implying a play of prescriptions that designate both exclusions and choices. These processes,
of formation and constraint, production and exclusion, are inseparable. More than this, such processes are both complimentary to and
constitutive of one another; discourse is formed and exists through their
mutual constitution. Both are contrary replies to the same fundamental
anxiety

> about what discourse is in its material reality as a thing pronounced
> or written... anxiety at feeling this activity... [its] powers and dangers
> that are hard to imagine; anxiety at suspecting the struggles, victories,
> injuries, dominations and enslavements, through so many words.
>
> (1981a, p. 52)

One may note a sharp distinction here between Foucault's notion
of discourse and commonplace notions of ideology. As Purvis and
Hunt (1993) insist in their comparison of the two concepts, discourse
cannot be treated merely as an extension and instrumentalization
of power, as that which masks or translates power; power, rather is
inscribed *within* discourse, it is – here quoting Foucault – 'the thing
for which and by which there is struggle' (1981a, pp. 52–53) This
does not of course mean that there are no potential attempts at the
management of discourse. There certainly are; the 'order of discourse'
points our attention to precisely the economy of such managements of
discourse.

   The above distinction between formative and constraining processes
structures Foucault's approach here to the analysis of discourse. Each
of these processes requires a discrete analytic process. While a critical
form of analysis is required to examine the functions of exclusion,
the processes of depletion and the institutional role in the operation
of discursive practices, a genealogical mode of analysis is necessary to
examine the *formation* of discourses. Importantly, although the later

Foucault will prove suspicious of any prohibitive notions of power, and particularly cautious regards prohibitive or constrictive notions of discourse – backtracking somewhat on the emphasis here – it is nonetheless important to explore his conceptualization of exclusion, prohibition and exclusion in *The Order of Discourse*. The interplay of positive and negative elements in the production of discourse affords a degree of complexity to Foucault's mode of analysis which, as a result, is able to grasp discourse as it emerges in the dynamic of 'push' and 'pull' forces and is well placed to appreciate the collateral relations existing between processes of generation and constraint. The parameters of what can be said at a given time of place then emerge only as a compromise between these two operations. I would argue that we need to remain receptive to the analytical possibilities of such a conceptualization, despite Foucault's understandable concerns that focussing on the constrictive runs the risk of his notion of discourse being assimilated as yet another prohibitive theory of power.

External systems of exclusion

Before turning to the productive forces of discourse, Foucault concerns himself with what he takes to be the overtly exclusionary mechanisms effecting discourse. The first exclusionary mechanisms he identifies are the social procedures of prohibition which correspond roughly to taboos, rituals and privileges of the speaking subject. These forms of prohibition seem fairly straightforward and Foucault does not spend much time in elaborating them, noting merely that where the (intersecting) grid of prohibition is tightest is in the regions of politics and sexuality.[3] Joining the forbidden speech of politics and sexuality is another form of exclusion, not a straightforward prohibition this time, but more of a division and a rejection: the opposition between madness and reason. With the exception of a number of largely peripheral changes, Foucault claims, this old division is still in operation. The speech of the mad is still 'a noise to discourse' that retains a capacity to truth. Foucault points here to the 'framework of knowledge', that 'whole network of institutions' and qualifications that allows the doctor or psychologist to be able to listen, with a learned and discerning ear, to those elements of truthfulness within the speech of the disturbed.

A third exclusion operating within the order of discourse is the opposition between true and false. Our sense of 'the true', our 'will to truth', is Foucault claims, evoking the Nietzschean concepts, something 'like a system of exclusion, a historical, modifiable, and institutionally constraining system' (1981a, p. 54). The example he uses to unseat an ahistorical sense of the truth is that of the Greek poets, for whom truth was that 'which inspired respect and terror, that to which one submitted because it ruled, that which was pronounced by men who spoke as of right and according to the required ritual' (p. 54). For a significant historical period then this was the highest order of truth, but, as Foucault explains, a day came when truth was displaced from the ritualized, efficacious act of enunciation, 'towards the utterance itself, to its meaning, its form, its object, its relation to its reference' (p. 54). The question of truth hence no longer became the question of what the discourse was, or what it did, but deferred instead to the question of what that discourse *said*. This has not however been the only shift in our 'will to truth'; there are ongoing mutations, continuing changes in the types of divisions that govern the terrain of legitimate knowledge. So Foucault puts it, the 'will to truth' has its own history, which is a history that varies according to the range of objects to be known, the functions and positions of the knowing subject, and the material, technical and instrumental investments of knowledge.

Our will to truth, like other systems of exclusion, can be shown to be contingent. This contingency can be demonstrated perhaps chiefly through the identification of institutional supports and the 'whole strata of practices' underlying the production of truth, such as pedagogy and library-, publishing- and university-systems. These basic material conditions of possibility cannot be reduced, avoided, if we are to properly gain a fix on the formative and constraining systems governing discourse. These are institutions, social structures and practices that limit and constrict the free flow of discourse, which both reinforce and renew it, and as such they need take their rightful places within a thorough analysis of the power of discursive practices.

The 'will to truth' (the way in which knowledge is put to work, valorized and distributed) makes for a vital component in the workings of a successful discourse, and is as such a nodal point of analysis. The strongest discourses are those that have attempted to ground themselves on the natural, the sincere, the scientific – in short, on the level of the various correlates of the 'true' and reasonable. This situation is aptly characterized by Edward Said:

> the will to exercise...control in society and history has also
> discovered a way to clothe, disguise, rarefy and wrap itself

systematically in the language of truth, discipline, rationality, utilitarian value, and knowledge. And this language in its naturalness, authority, professionalism, assertiveness and antitheoretical directness is.... discourse.

(1983, p. 216)

Will to power against will to truth

The methodological imperative stemming from these formulations is an unrelenting skepticism towards all those rationales, explanations and statements that would validate themselves on the grounds of their proximity to a supposed truthfulness. The injunction here is to replace these 'true' explanations with some other form of answer which is more conditional, which can demonstrate that what counts as 'the truth' is a product of discourse and power: a displacement of the will-to-truth by the will-to-power. This is a methodological tactic which will not only make overt certain conditions of possibility (certain contingencies underlying 'the truth'), but that will likewise prove a vital means of sensitizing the analyst to the pervasiveness of the power-knowledge complex.

What is being called for is not some naive debunking of the 'truthful' for its own sake. Indeed, to realize that truth is a function of discourse is to realize that the conditions of truth are *precisely* rather than *relatively* contingent on current forms of discourse. It is in this way ludicrous to read Foucault as suggesting that truth is 'relative', in the open sense of the term, where all possible truth-conditions are equal, depending merely on context or interpretative perspective. Foucault views truth-conditions as extremely stable and secure, as situated in a highly specific and idiosyncratic matrix of historical and socio-political circumstances, which give rise to, and are part of, the order of discourse. A skepticism of truth here defers not to a 'baseless' relativism, but instead to a carefully delineated set of conditions of possibility under which statements come to be meaningful and true. By 'conditions of possibility' Foucault here is referring to materialist conditions that are historically specific and contingent in themselves, rather than in any way 'transcendental'.

Both Parker (1992) and Potter and Wetherell (1987) are rightly explicit about the fact that attaining truth is not the goal of discourse analysis. They do not, however, expend enough energy on demonstrating the bases of power that underpin, motivate and benefit from the truth-claims of the discourse in question. Parker (1992) seems to shy away from destabilizing the notion of truth as entirely discursive-effect, and one suspects this is because he does, ultimately, want to take on a strong political position, something which would be largely untenable in the absence of any grounding moral/political/ethical truism. Potter and Wetherell (1987) appear to supersede questions of how truth *is attained in discourse* with questions instead *of the active function and outcome of acts of discourse*; as a result they pay little, if any attention, to the underlying forms of knowledge in which truth-claims are rooted. This being said, there is a stronger Foucauldian engagement with issues of truth in Potter and Wetherell's later (1992) work; as Willig (1999) observes, 'They invoke Foucault's argument that one way to undermine "truth" is not to counterpose it with another "truth" but to examine the discursive processes by which true and false statements become distinguished' (p. 6).

Neither of these respective methods hence pays enough attention to what underwrites what counts as reasonable and 'qualified' knowledge within a circumscribed socio-historical milieu. Although they may provide schematic details as to what counts as important or dominant forms of knowledge (science, psychoanalysis, psychology and empiricism), they do not properly detail the underlying forms/conditions/criteria of reasonable knowledge on the basis of which truthful statements can be made. What are the underlying supports, in other words, that make the analysed discourse in question feasible in the first place? Careful examination of this sort would expand the generalizability of discursive analytic work (and enable a 'latitudinal linking' of texts) beyond the level of the targeted, analysed text, something which neither Parker (1992) nor Potter and Wetherell's (1987) models can manage. These models fail to properly replace the 'will to truth' with the 'will to power'; what counts as knowledge, and the various systems through which knowledge is qualified/disqualified (in particular the systems of exclusion operating upon discourse) are not traced back far enough to *the material conditions of possibility*, that is, to the multiple institutional supports and various social structures and practices underlying the production of truth. As a result, discourse is not sufficiently grasped in its relation to power; the power of discourse is insufficiently engaged, and discourse analysis becomes more a project of reading the text than of engaging the discourse.

Parker's (1992) method, unlike Potter and Wetherell's (1987), does contain auxiliary criteria specifying that institutions reinforced/attacked by the use of a given discourse should be identified. It seems though that this awareness of institutional links and associated discursive practices is not properly integrated into his methodology in a way that is reasonably achievable within the frame of textual analysis. It would seem that these are goals better attained in a methodology (like genealogy) that does not prioritize textual forms of data at the cost of material forms – as do both Parker's (1992) and Potter and Wetherell's (1987) – and in a methodology which favours a latitude of diverse data forms.

Internal systems of exclusion

There are also a number of exclusions which work internally to discourse – the predominant amongst these are the functions of the discipline, the author and the commentary. Each of these allows the generation of new discourses virtually *ad infinitum* – although within certain limits of constraint. In terms of *the commentary*, Foucault (1981a) is speaking of the discourses based upon the major foundational narratives of a society, and the interchange between these primary (foundational religious, juridical or scientific texts) and secondary cultural texts (commentaries). It is due to the 'top heaviness' of primary texts that they will remain permanent, yet ever capable of being brought up to date, revisited for hidden or multiple meanings.

Each form of commentary obeys the simple directive of recitation; each gives us the opportunity to say something other than the text itself, but on condition that it is the text itself which is uttered (Foucault, 1981a). Foucault's suggestion here is that we overplay the importance of originality and freedom in everyday discourse when in fact much of what is spoken is really the product of repetition, the re-circulation of discourse. By playing up the 'finitude of discourse', Foucault is making us aware of the presence of the limits within which we speak. As such, the questions of innovation, novelty and our presumed ability to utter whatever we will, refers not merely to what is said, but instead to the reappearance of what has been said before.

A complimentary principle of internal exclusion is that of *the author*. Foucault means the author in the sense of a principle or grouping of discourse, a focus of coherence, a unity and origin of meaning. Whereas commentary limits the hazards of discourse through the identity of repetition and sameness, the author limits this same chance element through the identity of individuality and 'I'. Although the principle of the author is obviously not to be found in each instance of discourse, it is a crucial grounding point of the veracity of certain statements. In the Middle Ages for example, a proposition was considered as drawing its scientific value only with reference to its author. Today, by contrast, it is increasingly the case that it is the author who is asked to carry the authentification of the hidden meanings traversing the texts carrying his/her name. Foucault extends these views later, in *What is an author?* (1977e), where he asserts the 'author-function' not as a creative, originating capacity, but rather as a complex and variable discursive function which points to the existence of certain groups of discourse (associated with the author in question) and affirms their status within a given society. Asking 'What matter who's speaking?' (1977e, p. 138), he inverts the typical causal assumption that it is the author who generates discourse to ask how *discourse instead give(s) rise to subjects* (like authors) with privileged positions (and a series of related possible subject-positions). Instead of asking about what is revealed by authors in their texts, Foucault (1977e) suggests we ask instead about *what possible subject-positions are made possible within such texts.*

Suffice to say then that for Foucault, we typically overrate the ability of individual authors/speakers to say something genuinely new, unprecedented. Rather than trusting that individuals themselves are the basis for the emergence of statements, we need to look to how discourses operate as 'parameters of sense-making' within which individuals speak. To paraphrase Said's (1983) discussion of Foucault: the subject is an insufficient cause of a text. Or more directly: 'Over and above every opportunity for saying something, there stands a regularizing collectivity...called a discourse' (1983, p. 186).[4] As such we can far better track the action of a text, trace its political force by connecting it to the formation of discourse of which it is part, than by limiting it to the author principle. None of this is to say that there is not a range of representational outputs afforded by discourses operating as 'parameters of sense-making'. To be sure, there is a great deal of activity, even resourcefulness, in the discursive production of meanings and representation; hence, Said's characterization of discourse as a regularizing *collectivity*. Thus it often makes more sense to speak of a 'field of discourse', a 'discursive formation' so as to emphasize the possibility of adaptability and variation within a coherent political matrix of knowledge. In this way we are able to accommodate variation and flux within a generally stable constellation, rather than implying a singular static structure or 'definitiveness' to a discourse. Importantly, this situation does not leave us with a 'formless chaos of knowledge'. Certain patterns of force, meaning and control do emerge as stable and go on to attain formidable degrees of authority, and prove, practically, very difficult to challenge. So although certain specific discourses certainly do carry more power in contemporary society than others – we are by no means assuming an 'even field' of diverse relations of power here – all exist in a mobile array of intersecting forces and interests. Discourses, one might say, are always multiple, in combination, always in relative stages of formation. The 'surface' of discourse – to speak for the moment of the entire field of discursive relations – makes for a vastly uneven terrain, a topography that is infinitely complex in its details, that resists division into simple basic mutually exclusive categories. For these reasons, it is not generally appropriate – as is often the case in speaking of ideology – to speak of a single or *dominant* discourse, as if the discourse in question possessed anything like the singularity or overall dominance of capitalist ideology (the ideology that is to say serving those in possession of the means of production).

Discussion 3.1: Differentiating discourse from ideology

It is useful here to point to a series of basic distinctions between the Foucauldian concept of discourse and traditional Marxist notions of ideology. In the latter, as Dolar (1999) notes, there is a strong emphasis on the problems of the type of consciousness that makes power-relations possible, on 'its inherent illusions, its essential blinding, the false consciousness that enraptures individuals and turns them into subjects, the intertwining of recognition and misrecognition' (p. 82). In speaking of ideology in these terms, social critics often have in mind something akin to large mutually opposing 'blocks of consciousness' which, in the classical Marxist formulation, fall on either side of the truth/falsity divide (Purvis and Hunt, 1993). Neither of these postulates holds good in the case Foucault's notion of discourse, which is less singular in nature, and which cannot be conceptualized as a 'form of consciousness', or as an overall state of being-in-the-world. Foucault's focus on the 'pure exteriority of power', as Dolar puts it, does not entail, as do many understandings of ideology, the assumption of 'a space of interiority and a mechanism of repression' because these are 'the very entities he is trying to do away with' (p. 82). Much talk of ideology presupposes the existence of a humanist subject (with their innate faculties of consciousness, interiority) – precisely those facets of subjectivity that Foucault demands we account for rather than assume. Furthermore, ideology for Foucault always stands in virtual opposition to something else which is supposed to count as truth:

> The problem is not changing people's consciousness...but the political economic, institutional regime of the production of truth...The political question...is not error, illusion, alienated consciousness or ideology; it is truth itself.
>
> (1980a, p. 118)

Arguing that truth does not stand outside of discourse, that discourse is a far less singular entity than, say, bourgeois ideology is not to maintain that certain discourses do not hold more sway than others. Particular productions of knowledge do, no doubt, attain a greater weight of truth than others, although this is often a question of historical location. Paedophilia today, for example, is more authoritatively understood as an issue of pathological desire, indeed, as *psycho*pathology, than as the result of bodily aberration, or physical degeneracy within the figure of the paedophile (although the historical residue of such earlier types of explanation has not completely evaporated). 'Discursive fronts' as we might put it, extend their power and their associated prerogatives on exactly this basis, as being 'more the true' than aligned and/or competing modes of explanation (which are not always wholly discrete from them). Discourse at its most forceful manages just this, to claim the status of 'the truthful', hence Foucault's reference to discourses as 'regimes of truth'. To reiterate the above point: discourses, unlike the basic Marxist 'blocks' of ideology, cannot easily be distinguished with reference to the categories of what is 'true' or 'false'. Moreover, unlike many critical applications of the notion of ideology, a given discursive formation cannot easily be located on either side of a key line of antagonism that splits the social field. The lack of such clear-cut criteria (such as that of a class divide), of such principles of cohesion and/or discretion (such as class interests), make it harder to divide discourses up into a small number of fundamental categories.

It is worth emphasizing here also that discourses are never complete or absolute in the range of influence that they are able to exert. Various historical and political forces are continually making their influence felt such that, although relatively stable for given historical periods, the overall field of discourse is never static, never simply contained, controlled by any one institution or constituency. Despite an underlying constancy, discourses are thus subject to change, adaptation and reformation along slightly different lines. To miss this fact is to miss part of what is most fundamental to Foucault's account of the discursive: the field of discourse is always thoroughly composite, crisscrossed with conflict, and open to resistance.

Operations of constraint

The third internal principle of discursive limitation is that of the discipline. A valid disciplinary statement is contingent upon a variety of conditions, Foucault (1981a) reminds us, upon the appropriate domain of objects, theories, methods, propositions, rules, definitions, techniques and instruments. In this sense, statements made from within a discipline need to fulfil certain conditions more complex than those of simple truth. At the same time, however, disciplines consist of both errors and truths.

Although each scholarly discipline entails a variety of 'complex and heavy requirements' that 'pushes back a whole teratology of knowledge', that discipline always risks the possibility that one may hear truthful statements 'in the spaces of a wild exteriority' (Foucault, 1981a, p. 61).

In his attempts to rupture the integrity of the principles of the author, the commentary and the discipline, and by showing them up as limiting conditions that operate to re-circulate given understandings, Foucault is arguing that we have dangerously overestimated the creative and resourceful abilities of speaking subjects. It will be impossible, he demands, to account for the positive and multiplicatory role of these broad principles 'if we do not take into consideration their restrictive and constraining function[s]' (1981a, p. 61). Discourse analysis should hence busy itself not merely with the search for a plenitude of meaning, but rather with a search for the scarcity of meaning, with what *cannot* be said, with what is impossible or unreasonable within a certain discursive locations. Again, it is necessary to note that the later Foucault of *The History of Sexuality* will look, by contrast, to explosions of meaning, stressing the massive productive energies driving the constitution of sexuality within a given discursive field. Perhaps the obvious point to be made here is that different formations of discourse will emerge and operate under different conditions. There can be no one trans-historical rule: various economies of discourse will involve different combinations of production and restraint. An awareness of productive and constrictive procedures alike will be necessary; not all formations follow the same pattern as that of modern discourses of sexuality. The clear suggestion in Foucault's subsequent work though is that productive forces tend to predominate in modernity. Furthermore, we need avoid viewing the productivity of power as a subcategory of a larger power of constraint and endeavour to grasp the more paradoxical notion that, very possibly, relations of exclusion, prohibition and scarcity are subcategories of massive relations of discursive generation.

Parker's (1992) model of discourse analysis holds up relatively well in reference to Foucault's commentary on the limiting principles of author and discipline. Demonstrating a strong antagonism to psychologizing modes of explanation, Parker emphasizes that discourses are trans-individual, that 'there need not be an author behind a text', and that one should look beyond individual intentions when attempting to grasp meanings within a text. In this regard, one should note that much of the animating impetus of Parker's work (and this is shared, although perhaps to a lesser extent by Potter and Wetherell's (1987) *Discourse and Social Psychology*), lies precisely in the critical imperative to critique and question the conventions, norms, values and practices of established,

Table 3.1   Systems of exclusion/constraint governing discourse

External systems of exclusion/ constraint	Internal systems of exclusion/constraint	Determining conditions of application
i. Social procedures of exclusion (prohibition) ii. The division between madness and reason iii. The division between true and false	i. The principle of the commentary ii. The principle of the author iii. The principle of the discipline	i. Rituals of speaking ii. 'Societies of discourse' iii. The principle of doctrine iv. The social appropriations of discourse (as in education, or in institutional systems like that of law and medicine)

mainstream Western psychology. In this sense *Discourse Dynamics*, like a variety of his other texts (Parker, 1989, 1999; Parker *et al.*, 1995) certainly demonstrate an awareness of the inhibiting discursive powers of the discipline, and a willingness to disrupt and destabilize these boundaries for strategic purposes. Then again, it is questionable the extent to which this awareness is effectively (and critically) implemented within his discourse analytic methodology. Furthermore, both Parker and Potter and Wetherell suggest, in accordance with Foucault, that texts play a role in generating, enabling and limiting empowered/disempowered subject-positions (Table 3.1).

Determining conditions of application

A third group of procedures permitting the control of discourse are what Foucault refers to as determining conditions of application. Neither internal nor external to discourse itself, these procedures impose rules and restrictions of access on speaking subjects. Without dwelling too long on these we may identify them as ritual, doctrine, conditions of social appropriation and what Foucault calls societies of discourse. In general, Foucault is pointing out that not all regions of discourse are equally open, that some are almost totally forbidden while others are seemingly at the disposal of every speaking subject, without prior restrictions. With 'ritual' Foucault refers to the set of gestures, behaviours, circumstances and signs which accompany (and extend the warrant of) the qualified speaker of discourse and which are present in the political, juridical, religious and therapeutic instances of speech. This is more than an urging towards greater contextual specificity in our analyses; it is a direction to pay attention to the institutional props, to the behavioural extensions (the bodily significations, one might say) of the verbal performance of discourse.

'Societies of discourse' says Foucault, 'function to preserve or produce discourses, in order to make them circulate in a closed space, distributing them only according to certain rules' (1981a, pp. 62–63). There are various schemas of exclusivity and disclosure which mark different 'societies of discourse', as may be seen in the cases of technical or scientific jargon, the diffusion and circulation of medical discourse, or as in case of those who have appropriated the discourses of politics and economics. The analytical focus here is on institutionally bound networks that operate their own laws of discretion and exclusion when it comes to what can be said, and how.

Doctrines, by contrast, are those philosophical, religious or political texts that tend to be diffused, circulated and transmitted amongst an ensemble of individuals sharing a joint allegiance. Doctrinal speech requires conformity to a set of validated discourses (appropriateness of content). Reciprocally, however, it also in a sense requires the conformity of the discourse to the speaker (appropriateness of the speaker), given that the doctrine always stands as a sign, manifestation and instrument of a prior adherence to a particular class, a social status, a race or nationality. This is not only about the entitlements and prerogatives of certain elected speakers; it draws attention to the fact of a double subjection that comes about in doctrinal societies, the subjection of the speaking subject to discourses, and of discourses to the group of speaking individuals.

Education is a central concern for Foucault when it comes to issues of social appropriation: although education is thought to be the individual's route of access to whichever discourse he/she would like to enter, it remains always preventative, its distribution marked out along lines of social distances, opposition and struggle: 'Any system of education is a political way of maintaining or modifying the appropriation of discourses, along with the knowledges and powers which they carry' (1981a, p. 64). There can only ever be an artificial separation between the various broad determining conditions of application, precisely because these various procedures of subjugation are often effectively linked in social or educational systems. 'What', after all, he asks, 'is an educational system, other than a ritualization of speech, a quantification and a fixing of the roles for speaking subjects, the constitution of a doctrinal group, however diffuse, a distribution and an appropriation of discourse with its powers and knowledges?' (p. 64).

These determining conditions of application cut across the epistemological, societal and performative dimensions of discursive production; they add a broader sociological focus to the analysis of discourse. These considerations do not feature to any prominent degree in the methodological steps offered by Potter and Wetherell (1987) or Parker (1992), although the latter does direct attention to what can and cannot be said within the speaking positions of particular subjects of a given discourse. In fairness, one should note that the analytical interests of Potter, Wetherell and Parker are invariably more micro than those of Foucault – often texts of 'individual' speakers (interview material), or key examples of widely distributed 'public' texts – whereas Foucault typically seems more interested in broader formations of knowledge, in tracing these conditions of application from the perspective of a far wider frame of reference. Importantly, both Parker and Potter and Wetherell do make a contribution in this general area of analysis: both pay attention to the issue of positioning, considering how subjects are positioned in and through discourse as particular kinds of person with differential rights and prerogatives. Also important here is the notion of discursive warrants, that is, an awareness of how certain locations and roles put the speaker into a privileged position of knowledge or authority; variations of these ideas are present in both Parker (1992) and Potter and Wetherell (1987) (see also Gergen (1999) for further discussion of the idea of 'discursive warrants').

Valuable as such contributions are, they do, from a strictly Foucauldian perspective, bring with them a possible problem: the risk of insidiously re-establishing the category of the individual agent. So why they do well to focus on the subject as *positioned*, commensurate with a Foucauldian view, they also imply the possibility of 'making self' through discourse, a situation in which one's 'subject–position' effectively becomes one's 'individuality'. We should as such be wary of this application of 'positioned subjects' as potentially recuperating a sense of singular agency of discourse. The risk, moreover, is that such a level of analysis returns us to a focus on individuals – or subjects – where it is perhaps more appropriately focussed at a more trans-individual level.

Philosophical themes of limitation and exclusion

Having uncovered the predominant means of exclusion operating upon discourse, Foucault is now concerned with identifying the correlating philosophical themes that reinforce these activities. His question, in essence, is how modern western society has been so successful in eliding the presence and actions of discourse. The themes he identifies collude: they all propose an ideal truth as a law of discourse, they all adopt an immanent rationality as the principle of their behaviour, and they all address themselves to an ethic of knowledge which promises to give truth only to the desire for truth itself. These themes are all party to ensuring that 'discourse should occupy only the smallest possible space between thought and speech', to enforcing that speech should appear 'as simply thought made visible by means of words' (Foucault, 1981a, p. 65).

The first means of concealing the reality of discourse is found in the Heideggerian idea of *the founding subject* who is thought to directly animate the empty forms of language with their aims. This founding subject has at their disposal signs, marks, traces, letters, but is somehow immune to the need to pass via the filtering mechanisms of discourse in order to manifest these signifiers. It is through the intuition of this subject that meaning is grasped, that horizons of meaning are founded, where sciences and deductive reasoning have their ultimate grounding. A second theme, that of *originating experience*, turns on the supposition that at the very basis of experience there were prior significations, things already said, wandering around the world. In this idealist conception the world is occupied by 'things...already murmuring meanings which our language has only to pick up' (1981a, p. 65). This language, moreover, has always already been 'speaking to us of a being of which it is like the skeleton', and, we exist within 'a primal complicity with the world' (p. 65).

Universal mediation is a third theme which indicates the presumption of an omnipresent *logos* elevating particularities to the status of concepts and allowing immediate consciousness to unfurl in the end the whole rationality of the world. Through the reification of this logos, discourse becomes little more than 'the gleaming of a truth in the process of being born to its own gaze' and 'things themselves, and events...imperceptibly turn themselves into discourse as they unfold the secrets of their own essence' (Foucault, 1981a, p. 66). It is through these three dominant and pervasive philosophical themes, of the founding subject, originating experience and universal mediation that discourse is reduced to little more than a play, of writing, in the case of the first, of reading in the second, and of exchange in the third. These admitted activities of discourse are the only most superficial qualities (markers) of its actions; this writing, reading and exchange never puts anything at stake except signs: discourse is hence annulled in its reality and put at the disposal of the signifier (Foucault, 1980a). Here then is perhaps Foucault's strongest warning that the analysis of discourse should not defer simply to a reading of textuality, to a study of powerful significations (Table 3.2). What follows here is

a refusal of analyses couched in terms of the symbolic field or the domain of signifying structures, and a recourse to analyses in terms of the genealogy of relations of force, strategic developments, and tactics...The history which determines us has the form of a war rather than that of language: relations of power, not relations of meaning.

(Foucault, 1980a, p. 114)

Table 3.2 Philosophical themes that elide discourse and corresponding counter-themes.

Philosophical themes that elide the reality of discourse	Corresponding counter-themes that enable us to fix the 'reality of discourse'	Corresponding methodological imperative
i. The idea of the founding subject (*as corresponding to* the activity *of signification* of writing) – as exemplified in phenomenology	i. A persistent questioning of our 'will-to-truth'	i. The need to analyse discourse with reference to its *conditions of possibility*
ii. The idea of originary experience *(as corresponding to* the activity *of signification* of reading) – as exemplified in hermeneutics	ii. The restoration to discourse of its character as *event*	ii. The need to analyse discourse with reference to *action*
iii. The idea of universal mediation *(as corresponding to* the idea *in practices of signification,* of exchange) – as exemplified in Neo-Hegelianism's 'movement of transcendence'	iii. The 'throwing-off of the "sovereignty of the signifier"'	iii. The need to analyse discourse in terms of *material effects*

These comments asserts a formidable problem for many instances of discourse analysis, certainly for Parker (1992) and Potter and Wetherell (1987), indeed, for many critical linguistic practices which, within the context of their analyses, focus on power as a function of the text alone. Foucault's claim is that such forms of analysis typically attribute undue power to the internal properties/structure of language. Against a pan-textualism which might claim that everything can ostensibly be analysed as a text, as a language, Foucault (1981a) argues that the power in language links to, and stems from, external, material and tactical forms of power. Power cannot be fixed, or apprehended in the meanings and significations of texts alone; rather it must be grasped and traced through the analysis of tactical and material relations of force.

If one is thus attempting to engage critically with discourse, as Foucault understands it, then those forms of analysis based on the 'turn to text', that define discourse as 'a system of statements that construct...an object' (Parker, 1992, p. 5), as 'forms of spoken interaction...and written texts' (Potter and Wetherell, 1987) that consider discourse to refer to a set of meanings, representations, images, stories and statements (Burr, 1995), will remain woefully limited in their attempts to apprehend the full capacity of the power of discourse. These approaches come dangerously close to reducing discourse to narratives, to forms of representation, to language, or text alone. Potter and Wetherell (1987) are certainly guilty of this (although their later (1992) study includes more of a material focus on the effects of racist discourse), as to an extent is Parker (1992), although the latter, in a secondary capacity, does emphasize that discourse may also take material forms, and be 'embodied' in various kinds of practice. Even when authors such as Parker (1992), Burr (1995) and Wetherell and Potter (1992) signal that they are aware of the importance of material correlates of discourse, of discursive practices in the operation of discourse, they are unable to provide adequate means through which to involve the analysis of these material and extra-textual practised forms of powers within their methodology.

Closer to Foucault's insistence that discourses are, at basis, *forms of practice*, is the analytic approach of Fairclough (1992), who speaks of discourse in the terms of 'social action and interaction', and who is careful to emphasize *both text and context*, in the study of discourse, both that inside of *and outside of,* the studied text as part of the discourse in question. Some of Potter and Wetherell's work (Potter and Wetherell, 1987; Potter *et al.*, 1990; Wetherell and Potter, 1992) also takes cognizance of the importance of the context of discourse (i.e. along the lines that one needs to understand the political and interpersonal contexts in which speaking is being informed if one is to properly gauge its power and its purposes). While this relation of discourses to contexts beyond the immediate level of the text is important, and while this emphasis on the performative focus on discourse *as action* would no doubt be well placed for Foucault, even this attention to contexts and to textual *action* would not go far enough for him in terms of concretely tying discourse to physical and material arrangements of force. Ultimately, Potter and Wetherell's (1987) focus on the variability of linguistic form (according to context and function) simply defers to *a restrictive focus on linguistic content* which marginalizes the breadth of discursive phenomena beyond the text (as noted by Fairclough, 1992).

The principle of reversal – event versus creation

Foucault's first explicit methodological priority is the principle of reversal. He means reversal here in the sense of a subversion or an over-turning (Young, 1981), as a means of refuting and inverting assumptions of origin. Those traditional sources of discourse which appear to play a positive role in the production of discourse must be refuted through the demonstration instead of how they act to cut up, limit and 'rarefy' discourse. These are the traditional 'sources' that typically derail our analytic attempts, and separate, in an artificial way, individual voice, the drive to truth and the realm of technical expertise from the political field more widely.

The methodological counter-term supplied by Foucault here as a way of enforcing the principle of reversal is the idea of *discourse as event* which he sets up in opposition to the idea of *discourse as creation* (1981a). In a later interview (1981b), he qualifies the methodological prospects of the notion of eventualization as '[a] breach of self-evidence, of those self-evidences on which our knowledges, aquiescences and practices rest....' (p. 6). Continuing, he notes 'eventualization means rediscovering the connections, encounters, supports, blockages, plays of forces, strategies and so on which...count...as being self-evident, universal and necessary' (p. 6). The principle of eventualization amounts to a procedure of causal multiplication, it means effecting a multiplication or pluraliza-tion of causes such that the object of analysis (the event) is analysed by tracking the multiple processes which constitute it. Analysis hence proceeds by progressive and necessarily incomplete saturation, from the consultation of ever more sources of origin and realization, ever more analytical 'salients', to an increasingly polymorphism of elements, relations and domains of reference that play their role in bringing the object in question into being.

Thinking discourse as event thus enables us to look beneath the alibis of creation, and to isolate very different (and multiple) origins of discourse, which Foucault (1981a) suspects will reveal functions of exclusion. These objectives of 'breaching self-evidence' and 'rediscovering connections, supports, blockages, plays of force' lead us to a determined identification of the material components acting upon and within discourse, to an analysis of the multiple analytical 'salients' underlying the successful production of discourse. It seems that Foucault's suspicion (1981a,b) is that the more we follow a polymorphism of analysis, the more we will be able to tie discourse to the motives and operations of power-interests, the more analytically visible discourse will become, and, as a result, the more politically (and ontologically) robust our analyses will become. The principle of reversal hence may be seen as a way of *politicizing the de-politicized*, self-warranting accounts of discourse, as way of making discourse visible, and visibly connected to multiple prospective origins and forms of realization.

Said (1983) similarly emphasizes the importance of re-relating discourse to a greater network of power-relations when he notes that Foucault's method of critically engaging discourse is to strip it of its 'esoteric or hermetic elements and to do this by making [it] assume its affiliations with institutions, agencies, classes, academies, corporations, groups, ideologically defined parties and professions...[These critical engagements]...forcibly redefine and reidentify the particular interests that all [discourses] serve' (p. 212). Re-emphasizing the importance of this form of 'reaffiliation' he notes that '[e]ach discourse...is to some degree a jargon...a language of control and a set of institutions within the culture over what it constitutes as its special domain' (p. 219).

Here it should again be noted that Parker's (1992) method does make allowance for the identification of institutions; similarly, it makes mention of the fact that discourses reproduce power-relations. However, in both of the above cases, Parker (1992) fails to properly explain how the identification of institutions, like the identification of those who will/will not benefit from the mobilization of the discourse, may be properly accommodated within a methodology that treats discourse chiefly as a form of language. Again one feels that a broader definition of discourse, and a broader analytic scope than one limited basically to the analysis of *texts* will be necessary if this method is to comply with Foucault's demands. Similarly, Parker (1992) is anxious about how one might imply the omnipresence of power by emphasizing the inextricability of power and discourse, and thereby lose sight of the prospects of resistance. This is clearly antithetical to Foucault's approach, which seeks precisely to emphasize how *enmeshed* power is within discourse. (Importantly here, an emphasis of the intimacy and inter-connectedness of power and discourse need not, for Foucault, mitigate against the possibilities for resistance, particularly given that, in his conceptualization, resistance is a feature of every power relationship; there can be no relation of power *without* resistance (Foucault, 1982)).

Another pragmatic upshot of prioritizing discourse as event becomes clear: one should approach discourse not so much as a language, or as textuality, but as an active 'occurring', as something that implements power and action, and that also *is* power and action. Rather than a mere vocabulary or language, a set of instruments that we animate, discourse *is* the thing that is done, 'the violence', as he puts it, 'which we do things' (Foucault, 1981a, p. 67). Indeed, in Foucault's 1976 Collège de France lectures, discourse is understood as a battle or struggle; as both place of an instrument for confrontation. Discourse does not here simply express or reproduce social relations that have already been constituted:

> [T]he mere fact of speaking, of employing words, of using the words of others . . . this fact is in itself a force. Discourse is, with respect to the relation of forces, not merely a surface of inscription, but something that brings about effects.
>
> (Foucault, 2003a, p. xx)

Said is again a valuable point of reference here, especially so in his insistence that the predominant goal of discourse is 'to maintain itself and, more important, to manufacture its material continually' (1983, p. 216). Many of Foucault's later works take this material level of discourse as their prime focus. *Discipline and Punish* (1977a) is a case in point where Foucault maps, in rigorous detail, power's various and developing investments in the body. Here, each facet of discursive commentary is led and substantiated by the minutia of various corporeal rituals of bodily discipline, which, in their impact, would seem clearly irreducible to an exclusively textual focus.

It is worth commenting on one aspect of Potter and Wetherell's (1987) conceptualization of discourse here. While they do not take enough steps to adequately relate discourse to a wider realm of material forms of power – they have been criticized, as Burr (1995) notes, for looking at the internal workings of a piece of text at the cost of its wider political implications – they *do* importantly treat discourse as action, or, more specifically, as a 'potent, action-orientated medium' (Potter and Wetherell, 1987, p. 28). The performative quality that they grant discourse in their conception resonates well with Foucault's conceptualization of discourse as 'a violence we do things', and is somewhat helpful in mitigating against the notion of discourse as individual creation. Then again, their notion of interpretative repertoires, that is, the linguistic resources available to speakers in the construction of their accounts (Potter and Wetherell, 1987), regrettably restores what Fairclough (1992) considers to be a 'one-sided individualistic emphasis upon the rhetorical strategies of speakers' (p. 25). This is an emphasis that in many ways recuperates exactly the sense of authorial and creative capacity that the notion of discourse as event had attempted to circumvent.

The principle of discontinuity – series versus unity

Foucault's second explicit methodological injunction in *The Order of Discourse* is that of discontinuity. Perhaps the most straightforward aspect of this principle is the distrust it displays in cause-effect patterns of explanation. As Foucault (1970) had already suggested in much of his earlier works, linear causality and narratives of progress, continuity and evolution are not always the most profitable methodological tools of analysis. The reason for this distrust of continuity as an explanatory concept stems from the suspicion that, as an historical form of explanation, it will remain limited, insulated within the context of its analytical activity. Butchart (1998) signals this trepidation in his comment that historical analyses emphasizing continuity run the risk of projecting backwards from the present the concepts that their analysis will ultimately 'reveal'.

The important distinction here – and in this regard Foucault is explicitly reliant on Nietzsche's notion of 'effective history' (cf. Foucault, 1977b) – is that between a 'history of the past' and 'a history of the present'. A 'history of the past' is essentially a work of the present, strongly anchored in the current socio-political realm, and produced as a way of understanding what happened in a previous era. Because it is essentially a product of the present, it risks reproducing as much about the author's historical and political context as it does about the subject matter under study (Butchart, 1998). Rather than anchoring itself in current socio-political understandings and alienating the past, a history of the present, by contrast, prefers to interrogate the present, to examine *its* values, discourses and understandings with recourse to the past as a resource of destabilizing critical knowledge.

In equivalent terms then, rather than grant a privileged status to the content of discourse (as Parker (1992) and Potter and Wetherell (1987) do), discourse analysis needs to decentre and destabilize such meanings, undermine their authority and uproot the coherence, unity or 'ahistory' upon which such 'truthful' meanings are reliant. The fixing of discontinuities makes for a nodal point of analysis precisely because 'it disturbs what was previously considered immobile... fragments what was thought unified... [and] shows the heterogeneity of what had been considered consistent' (Foucault, 1977b, p. 147). In this way the workings of discourse become much more discernable, the effects of what had appeared as a 'transparent medium of communication' become fixable, just as some of our most fundamental concepts, like those of the psyche, sexuality and society become apparent as largely discursive entities. Hence one starts to see the absolute reliance, for Foucault, that any critical, or politically efficacious, project of discursive analysis will have upon effective forms of history; for him this is an important font of critical 'counter-knowledges' (Foucault, 1980a) well-suited to destabilizing current hierarchies of knowledge, to resistance and struggle. Without this historical dimension we will be limited to 'scratching the surface of discourse'; our results will remain loaded with contemporary values, more a product of contemporary discourse than a critical analysis of it.

Parker's (1992) method does suggest that 'discourse is historically located', in conjunction with the warning that discourse analysts should be wary of disconnecting themselves from history (p. 16). While these stipulations are commendable, it seems that this use of history can only possess a limited, peripheral and descriptive capacity if not centralized as a prime methodological component. Parker's (1992) appeal to history has an 'after the fact' feel, and as such, one supposes, it loses much of its destabilizing and critical potential. Ultimately, this reference to history lacks an explanation of how such contrary counter-knowledges may be put to use in *contesting* current discursive knowledges.

The methodological opposition Foucault (1981a) brings to play as a way of enforcing the importance of the principle of discontinuity is that of *series versus unity*. Rather than assume a shared likeness then, or suppose that each component of the analysis will be of the same type, the discourse analyst must be prepared to search for similar functions across a variety of different forms (language, practices, material reality, institutions and subjectivity). Similarly, rather than following linear successions of development (vertical patterns of analyses), the discourse analyst must be able to accommodate a lateral range in their analytic focus, mapping parallels of regularity (horizontal, 'sideways' patterns of analysis). Here the priority given to textual forms of discourse in Parker (1992) and Potter and Wetherell (1987) is again problematic; without the realization that textuality is only one 'realization-point' of discourse, without the breadth of analysis that would consider a variety of diverse forms, these forms of analysis will only be able to mount impoverished accounts of the greater powers and capacities of discourse.

Foucault's notion of the series is a vital methodological concept in alerting us to the fact that discourse works in discontinuous and often contradictory ways. If we are to successfully identify discourse, and to gauge it in the fullness of its various capacities, then we need a notion that can join together an ensemble of discourse's various components, despite their diversity. Said's (1978) assertion of the idea of 'flexible positional authority' is invaluable here. Flexible positional authority characterizes that factor of discourse that enables fragmentary, 'un-unified' and immanently dissociable discursive acts to work together in powerful conjunction. Thus Foucault's assertion, 'discursive events must be treated along the lines of homogenous series which, however, are discontinuous in relation to each other.' (1981a, p. 69)

Both Parker (1992) and Potter and Wetherell (1987) do attempt to accommodate a sense of the flexibility and discontinuity within the workings of discourse. (The notion of flexibility of use is integral to Potter and Wetherell's (1987) problematic notion of interpretative repertoire. Parker (1992) speaks of how a discourse might refer to other discourses as a way of extending itself, and reiterates the inter-textuality of discourse.) However these attempts once again fail to pay enough attention to extra-textual forms of discourse. Given then that discourse is able to work in *discontinuous* ways, that discursive practices are able to cross and juxtapose one another with 'mutual unawareness' (Foucault, 1981a), we cannot simply speak against discourse, or attempt to liberate a network of repressed discourse lying beneath it. To attempt to 'give voice' to a great unspoken risks simply reproducing the criticized discourse in another way. Indeed:

> the fact that there are systems of rarefaction does not mean that beneath them...there reigns a vast unlimited discourse...which

is... repressed by them, and which we have the task of raising up by restoring the power of speech to it.

(Foucault, 1981a, p. 67)

It is not the case that there is a great 'unsaid' or great 'unthought' which runs throughout the world 'and intertwines with all its forms and all its events' (p. 67). Foucault is pointing out that the model of repression will be inappropriate here in describing the functioning of discourse because it is quite simply *not* the case that the attempt to utter those meanings excluded, marginalized or 'repressed' by discourse will bring us to truth. There is not a vast and unlimited, continuous and silent discourse 'quelled and repressed by various practices', and subsequently, it is markedly not our task to 'raise up the restored power of speech to it' (p. 67).

This is a difficult point in the sense that it frequently does appear to be Foucault's task to do just this, to give voice to those de-legitimized sources so thoroughly disqualified from predominant discourse (Foucault, 1980a). While this may no doubt be the case, it is worth bearing in mind that this kind of genealogical recovery of subjugated voices does not occur under the auspices of confronting a great untruthfulness with the force of an indisputable truth. It occurs rather under the auspices of tracing discursive formations of power and control, by assembling a strategically organized ensemble of historical knowledges that will be capable of opposition and of struggle against the coercion of presiding discourse (Foucault, 1980a).

The analyst of discourse is predominantly then concerned with exploiting the gaps or shortcomings of a given discourse, with systematically demonstrating its contradictions and discontinuities; these are the seams to be pulled, the joints and weaknesses to be stressed. (Parker's (1992) method does make provision for such an emphasis on the internal contradictions within discourse in that he suggests analysts 'set... ways of speaking against one another' (p. 14).) Exposing these points of vulnerability is infinitely preferable to the attempt to unravel the great 'unsaid' precisely because the latter risks simply reproducing discourse rather than arresting its activity.

The principle of specificity – regularity versus originality

In speaking of specificity Foucault is worried about those overgeneralizing forms of analysis that would resolve specific and particular discursive forms into 'a play of pre-existing significations' (1981a). The activity of a 'general reading' of discourse will not suffice; discourse analysis must not be reduced to an exercise in interpretation, to do so returns us to an assumption of inherent meanings within the world which are simply to be decoded and translated. In strong opposition to such assumptions, Foucault warns that 'the world is not the accomplice of our knowledge; there is no prediscursive providence which disposes the world in our favour' (p. 67). It is not the case that varieties of discourse more or less approximate the true or intrinsic values of things; by contrast, we come to know meanings and to distinguish truth-claims *precisely on the basis of discourse.* An important word of qualification stems from this point. To proclaim that 'there is no prediscursive providence' is not to subsume everything within the world into discourse. Indeed, to suggest that our knowledge of the world, our estimation of truth, and our speaking capacity (the scope of things that can reasonably be said) is governed by certain discursive formations is clearly different to saying that there is nothing beyond the text, that everything that happens within the world is reducible to certain textual markers.

In contrast to suggestions that discursive practices can be largely reduced to textuality (as seems so often the case in predominantly textual focus of Parker (1992) and Potter and Wetherell (1987)), Foucault's warning is that we must resolve to 'throw off the sovereignty of the signifier' and look further afield to identify a wider array of discursive effects. Similarly, he demands that one does not reduce the analysis of discourse merely to the 'markings of a textuality', but that one fixes it also in the *physicality* of its effects, in the *materiality* of its practices. As such, critical readings, like interpretative exercises, will be insufficient, they will allow one to deny the materiality of discourse, to elide much of its force, and will hence result in the crippling of the political impact of our analyses.

The opposition Foucault draws on here is that between *regularity and originality.* His point here is to impress upon us the fact that similar discursive acts can occur in a multitude of different ways, in various different forms which stretch from what has typically been considered 'discursive', that is, the textual to the 'extra-discursive', the material level of discursive practices. Foucault's use of the term 'discursive practices' here is noteworthy; not only does it suggest a plurality of significations and acts that nonetheless maintains a unified function, it also makes it difficult to separate the material and the textual, to grant either a separate (and mutually exclusive) integrity beyond the other.

The collapse of this textual/material, 'discursive'/'extradiscursive' division seems strategic on Foucault's part, his agenda, it seems, is precisely to complicate and problematize the division. Once we consider the discursive utterance (say, for example, the diagnosis of someone as a 'pervert') as an action, as a practice or an event, then this utterance seems to start verging on the territory of materiality, and becomes more easily linked to the array of physical activities through which such a diagnosis may be made in the first place. On the other hand, more obviously material practices like procedures and treatments – say the regimes of rehabilitative or punitive operations that follow on from the incarceration of such a 'pervert' (the paraphiliac, the paedophile) – would clearly appear to be of a different ontological nature (physical acts, bodily confinement, routines of examination), able to support, extend, affirm textual elements of discourse, without being exhausted by it.

The collapse of such a division also brings serious problems with it – most obviously an overemphasis of textuality. Two distinct errors are to be found here. The first resides in seeing nothing beyond the 'discursive', nothing beyond the text, seeing torture, for example, as a form of dialogue. The second resides in granting a kind of overempowered status to language alone. A case in point here would be the deployment of political-correctness as a way of trying to change the world in isolation of certain fundamental material conditions. These errors signal a myopia of the text, an overvaluation of the linguistic and representational powers of language in isolation of the material arrangements of power in which they are enmeshed, and which they in turn extend.

The breadth of a focus on 'discursive practices' (so conspicuously absent in Parker (1992) and Potter and Wetherell (1987)) mitigates against exactly such a myopia. As problematic as it is to threaten the collapse of this distinction on an ontological level, there is nonetheless a critical methodological efficacy in a cautious, pre-cursory exploration of the blurring between the textual and the material, the 'discursive' and the 'extra-discursive'. This distinction implicitly undermines the activity of critical analysis inasmuch as it aids and abets the contemporary effacement and denial of the potency of discourse's material effects. Being able to cautiously blur these lines will keep the analyst from underestimating *the discursive effects* of the material, and *the material effects* of the discursive.

It seems that by being able to work in two analytic domains, to substantiate critical textual assertions on the basis of materially focussed analyses, and vice versa, that Foucault lends a unique epistemological

Table 3.3 Methodological requirements for the analysis of discourse

Methodological principles	Key corresponding methodological oppositions	Directions for theoretical elaboration (the fundamentals of the genealogical method to come)
i. The principle of reversal (facet of critical analysis)	i. *The event* as opposed to the idea of *creation*	i. A 'materialism of the incorporeal': an emphasis on the importance of *the material*
ii. The principle of discontinuity (facet of genealogical analysis)	ii. *The series* as opposed to *unity*	ii. A theory of 'discontinuous systematicities': an emphasis of the importance of *the discontinuous*
iii. The principle of specificity (facet of genealogical analysis)	iii. *Regularity* as opposed to *originality*	iii. The idea of chance as a category in the production of events: an emphasis on the importance of *chance (alea)*
iv. The principle of exteriority (facet of genealogical analysis)	iv. *Condition of possibility* as opposed to *signification*	iv. An overview of surface conditions as opposed to the deep analyses of meaning

strength to his work, a strength lacking in both Parker (1992) and Potter and Wetherell (1987). There can be little doubt that Foucault's priority is not that of 'reading', textuality or signification, but rather that of materiality, conditions of possibility and historical circumstance. Hence one might contend that Foucault's analysis of discourse occurs fundamentally *through the extra-discursive* – a fact which brings his approach to discourse into strong conflict those of Parker and Potter and Wetherell (Table 3.3).

The principle of exteriority – conditions of possibility versus signification

Rather than moving from discourse towards its interior, towards the 'hidden nucleus' at the 'heart of signification', discourse analysis should move forward on the basis of discourse itself, on the basis of those elements which gives rise to it and fix its limits: its external conditions of possibility. Foucault's methodological injunction here is that of *exteriority*. Critical readings, he claims, will prove inadequate: looking at what can be shown to be within the text is insufficient because alternative 'showings' will always be possible. This is the problem of textual relativism, where any reasonably supported textual interpretation will hold, within relative confines, as well as any other. Hence the results of our analyses will be of little significance beyond the scope of the analysed text.

This problem of textual relativism as mitigating critical/political utility is one of which many practitioners of discourse analysis (Burman, 1990, 1991; Burr, 1995; Parker, 1992) are themselves aware. As Burr (1995) notes, the relativism of much discourse theory makes it difficult to justify adopting one 'reading' of a text rather than others. Because a discourse analysis cannot be taken to reveal a 'truth' lying within the text, it must acknowledge its own research findings as open to other potentially equally valid findings; due to the absence of notions of truth and falsity as reasonable or secure points of reference in discourse analysis, all we have is 'a variety of different discourses or perspectives, each apparently valid' (Burr, 1995, p. 60). Burman (1991) likewise points to this inability to ally oneself to any explicit political position from within such approaches, and comments that it thereby becomes difficult 'to elaborate a position where it is possible to privilege or maintain a commitment to one reading rather than another' (p. 331).

It is clear in this way that the analyst of discourse needs to appeal to certain stable reference points outside of the text (although not those of truth and falsity, for obvious reasons). Indeed, if the critical efforts of the discourse analyst are to possess any real political weight then these analyses will need be substantiated with reference to a different epistemological order than that of textuality. The point here is that one needs to reference one's analytical conclusions, wherever possible, to a double epistemology; to corroborate findings to extra-textual dimensions, like those of space (geo-politics, or the analysis of heterotopia (see Chapter 5)), time (history), architecture or material forms of practice (Foucault, 1977a). Analysing text alone should not be seen as an adequate means of 'getting to grips' with power; power would seem to be a far more sophisticated thing than textual discourse alone.

There is another way of exploring the limitations of merely textual interventions, by drawing attention to the distinction between discourse as objective of power (discourse as 'the thing *for* which there is struggle', as *power itself*) and its means of implementation ('the thing *by* which there is struggle'). If we produce texts as a means of critiquing discourse, that is, if we generate discourse as the basis of opposition, we may very possibly act to provide an oblique support or adjunct to the discourse we are attempting to contest. To focus too much on the textual level of discourse (to confuse its textuality with 'all that power is') is to leave our critical readings and writings open to the subsumption of facets of a rival set of discourses, to allow our discursive productions to become the instruments of political interests to which we are opposed. In other words, the risk we take in engaging discourse chiefly at the textual level is in assuming that *this itself is power*, and assuming this at the expense of attending to how this textuality – like our own textual interventions – can be differentially utilized by different political interests.

Foucault is warning us that we are making a mistake in attempting to reduce the function of discourse to one comfortable role in the operation of power. One needs to only briefly consider the complexity of the mutually beneficial and interdependent relationship of the material and the discursive in the operation of power to be aware that discourse often appears as both *instrument* and *objective* of power, both its antecedent and its result. Discourse facilitates and endorses the emergence of certain relations of material power, just as it justifies these effects after the fact. Similarly, material arrangements of power enable certain speaking rights and privileges, just as they lend material substantiation to what is spoken in discourse. The mutual reliance of this relationship should not be underestimated; the attempt to isolate either aspect of power from the other in the analysis of discourse risks severely undercutting the efficacy of one's analysis, and colluding in the ongoing production of power.[5] I can phrase this differently: remaining *within* the text means that the analyst of discourse will not be able to properly engage with the text's diverse possible instrumentations, with how its particular discursive logics, rationales and formulations may come to *be differently utilized by a variety of political interests*. If the analyst stops short of plotting an overview of the matrices, interconnections and networks of material-to-textual and textual-to-material directions of power, they open themselves up to the possibility that their own critical work may become instruments of the discourses they are attempting to critique. Foucault's notion of the 'repressive hypothesis' (1978a) is useful here in demonstrating that an over-riding concern with the content and overt effects of discourse result in a lack of awareness of the means in which *the criticism of discourse itself may become the insidious instrument of power.*

Discussion 3.2: The relationship between politics and discourse

A Foucauldian analytics remains aware of the dangers of conflating discourse and power. Clearly, discourse is not all there is to power; other 'faculties', components and dimensions need to be taken account of in any sufficient political analysis of relations of force. Furthermore, these other components do not necessarily concur with, reiterate or support the kinds of discourse with which they have come to be associated. As Homi Bhabha (1994) warns, we must not make the mistake of assuming that a simply deterministic or functionalist relationship exists between discourse and politics. The importance of this point may be underlined with reference to an oft-cited example. Towards the end of the 1980s many prominent US feminists came together with representatives of the Christian right in adopting a strong anti-pornography platform as a basis for many of their political activities. At a surface level these two parties appeared to share a similar 'discourse', to make use of a similar set of statements, positions, slogans and so on, although of course their underlying politics were opposed in often quite fundamental ways. A crusader for the religious right could use virtually the same anti-pornography arguments and rhetoric as the feminist, but to conservative and patriarchal ends, rather than to further the objectives of anti-sexism. So while it is the case that discourse itself is powerful, that to exercise discourse successfully is to afford oneself a certain power, to claim a certain privileged enunciative role, it is also the case that conflicting political interests may attempt to utilize a similar kind of discourse.

This example alerts us to the risks of a merely discursive intervention in the world of power. The production of discourse is not necessarily a sufficient means of doing politics, of challenging or over-riding particular relations of power. We need be aware that in producing discourse (as in the case of a vocal anti-pornography position) we may be unwittingly providing instruments (arguments, rationales and 'discursive tools') that may be taken up and utilized by precisely a broader arrangement of power (a larger regime of patriarchal relations) that we had initially hoped to contest. Foucault makes the point clearly in *The History of Sexuality*:

> Discourses are not once and for all subservient to power or raised up against it . . . We must make allowances for the complex and unstable process whereby discourse can be both an instrument and an effect of power, but also a hindrance, a stumbling block, a point of resistance and a starting point for an

opposing strategy. Discourse transmits and produces power; it reinforces it, but also undermines and exposes it, it renders it fragile and makes it possible to thwart it.

(1978a, pp. 100–101)

The conceptual opposition that Foucault attaches to the principle of exteriority is that between signification and the conditions of possibility (1981a). Drawing analytical attentions away from significations alone, Foucault's imperative is thus to identify the various overlapping forms of support which limit the discourse under study, and in the absence of which certain discursive statements could not have been made. Analytic attentions hence need defer to a variety of circumstantial variables, stretching across the material, institutional and historical circumstances that make certain acts, statements and subjects possible at certain specific locations. Rather than just locating discourse within a web of discursive effects then, one might also unearth certain of its various potential instruments.

Perhaps the most important point of this position, for the present discussion, is that it plays up the extent to which certain forms of discourse analysis inevitably defer to a kind of interpretative activity, which, in a sense, recuperates the principle of the author within the interpretative researcher. (It should be noted here that Abrams and Hogg (1990) have criticized Parker's criteria for the identification of discourses, arguing that his stress on the way in which 'discourses are realised in texts' obscures the role of the analyst of discourse as interpreter. Similarly, Marks (1993) claims that despite attempts at reflexivity in discourse analysis procedure, typically the researcher's 'reading' carries the most weight (relative to that of research subjects), a fact that is also conceded by Parker and Burman (1993)). Lacking the breadth or latitude of a broad-based *genealogical* approach to critical investigation, discourse analysis unavoidably continues to follow 'a vertical line of investigation', to adopt 'a depth-approach' to the text. Hence, as Potter claims of Parker (in Burr, 1995), one's own less than explicitly contextualized political position comes to assume the anchoring-position once provided by the provision of the notion of 'truth'. Basically, discourse analysis, in the models provided by Parker (1992) and Potter and Wetherell (1987) cannot rescue itself from claims that it functions as an interpretative activity, which reifies the text, recuperates the author-principle (in the figure of the interpreter), and restores a central anchoring point, not this time in the form of truth, but in the authoritative interpretation, which performs much of the same function. Given that there is no 'prediscursive providence', any activity which is interpretative in some means or form, will only again uncover discursive effects. To critically engage with discourse one does not need implicitly interpretative approaches, one needs, by contrast, to map discourse, to trace its outline and its relations of force across a variety of discursive forms and objects.

Conclusion: shortcomings of discourse analysis

At the outset of this chapter, it was noted that there exists no strictly Foucauldian method of discourse analysis. The reason for this by now appears to be quite apparent: the various methodological injunctions prioritized by Foucault can be better accommodated within the ambit of critical genealogical work than they can within forms of discourse analysis that separate themselves from broader analyses of power, the consideration of history, materiality and the underlying conditions of possibility underwriting what counts as reasonable knowledge. One of the general conclusions that can be drawn from the preceding examination is that Foucault's conception of discourse is situated far more closely to knowledge, materiality and power than it is to language. As McHoul and Grace's (1997) note, Foucault moves the concept of discourse away from a linguistic system towards the understanding of a discipline – that is both in the scholarly sense (of science, medicine, psychiatry, sociology and so on) and in the sense of the disciplinary institution (such as the prison, the school, the hospital, the confessional and so on). It is exactly the omission of these three dimensions of analysis that so undermines the epistemological strength, the explanatory power and the political abilities of both Parker's (1992) and Potter and Wetherell's (1987) approaches.

It is with reference to these three pivotal conditions of discourse, and as way of tying together the underlying basis of many of the foregoing methodological/theoretical arguments that four basic arguments may be articulated. First, Foucault's conceptualization of discourse indispensably requires the role of historical contextualization; discourse analysis only finds its real usefulness within the agenda of a 'history of systems of thought' (Foucault, 1977c). To preclude the dimension of history from the critical analysis of discourse is to risk producing an analysis insulated within the socio-political discursive context in which it was produced, that is, it is to risk reproducing precisely the kinds of discourses one had hoped to interrogate. In this connection, both Parker (1992) and Potter and Wetherell (1987) arguably involve historical forms of analysis, *if at all*, in only a peripheral and hence insufficient capacity. Secondly, for Foucault, a study of discourse must necessarily entail a focus on discourse-as-knowledge, that is to say, a sustained attention on discourse as a matter of the social, historical and political conditions under which statements come to count as true or false (McHoul and Grace, 1997). Without reference to the underwriting conditions of knowledge and to the frame of what constitutes reasonable knowledge, discursive analytic procedures such as Parker's (1992) and Potter and Wetherell's (1987) will only be able to make isolated comments, comments with a generalizability and political relevance limited to the reference point of the actual analysed text. Third, without reference to materiality and the wider technologies of power in which such practices come to be rooted, discourse analysis remains largely condemned to 'the markings of a textuality', a play of semantics, a decontextualized set of hermeneutic interpretations that can all too easily be dismissed. More than this, by fixing on textual effects *as power itself*, at the cost of an awareness of textuality as a variously utilized instrument of power, discourse analysis aids and abets in the contemporary effacement and denial of the material effects of discourse, and appears to risk a dangerous reductionism in thinking power (Table 3.4).

Table 3.4 Foucault's methodological requirements for the critical analysis of discourse

Methodological principle	Corresponding conceptual opposition	Methodological imperative	Directions for theoretical elaboration (imperatives of the genealogical method to come)
The principle of *reversal* – (subvert attributions of the origin of discourse) (facet of critical/ archaeological analysis)	Discourse as *event* as opposed to *creation*	Tie discourse to motives and operations of a variety of power-interests and actions	An emphasis on the importance of *the material*; attempt to fix discourse within the category of *event*
The principle of *discontinuity* (being wary of the risk of projecting current discursive values into the analytical field) (facet of genealogical analysis)	Discourse as *series* as opposed to *unity*	Rather than as formal unity, grasp discourse as a 'laterality' of forms, as a horizontal series	An emphasis on the importance of *the discontinuous*

Table 3.4   (Continued)

Methodological principle	Corresponding conceptual opposition	Methodological imperative	Directions for theoretical elaboration (imperatives of the genealogical method to come)
The principle of *specificity* (avoidance of the assumption of inherent or intrinsic universal meanings) (facet of genealogical analysis)	Discourse as instance of *regularity* as opposed to instance of *originality*	Rather than resolving discursive forms into 'pre-existing significations' focus on the particular physicality, the precise materiality of discursive practices	Oppose teleological explanations of a universal or finalizing origin with descriptions of regularity; an emphasis on idea of chance (*aléa*) as a category in the production of events
The principle of *exteriority* (facet of genealogical analysis)	The analysis of *conditions of possibility* as opposed to the analysis of instances of *signification*	Rather than moving towards a hidden interior 'nucleus' of discourse, look to those elements which give rise to and fix its limits	An emphasis on the 'surface' conditions of possibility as opposed to an analyses of depth or 'inner meaning'

As a way of uniting the above three conditions of discourse in one over-riding methodological imperative, one could suggest that the analysis of discourse, according to a Foucauldian perspective, cannot remain simply *within* the text, but needs to move, in Said's (1983) formulation, both *in and out* of the text. If one is to guard that one's analytic efforts do not result in mere 'markings of textuality', with limited political relevance, restricted generalizability and stunted critical penetration, then it will be necessary to corroborate the findings of textual analyses with reference to certain extra-textual factors (history, materiality and conditions of possibility), to do exactly what Parker (1992) and Potter and Wetherell (1987) fail to do, to drive the analysis of the discursive *through the extra-discursive.*

There is another important distinction between Foucault's approach to the analysis of the discursive and the models advanced by Parker and Potter and Wetherell. As evidenced above, Foucault's approach to analysis parts way with the internal preoccupations of critical reading methods such as those of structural linguistics, deconstructionism and semiotics; his primary focus lies with the external or social conditions under which discourses are formed and transformed. As Purvis and Hunt (1993) emphasize, Foucault's is a rigorously social, even materialist examination of the formation of discourse; the notion of the 'order of discourse' directs our attention precisely to the economy of discourse constituted by these (material, historical, practical and technological) elements. This is a crucial component that is missing from Parker and Potter and Wetherell's models: an attention to the economy of forces within which particular discourses come to operate. Attention to this shifting field of intersecting and opposing forces permits a degree of sociological depth to Foucault's analyses; it allows us to begin outlining the points of articulation between a given society and the discursive formations that come to attain particular degrees of prominence. Here we might advance a cautious analogy. Discourses are like symptoms: if they are to be properly understood, they need to be placed in relation to the economies of conflict which they both express and constitute. Without this broader frame of analysis, discourse analysis is akin to a reading of symptoms that occurs without reference to the dynamic of forces, the matrices of formation, within which they come to take on a particular form.

Although this chapter has attempted to provide an explication of Foucault's theory of and analytical approach to discourse, and while it has attempted to explain his understanding in as accessible and as straightforward a manner as possible, it has not meant to imply that Foucault's position on discourse was unchanging, clear, simple or unproblematic. While I will not undercut the analytical efficacy of the analytical maxims supplied above by now introducing a lengthy critique of the shortcomings of Foucault's notion of the discursive, it is worth foregoing that Foucault's thinking in relation to the concept and methodology of discourse was certainly complex, difficult, nuanced, and at times, contradictory. There is, however, one issue that does demand to be addressed. In critiquing forms of discourse analysis, this chapter has frequently pointed towards the genealogical method as a superior means of critical engagement, yet it has failed to fully describe what such a genealogical approach would entail. In many ways then, this chapter begs a companion piece, an elucidation of the genealogical method as it may improve upon certain methodological problems specified above, how it may more efficaciously enable the project of political criticism, and how it may usefully be put to use within the domain of psychology. This is the focus of the following chapter.

Discussion 3.3: Activity as basis for 'counter-discourse'?

Despite that the focus in much of Foucault's later work shifts from the notion of discourse to that of the dispotif – perhaps precisely as means of accommodating the breadth and heterogeneity of what 'the discursive' might be thought to entail – the concept of discourse remains absolutely crucial to his work. Without disputing the importance of this notion, it seems nevertheless useful to briefly reflect on some of what is excluded from the critical frame of Foucault's approach to discourse.

The factor of *activity* as separable from social thought – as happening 'prior to', or *in opposition to* the formalization of discursive intelligibility – provides our first point of consideration. The possibility that seems to have been missed in Foucault's theorization of discourse is that physical actions – the *doing* of practical activity – might challenge, or refute, a particular set of discursive representations. This is by no means to suggest that the realm of activity exists in some ideal sphere beyond the 'jurisdiction' of the discursive. It is rather to open up the possibility that the doing of activity might work as a condition of contradiction of various forms of accepted social knowledge, indeed, that it might provide a critical dimension of reformulation or resistance.

Here it is worth pointing to a key theoretical precedent, the fact that Marx's theory of ideology is rooted in an *action theory*, which, as Purvis and Hunt (1993) emphasize, is organized around the dualism of action and consciousness. Marxism then, like activity theory, holds out that some form of lived experience, or, more to the point perhaps, *actual daily practice*, can start to challenge a whole series of hegemonic representations of reality. The possibility of discomforting juxtapositions of this sort is of course the basis for various forms of 'consciousness raising'.

Without framing this problem within the register of Marxism or with reference to correlated notion of consciousness, we might nevertheless question whether the domain of activity might provide a basis for 'counter-discourse'. If the premise asserted by Lev Vygotsky (1978) is taken seriously, then we should try to track activity not merely as 'following after' discourse, as strictly limited to the significances afforded it by social thought, but as itself a resource of thought and indeed, by extension, means of the refutation of more solidly anchored discursive practices. Jäger's (2001) criticism of Foucault's concept of discourse develops along very similar lines. He finds it strange that 'The psychologist Foucault . . . . did not know the activity theory based on the materialist psychology of the early 1930s', conceding eventually that 'possibly he rejected it as appearing . . . to be too subject-based' (p. 43). In a way, *Discipline and Punish* implies the possibility of activity as a means of refutation and resistance, precisely by virtue of its emphasis on how disciplinary operations thoroughly colonize the body, disciplining even its smallest movements and actions in order that they are brought into alignment with the implementation of discursive norms. The suggestion that bodily activity might be somehow 'counter-discursive' is also evident in the closing passages of the first volume of the *The History of Sexuality*. Here Foucault holds out the possibility that bodies and pleasures might exist outside of the discursive codification of sexuality: 'the point of leverage for the counterattack against the apparatus of sexuality must not be sex as desire, but bodies and pleasure' (1978a, p. 159).

4
Foucault's 'philosophy of the event': Genealogical Method and the Deployment of the Abnormal

With Brett Bowman

> And this is what I would call genealogy, that is, a form of history which can account for the constitution of knowledges, discourses, domains of objects etc., without having to make reference to a subject which is either transcendental in relation to a field of events or runs in its empty sameness throughout the course of history.
>
> (Foucault, 1980b, p. 117)

This chapter can be read in at least two ways. It is first and foremost a close-text exposition of Foucault's approach to genealogy, undertaken so as to avoid the shortcomings of many standard forms of discourse analysis as practiced within psychology.[1] It is also, more generally, a commentary on the strategic value of 'effective history' as it might inform qualitative research as a mode of critique. Foucault offers us less than a structured 'methodology' of genealogy; his late genealogical works create a methodological rhythm of their own, as Tamboukou (1999) puts it, ensuring no certain procedures of analysis. What Foucault does offer is a set of profound philosophical and methodological suspicions towards the objects of knowledge that we confront, a set of suspicions that stretch to our relationships to such objects, and to the uses to which such related knowledges are put. Foucault's genealogical method, in short, is a methodology of suspicion and critique, an array of de-familiarizing procedures and re-conceptualizations that pertain not just to any object of human science knowledge, but to any procedure (or position) of human science knowledge-production.

Following the style of the previous chapter, my discussion here will take the form of a reading of Foucault's most pertinent single document regards the question at hand, in this case Foucault's (1977b) essay *Nietzsche, Genealogy, History.* I illustrate many of the methodological maxims introduced with reference to a series of examples drawn from a recent study on the historical formation of paedophilia within South Africa between the years of 1944 and 2001. Given this third component of the chapter, I have elected also to include a series of speculations on the historico-discursive production of abnormality derived from Foucault's recent (2003b) *Abnormal,* a series of speculations which I believe exemplify many of the methodological injunctions of genealogy.

Subjugated knowledge, buried historical contents

In a 1976 Collège de France lecture, Foucault (2003a) remarked on a remarkable upsurge in the originality and diversity of local forms of criticism which, he felt, had rendered a range of human sciences discourses and institutions unusually vulnerable to contestation. He had in mind a variety of events, including recent student uprisings, the anti-psychiatry movement, and a number of attacks on the legal and penal systems in France. Speaking with an uncharacteristic sense of optimism, he noted that many of the most familiar and intimate of everyday practices and self-relations had become questionable; commonplaces of everyday human existence had seemingly become reversible, open to new and seemingly radical interrogation.

The uncoordinated and even fragmentary occurrence of such invectives did not pose a problem; the lack within anti-psychiatry, for instance, of any systematic principles of co-ordination, or of any over-riding system of reference, proved less important than its potential to produce a variety of autonomous critiques independent of the substantiation afforded by allegiance to systematizing theoretical frameworks. These sporadic invectives, for Foucault, were only made possible by virtue of an 'insurrection of subjugated knowledges'. Two conjoined ideas are involved here. First, the use of historical contents that have been neglected, filtered out and actively de-prioritized by the organizing structures of orthodox systems of theory and knowledge. Secondly, Foucault has in mind those kinds of knowing that are routinely rejected and dismissed, that cannot emerge from the practices, foci and priorities of a science of a recognized or 'reasonable' branch of knowledge. Not always traceable to written sources, such modes of understanding include the spoken knowledges of the subjugated, the differential and opposition counter-knowledges of recipients of disciplinary healings and corrections.

Foucault hence presents a potent combination for critique: a bringing together of the past and the forgotten with the deliberately excluded. Only by setting these two kinds of work alongside one another – the reactivation of neglected historical contents and the tapping of unsystematized oppositional contents – can one show up the divisions, the contestations and countering knowledges that 'functional arrangements [and]...systematic organizations are designed to mask' (Foucault, 2003a, p. 7). It is only through the contexts of exclusion and disqualification – contexts marked by struggle, conflict and the violence of marginalization – that we can properly grasp the *political force* of knowledge which is, in effect, the objective of genealogy. An unconventional means then for how we should mobilize such forms of counter-knowledge: by applying scholarly methods to them; the scholarly treatment, in other words, of that which has long since been ejected from the field of the scholarly. This poses an interesting challenge: the utilization of differential set of local and historical knowledges 'incapable of unanimity' via the tools of 'historical, meticulous, precise, technical expertise' (2003a, p. 8). Yet it is exactly this coupling that establishes the astonishing efficacy of the 'discursive critiques',[2] as Foucault refers to them, of the various scattered critical offensives mentioned above.

We are pointed thus in the direction of a rather unorthodox form of analysis whose yield is the recovery of conflicts and dissension, the revival of contestation against formations of truth. We may base an outline of genealogy on just such terms: genealogy is a coupling of scholarly erudition and local memory that 'allows us to constitute a historical knowledge of struggles and to make use of this knowledge tactically today' (2003a, p. 8). A principal objective is thus to 'make heard' the claims to attention of discontinuous, disqualified knowledges against the unifying centrifugal pull of theory. Hence the characterization of genealogies as 'anti-sciences' which do not necessarily work against the methods or concepts of a science, but whose overall function is to oppose the centralizing *power-effects* of institutional knowledge and scientific discourse.

If we follow Foucault's assertion that knowledge is inseparably bound with the practice and maintenance of institutional power in modern societies, then we understand that genealogies aim to fight the power-effects of any discourse that attain the status of 'science'. Buried historical contents and subjugated knowledge are such vital resources for genealogical work precisely because of their potential to disrupt the dynamic between power and knowledge; free of association from unitary discourse, they have yet to be integrated into the 'power-knowledge circuit', as Ransom (1997) puts it. This does not of course mean that such combative forms of knowledge may not be co-opted; as Foucault warns, in releasing such fragments of genealogy we run the risk that they may be 're-codified', assimilated back into human science usage, made useful aspects of disciplinary forms of power. Furthermore we should be wary of the temptation to synthesize these combative knowledges into a new globalizing theory with its own aspirations of scientificity. Indeed, we must not lose sight of the overarching objective of genealogy, which is that of the 'insurrection of knowledges against the institutions and effects of the knowledge and power that invests scientific discourse' (Foucault, 1980a, p. 87).

An epistemology of critique

Although Foucault does suggest that it is from beyond the parameters of qualified knowledge that the most forceful forms of criticism can be tapped, we must remain cognisant of the fact that these counter-knowledges are not necessarily an end in their own right. In short, not all that might qualify as oppositional knowledge serves the purposes of genealogical history. Genealogy must be distinguished both from the defence of ignorance – from, as it were, anti-knowledge, non-knowledge, a withdrawal from attempts at critical or intellectual engagement – and from appeals to the personal irreducibility of the phenomenology of direct experience, from romantic notions of a consciousness beyond formulation.

The empirical materials that Foucault looks to utilize need attain a certain factuality, must qualify as documents of sorts; the recovered memoirs of Pierre Rivière (Foucault, 1978b) and Hercule Barbin (Foucault, 1980f) make for two cases in point. The value, furthermore, of such documents or records is also largely contingent on how they are tactically put to use, linked to a greater strategic offensive. They constitute an important empirical resource, but one that needs to be linked to the operations of critical history, to a cogent 'epistemology of critique', if they are to be effectively utilized.

What though is entailed by what I am calling an epistemology of critique, how might this be given as the over-riding impetus of gene-alogical work and what is its relation to a conventional 'epistemology of truth'? It proves helpful in this respect to review the objectives of genealogy. For Smart (1983), genealogy disturbs formerly secure found-ations of knowledge and understanding, and does so not in order to substitute an alternative and more secure foundation, but to 'produce an awareness of the complexity, contingency, and, fragility of historical forms' (p. 76). The rival (or counter-) knowledges that genealogy produces are not thus *more truthful* – something that attacks on Foucauldian genealogy frequently misunderstand. In genealogy – developing here a theme introduced in the previous chapter – it is more of a question of increasing the *combative power* of potentially subversive forms of knowledge than of simply attempting to amplify their 'truth-value', more a tactics of sabotage and disruption than a straightforward head-to-head measuring up of 'supposed truth' with a 'truer' counter-example. Genealogy thus involves the showing up of certain formations of knowledge which it in part unforms; genealogy, for Dean (1994), is a form of analysis that 'suspends contemporary norms of validity and meaning as it reveals their multiple conditions of formation' (p. 33).

Genealogy is not then directed primarily towards the cultivation of knowledge – and certainly not towards the 'discovery of truth' – but rather towards the generation of critique. It maintains an impetus to counter-intuition; it pushes forward an unravelling of the self-evident, and does so to the ends of an awareness of the discrete violences and sanctioned subjections enabled by formations of human science knowledge. One may understand this as the attempt to render the alterity of those moments in knowledge that have remained outside of the prevailing structures of scientific discourse; it is a means of guarding against the effect of these structures which either dismiss such counter-knowledges, or neutralize their otherness by translating them into more familiar, less oppositional terms of intelligibility. A kind of epistemology remains a crucial aspect of such an initiative. The project of deploying oppositional knowledges capable of contestation – like the attempt to defamiliarize, to upturn commonplace contemporary norms and values – requires a weighty 'counter-evidence' that cannot simply be dismissed as a function of fiction or crass subjectivism.

Knowledge for the genealogist does not thus cease to be an epistemic project, as May (1993) seems to conclude. Rather it is the case that issues of knowledge are no longer exclusively epistemic, governed that is, exclusively by their relation to truth, but are now primarily *political* in nature. We might put it this way: genealogy, like other critical research methods, does thus apply itself to knowledge production and the generation of kinds of 'truth' (or, as Foucault might prefer, '*truth-effects*'); however, these are *operative, action-directed* 'truths', capable of opposition and/or resistance, rather than 'truths' of a static or merely factual variety. Genealogical research is thus tactical rather than unconditional, or indeed, positivistic, in its relationship to 'truth', a position neatly summarized in Foucault's comment that 'knowledge is not made for understanding; it is made for cutting' (1977b, p. 154).

Discussion 4.1: A methodological relation to truth

Truth, for Foucault (1980b), is linked in a circular relation with the 'systems of power which produce and sustain it...to effects of power which it induces and which extend it' (p. 133). If this is the case, then we understand both that Foucault's genealogies would *not* want to be received as 'truth' – certainly not if it meant that they were thus conducting the effects of scientific/institutional power – and that they *would* want to be received as 'truths' – in as much as that they would hope to be forceful enough to disrupt the power-effects of human science knowledge.

The attempt to induce truth-effects outside the sanctioned structures of human science knowledge points us in the direction of aesthetic production. It is in this sense that we should approach Foucault's oft-quoted comments on the truth-status of his own works: 'I have never written anything other than fictions....[although it] seems possible....to make fictions work within truth, to introduce truth-effects within a fictional discourse' (1980d, p. 193). In this mode of fictioning, one might fabricate something that does not yet exist – an usual aim of critique – one might 'fiction' history 'starting from a political reality that renders it true', or, similarly, one might 'fiction' a politics that 'does not yet exist starting from a historical truth' (p. 193). The clarification of Foucault's methodological relation to truth is likewise apparent in his reflections on the use of historical documentation:

> *Discipline & Punish* makes use of 'true' documents, but in such a way that through them it is possible to effect not only a certification of the truth, but also an *experience* that authorizes an alteration, a transformation in the relationship that we have with ourselves and out cultural universe...with our knowledge.
>
> (Foucault, cited in Miller, 1994, p. 211)

It is on this basis that Foucault (1988a), perhaps surprisingly, advances that 'knowledge can transform us' (p. 4).

The singularity of the event

Perhaps the primary conceptual and methodological challenge of genealogy – turning now to *Nietzsche, Genealogy, History* – lies in the attempt to grasp the complexity of 'the event' as a category of critique. The methodological objective behind this notion lies with holding in place the specificity of particular historical occurrences. It is a means of protecting against unwarranted generalizations; it guards against extrapolations which treat the event merely as an extension, a function of a historical era. McNay (1994) usefully paraphrases Foucault in this regard, arguing that much traditional history exercises a type of 'transcendental teleology' in which events are inserted in universal explanatory schemas and linear structures are thereby given a false unity.

The category of the event also interrupts methodological assumptions of necessary similarity between the analyst and what is being analysed. This means guarding against explanations that assume a trajectory of straightforward linear development, that are insensitive to disjuncture, to ruptures in the lineage of a given object of knowledge. The danger here is that of failing to accord a unique place or set of circumstances to the object in question, assimilating it instead into a series of epistemological assumptions continuous with the 'now' of the analysis. This is the problem of reading the object through its 'extensions' – through later objects or previous 'incarnations' with which it may not in fact be commensurate. The specific configuration of a discursive entity like insanity, for example, is best grasped not on the basis of an underlying similarity, but through the appreciation of radically different conceptualizations/treatments/experiencings of this discursive entity that are so dissimilar that it can no longer be considered to be historically continuous. Of course this is not to say that one's analysis is not to be guided by a rough thematic, as it would be in the case of a general study of madness. The point is that this theme will be broken into a series of qualitatively different pieces, dissimilar to the point where the supposed underlying essence of the thing starts to break apart altogether.[3]

Genealogy works against the grain of totalizing assumptions of essence or identity. Against beliefs of unifying structure, its task is to break up apparent progressions of events, to fragment the cohesion of objects and to deliberately oppose comparisons of 'necessary sameness' (that the 'now' is necessarily like the 'then'; that the 'here' of the analytical context is necessarily like the 'there' of that being analysed). Just as the genealogist avoids the temptation to thread narratives of events through a smooth trajectory of development, so she/he opposes all universalizing trends of explanation, and all tendencies to make objects or events of our analyses somehow immanently like us. The more historiography obeys a logic of identity, the more it necessarily covers over and supplants the disruptive influence of alterity. Importantly, this is not just an assertion of the analytical importance of the *specificity* of the object/event being analysed, it is also a willingness to fragment one's own current position of explanation, to allow the uncertainities of this object/event to cast a shadow of doubt on the norms and principles of the location from which the analysis is being conducted.

Here it pays to return to the methodological directive of eventualization as discussed in the previous chapter. Against an analytics of sameness, the injunction of eventualization is to explode the solidity, the historical continuity of the object via an investigative engagement with the innumerable processes and causes that play a productive role in its historical elaboration. This might be more easily phrased by suggesting that the given object (indeed, *event*) of analysis is best grasped as *a complex of factors*, a poised moment of converging contingencies and intersecting lines of force rather than as a self-sustained, autonomous entity. It is difficult to overstate the importance of this analytical category; Foucault indeed refers to genealogy as the philosophy of the event (1981a).

Discussion 4.2: Three figures of abnormality

In Foucault's 1974–1975 Collège de France lectures, he focuses on the historical emergence of the abnormal individual. What makes Foucault's concerns with abnormality so distinctive is that he departs from ideological and institutional analyses, eschewing both a sociological history of illness and 'a history of mentalities', to instead concentrate on the innovation of distinctive technologies of abnormality which occur in tandem with a series of regular networks of practical knowledge.

There are three principal figures in which the problem of abnormality is posed: the monster, the incorrigible (the 'individual to be corrected') and the onanist. Each represents a paradox, a contradiction of power-knowledge that Foucault is eager to make overt. The monster, prototypically, is a mixture of two realms, two types of body (as in hermaphroditism), or an apparent conjunction of the animal and human. As such 'monsters' present a violation of both the laws of society and, seemingly, of nature itself; they confound and confuse law by transgressing the 'natural order'; they present a 'natural form of the unnatural' (2003b, p. 56). The monster hence emerges from within the juridico-biological domain and combines both what is thought to be impossible and what is forbidden in the same figure. For a significant historical period, insists Foucault (2003b), the monster stands as the basic model of every little deviation; until the end of the nineteenth century, the abnormal individual is essentially an 'everyday monster'. Gradually this category of monstrosity undergoes a transformation, such that physical and natural disorder comes to be transposed on proto-psychological characteristics: conduct, moral disposition or 'mind'.

The incorrigible represents a different category of knowledge and intervention. Less important here are legal constraints and the paradigm of nature and society; this figure is strictly contingent on a new array of disciplinary techniques as they are established 'in the play of relations of conflict and support that exist between the family and school, workshop... parish, church, police, and so on' (2003b, pp. 58–59). (We see here then why a singular institutional focus will not suffice for Foucault, he requires an awareness rather of *inter-institutional* modes of knowledge which rely on shared 'technico-institutional' interventions.) Whereas the monster is the exception whose deviance is explicit, the incorrigible individual is an everyday phenomenon, so much so that they become, as Foucault puts it, regular in their very irregularity. In more straightforward terms, this figure is characterized by their everyday ordinariness – in a disciplinary society after all, we could all, in our unexceptional everyday status, be deviants – this, paradoxically, is part of what makes this figure recognizable.

With the figure of the masturbator, Foucault is concerned with a narrower frame of reference than either the juridico-biological domain or that of inter-institutional disciplinary spaces; his interest now lies with the more intimate confines of 'the bedroom, the bed, the body' where the supervisory figures are the parents, the siblings and the doctor, where the locus of control is 'a kind of microcell around the individual and his body' (p. 59). As Foucault demonstrates, the anxious language of onanism proves to be a particular fecund discourse of causality in the context of eighteenth-century aetiology. Masturbation possesses a kind of polyvalent causality which means that virtually the entire spectrum of physical, nervous and psychiatric illnesses may stem from it; it is for Foucault 'the explanatory principle of pathological singularity' (p. 60).

The nineteenth century abnormal individual is a composite of these three figures which had previously remained distinct; from this point aspects of the discursive and technological repertoires afforded each can now be exchanged and combined. The sexual monster is one of the earliest and most immediately recognizable of these hybrids. We have thus a monstrous individual who represents both a curative impossibility and an epicentre of sexual danger. Their acts are not simply a matter of deviance, nor are they merely criminal, or a matter of isolated sexual misdemeanour: they amount to something far more volatile, something greater than the sum total of these parts.

Foucault emphasizes how each facet of abnormality becomes the concern of a particular human science discipline, stressing also how various sectors of knowledge are divided, deplored to disciplinary ends. The monster becomes the object of politico-judicial powers and corresponds to knowledge of natural history; the incorrigible is the focus of reorganized functions of the family and incurs a rise in pedagogical techniques; the onanist demands a reorganization of the powers surrounding an individual's body, and relies upon the nascent biology of sexuality (Foucault, 2003b). The conceptual challenge Foucault faces is to explain how the organized control of abnormality that the nineteenth century makes possible manages to 'systematize, codify, and link together these bodies of knowledge and power that [had] functioned separately in the eighteenth century' (p. 62).

Against origins

Beneath Foucault's distrust of assumptions of continuity lies an even more ardent distrust, that of 'originary' explanation. This seems surprising in as much as genealogy is often understood as the exploration of roots, an excavation of underlying precedents. Foucauldian genealogy might indeed be said to be interested in origins, not in the teleological sense of the term – in the sense of an ultimate underlying meaning or essence – but rather in the sense of a previously given 'reality of substance'. The work of genealogy, we might say, is to locate a *precontext*, to sketch a complex of events and circumstances that makes a particular historical 'surface of emergence'. This is one of the several ways in which Foucault opposes genealogy to metaphysics: rather than an attempt 'to capture the exact essence of things, their purest possibilities' or to assume the existence of 'immobile forms' (Foucault, 1977b, p. 142), the genealogist favours a lineage of accidents and successions, opposing all images of primordial truth and/or 'originary' identity, always wary of transcendent categories of explanation.

Part of the richness of genealogical analysis is that of the 'grey, meticulous, and patiently documentary' collection of 'entangled and confused parchments.... scratched over and recopied many times' (Foucault, 1977b, p. 139). Genealogy, Foucault points out, requires 'relentless erudition', 'a knowledge of details and ... a vast accumulation of source materials' (p. 140). Foucault is hence looking for a kind of historical density, a juxtaposition of varying circumstantialities and perspectives that underlie the production of knowledge; collecting layers of historical sedimentation of this sort demonstrates how origins are continually overwritten, re-inscribed or overwritten. *These* are the origins that genealogy is interested in: dissipating, conflictive, contradictory origins that are never singular, determinant: 'What is found at the historical beginnings of things is not the inviolable identity of their origin; it is the dissension of other things... disparity' (Foucault, 1977b, p. 142). Or in McNay's words: 'Far from being teleologically governed, the historical processes that give rise to the emergence of events are in fact discontinuous, divergent and governed by chance (*aléa*)' (1994, p. 89).

The problem with originary talk is not only that it imports a notion of truth into beginnings – origins thus effectively stand for the foundations of a given discourse – it also assumes an essence behind the phenomena, a being behind a becoming; a single source which provides 'both the material and the motivation for the flowering of a discourse or a practice' as May (1993, p. 74) puts it. Talk of origins brings with it a series of metaphysical assumptions; it is as if, paraphrasing Foucault, one is thus encountering objects at their purest. There are a number of interconnected problems here, the first is a kind of epistemological tautology, neatly described by Foucault: 'the origin makes possible a field of knowledge whose function it is to recover it, but always in a false recognition of its own speech' (1977b, p. 143). We have here the problem of 'foreclosed objects' that are implemented by the disciplines that claim to discover them. It is also the problem of a regime of truth, an 'order of knowledge', whose claims to truths flow from the field of objects that it has foreclosed. Not simply an epistemological tautology then, but also the political problem of the regime of truth (and truth-*effects*) established on the basis of this tautology. Macey gives the example of sexology: from the genealogist's perspective there can be no hidden or inner truth in a category such as gender; this, the object of such a field of study, must instead be grasped as that which is 'constructed by the bodies of knowledge that claim to be able to explain it' (Macey, 2000, p. 157). It is not so much the case then that a field of knowledge arranges itself around an essential object of analysis that poses a 'challenge of understanding'; it is rather the case that the objects in question are constituted by the relevant bodies of knowledge as components of their own conditions of possibility. These are objects, furthermore, that they come to 'own', to exercise a disciplinary prerogative over.

Discussion 4.3: Formations and deformations of apartheid childhood

A useful means of illustrating many of the above methodological principles is found in a study of the historical formation of paedophilia in South Africa (Bowman, 2005; Hook and Bowman, 2007). The first tier of the study was an interrogation of discourses of childhood sexual abuse within South Africa between 1944 and 1978. This component of the analysis yielded a potent discursive figure: the threatened child as a cherished emblem of the future and hope of a 'biopolitical family of whiteness'. Given the racist colonial and apartheid back-drop to the study – a pervasive racism that permeated virtually all the analysed materials – it proved crucial to examine the way power intersected with 'race' to produce particular subjects and objects in South Africa.

A series of historical anomalies and contingencies particularized the gradual construction of the threatened object of paedophilia (and the paedophile themselves) during this period:

- Early reporting of child–adult sexual contact (*c.* 1944) registers neither a sense of psychological damage nor of childhood trauma – both of which are to prove subsequent inventions – and hardly acknowledges the apparent criminality of such acts; euphemisms of 'interference', 'improper examination' and 'offence' do not register such events within a lexicon of injury; ages of children are not initially supplied, perpetrators are not accorded any detailed description; when, eventually, the terminology of physical abuse does come into play, such acts are framed in terms of *moral impropriety* rather than in those of traumatizing sexual action or fundamental criminal infraction.
- By 1948 there are popular media reports of 'indecent assault' and 'sexual aggravation' of children by adults (understood for the most part as incidents of incest); no standardized protocols of investigation are in existence for how to respond to such acts (intervention in such cases meant the removal of children from their homes); such acts are instances of a disturbance of social roles, or of moral transgression, but have not as yet assumed a powerful medico-legal status; an unsanctioned intrusion of adult knowledge, practice and desire into the world of the child comes to underwrite the nature of child–adult sexual contact.
- By the early 1950s, although no special distinction is drawn between the forensic assessments of adults and children, a series of bodily measurements and observations of a medical variety become key means of qualifying and substantiating the damage suffered by the child. However, a 'crisis of injury' emerges: the problem is posed of how to qualify and quantify the damage of an act whose moral implications outweigh its physical infringements. So while physical injury initially grounds the severity of the act of child–adult sexual contact, this comes to be supplanted by a more abstract disruption of the natural psychology and moral purity of childhood. A first step towards a psychological qualification of damage comes with the obligation to specify the age of the affected child; once this is linked to notions of chronologically specific stages of childhood, the notion of lingering psychological damage becomes a point of increasing importance.

- In the 1950s the figure of the 'child molester' or 'paedophile' becomes a recognizable entity in popular newsmedia; the bodies of such persons – also understood as sexual deviants – is subjected to the scrutiny of the medical gaze, scanned for a biological means of substantiating the apparent moral pathology in question. One witnesses here the failed attempt to root the moral monstrosity of paedophilia within a set of physical co-ordinates (items on a sexological examination of the time include the following observation categories: testicles, prostate, scrotum, sternal notch length, distribution of subcutaneous fat, auricular orifice, lobe of ear (see Hook and Bowman, 2007)); this failure impels a different order of problematization, one which prioritizes sexual predilections and practices – indeed, a para-psychological order of attributes – rather than external organic or anatomical qualities (standard sexological queries cited by Hook and Bowman (2007): details of first conscious sexual experience; feelings towards intercourse with a child; reactions to pederasty, fellatio, mutual masturbation, interfemoral coitus and so on). This linking of bodily and behavioural questioning to more detailed sexological and psychological examination means that the acts in questions are shifted from the domain of the contingent, to the domain of the inevitable.

The history of truth

A particular research focus for genealogy is thus implied: an interest in the scrutiny of 'objects without origins' in Butchart's (1997) phrase, an analytical preference, in other words, for those objects which appear to have no history, be it the notion of morality (Nietzsche, 1899), the social scientific category of homosexuality (Foucault, 1985) or the advent of the idea of childhood (Ariès, 1962). Genealogy is anti-essentialist, belligerently historical, adamant both that histories can be written of seemingly ahistorical entities, and that even apparently unchallengeable origins possess a surface of emergence which might be plotted with reference to a set of poised contingencies and accidents. Foucault hence opposes history to truth, certainly so insofar as truth is determined on the basis of *trajectories of development, origins of final cause* and epistemological stabilities of *unity, continuity* and *identity*. What Foucault, following Nietzsche (1983), understands as 'effective history' is the force of critique that can destabilize such presumptions. Effective history distrusts these types of narrative, which lend a definitive sense of cohesive and sequentiality and thus solidify the subject-matter of attempts at knowing into substantive objects of truth. The crucial point to grasp here is that what counts as truth can itself (and should) be historicized:

> the very question of truth, the right it appropriates to refute error and oppose itself to appearance, the manner in which it developed...does this not form a history, the history of an error we call truth?
>
> (Foucault, 1977b, p. 144)

Another area of particular scrutiny for the genealogist is the domain of established 'truths'. 'Truth' insists Foucault 'has had a history within history from which we are barely emerging' (1977b, p. 144). The work of the genealogist is to radically historicize truth, to historicize a metaphysics of substance. A crucial target here is trust in the 'interior of consciousness', the conviction basic to much psychology, in other words, that the interpretative efforts of the dogged social scientist will ultimately yield an inner kernel of subjective truth within their objects/subjects of analysis. In Dreyfus and Rabinow's (1982) terms: 'Genealogy's coat of arms might read: Oppose depth, finality, and interiority' (p. 107). Foucault's anti-essentialism comes strongly to the fore here; if the genealogist listens carefully to history, she/he finds that that there is something altogether different behind things, 'not a timeless and essential secret' but rather the secret that there is no other than a fabricated essence, composed 'in piecemeal fashion from alien forms' (1977b, p. 142).

The methodological point at hand – returning here to Foucault's emphasis on exterior conditions of possibility as opposed to the excavation of *inner substance* – is that once viewed at the right distance, from the right perspective, anything will yield an impressive visibility. In an earlier essay, *Nietzsche, Freud, Marx*, Foucault makes this point:

> Whereas the interpreter is obliged to go to the depth of things, like an excavator, the moment of...[genealogy] is like an overview, from higher and higher up, which allows the depth to be laid out in front of him in a more and more profound visibility; depth is re-situated as an absolutely superficial secret.
>
> (1977d, p. 187)

The project of interpretation itself is hence interrogated: what underlies the efforts of interpretation? The answer is more interpretation. 'If interpretation is an unending task, it is simply because there is nothing to interpret' (p. 189).

The dissolution of the object

How then to locate 'precontexts', to track conflictive 'lineages' of objects without relying on assumptions of origin? Here it is necessary to introduce the principle of descent (*herkunft*), an analytical term Foucault borrows from Nietzsche (1983), and which Butchart describes in the following way:

> Methodologically, descent means that genealogy avoids the assumption that any concepts are simply static in favour of documenting the profusion of events in which such concepts form and fade [it means] outlining the discursive regimes that make them formalized objects of knowledge and targets for intervention.
>
> (1998, p. 9)

Tamboukou's (2003) description concurs: in analyses of *descent*, the past 'can never be revived or reconstructed... there is not a final destination, a place where things originated in the first place' (p. 199). The analysis of *descent*, as she nicely puts it, 'is about revealing the contingency of human reality, describing its complicated forms, and exploring its countless historical transformations' (p. 199).

The procedure of descent thus must be distinguished from both the attempt to establish origins, and from the notion of a progressive or linear development (i.e. 'ascent'). In the case of the former, the idea of descent carries less of an implication of finality than does the notion of origins. Descent – like the attempt to trace a lineage – seldom yields an unmixed line of heritage, revealing more typically a scattered set of antecedents. It is just such a scattered set of antecedents that the principle of descent endeavours to explore.

Against trends of unification – or projects whose aim is the fabrication of a coherent identity – genealogical analysis permits 'the dissociation of the self, its recognition and displacement as an empty synthesis' (Foucault, 1977b, pp. 145–146). Genealogy moves its focus away from capturing a precise category – a precise subject or object – to fixing instead a vector of forces, a network of elements within which an object of knowledge attains epistemological coherence. We are thus looking to describe a surface of emergence that is not a stable originary basis, but a shifting set of coordinates which are themselves the articulation points of struggle.

Therefore it is not really an object of knowledge that genealogy is concerned with, but rather the field of historical action in which this object is brought into being. A field of action, furthermore, that cannot be reduced to the influence of a single actor; we are concerned with a particular realm of power-knowledge that isolates this object as a point of focus, that makes it susceptible to certain kinds of knowing, that animates it within a routine of practices. Rather than concentrate on a given object (the figure of the paedophile, to take an example), we should seek to grasp this ostensible object within the motion of history (from the non-existence of such a category of subject to the emergence of pederasty in nineteenth century medical texts, to the highly specific diagnostic category of paedophilia that exists today in the taxonomy of the Diagnostic Statistical Manual). Such an object should likewise be grasped at the intersection of multiple vectors of control – as in the case of the various medical, legal, psychiatric and forensic procedures that make the paedophile 'practicable'.

If such a de-prioritization of the object seems odd, then it is worthwhile playing out certain of the epistemological implications of maintaining the object as a privileged category of explanation. The category of the object implies a static, discrete and ahistorical form of existence, one which is easily detachable from a given time, place and social context. The object thus risks becoming a transcendental category of explanation. Moreover, an epistemological focus on the object implicates the participation of a subject, for to conceive of an object is necessarily to conceive also of a subject by virtue of which this object gains an elementary meaning, function or value. The category of the object might thus be said to imply the role of an individual actor, and with it, the category of singular agency. These are explanatory factors that Foucault is clearly opposed to, which are all too easily accorded a degree of analytical priority.

The status of the object of knowledge in genealogy is thus never to be presumed or generalized. In genealogy it is rather – and this is exemplified in Foucault's later works – the *organization*, the *coherence* and the *practices* that produce objects of knowledge that we are concerned with. The 'object' that genealogy studies is never more than a catalogue of the set of historical vicissitudes against which it gains coherence; this field of events is the 'ontology' of the object in question. We are focussed thus on the particular networks of interwoven forces and occurrences that give such entities a viable 'objectivity', a minimal 'knowability'. Importantly, this implies not only a commitment to history but also a focus on the *materiality* of practice, the role of subjugation. As Dreyfus and Rabinow (1982) point out, the genealogist does not seek to discover substantial entities (subjects, virtues, qualities), or to reveal their relationships with other such entities; rather she/he sets out to study the emergence of a battle that defines and clears a space in which the ostensible 'object' of analysis becomes visible.

Such a directive to engage the practices (events) of knowledge that set objects into historical motion entails a shift in research focus. This is not only a shift in what constitutes the genealogist's given research domain, it is also a shift in the genealogist's *relationship to the discipline* within which they work, a point I will return to later. Suffice for now to say that there can be no genealogy of a psychological object – for example, intelligence, personality and depression – which is not also a critical history of that domain of knowledge and practice – psychology itself – from out of which this object has emerged. There is a different way of extending this point: descent, Foucault emphasizes, entails a 'dissoci-ation of the self'. Traced stubbornly enough, the route of descent will take us to the point where we lose the standard epistemological relation-ship we have with the ostensible object of knowledge, to a point *before* its established history begins, a point before the social and human science disciplines, which our research efforts represent, and which themselves have a history.

Rather than a predetermined course of history, the complex course of descent shows up 'the errors, the false appraisals... the faulty calcu-lations that gave birth to those things that continue to exist and have value for us' (Foucault, 1977b, p. 146). Accidents rather than essences, we might say, lies at the basis of what we are and what we know; dissol-ution rather than unification underlies what we qualify as 'substance'.

Discussion 4.4: Formations and deformations of apartheid childhood (cont...)

- By the mid-1960s the category of the paedophile attains the status of human scientific fact (the second edition of the Diagnostic and Statistical Manual (DSM II) is published in 1968); this figure emerges as an undeniable object of moral, legal and psycho-medical discourse and practice, they are possessed of a distinctive aetiological profile and a set of typical sexual predilections, life experiences and moral characteristics. A variety of bio-political and disciplinary technologies (questionnaires, interviews, physical examinations, psychological and psychiatric assessments) play their part not only in objectifying but also in thoroughly individualizing the paedophile, a figure not merely discovered or identified, but actively produced within established networks of human/social science knowledge and practice.

- In the mid-1960s apartheid's political logics of race over-ride virtually all other factors of judgement and evaluation; an instance of 'inter-racial' paedophiliac violation is problematized more as a transgression of 'race' than as a violation of childhood; much by the same token, the political imperative behind building a political community of whiteness exceeds even the apparent affront to the conservative values of Christian National Education: anonymous sperm donation and artificial insemination are advocated as a means of increasing white population growth; similarly, abortion should not be viewed as contradicting the values of the Dutch Reformed Church in the case of a white woman being raped by a black man.

- The importance of 'white generational succession' as a key theme of the longevity of the apartheid system of governance plays a crucial role in popular representations of (white) childhood and in the prioritization of issues of childcare, parenting, infant hygiene and health during the late 1960s; the figure of the paedophile, already a moral, medico-legal and behavioural-psychological deviant now takes on a new political significance as a threat to white childhood; only white children qualify as victims of such acts in this period of apartheid, only 'European' assailants are identified, hence it is not effectively possible for a paedophiliac act to be perpetrated if either the assailant or the victim is black (ethnographic studies maintain that no paedophilia occurs in 'Bantu' populations (Bowman, 2005)).

- The 1970s sees an increasing racialization of childhood in South Africa; the hope, promise and preciousness of white childhood is a recurring motif in popular media and advertising forms; powerfully idealized and individualized white children are viewed as belonging to the white community as much as to their own families; a familial dynamics is introduced into the protection and appreciation of white children as embodiments of a white suprematist political future; a certain structure of positioning is deployed which generates an imagined community of whiteness, and along with it, a shared set of para-familial responsibilities and obligations to a bio-political communal family of whiteness.

- Miscegenation is construed as a major threat to the future of the white population, the miscegenated child is fixed in one newspaper report as having no future in South Africa (Bowman, 2005); white anxieties about the unprecedented growth of the black population means that black children are increasingly represented by apartheid media as a threat to bio-political whiteness; the rise of Black Consciousness means that black youth are increasingly viewed as dangerous; thus excluded from full citizenship and, indeed, from the status of childhood – neither precious, nor the embodied hope of a future generation of white privilege, black childhood was not invested with the same aura as white childhood – black children become a threat to the future of white apartheid South Africa.

The body against the human

Given Foucault's strong brand of anti-idealism, it is unsurprising that his genealogical method evidences a strong commitment to materiality, indeed, to *corporeality*. Descent, he notes, 'attaches itself to the body' (1977b, p. 147). Now while at first it seems that Foucault is speaking metaphorically – and at some level the metaphor holds, the metaphysician dissects the human soul, while the genealogist treats the soul as an object-effect of the various technologies of the body that have given rise to it – it quickly becomes apparent that his meaning is also literal. The body is a privileged object of analysis for the genealogist. The body, its forces, its various attributes, prove demonstratively malleable. Indeed, 'nervous system... digestive apparatus... faulty respiration... improper diets... the debilitated and prostrate body' (p. 147) are all 'points of inscription' of assorted historical and political forces.

As discussed in earlier chapters, the body in power and discourse is a recurring motif throughout Foucault's work; it is an important ground or rooting point through which various procedures of power may be conducted. In emphasizing the materiality of power and the body's recurring role in those relations of force that underlie all vectors of origin, Foucault's objective is to explore the changes of the body as a *variable form* marked by differing institutions of historical and political force; how this variable body is manifest, known, observed and 'occupied' will provide a useful set of indices of the regimes of knowledge and control that predominate at any given time.

In the body we have also a reminder of the most *human* of circumstances underlying events. Here I mean 'human' in a non-humanistic sense, as in Foucault's remark to the effect that the body 'gives rise to desires, failings, and errors' (1977b, p. 148). Such 'bodily' circumstances – evoking here a sense of non-permanence, fallibility and mortality – found to underlie great events help to decentre idealist, humanist narratives that would seek to explain pivotal historical moments as a function of transcendent, universal human traits. Perhaps the best way to understand Foucault's use of the body as a priority of genealogical analysis is hence through the opposition of *the body against the human*; the body here meant as the depersonalized 'inscribed surface of events', or as 'locus of a dissociated Self' (p. 148). One cannot dispense of this corporeality in genealogy: the body and everything that touches it, as Foucault emphasizes, is the concern of descent; it is through the notion of descent that genealogy hopes to understand *the articulation of body and history.*

Foucault's subsequent work elaborates upon this methodological priority. The task of genealogy, as he argues in *Discipline and Punish*, is to show that

> the body is...directly involved in a political field...[and to demonstrate that] power relations have an immediate hold upon it; [that] they invest it, mark it, train it...force it to carry out tasks, to perform ceremonies, to emit signs.
>
> (1977b, p. 25)

Importantly, by focussing on how the body has become an essential component for the operation power in modern society, Foucault not only directs our attention to how the body is divided and manipulated by society, he also links the body in all its biological functioning to institutional apparatuses of force, as Dreyfus and Rabinow (1982) argue.

Emergence

Concerns with subjugation are increasingly emphasized in Foucault's next principle of genealogical analysis: emergence. Tamboukou (2003) again provides an apt description in this regard. *Emergence*, she emphasizes, is not the effect of individual tactics, 'but an event, an episode in a non-linear historical process' (p. 200). The analysis of emergence, furthermore 'is not about why, but about how things happened; it is about scrutinizing the complex and multifarious processes that surround the *emergence* of the event' (p. 200). We should operationalize the principle of emergence (*entstehung*) in opposition to the logic of culmination, in opposition to those objects or entities treated as 'end-points' of historical development. For Foucault such instances of the logic of culmination endeavour to deliver the present from a critical historical sensibility, to make it instead somehow permanent, outside of the flux of historical forces. The 'final' resting points of contemporary events or objects must, by contrast, be viewed as merely current episodes in an unstable chain of subjugations.

The overtly political role of genealogy here comes to the fore, its analysis proceeds not along the lines of establishing 'the anticipatory power of meaning', but rather so as to unearth 'various systems of subjection...the hazardous play of dominations' (Foucault, 1977b,

p. 148). Emergence is always produced through a staging of forces, by plotting this interaction, the dynamic struggle of forces waged against one another. There are no 'solid forms' here, no stable, crystallized historical moments. Hence one of the reasons why genealogy is so appropriate for the analysis of power: one of its fundamental tasks is to foreground the historical 'entry of forces'.

We should not be too quick to guess the identities of the adversaries in question, still less to presume a closed field of struggle foregrounding a contest between equal forces. Rather we are seeking to plot the contours of a battle that is less symmetrical than the notion of rival forces might imply, more multiple than categorical groupings of 'winners' versus 'losers'. The 'object' of our analytical attentions is best understood as an accidental assemblage, an unstable collection of events, ridden with faults and with heterogeneous layers that threaten its cohesion from both 'within' and from 'behind', in the terms of both its seeming essence and its apparently fixed path of ancestry. The notion of the constituting subject is again denounced; rather than view the subject as the start, the 'inaugural point' of the object or event, the genealogist must view the human subject as itself something that needs to be accounted for within the reckless flux of forces that its work traces. No one is responsible for an emergence, states Foucault bluntly, 'since it always occurs in the interstice' (1977b, p. 150).

Here one notes a crucial distinction between Foucault and Nietzsche. The latter grounds morality and social institutions in a 'will to power' that is itself a factor in the tactics of individual actors. Wary of implying too readily the agency of the individual subject and hostile to explanations that assume a locus of unique subjectivity or psychology, Foucault takes a different tack. In contrast to Nietzsche, he 'totally depsychologizes this approach [seeing]...all psychological motivation not as the source but as the result of strategies without strategists' (Dreyfus and Rabinow, 1982, p. 109). There is both a strong anti-psychologism and a fervent anti-humanism at work here, a trepidation towards the tendency to understand truth or power as somehow the result of psychological motivations on the one hand, and an aversion to traditional history's habit of locating the self-reflective subject at the centre of the event on the other. As McNay (1992) remarks, Foucault's concern is that by privileging the individual actor such modes of explanation 'place an emphasis on what are considered to be immutable elements of human nature....[hence] history is implicitly conceived in terms of a macroconsciousness' (p. 13). The attempt to explain the social world hence comes to be centred on the affirmation of essential human characteristics; a 'psychologization' of history, as one might put it. This is clearly not the vice of historical explanations alone; this is a pressing consideration in the explanations of any of the social sciences where the 'traits' of 'man' are foregrounded above and beyond their moving social and political grounds of location. Practices of knowing thus come to operate around a logic of identity and subjectivity – a kind of projective anthropomorphism – in which apparent human qualities lie at the explanatory heart of virtually all objects/events of analysis.

Discussion 4.5: Childhood and sexuality: The expanding domain of the psy-disciplines

Sexuality, advances Foucault (2003b), plays a vital role in consolidating the three disparate prototypical figures of abnormality (the monster, the incorrigible and the onanist). There are a number of important intersecting notions here – the idea of formative infantile/childhood experiences for one, the concept of instincts, for another – which likewise play crucial roles in the expanding disciplinary mandate of the psy-disciplines. Foucault, however, seems particularly intrigued by the priority placed on a particular dimension of human existence – a variously understood 'sexuality' – as a kind of foundational principle, as a integral aspect of virtually all types of mental illness and behavioural disorder. It is useful in this respect, Foucault thinks, to link this new prioritization of sexuality to a series of older measures of problematization; the question asked thus is how is it that the Christian flesh – problems, in other words, of the sins of lust – are transformed into the human science objectification of sexuality.

Despite a series of fundamental shifts, there are a number of historical precedents to be detected in respect of how the libido of the theologians becomes that of the human sciences, in how, as Davidson (2003) puts it, the concupiscence of the flesh becomes the psyche of the abnormal. Three shifts are singled out by Foucault as of particular importance in the historical transition from Christian apparatuses of confession to modern psychiatric modes of conceptualization. First, the *spiritual* dilemma of sins of the flesh came to be delimited and focused on the problems of the physical and sick body (a new focus thus on *somatization*). Secondly, a 'regressive' analysis came to play an increasingly important role in grappling with issues of the flesh, that is, credence was given to a belief in *the formative role of infantile sexuality* on later sexual habits (a focus thus on *infantilization*). Thirdly, medical rationality and expertise come to predominate as the means of understanding a sexuality which is no longer only a spiritual or religious issue, but also now a *scientific* concern. Fourthly, and perhaps most importantly, the problematization of sexuality no longer relies merely on a list of prohibited acts, nor does it operate on the basis of relational laws (what kind of act is or is not permitted with whom). Sexuality is now thoroughly internalized and individualized – *psychologized* – opened up into a domain of thought, images, imaginings, 'impressions communicated from the body to the soul and the soul to the body' (Foucault, cited in Davidson, p. xxv), such that it always exists in the form of *a fundamental relation a subject has with his or herself.*

Childhood itself – like sexuality, another crucial focus of psy-discipline inquiry – is also implicated in this line of emergence, linked to sexuality by virtue of the idea of the formative nature of infantile experience. We see an essentially new idea emerging in how disciplinary knowledge about individuals is generated: the folding back of recent biographical details onto the history one's early life. The very idea of history-taking, of subjecting individuals to processes of biographical documentation is, at first, something of a novelty for the psy-disciplines. This soon changes. For as Foucault (2003b) insists, it is only inasmuch as an adult resembles their childhood, inasmuch as continuity can be traced between childhood and adulthood, that one can confidently identify a given psychiatric or psychopathological condition. 'Childhood' thus becomes an elementary and an indeed irreducible component in how new forms of psychological knowledge function. This is not simply an aetiological issue, although, to be sure, the ability to make recourse to childhood experience greatly amplifies the aetiological powers in question. The folding back of child onto adult, of adult onto child, this plotting of telling continuities and discontinuities, becomes a fertile means of understanding tendencies, dispositions, traits and personality, a means of predicting future human behaviour generally. In many circumstances, subjects can only be psychiatrized – located, that is, within the horizon of a proto-psychological knowledge – by establishing the ways in which the child lives on in the adult.

Childhood, insists Foucault (2003b), as both developmental stage and general form of behaviour, becomes a source of profound identity. This also means that psychiatric knowledge needs no longer be limited in its ambitions to the understanding of illness, or to the scrutiny of its organic correlates: 'childhood [is] ... one of the historical conditions of the generalizations of psychiatric knowledge and power' (p. 304). This then is also the point at which we might speak of a properly psychological knowledge, a concern with human behaviour, its motivations and experiences, which while always essentially linked to concerns with normality, deviance and abnormality, need not constitute itself, as psychiatry had, as simply a study of human illness.

The thematics of war

Against a privileging of the terms of human experience, and as means of escaping the dimensions and capacities of the human, an anti-phenomenological Foucault attempts to grapple with the strategies of power that may have conditioned and produced such modes of description. Against a 'script' of implicit human meaning, and contrary to the naïve belief in a self-thematizing subject, Foucault adopts a thematics of war; effects of domination should not be fixed within a framework of human qualities but should instead be grasped in an analysis of tactics, manoeuvres, techniques, procedures and functions.

A model of history as a series of struggles is directed against the dialectical notion of the self-reflective subject as a turning point of historical change. Here emerge two of Foucault's favoured targets: the dialectic (a way of evading the 'always open and hazardous reality of conflict by reducing it to a Hegelian skeleton' (Foucault, 1980b, pp. 114–115)) and semiology (a way of avoiding the violent character of this conflict and 'reducing it to the calm Platonic form of language and dialogue' (p. 115)). Foucault is opposed thus not only to 'the shape of the human' as it informs categories of analysis, that is, to a set of concepts derived from human forms and qualities, he is also opposed to visions of a world that privilege categories of human experience and human meaning.[4] Foucault clearly prefers the 'intelligibility of struggles, strategies and tactics' to either of these modes of description. The analytical language best suited to grasping history and power – and by extrapolation, ostensibly 'human' objects and events – is that of a thematics of constant war.

'Humanity' proclaims Foucault, 'proceeds from domination to domination installing each of its violences in a system of rules' (Foucault, 1977b, p. 151). We should not expect to reach a point of cessation in this respect, that is, in the terms of the intersecting lines of multiple force relations, that, for Foucault, qualifies the social realm. Such changing configurations of authority, control and resistance are a central focus of genealogy, a focus that must be tracked even despite the façade of lawfulness and peaceful reconciliation. The shifting grounds of tactical arrangement and strategic gain, of violent marginalization and selective disqualification – the conditions, that is, of an effective social war over what is knowledge – are constant and ongoing. Foucauldian genealogy is opposed to all versions of the 'end of history' claim that attempt to removes present conditions from historical scrutiny. The principle of emergence does not yield 'stationary histories'; it does now view the present as an historical end-point. Identifying points of emergence should not result in a concurrence of identities nor in a succession of culminating meanings, but rather in a display of *substitutions, displacements* and systematic *reversals*.

In this respect, we might oppose the principles of emergence and interpretation. Foucault opposes the notion that interpretation involves a gradual exposure of meaning, an 'inward journey' to a truth that might allow us to unfold 'the development of humanity'. Interpretation, pursued in this manner, may, in fact, be *the very subject of genealogical investigation*. Processes of interpretation, no less than appeals to the search for knowledge, are instances of an imposition of direction, a kind of participation that bends the events and subjects it hopes to disinter to a new will.

Discussion 4.6: Fragments from a genealogy of South African paedophilia

As Bowman (2005) and Hook and Bowman (2007) show, the staggered lines of emergence and descent that characterize discourses of paedophilia in South Africa in the 1980s yield a less than unified object. The psychological or essentially psychopathological core than one may have expected to find at the heart of paedophilia is, furthermore, radically displaced, supplanted by a series of shifting socio-political contingencies. As above, I cite only select historical events affecting the production of paedophilia and the associated construction of childhood:

- The social, economic and political war waged by the apartheid state on (its own) black children begins to subside by the late 1970s; the subjectivity and living conditions of black children emerge as significant social science and public health issues; by 1985 the *South African Medical Journal* proclaims that child molestation poses a serious threat to the children of the country – doctors, lawyers, psychologists, the police, even children themselves are called upon to fight this growing threat; popular representations of paedophilia often take the form of moral outrage and panic, a hysterical quality characterizes such depictions; a degree of suspicion comes to be placed on all those pastoral roles bridging the worlds of child and adult that had previously been presumed innocent (teacher, minister, doctor and guardian); in 1986, the year after a state of emergency is declared, allowing the apartheid government to take extraordinary measures to suppress resistance to its policies, the South African Police establish the Child Protection Unit, with a predominant focus on child sexual abuse.
- The year 1987 sees the first extensive criminal cases describing paedophilia gain widespread public attention; the third edition of the Diagnostic Statistical Manual refines criteria for paedophilia along the following lines: *recurrent, intense sexual urges and sexually arousing fantasies involving sexual activity with a prepubescent* child; the indistinct outline of the South African paedo-

phile now takes on a rigid categorical form which necessitates a strong psychological aspect (as in the case of 'urges', 'fantasies' and 'attractions') and which necessarily excludes a variety of acts and persons who would previously have been included (not all child–adult sexual contact is paedophiliac, desire needs be present; the victim must be prepubescent); rather than being primarily anchored in the aberrant body of the offender, the causes of paedophilia must now be gauged as problems of desire, problems understood with reference to a psychological vocabulary of the *obsessions* that precipitated the act, the *thoughts* that accompanied it, the *images* that surrounded it.

- The mid- to late 1980s produced sporadic accounts of the sexual abuse of black children; importantly, however, the black offenders of such acts could not, technically, be considered paedophiles. Given the lack of psychological subjectivity accorded the black subject in apartheid – who, although subject to massive racist objectification, was not afforded the same degree of psychological individualization assumed of whites – the black man or woman could simply not present as a paedophile inasmuch as this designation required the depth and texture of a disturbed psychological life. By a quirk of the racist system of values that had refused to acknowledge the full psychological existence of black subjects, sexual offences against children committed by black subjects could only be qualified as acts of criminal violence, not as the full blown psychological aberration of paedophilia. Similarly, given the representations of township children around this time – still viewed as delinquents, lacking moral sense, prone to violence and criminality – it is hardly surprising that they did not represent the same sacrosanct object of protection as did white childhood. We have here then a striking example of Foucault's analytical principles of reversal and exteriority, a set of racist material conditions of possibility that limit both the internal origins (or 'inner meaning') of paedophilia (and its associated object, childhood) and its apparent universality, its generalizability across different times and places.

Wirkliche Historie

All this calls for qualification: how does the effective (*wirkliche*) history derived from Nietzsche distinguish itself from traditional models of history? Well, for a start, effective (genealogical) history dispenses with those types of historical explanation that imply a suprahistorical perspective, or that attempt to effect an easy form of reconciliation of present to past. Critical *wirkliche* history, attempts, by contrast, to set in motion that which has been considered to be immutable, immortal in 'man'; effective history, unlike traditional forms, accepts no constants: 'Nothing in man [*sic*] . . . is sufficiently stable to serve as the basis for self-recognition or for understanding other men' (Foucault, 1977b, p. 153).

Effective history carries with it something of an alienating tendency; it opposes a 'play of recognitions', insisting, as a methodological pragmatic, that there is far more that *distances* than that *unifies* the discursive and subject formations of past and present. Genealogy aims to counter those explanatory trends that indulge in the recovery of ourselves, in past times, events or objects. Genealogical history is less a mirror than its opposite: it yields a kind of opacity where we had hoped to find a set of historical reflections. Effective history, notes Foucault bluntly, 'introduces discontinuity into our very being' (1977b, p. 154).

In a reversal of traditional history's preference for examining things furthest from itself, effective history studies what is closest to itself, immediate forms of normalcy, but in a defamiliarizing vein, recalling that such entities are themselves historical objects. Perhaps the best way of making this point is to think of a contrast between those forms of explanation which fail to sufficiently interrogate the present – instead effectively (if implicitly) naturalizing, reifying present values, norms and ideas – opposing these modes of knowing to a more strategic use of history which is willing to shorten its vision to those things nearest to it, to as such 'estrange ourselves from ourselves', to denature, to make strange that which exists within the sphere of the everyday and accepted.

Effective histories, moreover, are aware of their own presence in the field of observation. Whereas traditional historians or social scientists are thought to take unusual pains to erase those elements of their work which reveal their grounding, effective histories do not seek to conceal such reference points, they are 'not given to a discreet effacement before the objects [they]...observe' (Foucault, 1977b, p. 157). Armstrong (1990) makes the same point in a somewhat different context when he compares genealogy with qualitative and quantitative research approaches. Despite all the emphasized differences between this pair, they share basic similarities: both elevate to primacy their objects of study and ignore their own presence within the analytic field. In doing so their results come to appear as *given*, as independent of the methods used to define them, whereas in fact, as Butchart (1998) avers, they are inseparable from the contemporary universe of explanation and methodology which has produced them. The best defence genealogy has against this problem of 'explanatory anachronicity' comes in the form of the joint principles of descent and emergence, which, as discussed above, hope to fragment that which is presented as unitary and ahistorical, on the one hand, and to destabilize assumptions of origin and continuity, on the other.

It is crucial then that the objects of analysis and the knowledges produced in their scrutiny are put back into a relation of sorts with the historico-discursive position of the researcher, and not a relation of an avowed subjectivity, or of scholarly or scientific neutrality. Here one of the most difficult challenges faced by the genealogist: an obligation to mark his or her own presence within the analytical field. This in contrast to the usual procedures of detachment thought to protect the truth-claims of historico-empirical study: 'proofs' of objectivity, recourse to the accuracy of facts or similar such safeguards against subjectivity. What Foucault has in mind here is not a monitoring of researcher subjectivity or a greater reflexiveness regards the idiosyncracies of one's analysis – far from it. What is called for instead is a version of historical aware-ness, a tracking of an 'entry into knowledge', an entry which is both that of the researcher and that of the discipline in question. I should say 'researcher-function' here rather than 'researcher' so as to avoid any equation with psychological individuality, to point rather to a historico-discursive location, to a relation to a formation of knowledge to which such a researcher is expected to contribute. I have in mind, furthermore, an awareness of the history of interpretations into which such 'contri-butions to knowledge' are being slotted, or, put differently, an attention to the historically varied formation of knowledge (or discipline) within which one acts as an active participant. What is required, to put it differ-ently again, is an awareness of the formative powers that accrue to the historical and disciplinary location from which the researcher speaks.

Discussion 4.7: Fragments from a genealogy of South African paedophilia (cont…)

- The 1988 interrogation of Benjamin Wentzel emphasizes a new element within the growing human science knowledge of paedophilia in South Africa: the notion of the paedophile as *victim of their own sexual abuse*; although not unprecedented, this case marks an important benchmark in the emergence of the *abused–abuser discourse* within public representations of paedophilia in South Africa; a comprehensive history of the subject and their psychological life becomes a necessary component of assessment; moreover, a troubled developmental biography becomes a vital explanatory element in accounting for such events; the acts of the paedophile come to act as a 'double proof' of the psychological damage of child sexual abuse, we have, in other words, a chain of damage into which the paedophile is inserted as both cause and effect.

- The discursive objects of the paedophile and the child thus come to be increasingly intertwined in a way that accentuates the discursive influence of each, so, even in emphasizing all that is aberrant and damaged in the paedophile, the status and fragility of the child is affirmed; by exaggerating both the threat of paedophilia to the child and the threat to a bio-political community of whiteness both such subjects of threat are reified as fragile, as in need of special measures of care, protection, and, indeed, of a particular order of preventative vigilance.
- The body of the paedophile again becomes an important focus; this is not the deformed, monstrous or degenerate body of earlier depictions, but the normal body subject to the moral corruption of damage; physical and emotional violence, alcohol abuse, emotional deprivation, dysfunctional family dynamics all become crucial aetiological features of Wentzel's case; no longer linked to a natural or hereditary disposition which may call into question the racial purity of a community of whiteness, this paedophile is *made*, not born, a product of an abusive and deprived environment; despite then a change in how the paedophile is understood – given that they are locked into an abused– abuser model of causation – a commitment to a 'hygiene of whiteness' and a para-familial responsibility towards a community of whiteness is nevertheless affirmed and seemingly extended.

The relationship to knowledge

How then to think one's relation to knowledge, a relation which refers both to the researcher's location in the history of his/her knowledge – a relation to the *present* of their discipline, one might say – and to how one might put genealogical 'counter-knowledges' to the work of critique? Foucault devotes the very last section of *Nietzsche, Genealogy, History* to a series of inventive oppositions to traditional history. I would suggest that we can take up these oppositions as a means of responding to this problem, that is, as a series of critical orientations to knowledge which, at the same time, offer possibilities for how we put the counter-knowledges of genealogy to work.

The first of the oppositional types that Foucault suggests is history in the mode of the parodic. He intends here a severance of the connection to established certainties and memories, a muddying, an *unrealization* of the current historical realities thus affirmed. It helps here to outline what Foucault, following Nietzsche, is opposing: a reverential type of history in which past historical prototypes become the means of anchoring current 'essences', values and identities. Self-recognition here takes the form of reminiscence. This is a monumental order of history, stuck in the mode of veneration, which celebrates particular historical achievements and figures, lending to them a constant reifying attention, such that they become the iconic points of reference for a contemporary universe of values. In contrast, a parodic type of history – a parodic relation to knowledge – doubles, multiplies history; it explodes illusions of similarity that ensure the past is a known quantity to the present, that attempt to enclose the past in the present. Such a parodic orientation is duplicative: it leads to the profusion of a variety of historical moments and events – which are rendered uncertain, unreliable in the process – proliferating them to the point of entropy. Such an orientation not only works against the tendency to find historical constants – it shatters such bonds of similarity yielding instead a carnivalesque variety of forms – but also parodies such similarities, pushing this process to farcical excess. The multiple similarities evidenced occur in an ironic or mocking manner which in effect accentuates historical difference. No longer thus 'our faint identification with the solid identities of the past', but rather 'our "unrealization" through the excessive choice of identities' (Foucault, 1977b, p. 161).

The theme of *dissociation* extends these objectives; its target is the notion of identity, and the particular style of knowledge (or model of history) that it hopes to replace is that of continuity, tradition, succession. A sense of defamiliarizing plurality is again evident here. As in the recourse to the parodic, the hope is to fragment unifications of identity, showing up instead the 'countless spirits' disputing its cohesion, the numerous forces intersecting and competing in a finalized object of knowledge. Such an analytic principle – which is also a bastardization of pure objects and uncomplicated lines of ancestry – hopes to effect a collapse of cohesion, making apparent instead a complex system of multiple elements within any given identity which resist synthesis or mastery.

Dissociation thus avoids the principle of reduction to the one, to any whole, singular or regularly knowable identity autonomous within, commensurate with, itself. The whole notion of identity as it might be configured in these terms must be jettisoned. 'The purpose of genealogy...is not to discover the roots of identity, but to commit itself to its dissipation...it seeks to make visible all of those discontinuities that cross' (Foucault, 1977b, p. 162). This moves us towards the destruction of the category of the subject as locus of action, agency and knowledge. By the same token, it turns against any version of humanism or anthropomorphism that locates compatible human 'selves' across all periods in history. It also combats the historical stasis inherent in the idea that an identity has been *formed*, an 'identity' thus presumably resistant to the re-makings of historical flux. Again then a refutation of the logic of sameness that impedes thinking and critique, a comforting logic that should be eschewed by the intention 'to reveal the heterogeneous systems which, masked by the self, inhibit the formation of any form of identity' (p. 162).

Foucault seems deliberately ambiguous in discussing the *sacrifice* of the subject of knowledge. At a straightforward level he wishes to impress upon us, the Nietzschean tenet, that all knowledge rests upon injustice: 'there is no right, not even in the act of knowing, to truth or a foundation to truth' (1977b, p. 163). That the instinct for knowledge is malicious connotes a foregoing of any belief in the neutrality, objectivity or 'disinterestedness' in the forces of knowing. Giving up on the belief that knowledges are devoid of passions or are committed solely to truth, the genealogist advances, as a kind of analytical pragmatic, the view that all knowledge rests upon injustice. For Foucault we need disabuse ourselves of the belief that the will to knowledge achieves universal truth; its development is not tied to the constitution of a free subject; it has not simply 'detached itself from the initial needs from which it arose', and 'risen to the level of pure speculation subject only to the demands of reason' (p. 163). Rather this knowledge, an often transgressive and threatening force, creates dangers; it breaks down illusory defences and dissipates the unity of the subject, it 'releases those elements of itself that are devoted to... subversion and destruction' (p. 163).

This 'rancorous' will to knowledge seems at some level to attract Foucault inasmuch as it – here he paraphrases Nietzsche – 'sides against those who are happy in their ignorance, against the effective illusions by which humanity protects itself... [and] encourages the dangers of research and delights in disturbing discoveries' (1977b, pp. 162–163). It is as if, for Foucault, there is a kind of potential 'death-drive' in this will to knowledge which will eventually be focussed on the target of knowing subjects and institutions *themselves*, on, as it were, the destruction of those positions of knowing that ultimately maintain knowledge. It appears as if Foucault wishes to push the violence inherent to the will to knowledge to this last possible subject-area, that hallowed domain where such unforgiving, such destructive and dis-assembling energies are not usually allowed to turn: the location of subjects of knowing. I should be clear: it is not the case that the injustices, the destructive forces of the will to knowledge should go unchallenged. This forcefulness of knowledge – so brilliantly demonstrated in the account of disciplinarity – should not go unopposed or uninterrogated; precisely this is the point of Foucault's genealogies. What Foucault is implying though is that this violence of knowing may eventually 'return home' – a situation he seems to wish to advance – to those institutions, structures processes and certainties of human science knowledge. It is no longer 'a question of judging the past in the name of a truth only we can possess' (p. 164); it is instead the risk of the destruction *of the subject who seeks knowledge in the will to knowledge itself.*[5]

Three modes of history then, three approaches to the relationship to knowledge that diametrically oppose three basic platonic modalities of history: the veneration of monuments succumbs to parody; trust in historico-discursive continuities falls prey to systematic dissociation; the truth-production of privileged subjects of knowledge gives way to an order of counter-knowledge intent on targeting exactly such subjects. In this way, Foucault hopes to free critical historical work of a suprahistorical sensibility, to combat metaphysical and anthropological models of conceiving the world and to construct a form of counter-memory able to displace and interrogate the predominance of human science knowledge.

Discussion 4.8: Oscillation, paradox and conflation: Political tactics in discourses of paedophilia

- In the 1989 cases of Stephanus de Villiers and Don Lamprecht, a relatively new dynamic emerges in representations of paedophilia: a powerful oscillation between extremes of normality and abnormality. More normal than normal, as it were, both de Villiers and Lamprecht posed a problem vis-à-vis the established diagnostic categories of paedophilia. The biographical and everyday details of their lives – ordinary in virtually every way – proved insufficient in understanding the motivation and apparent perversity behind their paedophiliac acts. This discursive oscillation is ultimately productive (at least from the perspective of disciplinarity): even the most normal of events is rendered potentially (even *particularly*) suspicious; what is most disturbed or abnormal is put on a continuum with the normal.
- A second, similar contradiction in talk of paedophilia also becomes evident by the beginning of the 1980s. The discourse of the paedophile comes to be caught between the requirements of precise scientific diagnostic use and the demands of sensationalizing popular media representations (of moral outrage and so on) which emphasize the frequency and spread of child sexual abuse. The discourse of paedophilia is pressed into two incompatible functions. On

the one hand, it is used in a disciplinary capacity to *individualize* perpetrators, who are thus lent a distinctive profile of characterizing features, predilections, life-history elements and so on, in the process. On the other hand, it is used in a far more flexible and generalized manner to direct attention to paedophilia that may exist even within the most 'normal' of places and people. So just as this discourse must be particularized in its disciplinary use, it must be made generalizable as a strategy of bio-political anxiety; it needs function as a mobile and transferable template through which suspicion can be amplified and the imperative to secure children strengthened. A paradoxical discourse thus comes into play: the thoroughly individualized paedophile is someone the population cannot identify with – for they are, after all, perverse, psychologically abnormal – and yet they are also someone that must be immanently *identifiable with* in view of their very unextraordinariness.

- A tactic of conflation also becomes apparent in South African depictions of paedophilia during this time. Although the problem of child sexual abuse can be understood as a purely sexual disorder – a perversity rather than a psychopathology or deviant personality – these trends of explanation become progressively difficult to separate; the conflation between the act of child sexual abuse and a sociopathic character, between an aspect of desire and a disturbed personality structure, becomes firmly entrenched. Paedophilia in popular representations *is* pathology, a departure from previous eras in which it was possible to think of the paedophile in both pathological and non-pathological senses. Such a tactics of conflation is under-written by a tauto-logy: to have committed an act of child sexual abuse is to occupy a type, it is to sustain the suspicion of the presence of problematic desire and is enough hence to lock the subject into a future, a 'career' of psychopathology. Corres-pondingly to confess to such inappropriate desires is to fall within the ambit of such a type and to be tied forever thus into the disposition to act. There can be no innocent 'paedophile' (even if no act is committed); we have here a tautology in which to desire *is* to act, in which the act *is* the incontrovertible evidence of the desire. Desire and act come to imply one another in a spiral of problematization, which, thanks to a series of psychological notions joining these two (personality, psychopathology, tendencies, character), ensures that this subject is effectively a suspected criminal subject for the duration of his or her life.

Genealogy and psychology

What is to be said then about how genealogy and psychology might be used together? I should preface such comments with a note of caution. Foucauldian genealogies, as Young (1991) makes clear, focus on the possibility of making intelligible the strategies and techniques of local operations of power and do so without relying on either the dialectics of ideology or upon a belief in the consciousness of subjects. Genealogy, Young continues, is in fact relentlessly *anti-psychological*. On the one hand, it eschews the terms of a human science vocabulary of, amongst others, *psychological* concepts whose effects it wishes to apprehend rather than extend. On the other, it is continually wary of the powerfulness of a constant and often anomalous psychologism that places the self-reflective and transcendent human subject at the core of meaning. This psychologism – virtually characteristic of modernity, for Foucault – is the counterpart to the humanism he so detests, a kind of anthropo-morphism which casts shadows of human meaning and experience upon historical events and social structures in a way that means we inevitably misapprehend the functionality of power.

In the case of applied genealogical analysis that illustrates this chapter, I have tried to show how genealogy unmakes psychology. I have attempted to emphasize not only that genealogy's radical historicism immediately puts it at odds with psychology – a discipline not typically renowned for its historical sensibilities (Butchart, 1997) – but that the effect of Foucauldian genealogy is to destroy the individual psycho-logical subject as a primary vehicle of explanation. Genealogy opposes exactly the notion of a necessarily individualized internal psychological universe, exactly that object which is psychology's privileged subject, *the* object of analysis it cannot dispense with if it is to maintain its viability as a discrete discipline of knowledge.

These incompatibilities noted, I think it is important to draw attention to at least three possibilities. First, the very fact of this noted incompat-ibility makes the argument *for* a genealogical engagement with psycho-logy. Indeed mainstream, individualizing psychology in its tendency towards 'ahistorical', universalizing, internal and depoliticizing trends of explanation (Heather, 1976; Parker, 2003) seems one of the human science disciplines most in need of genealogy's attentions. So the best form of combining psychology and genealogy, following this line of argument, comes with the prospect of performing a genealogy of various types of psychologies – which itself might qualify as a type of critical psychology. Such a project would address the historical emergence and descent of the discourse and procedures of psychology; following once again the model set by the work of Nikolas Rose (1991, 1996a), it would focus on a critique of the formation and operations of a regime of know-ledge that invents human objects and makes them practicable within a broader web of social power.

A second possibility: genealogy may be one of a series of critical means of approaching a set of problematics (racist talk, subjectivity, spatio-discursive location and so on) that have typically, although not necessarily, been construed as psychological in nature. What I have in mind here is not only a deposing of a series of standard psychological objects (although that itself is an attractive critical goal), but the possibility of approaching such object-events in a variety of ways, an overlaying of different grids of analysis. One should bear in mind in this respect that the practice of genealogy need not completely supplant other research modes. Tamboukou and Ball cite Colin Gordon (1980) in this regard: Foucault had not intended to 'supplant or invalidate... parallel investigations such as those of sociology and ethnology, but to make available to historical analysis a whole additional range of objects and relations' (p. 236). The various instruments of genealogy or, put differently, the types of *questioning* and *historical defamiliarization* that Foucault's philosophy of the event brings with it, might prove a means of radicalizing a qualitative research project. Tamboukou and Ball (2003) make several instructive suggestions regards how this might be possible. A genealogical framework may be helpful, they argue, by: shattering norms and certainties about what can and should be researched; interrogating how we define what counts as knowledge, truth and scientificity; recovering excluded subjects and silenced voices; restoring the political dimension of research; highlighting the centrality of the body to power; opening previously unthought areas of investigation; and by guarding against the temptation to recognize oneself in the data analysed (Tamboukou and Ball, 2003).

There is also a third possibility. Willig (2005) argues that attempts to grapple with the varieties and dynamics of subjective experience need not be incompatible with the procedures of genealogy. We can be interested in subjectivity without buying into humanistic version of the psychological subject, a fact evidenced in Lacanian psychoanalysis, and, indeed, Willig claims, in Foucault's own interest in technologies of individual domination, in the history of how individuals act upon themselves through technologies of the self. This, I think, is an argument not to be neglected; there are certainly facets of Foucault's earlier work that are more willing to foreground experience as a crucial politico-discursive factor – one is reminded particularly here of Foucault's own reference to *Madness and Civilization* as 'an experience book' (Foucault and Trombadori, 1991, pp. 35–36). To treat subjective experience as itself subject to historical eventualization, as a contingent formation of an array of warring forces, that is, as the complex, variable outcome of conflicting economies of knowledge, discipline and discursive positioning, 'may help us to...facilitate alternative subjectivities' (Willig, 2005, p. 33). We return to a problem I have tried to echo across several of the foregoing chapters, be it with reference to the critiques of Butler, Dolar or Badiou. We cannot simply forego the question of the psychic life or psychic economy of power, the issue of the ontology of the subject, or, in the terms of my own argument, the fact of how certain psychological/psychic capacities are instrumental factors in the workings of political control or influence.

Another question emerges here. If genealogy is not to be limited to the critique of human science knowledges, as it typically is in Foucault, if it is to be applied to a wider domain and not always returned to an attack on the institutions of humanism – which is not to deny that this may still be its most appropriate focus – then would this allow us some strategic access to certain of its concepts, so long as they are approached in a provisional and historicized manner?[6] Is it not the case that genealogical analyses of a Foucauldian type can and perhaps should be complimented by further investigation of 'psychological' dynamics and mechanisms of power which are not completely explained away by critical historical and discursive analyses of truth, knowledge and materiality? Is it not possible for the two to work hand-in-hand, for concepts like affect to be put into a relation of historical motion, to be effectively genealogized even as we engage with their psychological role as component aspects of a (less than fully conscious) technology of self? Surely it is possible to envisage a study of, say, racist affect, which will trace such a subject-area in historical formations of descent and emergence, and do so without ultimately being limited in its critical horizons only to a critique of the human science usage and application of 'affect'. Might such a critique not be commensurate with genealogy's attempts to plot the strategies and techniques of local (and indeed governmental) operations of power? I think so.

Conclusion

At the end of the previous chapter I made a series of claims, foremost amongst which was that a critical analysis of discourse requires more than a preoccupation with textual relations of meaning. Discourse cannot be adequately critiqued, I argued, following Foucault, unless we apprehend its underlying conditions of possibility, that is, the dimensions of *history, discourse-as-knowledge* (factors underwriting what constitutes reasonable knowledge) and *materiality* in which it is embedded.

I hope thus to have shown how genealogy or 'the philosophy of the event' furthers these methodological imperatives, particularly perhaps in its prioritization of *effective* history, its scrutiny of the relation to knowledge and its attention to a thematics of war. This, I should add, is not to totally preclude the analysis of the internal dynamics of large-scale discursive formations; I have not meant to imply that there is no critical value in attending to the rules of production and transformation of discursive practices. This is precisely the course of Foucault's own methodological shift from archaeology to genealogy, aptly described by Smart (1985), as a move from the internal dynamics and functioning of discourse towards an analysis of social institutions and practices; the later Foucault favours genealogical analyses precisely inasmuch as they enable scrutiny of 'the complex relationships between discursive and non-discursive practices, in particular relationships between power, knowledge and the body' (p. 43).

A related issue raised in the foregoing chapter was the problem of extricating ourselves from the gravitational pull of a given socio-historic sphere of discursive values. The methodological and philosophical measures recommended by Foucault in this chapter (parodic, dissociative, sacrificial relations to history, to knowledge) seem crucial in this respect. They provide a way of 'making strange', a possibility for retrieving the counter-knowledges of marginalized, forgotten or disqualified sources, a means, perhaps, of evoking alterity. The same could be said of Foucault's dismissal of a series of standard philosophical ways of knowing, namely the platonic, humanistic, anthropological and psychological traditions of understanding that genealogy works so hard to combat. Here I should also stress that many of Foucault's most valuable methodological tactics of defamiliarization – injunctions regards the dissipation of the object, the prioritization of the bodily, the emphasis on the analytical category of the event, his espousal of procedures of emergence and descent – should not be seen as limited in their relevance to the domain of historical studies. While the domain of genealogical history no doubt represents the area of their most effective application, I would suggest that each such analytical priority can make its contribution, within the general ambit of qualitative research, to advancing the work of critique.

The distinctive role of Foucauldian critique as cut apart from the agenda of 'knowledge for knowledge's sake' has been another of my governing concerns in what has gone above. As I hope is clear by now, genealogy does not thus take a place alongside other procedures of knowledge; genealogy is instead an approach to interrogating the role and function of particular forms of knowledge – particularly those of the human sciences – which come to play their part in the ordering and regulation of society. *The political operation of systems of knowledge,* rather than objects of knowledge in need of further discovery, is the proper target of genealogical investigation. Indeed if we are to delineate an appropriate area for genealogical study, it would not be a particular topic, a given social object or subject area, rather it would have to involve the field of knowledge along with the objects it gives rise to. Butchart has put this well: 'there can be no objects of knowledge in the absence of methods for their production' (1998, p. 184). Looking to the example of Foucault's own work, it is not possible to locate a genealogical study that is not at the same time a critical engagement with the human sciences; the human sciences are a crucial part of the 'organized and organizing practices' of society (Dreyfus and Rabinow, 1982, p. 103).

A final observation that may help to consolidate some of what has gone above: genealogy works against ontology; indeed it offers us exactly a series of de-ontologizing procedures. It is anti-ontological in a dual sense. Not only does it contest the existence of the standard epistemological objects presupposed by the theories of the human sciences, it also opposes metaphysical speculation on the foundational nature of being.[7] I mention this so as to anticipate a predictable line of criticism: despite the claim that Foucault is not attempting to construct a general theory, is it not the case that his methodological pragmatics do in fact insist on a worldview, precisely by virtue of their anti-humanistic, anti-psychological, anti-platonic perspective? Is there not a surreptitious affirmation of a quasi-theoretical position going on here?

I should be clear here: there can be no essence to genealogy; genealogy has no positive content of its own. What would appear, by virtue of the force of its attack, to be *the positive* of a genealogy's counter-knowledge must be viewed in the light of which it attempts to critique. Arguably, there is nothing essentially anti-humanistic, anti-psychological, anti-Platonic about genealogy; that a Foucauldian genealogy may be characterized in this way is result of the hegemonic position such trends of thought (humanistic, psychological, Platonic) have attained in Western society. We only access genealogy, as it were, in the negative; genealogy is against the power of such hegemonized trends of thought; and *that*, the force of *the against*, is what genealogy is.

Discussion 4.9: Bifurcating paedophilia: Sovereignty and disciplinary bio-power as modes of discourse

In 1989, a year before the release of Nelson Mandela, Gert Van Rooyen – still today South Africa's most notorious paedophile – is arrested. The investigation that followed and the subsequent media furore saw unprecedented levels of public concern over paedophilia, just as white anxieties over the prospect of black rule (and the demise of white leadership) were at their highest. The case represented a turning point in the public portrayal of paedophilia in a number of ways. For a start, although the shadow of moral evaluation had never been completely lifted from portrayal of paedophilia – this aspect had receded somewhat in psychological, medico-scientific understandings – we encounter in presentations of Van Rooyen a stark set of religious morals and not only this, but an unguarded characterization of his acts and person as evil.

The figure of the paedophile, more than ever before, starts to work as a figure of counter-identification for an entire community of values; there is, in other words, a kind of discursive short-circuit – extending the conflations discussed above – which means the paedophile starts to work as an emblem of everything that is objectionable. Rendered not only as sociopathic and evil, Van Rooyen is depicted as a pornographer, a drug-user, an insatiable sexual sadist; he is accused of sacrificial practices, of involvement with a syndicate intent on kidnapping young girls; his house is likened to a house of horrors, his handwriting compared to that of Adolf Hitler (see Bowman, 2005). This dynamic is complicated further: Van Rooyen is portrayed as a Satanist – as forcible an ejection as one can imagine from the norms of the Christian National Education of the apartheid state. In line with the political paranoia of internal threat, the everyday 'monster within us', he is singled out as an evil coming from within the fold of white Afrikaner Christianity, as someone who had epitomized its values even to the point of taking on the vocation of minister. The discursive pattern thus is that of the ordinary good subject – popular, Afrikaner patriarch and man of God, who initially exists at the heart of the ideals and ideological values of a given discursive system – who is subsequently pushed to its outskirts as its most abhorrent exteriority, as the abject persona and point of absolute *counter-identification* against which it may ascertain and affirm its own universe of values and identifications at a time when they are most under threat. The discursive character of Van Rooyen thus lends a powerful form of identity to this system, even as he is expelled from it.

It is understandable thus that by the mid-1980s the discursive caricature of the paedophile had reached exaggerated proportions. The fact that this discursive category had come to operate as a virtual personification of social threat, an epitomization of villainy, meant that the figure, the paedophile, was now better suited to populate the terrain of popular culture and tabloid sensationalism than the domain of human and medical science discourse. Indeed the popular discourse of the paedophile is so bloated by this point (through the accumulation of various historical representation), so morally and politically volatile, that it is unable to maintain its integrity as a pseudo-scientific term. A bifurcation of the discourse results; this is a discursive shift of major importance, for, from here, there are two languages of causation and detection, two distinct but connected vernaculars of suspicion, scrutiny and reaction.

On the one hand, the various figures, component logics and productions of paedophilia cease to attain the coherence of a single discourse and fragment out into a far more complex and variable arrangement, one which is less bounded by the strict needs of scientific rigour. An informal, overblown discourse, irrationally charged with social anxieties of various sorts, this set of representations includes a cross-section of elements from across the archive of paedophilia. It obeys no injunctions against tautology and features frequent slippages between the causative categories of actor and act, between personality and desire, deviant sexuality and psychopathology. The second such language is formal and institutional in nature. It remains within a discourse of human scientific orthodoxy which requires a suspension of moralizing judgement along with the need for a cohesive model of practical intervention. This bifurcation appears to follow the logic of the Foucauldian distinction between modes of sovereignty and disciplinary bio-power. Whereas the former requires a singular, spectacular subject of power made known to all, the latter mode of power circulates in less than visible or personalized forms, investing a variety of moral orthopaedic or pastoral agencies. The combination of these modes of discourse means that the paedophile is made a spectacular ongoing presence within society – a visibility which affirms the *potentialization* of paedophilia (there is always the possibility that this or that person may be a paedophile) – and that paedophilia may be undetected, anonymous, occurring at all levels of society, a situation which implies a type of *inclusivity* (no area and no subject of social life should be excluded from the field of scrutiny).

This bifurcation corresponds to the split between the figure of the paedophile as they exist within the popular social imaginary – the subject of a prurient, sensationalized tabloid fascination – and the act of adult–child sexual contact, designated now as 'child sexual abuse'. It is this formulation which becomes the authoritative psychosocial and bio-political register of intervention and knowledge with which such future acts are to be comprehended in South Africa in the 1990s.

5
Space, Discourse, Power: Heterotopia as Analytics

Space is fundamental in any exercise of power.

(Foucault, 1993, p. 168)

Social ordering and the spatial

The notion that space plays a vital role in informing practices of subjectivity and power has received much theoretical substantiation of late. Soja's (1989, 1996) notion of 'spatiality' is perhaps the foremost example here, although, in differing ways, Bourdieu's (1988) notion of the habitus, Fanon's (1986) 'Manichean divisions of colonial space' and Foucault's (1997) conceptualization of heterotopia all interestingly lend themselves to further explorations of the intersections between space, power and discourse. Each such perspective provides a prospective means of theorizing the relationship of subjectivity to the management of space, and the management of space to the broader ordering of a given social milieu. What is crucial about writings of this sort is that they alert us to the fact that there may well be a missing dimension in our analyses of social subjectivity, namely the component of space itself.

How then might we go about talking about space? Without the training or expertise of the architect or geographer, one does not necessarily have an appropriate set of tools or vocabulary of space to conceptualize the qualities of space. It is important thus to reiterate that space is itself *an element of discourse*. It is this factor that makes it possible for those of us less equipped with the 'spatial language' of the geographer to apprehend something of the political role of space. Just as the notion of discourse opens up the domain of knowledge and representation as a fundamental dimension of political activity, so it enables us to grasp how space, through the particular mode of constructions it enables, its various significances and characteristic practices, is likewise a dimension of political activity amenable to critical analysis. As established in Chapter 3, discourse cannot be reduced to practices of writing and speaking. Discourses are heterogeneously realized in a variety of forms, not only in the textuality of representation and knowledge, but in the regulating principles and actions of institutions, in forms of everyday practice, in actual material arrangements such as that of architectural structure. Quite clearly then, the discursive by no means precludes the spatial: the identities, materiality and practical functionality of places, so long as they are social phenomena that produce and contribute to the construction of social meaning, are amenable to discursive forms of analysis.[1]

It is not difficult to imagine how certain spaces become loaded with practical significance, with distinguishing 'repertoires' of practice. Such differences are relatively easy to isolate: one needs to only look across the diverse functional sites of, say, the school, the hospital, the brothel, the airport, to gain a sense of their distinct practical 'identities'. To demarcate a place is also to demarcate an appropriate regime of behaviour and practice, a particular order of materiality. The identity and functionality of a place is hence importantly tied to forms of social practice, to the types of knowledge it engenders, that 'reside' within it, and which its space puts into play. The 'discursive relays' between politics and place hence make for important nodes in the critical analysis of power. Furthermore, practices, discourses and orderings of space may hence function as indexes of wider social networks of power, and may, accordingly, be enlisted to challenge or subvert exactly these broader varieties of meaning, value and practice.

Spatiality

Perhaps the best way to give theoretical form to these discursive relays between politics and place is through Soja's notion of 'spatiality'. 'Spatiality' is a conception of space that Soja (1989) uses to oppose what he refers to as 'the dominance of a physicalist view of space [which] has so permeated the analysis of human spatiality that it ... [has] distort [ed] our vocabulary' (p. 80). Soja (1989) points to a separation between space *per se*, space as a contextual given, and socially-based *spatiality*, the created space of social organization and production. Rather than imagining space as a white page on which the actions of groups and institutions are inscribed, Soja (1989) warns of *the social production of space*, and argues that the organization, meaning and functioning of space is a product of social translation, transformation and experience. 'Socially-produced space is a created structure comparable to other social constructions', he claims (pp. 79–80). Spatiality may thus be operationalized as socially-constructed and socially-practised space, space as intricately intertwined with socio-political and historical relations of power-knowledge, as *itself discursive*.

Discussion 5.1: A 'grounds of identity'

Discursive engagements with spatiality have begun to feature in social psychology, as is the case in Dixon and Durrheim's (2000) formulation of the notion of a 'grounds of identity'. Emphasizing the ways in which physical (and socio-discursive) space operates as an identity-resource, Dixon and Durrheim apply a specific formulation of the notion of *place-identity* which aims to emphasize the shifting, historical, cultural, discursive and socio-political nature of identity. They prefer this conceptualization to the traditional psychological notion of 'place-identity' that is based on an individualist, mentalist and apolitical approach to social reality. Their approach shifts a focus on mental (and specifically cognitive) processes from *within* the individual to an *interpersonal* level of social practice and interaction. This conceptualization is explicitly *discursively orientated*, that is, it engages both space and identity (and the relays which connect them) as thoroughly invested with social knowledge, meaning and power. Created through talk, a 'grounds of identity' is 'a social construction that allows subjects to make sense of their connectivity to place and to guide their actions and projects accordingly' (Dixon and Durrheim, 2000, p. 32). They stipulate that a discursive approach of this sort seeks to 'map how varying ways of discursively locating the self may fulfil varying social and rhetorical functions' (p. 33). Moreover, they discuss a 'grounds of identity' in the double sense of a *'belonging to place'* and a *warrant through which particular social practices and relations are legitimized*. Both of these senses evoke a powerful sense of subject-positioning.

A benefit of analyzing space as a discursive resource of subjectivity is that it brings into sharp relief the notion of the subject-position; subjectivity and space are tied together via discourse. Issues of 'identity' are as such strictly secondary to questions of subjectification, to issues of discursivity. Of course, one of the fundamental operations of discourse – often sidelined by Foucault's analyses for fear of re-centring notions of subjectivity – is the positioning and locating of subjects, the generation of 'subject categories' that are constructed differentially across ranging imbalances of power with marked asymmetries of rights, warrants, prerogatives and so on.

While Dixon and Durrheim are not expressly Foucauldian scholars – the question of identity still features too strongly in their work – they do provide a possible bridge between ostensibly 'psychological' analyses of the relation between space, power and identity, and properly Foucauldian concerns with the discursive critique of how the management of space is crucial to the ordering of the social milieu. Just as a critical analysis of discourse might supersede 'psychological' engagements which prioritize questions of personal identity, so a Foucauldian analysis of 'spatio-discursive topographies' might come to replace primarily psychological analyses of 'space-identity'.

Heterotopology

Having called attention to the political and discursive dimensions of space, we may now turn our focus to Foucault's most important analytical observations in this regard. He proposes the project of heterotopology, that is, 'the study, analysis, description and "reading"... of those different spaces, those other places [that enable]... both mythical and real contestation of the space in which we live' (Foucault, 1997, pp. 352–353). Such a project of study would focus on the analysis of 'heterotopia', that is, 'other' spaces – 'spaces' here understood in both a literal and a metaphoric sense – spaces of alternate social ordering. More precisely, by heterotopia one has in mind a particular 'analytics of difference', typically (but not exclusively) as applied to the study of bound spatial domains that possess a precise and well-defined function – a stable 'identity of purpose' as we might put it – within a given society (Airports, hotels, schools, jails, cemeteries might all qualify as heterotopia).

Given that heterotopia have well-formulated rationales and highly-specialized social functions and meanings, it stands to reason that one should be able to study the discourses and characterizing practices which 'institute' the place of the heterotopia and solidify its social identity. In this sense the study of heterotopia leads the analyst back to the overarching schema of political practices and discourses of the society in which it is localized. The concept proves useful precisely because it demonstrates how the logics and practices of given places transpose the rationality of power into material practice.

Foucault's description of the concept of heterotopia proceeds by listing a series of characterizing features. These features are both criteria for identification – the means for differentiating what might qualify as heterotopia from what does not – and rudimentary steps of analysis, that is, a means of generating analytical observations about the micro-geopolitics of discrete spatialities. It is useful to review these characterizing features in some detail before demonstrating how they might be applied in the analysis of a particularly striking example of such a space of alternate social ordering, namely the South African gated community.

Synchronies of culture and history

The category of heterotopia permits for a great deal of variation. Foucault is aware that the identities of purpose of such bound spatial domains changes significantly over time, and between cultural locations. As Soja (1995) emphasizes, heterotopia are always variable and culturally specific, changing in form, function, and meaning according to the particular 'synchrony of culture' and moment in history in which they are formed (p. 15). As one might expect, the changes that take place in heterotopia – the 're-inventions', reproductions or transformations in the maintenance of particular sites – function as an index of historical change more generally. The heterotopia, furthermore, is also a universal element of human societies, 'a constant feature of all human groups' (Foucault, 1997), despite that, as Soja (1996) adds, it has no absolute universal model and takes varied forms.

Differential spaces: The power of juxtaposition

Heterotopia are importantly related to other spaces. Despite that a given heterotopia will prove notably distinct from the spaces around it, it does connect with, and link to, its surrounding space, even if such connections more than anything work to create effects of contrast and difference. The role of the heterotopia is either to create 'a space of illusion exposings real space as still *more* illusionary', or, to create an *other* space 'as perfect, as meticulous, as well-arranged, as ours is messy, ill constructed, and jumbled' (Foucault, 1997, p. 356). (Soja (1996) refers to this as the 'external function' (p. 161) of the heterotopia). The heterotopia then, by definition, is a *differential space*, importantly related to, but always fundamentally different from, the places which surround it. Given this quality, it is unsurprising that the heterotopia 'has the power of juxtaposing in a single real place different spaces and locations that are incompatible' (1997, p. 354). This is to say that the analysis of the heterotopia typically yields a variety of contradictions and paradoxes 'that are not necessarily overt, initially evident. The variability of the heterotopia is again important here, as Soja (1995) notes '[T]his complex juxtaposition and cosmopolitan simultaneity of differences in space ... charges the heterotopia with social and cultural meaning' (p. 15). The incompatibility of the heterotopia's various internal combinations, thus, makes for an important focal point of critical analysis.

'Heterochroneity' and protected entry

Heterotopia are distinguished, furthermore, by the special nature of their time. Foucault (1997) notes that the heterotopia exhibits a 'pure symmetry of heterochronisms', that it is linked to 'bits and pieces of time', that it enables visitors to enter 'a total breach of traditional time'. Soja (1996) speaks of 'slices of time' which, borrowing on Foucault, he claims 'allows the heterotopia to function at full capacity' (p. 160), the suggestion being that this special chroneity accentuates the heterotopia's function.

Heterotopia also presuppose a system of opening and closing. The question of accessibility is central here and Foucault is particularly concerned with how a place is open or closed to public entrance, with how it maintains boundaries, barriers, gateways and *disallows* thoroughfare, loitering or anonymous entrance. It is at this dimension of space that power becomes, arguably, most palpable, and Foucault is adamant that all heterotopia involve a system of opening and closing that simultaneously isolates them and makes them penetrable. One does not access heterotopia purely by the force of will alone; access is accompanied by a form of submission or by a variety of a rite of exchange.

'Other' places: Sites of deviance, crisis

There are two fundamental forms of heterotopia: one of crisis, and one of deviance. Heterotopia of deviance, Foucault (1997) maintains, are those places occupied by individuals who exhibit behaviour which deviates from current or average standards of a society: asylums, psychiatric clinics, prisons, rest homes, schools for delinquents and so on. Heterotopia of crisis are generally recognized as those privileged or forbidden places reserved for individuals or societies in a state of upheaval, difficulty or breakdown. I have already noted that heterotopias are *differential spaces*; that they are typically sites of crisis or deviance only strengthens this differential quality. It is from this difference, their very 'otherness', that stems their ability to offer critical perspective on other places. Hence Foucault's (1997) description of the heterotopic place as that which is 'absolutely *other* with respect to all the arrangements that it reflects' (p. 352). Similarly, the heterotopia is 'a place that lies outside all places and yet is localizable' (p. 352). One surmises from this that the heterotopia is a place able to transcend its basic social function and to subvert or mirror the typical kinds of social intercourse of a society.

Discontinuous grounds – sites of resistance

As both places of 'otherness' and as a space possessed of a highly specified social function, it would seem that the heterotopia should be able to demonstrate a certain amount of friction between what is socially normative and what it peculiar to itself, between the day-to-day activities of a given society and how it departs from the rules and norms of this society. This would seem to be exactly the condition underlying its ability to represent a point of destabilization for current socio-political or discursive orders of power. It is this very overarching functionality that Hetherington (1997) targets in his definition of heterotopia as 'spaces of alternate ordering':

> heterotopia organize a bit of the social world in a way different to that which surrounds them. That alternate ordering marks them out as Other and allows them to be an example of an alternative way of doing things.
>
> (p. viii)

The role of the heterotopia as 'place of Otherness' – which, incidentally, is the literal translation of the original Latin term – is central to Foucault's elaboration of the term. This role has also proved central to the various ways in which the concept of the heterotopia has been developed as a viable form, or site, of resistance (Genocchi, 1995; Soja, 1995; Lees, 1997; Hetherington, 1997, 1998). Hence, in Lees's (1997) terms, the heterotopia is a 'spatially-discontinuous ground' that 'opens a critical space' which 'provides a real site of practical resistance' (p. 321). More directly, and more optimistically yet, Lees (1997) defines the heterotopia as a 'heterogenous field of potentially contestatory countersites for political praxis and resistance' (p. 322). Similarly, Genocchi (1995) speaks of heterotopia as 'socially-constructed countersites embodying... form[s] of 'resistance' (p. 36).

Real utopias – effectively realized political sites

There is an inevitable utopian quality about heterotopia; the quintessential 'alternate ordering' that helps define the heterotopia is based, as

Hetherington (1996a) puts it, on a variety of 'utopics'. In this way one starts to see how the heterotopia stands as Foucault's (1997) theoretical conversion of the idealized notion of *the utopia* into pragmatic, 'real-world' terms. Both utopias and heterotopia 'have the curious property of being in relation with all the other sites... in such a way as to suspect, neutralize, or invert the set of relations they happen to designate, mirror, or reflect' (p. 352). However, whereas utopias are ideal sites with no real place, and remain fundamentally *unreal*, heterotopia are 'real sites' of 'effectively enacted utopias' (p. 24).

Heterotopias are the potentially transformative spaces of society from which meaningful forms of resistance can be mounted. These are the places capable of a certain kind of social commentary, those sites where social commentary may, in a sense, be *written into* the arrangements and relations of space. Following on this, Lees (1997) claims that the practised politics of the heterotopia would not be merely *analogies* or *figurative comparisons* of resistance, as in the case of the imagined space of the utopia, but would instead constitute *real-world interventions* within the political fabric of society, *acted upon* rather than simply *spoken* forms of criticism *commensurate with the realized and actual field of political action and power*.

Discussion 5.2: Heterotopia-as-analytics

While the analytics of heterotopia holds innovative possibilities for critique – see for example the work of Connor (1989), Chambers (1994), Lyon (1994) and Hetherington (1996a, 1996b) – the underlying conceptual unity of the term is in need of elaboration and development. As noted by Soja (1995) and Hetherington (1997), there are only two texts in which Foucault makes reference to heterotopia. The first is a brief mention in the introduction to *The Order of Things*; the second is in a lecture, *'Of Other Spaces'*, that Foucault delivered to a group of architects in 1967, and that was only belatedly published, in an unedited form, shortly before his death. These two texts deal with the concept in significantly different ways – the possible articulation between these texts is not a point addressed by Foucault – although as Genocchi (1995) notes, these two uses of the term 'bear a strange consistency' (p. 37). It is worth bearing in mind thus that in speaking of heterotopia, we are dealing with a strictly provisional set of ideas, with what we might term an unfinished concept.

Another important point of qualification arises here: one should not automatically assume that the analytics of heterotopia refers exclusively to places. We should apply the notion of the heterotopia *as an analytics* rather than simply, or literally, as place; it is a particular way *to look* at space, place *or text*. Hetherington (1997) drives this point home when he insists that the heterotopia can be just as much a *textual* site as a geographical one, in fact:

> In the main, Foucault is interested in the heterotopic character of language and the way that textual discourse can be unsettled by writing that does not follow the expected rules and conventions... [He] does... go on to speak of heterotopia in relation to specific social spaces whose social meaning is out of place and unsettling within a geographical relationship of sites.
>
> (Hetherington, 1997, p. 8)

Similarly, in linking Foucault's two different descriptions of the concept Genocchi (1995) suggests that:

> In *The Order of Things* Foucault's discussion of heterotopia centres upon a discursive/linguistic site in contrast to... an examination of actual... locations [as in *Of Other Spaces*]... In each case the distinguishing feature of the heterotopia is [that it enables]... a form of discontin[uity]... a status which, in turn, gives each the ability to transgress, undermine and question the alleged coherence or totality of self-contained orders and systems.
>
> (p. 37)

We should not lose sight of this duality of the heterotopia as an analytical term. This may seem a minor point, because the spatial and the discursive would seem to be inseparable spheres of social life and meaning – indeed, in a Foucauldian vein, one might speculate that the spaces and practices of a given place like that of the gated community *may be seen as very materialized forms of discourse*. The importance of the discursive or textual dimension of the heterotopia lies in the fact that whereas Foucault does detail what we might refer to as a substantial 'epistemology' of the discursive, that is, a means through which it may be engaged, apprehended, criticized (Foucault, 1981a), he provides no thorough or comparable epistemology of the spatial. As such we should be wary of limiting the application of the heterotopia to an analysis of space alone. This is not to deny the application of the term at this level of critique – Foucault's concerns in *Of Other Places* are, after all, very much centred on the spatial – it is rather to warn against the assumption that the notion provides in itself an adequate epistemology of space. A related caution: one should guard against an overly literal application of the concept, to do so risks overlooking the more inclusive value of the term as an overarching 'style' of analytics.

Rearrangements: Alternate social ordering

Striking to the core of the analytical usefulness of the concept, Foucault characterizes heterotopia as:

> the real and effective spaces which are outlined in the very institution of society ... which constitute a sort of counter-arrangement, [an] effectively realized utopia, in which all the real arrangements that can be found within society, are at one and the same time represented, challenged and overturned.
>
> (1997, p. 352)

Importantly, however, this 'recycling', this re-representing and challenging, of the meaning and functioning of other spaces need not be used solely towards laudable or progressive political goals. The mechanism at hand, that of 'reforming', *reordering* space, makes for an apt description of colonizing activity. With this sobering warning, Foucault emphasizes what we should have suspected all along, that although the heterotopia may be a vehicle of progressive political aims and agendas, it is just as easily a site and means of reactionary politics.

Heterotopia are able to unsettle spatial and social relations directly, through material forms of 'alternative ordering', or less directly through representational means. As Hetherington (1997) insists, the otherness of heterotopia is established 'through a relationship of difference with other sites, such that their presence either provides an unsettling of spatial and social relations or an alternative representation of spatial and social relations' (p. 8). The representational 'alternative ordering' of the heterotopia, for Foucault, occurs through *similitude*. The representational order of similitude is best introduced by contrasting it to the notion of resemblance. In a relation of resemblance a given representation calls to mind that which it looks like, that which it bears an overt or conventionalised similarity to, and does so in a fairly direct or automatic way. There is, as we might put it, a certain 'stability of reference' in resemblance that means that we recognize without difficulty what is being referred to.

Quite in contrast to an order of resemblance, which relies on conventionalised associations of similarity, similitude works on the basis of unexpected or unusual associations. In a relation of similitude there is no obvious code, no direct referent and no immediate or obvious translation. Rather than solidifying a stable relation of reference, similitude is thus about the effects of juxtaposition, of bricolage, which confound the attempts to read a regular or stable code of meaning. Whereas in resemblance the relationship between a signifier and a signified is strongly conventionalized and formalized, in similitude the reference 'anchor' is gone and ' ... [h]ierarchy gives way to a series of exclusive lateral relations' (Harkness, cited in Hetherington, 1997, p. 43). Similitude can be likened to metonymy 'where meaning is dislocated through a series of deferrals that are established between a signifier and a signified rather than directly to a referent' (Hetherington, 1997, p. 43). Much like the oddity of combinations in dreams – Foucault takes the surrealist paintings of Magritte as an example of similitude – such eccentricities of arrangements work precisely to bypass existing codes of understanding, and, by extension, existing orders of social arrangement.

Heterogenous combination

Heterotopias do not exist in and of themselves. As Hetherington makes clear, there is nothing intrinsic about any site that might lead us to describe it as a heterotopia: 'It is the heterogeneous combination of the materiality, social practices and events that were located at this site and what they come to represent in contrast with other sites, that allow us to call it a heterotopia' (1997, p. 8).

This principle of heterotopia derives from the fact that they represent through similitude: heterotopias 'only exist in relation ... they are established by their difference in a relationship between sites rather than their Otherness deriving from a site itself' (Hetherington, 1997, p. 43). This point is useful in holding at bay the temptation to overly concretize the notion, to 'literalize it in space' rather than practice it as an analytics.

Discussion 5.3: Critical limitations in applying the notion of heterotopia

Genocchi (1995) rightly points out that heterotopia embody a kind of discontinuity (which we might understand, in the terms given above, as their ability to 'juxtapose incompatibilities'). It is this 'embodied discontinuity' that gives heterotopia 'the ability to transgress, undermine and question the alleged coherence or totality of self-contained orders and systems' (Genocchi, 1995). How coherent though is this conceptualization of the discontinous otherness of heterotopia, especially once the attempt is made to ground the heterotopia in question in an actual physical site?

How is it that we can locate, distinguish and differentiate the essence of this difference, this 'strangeness' which is not simply outlined against the visible...how is it that heterotopia are 'outside' of or are fundamentally different to all other spaces, but also relate to and exist 'within' the general social space/order that distinguishes their meaning as difference?

(Genocchi, 1995, p. 38)

As Genocchi (1995) argues, to concretize the notion as site, to literalize it as discrete, physical area is to undermine the concept itself through a form of self-contradiction. Or in Hetherington's (1997) terms:

trying to identify sites as heterotopia is self-refuting because...the concept depends on maintaining its undefinable incommensurate character...it is this which gives heterotopia their power; to locate a heterotopia as a site and name it as such is to remove all of its alterity and make it a space like any other.

(p. 47)

The upshot of this is to reiterate that we need to use the notion of heterotopia more as an analytics than as a means of describing places, indeed, as 'a practice...that challenges...functional ordering...while refusing to become part of that order, even in difference' (Hetherington, 1997, p. 47). As such heterotopias possess no singular autonomy in themselves, and exist only in a relational or comparative capacity, by virtue of incongruous juxtapositions or combinations through *effected* difference and otherness, in the effects of bricolage that Foucault considers so indicative of the signification of similitude. Our analysis of heterotopias then are never discrete to the spatial or textual site that they take as their immediate point of reference, but are rather readings exactly of the 'thoroughfare' of practice, meaning and value, engagements exactly of the discursive intercourse between this site and what surrounds and penetrates it. What makes the heterotopia – and what the analysis of the heterotopia yields – is as much its 'constitutive outside' as what is ostensibly bound by the boundaries of its space.

A heterotopology of the gated community

Having introduced the notion of heterotopia, it is helpful to put it to practical use, applying it to the challenge of conceptualizing a particular conjunction of space and power, namely that of the gated community. Before turning to a more empirically grounded engagement with an actual gated community – a particularly large and prestigious enclave,

Dainfern Estate, which lies to the North of Johannesburg – I need make a necessary qualification. Important as questions of discourse are in what follows, the analysis I will go on to offer here is not a discourse analysis. Although I will offer a series of tentative comments on the intersections of materiality and discourse in spatiality of the gated community, a far more rigorous engagement with the elements of knowledge, history and materiality would be required – as Chapter 3 makes clear – if this study were to qualify as an adequately Foucauldian analysis of discourse. Rather than an instance of discourse analysis, this study is a 'heteroto-pology', a case in point of an analytics of the heterotopia.

Fortress societies

What though is a gated community, and why should it interest us? A gated community is a type of residential area that has come about as a result of the aggressive privatization of a potentially public space. It is essentially a bought space, a fenced off domain that denies non-residents and non-affiliates entry, and that is marked by various material and symbolic measures of exclusion. As Blakely and Snyder (1999) explain, 'gating' refers not only to physical barricading – and to the extensive security measures that typify it – but also to attempts to cement upper-income suburban divisions that serve the objectives of exclusivity and prestige. Gating serves to consolidate a particular community lifestyle, a set of privileges that may not otherwise be possible. Herein lies its interest to us: the gated community is a zone of spatiality, a place where intensive regulations of space and parallel productions of discourse intersect in forceful ways, combining to create warrants of exclusion and privilege. Approaching the gated community through the analytics supplied by the notion of the heterotopia will help bring these mutually supporting combinations of discourse and space, *of spatiality*, to the surface.

A brief description of the gated community phenomenon is in order. Blakely and Snyder (1999) identify three main categories of gated communities: 'lifestyle', 'prestige' and 'security-zone' types. 'Lifestyle communities' hope to protect and engender a certain way of life. Typically located at a significant distance from the city, such communities are easily likened to holiday estates. Emphasis here is often placed on ample recreational facilities (golf courses, tennis courts etc.) and on rustic or natural surroundings; a high proportion of residents are retired. These developments reflect 'a notion of shared territory and exclusive rather than inclusive sharing values' (Blakely and Snyder,

1999, p. 55). 'Prestige communities' are about creating class distinctions, about exuding signs of exclusivity; often ostentatious in design, their object is to secure for residents a secure place on the higher rungs of the social ladder. The motivation for 'security zone communities' is predominantly the fear of crime and outsiders. Here residents or developers establish 'gating' in attempts to 'maintain' the values, identity and safety of the neighbourhood.[2] It is worth dwelling on the factor of security for a moment, because in many instances it proves to be the over-riding justification for gated communities.

Privatized governance

Blakely and Snyder (1997) argue that rapid demographic, economic and social change in the United States has resulted in anxiety about the future, invulnerability and uncertainty about the stability of neighbourhoods, of all of which comes to be reflected in an increasing fear of crime. The resulting assumption is that unregulated and uncontrolled residential space is dangerous space. Speaking of gated-community developments in Brazil, Caldeira (1996a, 1996b) notes that the fear of violence and crime has increasingly ensured segregation, distance and separation between classes – a division continually reinforced by popular discourses around crime. Continually repeated stories of crime contribute to a magnification of perceptions of the criminal threat, and to a gratuitous focus on counteractive security measures. Hence an aesthetic of security has come to impose a new logic of surveillance and distanciation, resulting in 'a city where different social groups are...closer in the city space, but...are separated by walls and technologies of security [such that they]...tend not to circulate or interact in common areas' (Caldeira, 1996a, p. 55).

That an agenda of separatism is enforced in gated-community living arrangements seems obvious. Blakely and Snyder (1999) observe how such communities function to reproduce an established order, hastening to mention that gated communities are frequently built and maintained on the basis of explicit 'deeds of lifestyle'. Many maintain their own internal bylaws, and are often governed by Home Owners Associations (HOAs) through which property owners come to share legal ownership of streets, sidewalks, gates and other facilities. For McKenzie (1994), this process is far less about extending community prerogative and far more about extending as extensive as possible control of space and capital. HOAs might be considered 'state actors' insofar as the authority they wield is similar to those of local governments. In such 'privatized governance', claims Lagerfeld (in Landman, 2000b), people can effectively set their own taxes, and use them for the services they choose, and restrict the benefits to those within the gates rather than complaining of using 'their' money for other peoples' problems. We see hence a withering of mutual social responsibility; the idea of what it means to be a resident of a community seems to have changed from speaking of *citizens* to *taxpayers* (Blakely and Snyder, 1999). The private world of gated communities hence shares little with that of their outside neighbours. Davis (1992) hence accuses the US government of collaborating 'in the massive privatisation of public space and the subsidisation of new, racist enclaves' (p. 227).

Separate development

Blakely and Snyder (1999) argue that 'fortress developments' allow select citizens to withdraw from public contact, while forcibly excluding others from sharing their economic and social privileges. The South African gated community is no exception, ensuring that 'freedom of movement is restricted, chance contact is eradicated and public interaction limited to that between self-defined, homogenous groups' (Bremner, 2000, p. 11). Instead of eliminating the dualism between public and private space in the establishment of a homogenous public domains, gated communities have destroyed public space and enlarged private domains that fulfil public functions in a deeply segregated way (Caldeira, 1996b). Watson and Gibson (1995) read such 'gatings' as emblematic of wider social systems of exclusion, domination and identity. Representing an increasing privatization of potentially public activity – an increasing independence from the general civic life of the social sphere – South African gated communities have come to create new forms of economic, social and class segregation. Growing divisions between city and suburb, and rich and poor, create new patterns, which reinforce the costs that isolation and exclusion impose on some (specifically the poor, marginalized and disenfranchised) (Weideman, in Landman, 2000b). For Landman (2000a) such developments have lead to fragmentation within the greater community, to a new elitism and intolerance. The spatial logic of apartheid has thus been given a new rooting-point and Johannesburg has become increasingly fragmented, dispersed and divided, such that Bremner (2000) claims that gated communities have obliterated public space from the urban realm.

Crime crisis

Foucault (1997) does not prioritize any of his designated criteria of heterotopia; as such I will proceed with my heterotopology in an order that suits the purposes and clarity of the argument I wish to develop. Given that heterotopias are those 'other' places which arise around points of crises (and particularly around crises of living space), it would seem as if there could be little doubt that gated communities qualify as heterotopia, at least in the sense that upper-income (and predominantly white) South Africa perceives the current crime problem as attaining crisis-proportions. As exemplified in Dainfern's promotional literature:

> In the present social climate, our very homes are sitting targets and our families victims of unprecedented violence.
>
> (Dainfern promotional brochure (henceforth DPB), 1999)

This characteristic of the heterotopia, that it is a spatial answer to a social problem, seems to be exactly what provides gated communities with the pragmatic rationale for their elaborate control of space. This quality of offering a spatial solution also provides the gated community with a precise and well-defined function within society, a function that, in Foucault's (1997) terms, should prove emblematic of presiding structures of power. Here it is crucial to reiterate that the gated community serves a series of overt functions, providing not only crime protection, but also ensuring 'the good life' and providing a special 'like-mindedness', that is, the opportunity of membership in an exclusive status community. These rationales jostle for ascendance in a Dainfern brochure whose target audience is clearly that of:

> discerning South Africans who yearn for the freedom of living in a secure...setting amongst people of like-minded persuasion...seek[ing] a lifestyle of real quality....We recognize the special nature of golf estate development, where superior lifestyle and security are paramount to a discerning audience....where standards are non-negotiable.
>
> (DPB, 1999)

Signals of distinction

One of the strengths of Foucault's analytics of the heterotopia is the way it suggests that one overturn routine explanations of pragmatic function to offer instead more critical explanations tied to broader socio-political agendas. This leads one to query how the rationale of crime prevention becomes a powerful warrant for various forms of exclusionism. One needs only to note the way in which the avoidance of crime is coupled with the attempt to bolster social class, as another brochure proclaims:

> Residents are 'escapees' from Bryanston, Sandton...people who can no longer abide the high crime rate and the upkeep of large estates. They have basically swopped that lifestyle, once the yardstick by which your success was judged in the 'old' South Africa, for living in one giant fully secured garden.
>
> (DPB, 1999)

Quality of life – much like the prospects of appreciating nature, or of living a truly natural life – becomes indissociably attached to security:

> You'll become part of a community of people who, like you, prefer country style living in a secure, natural environment, where you fall asleep to the call of the kiewiet, and wake up to the gentle flow of the Jukskei river... In maintaining a secure oasis at Dainfern...one of the key ingredients... is security consciousness and peace of mind.
>
> (DPB, 1999)

Exclusivity, social status and the assurance of a peaceful, quality lifestyle are all collapsed into a discourse of crime prevention. There is a tactics of conflation at hand here, where all-important codes of class are couched in the more defensible yet no less desirable codes of nature, safety and quality. Crime fear, class elevation and the right to exclude support to each other at every point, ultimately coalescing in an argumentative strategy of a 'rights' of privilege.

The new 'influx control'

The systems of admission, the rites of exchange necessary to obtain entry to heterotopia are strongly in evidence in gated communities; one needs to submit to a series of procedures, including the recording of entry and exit times, and, often, the provision of written personal details and motives for entry. These procedures of entry are typically accompanied by video-taped documentation of the appearance of visitors and their means of transport. Often permission to enter is contingent on the verbal confirmation of an appointment by a resident. Residents, on the other hand, once recognized, are admitted at the checkpoint rather than needing to undergo further scrutiny. Working counter to the objectives of integrating previously divided communities, such measures ultimately entrench previous patterns of forced division. Already powerful categorizations of race and class are thus re-inscribed in everyday ritual of access and exclusion, in the propositional materiality of barred-off roads, electrified fences, booms and razor-wires whose significations recapitulate the message of violent exclusionism embodied in their physical form.

Dainfern operates a particularly stringent series of access restrictions:

> Only two controlled entrances allow access to Dainfern's large suburban territory... [Dainfern has] high walls with electric wiring designed... to be... forcibly discouraging. 24-hour perimeter patrols... spot any undesirable activity before a problem can arise... [The e]ntire estate is surrounded by 2.4 m walls... Residents are issued with their own access cards; visitors are admitted only on resident's prior notice – or after telephone authorization on arrival... The entire perimeter is patrolled around the clock.
>
> (DPB, 1999)

The ritual of entry to Dainfern becomes, for visitors, a relation of contract; entrance requires a written acknowledgement of, and agreed adherence to, the estate's rules:

> Visitor cards are granted after signing a document agreeing to abide to the rules of the... Estate, and only after verbal confirmation of an appointment by a resident... [A residents'] access card gives... instant entry. If you are a guest... [a] phone call to your host will confirm your status... Builders are allowed on site only during specified hours and are not permitted to remain overnight.
>
> (DPB, 1999)

Talk of one's 'status' being 'confirmed', or differential entry-rights and necessary 'authorization' to access what is ostensibly a suburban area sit uncomfortably for many South Africans, especially when accompanied by tacit indications of race. The racism implicit in the above reference to 'builders' has not gone unnoticed, as in a newspaper report on the estate:

> Dainfern has been accused of racism because (black) builders cannot enter the estate without producing an ID whilst the (white) contractor

has never been asked for identification . . . . every morning the black workers . . . stand in a queue for their IDs to be examined. Some are turned away at the gate because the guards don't think their papers are authentic.

(Oliphant, 2001, p. 4)

These measures bear a striking similarity to past apartheid means of restricting the movement of black citizens (requiring the permission of empowered parties, possessing the correct 'documents' to obtain right of access). Of course these procedures do not simply duplicate the spatial regulations of apartheid; there is a new and potentially over-riding dynamic here, that of class:

A (black) driver says that when he is driving his luxury Pajero nobody asks him for an ID whereas when driving a van, one has to be shown.

(Oliphant, 2001, p. 4)

Contradictions of space and time

Foucault's criterion of 'juxtaposed incompatibilities' makes for useful application here. This criterion usefully draws attention to the ways in which the gated community is a compromise-function, a paradoxical balancing of lethal with safe spaces, communal with private, access-ible with impenetrable. Similar contradictions, ideas of 'a rustic setting' alongside those of 'sophisticated surveillance technology', notions of 'assured safety' despite 'urban detachment', are likewise apparent. Publi-city representations of high profile gated communities labour to make these contradictions seem reasonable. Promotional literature is hence filled with euphemistic paradoxes, especially so in connection with security concerns. We have a 'stringent yet unobtrusive security', elec-trified fencing which is 'not . . . lethal but forcibly discouraging', a 'high security entrance' whose approach is softened by 'landscaped gardens' (DPB, 1999). Threats of protective violence hence subsist alongside promises of escapist recreation; spaces of status and affluence are juxta-posed with those of fear and of fortified seclusion.

Analysis of the 'heterochroneity' of gated communities similarly yields a series of paradoxes. Given the extent of its broad and ample recre-ational facilities, one does get the sense of gated community time as markedly *leisurely* in nature; the objective presumably being that time within the gated community should approximate as closely as possible an 'eternal weekend'. As one Dainfern resident put it: 'You kind of get the feeling you are living at a holiday resort sometimes'. This variety of time is sharply contrasted by the stringent regulation of time as controlled by gated community surveillance technologies. The recording of times of arrival and departure results in a repetition and cataloguing of time; records of times of busy access and potential intrusion can be collected and analysed so as to assuage concerns of predictability, security and order. This documentation of time is accompanied by another means of ordering: the 'monochroneity' of the unceasing surveillance of 24-hour security. Time and space alike are thus carefully monitored, 'domesticated' such that the environment becomes ever more permeated with power.

Juxtaposed incompatibilities

The contradictory juxtapositions highlighted above lie at the heart of the analytical utility of the analytics of heterotopia. Such juxtapositions work both internally (within its own contrary representations and conditions of space and time) and externally (within reference to its surrounding space), to indicate the outcomes and continuance of a recent apartheid history of the race and class structuring of privilege and poverty. One of the strongest indications to this effect is to be found in the disparity between the internal living conditions of Dainfern and its immediately surrounding space. The son of a Dainfern resident's reflections on a neighbouring 'squatter camp' are evocative in this regard:

> [N]ext door is a place called Zieverfontein... It's a squatter camp and actually from my parent's house you can see [it]....Its like this big fucking contrast. And...you can hear the music at night...Some property company has bought the land and they going to move the squatters somewhere, wherever...If you stand on the top deck [of our house]...you can actually see the shacks. My parents...are concerned...But....I say....If you want to have such a rich area then you've got to have a contrast. There's the balance. And the balance unfortunately is right next door....You kind of expect the crime rate to be higher...You kind of expect to get hijacked once you hit the road. All of things you're trying to get away from are right outside the door. Its a large, large squatter camp...and this company has bought this farm and they are going to relocate the squatters.

Reading this one might be forgiven for thinking that no political transformation had taken place in South Africa, particularly in the reference to the 'relocation' of squatters. Interesting also is the suggestion that the gated community might boast – contrary to its best promises – a *higher* crime rate than other areas. Such stark contradictions, whether of an internal or comparative sort, work as powerful indicators not only of an historical structure of privilege, but of the extreme measures needed to ensure the maintenance of such massive social asymmetries of affluence and dispossession. The contradictions are indicative of a situation in which the ideal world of 'naturalized' privilege is necessarily predicated on forcible measures of exclusion, and on gratuitous levels of power and control. One might imagine that these contradictions, by the very fact of their discordance, would point to an untenable living situation, and to more than just that, to an *untenable social-political structure.* Yet this is to misunderstand how the discursive strategies of entitlement operate in this environment. Rather than indications of an inequitable system, these contradictions are taken up as exactly the measures necessitated by an unfavourable socio-political system, a tactic by which socio-political accountability is deferred and historical privilege is consolidated in the face of profound inequality.

A perfect world

The utopian rhetoric of heterotopia is evident in the description of one gated-community resident who is, however unintentionally, quite eloquent in this regard:

> What's happened in this country is that there's been a breakdown of rules...Nobody has regard for anyone...If you wish to take someone's car or break into a home and have your way with a poor housewife...you do. This is the new thing in South Africa, you take what you want, and you do what you like, whereas here there are laws. There are rules and if you do not abide by them you will be asked to please leave the estate. If you don't abide by the laws of Dainfern you will be asked to leave. So that is a very good thing. And we live here in harmony now...Sometimes you think thank goodness you can still live by certain standards.

The utopian rhetoric is even more present, perhaps unsurprisingly, in Dainfern's promotional material:

> Imagine a world of open spaces and freedom. A world of peace and tranquillity. A world of guaranteed security. Imagine this idyllic world within your world.

> (DPB, 1999)

Security is again a necessary component of the perfect world thus envisaged, as is the reiteration of a right of possession ('your world'), and a sense of exclusive ownership. A celebration of nature and personal propriety blend together with a sense of an exclusionary morality, and an even more exclusionary community spirit, to articulate a kind of 'rights' in the following extract (a continuation of the above resident's description):

> Everybody that lives here in Dainfern is very proud of what they own and they respect everything. So you don't have people damaging things. Its yours...You have pride in everything here...there's a beautiful river that runs right through Dainfern and its yours. You pay a levy here and it belongs to you. We have this wonderful sense of pride.

Such utopian flourishes often hark back to another ideological time (of apartheid?); their predominant function seems to problematize outside space:

> Dainfern...is like it used to be – before homes became fortresses and children had to be escorted to visit their friends.
>
> (DPB, 1999)

Disqualifying the exterior

As is the case of other heterotopia, gated communities promote themselves as the closest possible realization of certain social, political and moral ideals. This is not only the case in terms of how they promise an orderly and serene inner space, but also in terms of how outside space comes to be constructed. Representations of the gated community continually emphasize the treacherous and crime-ridden quality of the urban spaces of greater Johannesburg, whilst nonetheless presenting the gated community's own sanitized space as harmonious, orderly and natural. The key discursive tactic in the foregoing extract is to construct the outside world as perilous, damaged and irretrievably lost, and to do so in a way which provides a series of warrants for exclusion, separation and segregation. Note, for example the disqualifying tactics in the following extract, which neatly denies the possibility that 'real' parks might exist in the city:

> The harmony of Dainfern...make[s] an instant impact. Palm lined avenues...Classically designed parks, with...fountains and

water-features. A far cry for what passess for parks in the city. A place to stroll freely. No litter. No tension.

(DPB, 1999)

In this connection gated communities fulfil another of Foucault's criteria for heterotopia: they find their function in reference to alternate spatialities, in making overt the problematics and vulnerabilities of 'other' external and surrounding spaces. In fact, and here again in reference to its effectively realized 'utopian' qualities, the gated community is the closest permissible version of a pseudo-independent and sequestered mini-society – such as the proposed Afrikaaner 'Volkstad' – which hopes to maintain some variety of autonomous or demographic self-governance along with the enforced right to separation.[3]

One might here venture that gated communities need to overstate the crime–threat, so as to justify the multiple levels of avoid-ance, exclusion and separation they implement. If heterotopias do perform the function of representing, in miniature, aspects of the greater socio-political rationality of their broader context, then one could suggest that this is how the discourse of crime is operationalized more generally in South Africa: as a warrant to protect and consolidate past historical prerogatives and structures of privilege.

Divorced from the public realm

As I mentioned above, gated communities are attempts at secession from the public realm, sites of privatized government that main-tain their own basic municipal mandate and manage many of their own civic affairs. In the case of Dainfern such a self-sufficiency of amenities and resources has developed to the extent that the estate now boasts its own post office and postal code. The walled-in area of Dainfern now operates as a quasi-independent suburb, notwith-standing the fact that it is largely impenetrable to outsiders. Rather than rely on municipal water supplies, the estate draws its water from the nearby Jukskei river. Virtually all municipal maintenance – the removal of trash, the upkeep of roads, 'public' parks and so on – are managed internally. In perhaps the most dramatic evidence of its plans to separate itself off from the public realm of the country, Dainfern has its own school, 'Dainfern College'. The school is situated at the entrance of the estate ensuring that children may 'walk safely from home to school and back' (Anonymous, 1998). Established because of 'current fears about the possible deterioration in the government schooling system' (1998), the school, it appears, operates on a residence debenture system ensuring that ownership resides in the hands of the parents and governing body, and secures a child's place in the college.

The micro 'government' of space and community thus enabled exhibits a variety of formal similarities with the historical macro-politics of apartheid, particularly in the ways it consolidates relations of exclusion and division. By virtue of this self-owned 'micro-government' of space one might suggest that the gated community does function as a 'potentially transformative space of society', although obviously of a reactionary rather than progressive capacity. As in other heterotopias, gated communities perform the job of inverting social relations manifest in external societal contexts; reordering them, 'correcting' them, 'perfecting' them against an opposed political rationality, such that the interests of a particular minority might win out. Mirroring this suggestion, Davis (1992) has asserted that such 'fortified-enclaves' are forms of resistance with the primary aim of the reassertion of privilege.

Bearing in mind that the heterotopia is a site of 'alternative social ordering', what is the broader pattern of socio-political rationality that might be read out of the spatiality of the gated community? What argumentative strategies emerge here, what might its alternative representations of social reality tell us? In many ways the privatization of this gated-community domain, and the prerogatives it accordingly cedes to its inhabitants (to exclude 'undesirables', to protect oneself with force, to live in a removed geographical location) suggests a new kind of prerogative, a new 'rights' of exclusion and separation. We have here, behind the façade of pragmatic necessity, a set of co-ordinated operations of power. Despite being presented as little more than a series of crime-preventative measures, as the natural benefits of the affluent, such measures of control ultimately combine to implement a far broader logic of entitlement. The gated community's various systems of privilege come to support a central function: the generation of the right to divorce oneself from the new political agendas of the country, and to substantiate a 'rights' of privilege. In this way, accountability is deferred, calls of integration avoided, historical bases of privilege consolidated, and a new separatism is entrenched.

Inscribing power into space

What has this application of the analytics of heterotopia helped to show up about the gated community? It has demonstrated the extent to which such sites exhibit a line of continuity with apartheid structures of exclusivity, entitlement and exclusion (although, admittedly, exclusions of class now seem to over-ride those of race). More than this, it has helped to show up a series of social contradictions – brought together and epitomized in the paradoxical discourse of a 'rights' of privilege – that emerge in the application of the criteria Foucault provides for identifying heterotopia. These criteria lead us to precisely those intersections of space, discourse and practice where such social contradictions are at their most jarring. The factor of similitude is in evidence here, not only in terms of the juxtaposition of incompatibilities that enables this space to bypass existing codes of social and political order (such as the ideals of integration and non-separatism of the new South Africa), but also in view of how such juxtapositions are forced into a critical visibility. Put differently, an adequate critical appreciation of similitude – as enabled through the analytics of heterotopia – directs our attention to those 'triangulations' of materiality, representation and practice where asymmetries of power are at their most extreme.

'Crime fear' is clearly a central component of such a 'rights' of privilege here. It is operative in constructing the external world (the country beyond the gates) as irretrievably damaged, and doing so in a way that attempts to provide a series of warrants for broader projects of alternate social ordering, orderings in which a 'rights' of exclusion, distantiation and entitlement feature strongly. Crime fear is also a centrepiece in the discursive generation of a 'right' to divorce oneself from the new political agendas of the country, to defer accountability, elide integration and consolidate historical bases of privilege. A moral, naturalist 'utopics' functions in much the same way, to create an ideal world of naturalized privilege that is 'necessarily' predicated on measures of forcible exclusion, segregation and separation. It is through such utopian rhetoric that a tactics of conflation is managed, one in which the codes of class, affluence and status come to be couched rather in terms of appeals to nature, moral order, safety and quality.

On the basis of this analysis, one might advance that the driving force behind the establishment of gated communities may be less about providing security and a sense of community, and more about *inscribing historical structures of privilege into space*. Simply put, just because these arrangements of space operate beneath a powerfully legitimising rationale – that of crime prevention – and just because they have a predominantly spatial, that is, apparently *pragmatic* existence does not makes them innocent in the perpetuation of historical asymmetries of power. Their spatial regulations are not simply about protection; they are, far more fundamentally, about the creation of a separate world, a new social, moral and political enclosure, where subjectivities of prerogative and entitlement can be affirmed and extended. This may ultimately be the principal objective of the gated community: instituting a new and selective order of 'rights', a 'rights' of exclusion, of violent self-protection, and of self-governance.

Discussion 5.4: Heterotopia as symptomatic

The contradictions highlighted above show how we may isolate a political rationality at work in gated communities that far exceeds the reasonable objectives typically given for their establishment. This opens up an interesting possibility: that we may read heterotopia as symptomatic kinds of structures. Let me motivate this claim. One of the key contradictions yielded by research into gated communities is that crime anxiety — by far the most cited justification for 'gating' – is not necessary reduced by moving into a gated environment. Contrary to what one may have assumed, community park residents do not necessarily feel safer than they did before. As Landman (in Rossouw (2001)) argues: 'There's no evidence . . . that points to gated-communities actually reducing crime' (p. 6). Paradoxically, gated-community residents may well be subjected to a *systematic over-emphasis of the threat of crime*, thus becoming subjects of a discursive 'crime paranoia' mobilized to justify the secession from public space that such sites hope to make possible.

If one can convincingly argue that gated communities do not necessarily deliver on the pragmatic reasons that are provided for their establishment, then what is it that they actually *do*? Well, as is the case in the psychoanalytic notion of the symptom, their real motivating reasons may differ significantly from typically attributed causes. Such 'real' reasons may be of an inadmissible sort, even if they start to become apparent under careful scrutiny of the types of 'secondary gain' they enable. To ground this discussion somewhat, I might extend the argument offered above: the spatiality of the gated community does more than simply respond to the problem of crime. Rather 'crime' here becomes a pretext, a means of justifying a series of unreasonable political entitlements (separatism, succession from the public realm, the prerogative of self-governance) that would be otherwise very difficult to defend in a post-apartheid context. Here then an ostensibly symptomatic reading that prioritizes the 'secondary gain' aspect of gated-community spatiality over the more acceptable pragmatic reasons typically offered.

Interestingly, one might push the argument further, referring back to Dixon and Durrheim's notion of a 'grounds of identity' to suggest that one answer to what gated communities really do is that they *provide the basis for an entitled and exclusionary mode of subjectivity.* Such spaces provide the material and discursive resources that make such an order of exclusionary subjectivity not only possible, but also immanently *practicable.* One should not as such underestimate the warrants that a 'loaded' spatiality enables, or indeed, the political rationalities, the patterns of subjectivity that it is able to support, verify and substantiate with recourse to the proof of its surrounding environs. In other words – trading again pragmatic reasons for a different order of cause – it is perhaps necessary to look to *the particular mode of subjectivity* that a given type of spatiality makes possible if we are to explain why it was established in the first place.

Returning though to the analogy of heterotopia as symptom: one might suggest that heterotopia, like symptoms, operate as compromises between certain unspoken interests (of power), and explanations of a pragmatic rationality (of their well-defined social functions). If heterotopias do emerge in societies as kinds of 'compromise structures' between power and pragmatic necessity, then, as in the case of symptoms, we might expect that they would provide a cryptic indication of the underlying conflict of interests that has both brought them into being and given them their particular form. It is worth emphasizing here that both the psychoanalytic symptom and Foucault's heterotopia can be 'read'; both are taken to embody a type of meaning that is elusive, resistant to immediate interpretation. The heterotopia's function of representation-by-similitude seems relevant here: might we not consider the symptom as a particularly cryptic form of similitude, one that follows oblique or lateral lines of representation? Is the symptom not exactly that, *the disguised representation of a state of affairs* that must, by definition, take the route of an unobvious, detoured or unconventional representation? The heterotopia's function of representation-by-similitude would thus imply that 'heterotopic analytics' (heterotopia-as-analytics) enables *symptomatic* readings of place/text. This, in part, is what I have attempted to do with the above application of the heterotopia, to suggest that while certain heterotopia (such as the gated community) may quite blatantly embody aspects of popular moral or political discourse (anxieties of crime fear, imperatives of crime prevention) they also – perhaps more tellingly – hold *symptomatic indications* of a social, moral and political order (a 'rights' of privilege, exclusion and separation), in which relations of direct meaning are dislocated through a series of deferrals.

Conclusion: Reciprocations of materiality, meaning, spatiality

Edward Soja (1989) has consistently warned against analyses that understand space in a depoliticized way, that treat it as an arbitrary or unimportant dimension of power. Foucault (1993) likewise stresses that space is an instrumental means of transposing certain rationalities of power into the forms of material practice. The upshot of this is that we need 'read' arrangements of space, to study the alternative social orderings produced by differential, 'other' places to see how they parallel or support particular regimes of truth. I have tried to stress exactly these imperatives in this chapter: the necessity of engaging the spatial element of discourse, the importance of identifying those relays of meaning and practice that link everyday social values to the procedures and identities of particular places. In this way, we may grasp how meaning, materiality and space come together to implement relations of power and provide a 'grounds of identity', that is, a set of resources for subjectivity.

There is one final point of clarification to insist on. Spatiality, to be sure, is more than just an extension of textual power, more than just an index of discourse. Practices of power realized in arrangements of space may *themselves* function as points of discursive generation; elements of control embodied in particular configurations of spatiality may, in other words, serve as the basis upon which *further* relations of power may be justified, expounded and rationalized. I can put this differently: forceful arrangements of space *are themselves a means of construction*; we are dealing not only with a spatialization of meanings and of power, but with *spatialization as a means of making meaning and power*. We return thus to Soja's warning, which is itself a methodological guideline: spatiality does not simply *follow after*, duplicating established asymmetries of power; the formation of social space is itself a 'grounds' for the establishment of meanings and relations of control. The spatiality of the gated community, as I have tried to show, is at one end of a loop of power in which discourses of crime fear warrant a regime of material interventions and practices that in turn validate a variety of prerogatives and entitlements. Discourse as talk, as social value, reinforces itself as concrete, physical and potentiality violent materiality at each point in an unfolding spiral of social power in which historical structures of privilege and exclusion are continually reproduced.

206

(a)

(b)

Figure 5.1 Electrified perimeter walls are characteristic of most South African gated communities (see a), as are stringent security access points (see b). Courtesy of Michele Vrdoljak.

(a)

Figure 5.2 An 'autonomy of amenities': Dainfern boasts not only its own post office boxes and postal code (see a), but also its own power supply (see b). Courtesy of Michele Vrdoljak.

(b)

Figure 5.2 (Continued)

PRIVATE ROAD

USE AT OWN RISK
NO LIABILITY FOR DAMAGE
LOSS OR COST HOWSOEVER
CAUSED, INCLUDING NEGLIGENCE

THIS IS A PRIVATE ROAD AND ANYONE USING THE
ROAD DOES SO ENTIRELY AT THEIR OWN RISK, AND
NEITHER THE REGISTERED OWNER NOR THE HOLDER
OF THE RIGHT-OF-WAY SERVITUDE, ITS AGENTS,
REPRESENTATIVES OR EMPLOYEES (COLLECTIVELY
THE OWNER) SHALL BE LIABLE FOR ANY DAMAGE,
LOSSES OR COST WHETHER TO PROPERTY OR TO
PERSON ARISING FROM OR IN CONNECTION WITH
THE USE OF THE ROAD AND HOWSOEVER CAUSED
AND WHETHER DUE TO THE OWNERS NEGLIGENCE OR NOT

(a)

Figure 5.3 A case in point of the secession of gated community space from the broader social realm: Privatized roads. Courtesy of Michele Vrdoljak.

(b)

Figure 5.3 (Continued)

(a)

Figure 5.4 The discursive utopics of heterotopia are lent a formidable *material* component in many gated community living spaces. The use of natural features – here dams (see a), rivers (see b) and aspects of an apparently rural countryside (see c) – play their part in the construction of an idyllic 'more natural' living environment. Courtesy of Michele Vrdoljak.

(b)

(c)

Figure 5.4   (Continued)

(a)

(b)

Figure 5.5 One of the starkest contradictions of gated-community spatiality is realized in the disparity between the militarized security technology of its exterior, and the perfected recreational spaces (golf courses (see a), playgrounds (see b) and swimming pools (see c)) of its interior. Courtesy of Michele Vrdoljak.

(c)

Figure 5.5 (Continued)

6
Governmentality, Racism, *Affective* Technologies of Subjectivity/Self

> [T]here is nothing simple about the structure and the dynamics of racism. My conviction now is that we are only at the beginning of a proper understanding of its structures and mechanisms [of its]...complexes of feelings and attitudes, beliefs and conceptions.
>
> (Stuart Hall, 1992)

> Our relation with our racial selves is an evasive thing, often easier to feel than to express.
>
> (Paul Gilroy, 2004, p. 41)

I

How to approach racism's technologies of self...?

Foucault, as we have by now seen, provides a series of methodological injunctions for the effective analysis of power. He directs our attention to its 'micro-physics', its capillary functioning, and urges us to develop a bottom-up grid of analysis with which we might grasp this functionality in the attenuation of individualized forms. He directs our attention also to power's relational form, to the processes, activities and dynamics that underwrite its procedures. Crucial here are the mechanisms, strategies and techniques it utilizes, its 'instru-mentality', the fact of the transposition of certain of its rationalities onto political technologies of subjectivity and self.

The idea of the technology, as a category of analysis, is strongly focused on the minutia of the concrete instrumentation and mechanization of procedural applications of power. When this concept first enters Foucault's conceptual vocabulary, it is within the context of his illustration of the operations of disciplinarity (see Chapter 1). Here the technology is something like an expert system comprised of a discrete set of applied skills, techniques, practices, knowledges and/or forms of specialist language used, whether by experts or on deviant subjects, or by individuals on themselves, as a means of achieving a stated objective of increased mastery or control. Removed from a strictly disciplinary frame, Foucault's later (1988a,b,c) conceptualization of technologies took on a predominantly ethical form, focusing on repertoires of individual self-conduct as managed either through broader regimes of subjectivity, or the micro-techniques of a 'care of the self'. The vital distinction here, in ethical versus disciplinary uses of this notion, is a turn to *self* rather than institutionally operated systems of intelligibility and control. The notion of technologies of subjectivity – as I will go on to discuss in this chapter – refers to a broad set of self-regulative practices, a heterogeneous set of relays, in Rose's (1991) terms, which bring the 'varied ambitions of political, scientific, philanthropic and professional authorities into alignment with the ideals...of individuals' (p. 213). Technologies of self, by contrast, result when such mobile and multivalent technologies of subjectivity came to be 'enfolded into the person through a variety of schema of self-inspection, self-suspicion, self-disclosure, self-nurturance' (Rose, 1996a, p. 32). What one is able to plot here is a 'downward saturation' of power where certain vocabularies and instrumentations of subjectivity enable 'the operations of government to be articulated in the terms of the knowledgeable management of the human soul' (p. 231).

This influential notion of technologies of subjectivity/self provides a useful way of thinking the interchange between structural apparatuses of influence and a micro-politics of self, between totalizing and individualizing forms of power. It slots neatly into Foucault's account of governmentality, providing an articulation of that 'tricky combination' between 'political structures of individualization' and 'totalising procedures' (Foucault, 1982, p. 213). We have thus an analytical means for examining that 'go-between' area in which deeply private, individualized (and ostensibly 'internal') practices of self and subjectivity *are already* political operations, with broader political objectives and effects that may be dispositionally linked to macro forms of state power.

What I wish to suggest is that this conceptual template of governmentality and technologies of subjectivity/self, initially devised by Foucault and subsequently elaborated by Rose, provides us with a potentially novel way of thinking about racism and about forms of racialized subjectivity. I am not alone in this respect; Paul Gilroy, for example, mentions the role of Facism's technologies of self and solidarity, which he claims 'have proved as influential and attractive as the appeal of any of its systematic ideological features' (2000, p. 302). The same may, of course, be said about racialization and indeed racism, by virtue of the fact of the varying means – registers of seeing, speaking and enactment; bodily, spatial and performative routines – by means of which 'race' is constructed, substantiated, encoded and then enfolded within technologies of self. This much is made clear in Gilroy's description of racializing regimes, those programmes of action, 'structures of feeling and doing' which produce 'race' as an obvious, natural and seemingly spontaneous feature of social life. Gilroy speaks also of the 'systematic flow of racialized mentalities and identifications...of the visceral anxieties and pre-political concerns that speak to the currency of 'race' and absolute ethnicity' (2004, pp. 44–45).

What is thus enabled in the above reference to Fascism's technologies of self – and we should bear in mind that Gilroy's is at best a fragmentary application of Foucault – is a perspective on *affected subjectivity*; we have a level of penetration and consolidation within subjects that is reducible neither to the terms of psychological explanation, nor to sociological critiques of determining social structures. This affective subjectivization, to stress the point, cannot be accounted for along the lines of mechanistic ideological manipulation, as Gilroy makes clear in his reference to Richard Wright's comments on the solidarity of ideals, beliefs and assumptions that Wright had witnessed in Fascism: 'I am not speaking of the popular idea of regimenting people's thought; I'm speaking of the implicit, almost unconscious, or pre-conscious, assumptions and ideals upon which whole nations and races act and live'(Wright, in Gilroy, 2000, p. 207). For Gilroy thus we need be alive to fascism – and to racism – in its prepolitical, cultural and psychological aspects. One should hasten to add that these aspects should not be seen as immanently detachable from questions of state power; they should be taken up with a view to how certain lingering associated investments and ideas (rationalized ideals of nation, culture, patriotism, etc.) come to be played out as instruments of modern political administration.

To take up certain of the above Foucauldian injunctions in a rather unorthodox (and seemingly quite unFoucauldian) manner, and taking seriously Gilroy's concern with the 'flow of racialized mentalities and investments', I want to argue that we need to apprehend racism not only as a technology of subjectivity and of self, but as an *affective technology* of subjectivity and self. I have in mind here an awareness of how certain racialized affects come to be deployed, experienced and lived in a fully subjectivized fashion, even if the most important grounding co-ordinates of their ideological coherence may be sources elsewhere, at the level of governmental practice. Foucault's theory of governmentality – which I will introduce shortly – leads us to examine the conduct of various human capacities through a variety of indirect or 'dispositional' mechanisms. It shows us furthermore that many of our most private or internalized practices of subjectivity provide a means of articulation for larger-scale political rationalities. If we accept these two postulates, then it would seem that the question of the conduction of affect is something of an imperative for any critical apprehension of racism.

I have three objectives in this chapter. First, to provide an intro-ductory discussion on several of the notions mentioned above, espe-cially the ideas of governmentality, technologies of subjectivity/self and the associated concepts of the apparatus (or *dispositif*) and disciplinary bio-power. At this level of exposition, my aim is to build upon the account of the emergence of disciplinarity (discussed in Chapter 1) and methodological injunctions for the analysis of power (discussed in Chapter 2), and to do so by introducing the remaining concepts of Foucault's multifaceted understanding of modern power, namely the *sovereignty-discipline-government complex*. I hope in this respect to show how Foucault's later conceptualizations of power move beyond some of the apparent limitations of the notion of disciplinarity (that it is insufficiently differentiated; that it risks reducing all of modern power to the paradigm of discipline; that it slips implicitly into a negativist mode of domination hence foreclosing possibilities of resistance, etc.). Secondly, I hope to introduce the topic of racism, both in the terms of Foucault's account developed in *Society Must be Defended* (2003a), and, indeed, in the form of a challenge to the critical historico-discursive frame of analysis typically associated with Foucault. Thirdly, developing on this challenge, I wish to open up the terrain thus established in a provocative way, by providing a tentative outline for how an analytics of governmentality may be advanced in such a way that takes seriously the *affective* dimension of technologies of self. My goal in this respect – in accordance with a line of criticism running throughout this book – is to offer a Foucauldian frame able to engage with what we may cautiously refer to as the 'psychological' dimension of a given social phenomenon, in this case, racism. I have allowed myself more exploratory latitude than in previous chapters in applying a series of Foucault's conceptual motifs; my focus here, in bringing this book to a close, is to suggest a future possibility for a Foucauldian analytics of certain psychological forces.

The governmentality of 'affected' race

The idea that 'race' has itself become a principle of governance in Modernity, a formidable bio-political technology in its own right, is not, of course, a new idea (see for example Mbembe, 2001; Posel, 2001; Stoler, 1995); Foucault himself elaborates on this theme in his 1975–1976 Collège de France lectures (see Discussion 6.3). Here though it seems worthwhile posing a 'psychological' type of question not typically raised in analyses of this sort: surely such administrative technologies of race – whether their prime concern lay with rudimentary racial classification or with systematic segregation – gave rise, at each point of their application, to a set of affective responses and identifications in its subjects? It would seem psychologically naïve to speculate about these measures without considering the range of identity-effects, the intense 'affect-positions' they no doubt induced. We might take this speculation a step further: surely this range of affects and identifications should be thought of as no less subject to the procedures of racist governmentality, no less 'technologizable' than the particular bodies, arrangements of space, modes of civic interaction – each racialized, each *racializing* – brought into being by the apparatuses of the racist state.

I can make this argument more forcefully with reference to an example. In an important paper on racial classification in apartheid, Posel (2001) comments:

> What made the apartheid system of racial classification notoriously distinctive was its panoptic scope: Every single South African citizen was...compelled to register as a member of an officially designated race, on the understanding that this classification would then inform every aspect of that person's life.
>
> (p. 89)

Virtually every aspect of a person's daily life was racialized, made subject to racist state surveillance and restriction: the range of available employment, the level of taxes and levies, the type of public amenities, the class and type of transport and the possibility of land-ownership – all were determined according to racial type. Posel's account does not engage with the affective dimension of these restrictions and divisions, although she does note that: 'the daily...experience of race derived from the ordinary, immediate experience of how people...lived' (2001, p. 94), and furthermore: 'apartheid's racial grid was strongly imprinted in the subjective experience of race' (p. 87).

These quotes advance the argument I am trying to make. First, given the degree to which the fabric of daily life was suffused with an order of racial consciousness – an awareness of categorical prerogatives and their corresponding disentitlements – it seems impossible to imagine that the segregations and classifications of apartheid did not give rise to a series of identity-effects and affective positionings. Furthermore the order of affects and identifications thus incurred should not be viewed as merely incidental, as of secondary importance; they must rather be grasped as of crucial and indeed instrumental importance when it comes to addressing the tenacity of (post-)apartheid's logics of race. Put differently: rather than reading such affects and identifications as peripheral to an analysis of the structural factors and procedural components of state racism – as arbitrary by-products – surely these affective forces need be factored in as central consideration, if we are to produce an adequate account of racist governmentality? Indeed, would the strategic encouragement of certain identity- and affect-positions not ultimately prove as instrumental to an overall programme of racist governmentality as its more overtly material technologies of division?

One last contribution to this argument. It is by now a common-place of history that apartheid, as a state-legislated system, implemented racism at a variety of formal and institutional levels across South African society. Apartheid did not, however, legislate that whites *must* neces-sarily be racist in their everyday interpersonal dealings with blacks, even if it is true that such a tacit injunction can be said to have been implicitly written into the discursive ordering of the apartheid public sphere. Nevertheless racism was – and indeed *still is* – perpetuated at just such a micro-political level, through the means of everyday interactions, ordinary interpersonal practices – difficult to formulate or analyse – that appear pre*political* in nature. The personal racism of the white subject was not, as it were, enforced or regulated by the state. This notwith-standing, such forms of racism functioned, almost without fail – and at even the most micro, the most capillary levels of interpersonal contact – to extend and support the structural racisms of the state.

This, incidentally, raises the question of how racist regimes respond to the problem of those informal interactions between members of different racial groupings which provide the basis for bonds of friendship, affiliation, identification and so on; a difficulty arising from the fact that the whole domain of gestures, friendliness and momentary inter-subjectivities cannot ultimately be legislated. One response, interestingly analysed by Finley (2007), is the construction of the 'race traitor', who need not necessarily break any of the codified rules of racial contact, but whose emotional loyalties are thought to lie with 'racial others'.

In the notion of governmentality, the micro-political dimension of interpersonal racism may well prove crucial to sustaining broader macro-level components of racist state power; indeed, the latter may ultimately prove easier to remove than the former. Here then a case of how macro- and micro-levels of power might be seen as working together, in conjunction, each extending and supporting the other, without being carefully correlated, without their relationship being codified or fixed. It is exactly the conjoined effects of such multiple lower order governments of the personal to the general benefits of the higher-order government of the state which Foucault can help us to conceptualize. We are met here with an intriguing problem of causality, with a complex and potentially evasive – even discontinuous – pattern of political influence in which wide-ranging governmental measures aim to regulate all sorts of social life, down in fact, even to the realm of affective relations. The intuitive response to such a claim is that the affective is a largely prepolitical domain, one that cannot simply be legislated or regulated. Now although of course 'legislate' like 'regulate' is too strong a word, this is exactly what I want to argue: I want to make the case that many contemporary modes of governmentality do involve a strong *conduction* of affect, a streaming, or encouragement of certain affective bonds which in many instances do retain powerfully racializing elements. My argument is that we should bring these three terms (affect, technology and governmentality) together, for unless we are able to grapple with the vicissitudes of certain modes of affective formation, and, indeed, with how these modes come to be operationalized as technological elements of broader governmental logic, we fail to appreciate something quite fundamental about contemporary modes of race and racism.

Discussion 6.1: The limits of historicism as mode of critique

Towards the end of Chapter 1, I queried whether we should treat history as the absolute horizon of criticality within which to grasp all the objects of our analyses. I also queried whether constructionist accounts of certain objects of knowledge were sufficient in and of themselves. Now, while we should stop short of classifying Foucault as a constructionist — the historical depth of his writings, the clear attention to materializations of power and its instrumentation in various apparatuses/technologies cut him apart from many textually focused variants of social constructionism — some important questions do arise here. Can all objects of knowledge be historicized in the same way; are all such objects, as it were, equally constructed, or constructed in the same types of ways?

Questions of race and racism certainly make for important consideration in this light. As a series of authors have recently cautioned, we cannot explain prejudice and bigotry as merely sets of representational content, as simply the effects of asymmetrical social structure, or as only conscious beliefs and political effects (Cheng, 2000; Seshadri-Crooks, 2000; Žižek, 1998). For Lane (1998), racism's irrational forms 'elude explanation by sole reference to either conscious precepts or social history' (p. 2). Shepherdson (1998), similarly concerned with the limits of constructionism and historicism, questions whether issues of 'race' can be adequately grasped as only a matter of 'discursive effect or ... purely through symbolic formation' (p. 44). The full significance of the concept of 'race', he argues, remains irreducible to the analysis of historical and discursive context; to understand racism we need in addition an awareness of the *psychical representations* of 'race', only then can the peculiar tenacity of this concept be addressed. To be clear, Shepherdson's objective in grappling with the shortcomings of historico-discursive conceptualizations of 'race' is not to propose a return to the 'reality' of empirical facts, to the 'name of biological truth'. His objective is rather to question whether all phenomena can be historicized in the same way, to argue, furthermore, that the historicity of various phenomena may not have been 'prematurely reduced to a single form by the discourse of social constructionism' (1998, p. 44).

Winnubst (2004) offers a similar attack, noting that psychoanalytic theory provides the tools with which to answer 'what social constructionist approaches assume but never adequately account for', namely the fact of 'how race attaches to individual bodies and psyche ... while simultaneously operating through a trans-social logic' (p. 43). Psychoanalysis, she proclaims, provides opportunities to articulate how race is historically and socially constructed and yet individually embodied. Clarke (2003) also expresses reservations over the recent preponderance of sociological/discursive analyses of racism, many of which fail, in his estimation, to address a series of core issues:

> [F]irst, the ubiquity of forms of discrimination and *the affective component* of hatred; second ... the sheer rapidity, *the explosive, almost eruptive quality* of ethnic hatred ... Third ... the *visceral and embodied nature* of racism ... Finally, the *psychological structuring* of discrimination ... the psychological mechanisms that provide the impetus for people to hate each other.
>
> (2003, pp. 2–3, my emphasis)

What unites all of these accounts is racism's notorious recalcitrance in the face of historical, discursive and institutional change. To paraphrase Lane (1998): conventional emphasis on racism's material and discursive history tends to ignore this phenomenon's *impalpable forms*; to consider racism as merely the outcome of 'cultural fixation or residue of historical prejudice is not sufficiently helpful' (p. 3), he advances. It remains for us thus to interpret this phenomenon's intransigence, to grapple with the fact of apparently growing levels of intolerance, racist hostility and hatred even in societies where equality and democracy have become enshrined ideals.

To adopt the psychoanalytic perspective advocated by the above authors is not to condemn discussions of racism to irretrievably individualistic modes of conceptualization. Nor is it to fix the topic of racism within a 'vernacular of deviancy' which views racist phenomenon as no more than a psychopathological form, as the maladjustment of isolated 'asocial' subjects (which is not to say that previous psychoanalytic engagements with racism have not been guilty of these types of reductionism (see Cohen, 2002; Frosh, 1989)). A cross-section of recent psychoanalytic work on the topic of racism (Bhabha, 1994; Cheng, 2000; Riggs and Augoustinos, 2004; Seshadri-Crooks, 2000; Winnubst, 2004; Žižek, 1998) largely avoids such pitfalls of de-contextualization and psychological reductionism. Such critical applications of psychoanalytic theory have remained attentive to the interpenetration of psychological and structural factors, aware that procedures of identification, disavowal, projection and related 'psychological' mechanisms do not occur in a historical vacuum, or beyond the reach of forceful discursive practices. It is not here merely a case of historical representations and associated practices that perform and substantiate 'race', but also of the *affective* dimension of such representations and practices; it is a question also of the passionate attachments and investments in such categories which are continually reiterated in racist discourse and feeling.

In much the same vein Lane argues that '[w]e cannot comprehend ethnic and racial disputes without considering the implications of psychic resistance', unless we 'engage critically with the fantasies organizing the *meaning* of racial and ethnic identities' (1998, p. 1). Work of this type calls for an approach that looks neither to isolated subjects themselves in a way that is cut off from their historical and symbolic realms nor to a focus on symbolic structures abstracted out of their relationship with human subjects. It hopes rather to understand something of 'the complicated relationship between subjects and their symbolic structures' (Lane, 1998, p. 2).

II

The arts of government

Foucault's work on governmentality stems from a series of studies on sixteenth century political theory. The challenge that Foucault had set for himself in this respect was that of adequately conceptualizing 'the powers of state' without deferring to the traditional terms of sovereignty.

This work constituted his most significant attempt to flesh out the 'middle order' in his account of power, to connect, as Dreyfus and Rabinow (1982) note, a disciplinary focus on subjected individuals with a series of anonymous mechanisms of power operating on a broader social level, and to do so via a cautious assertion of limited elements of sovereignty.

One of the first misconceptions that Foucault (1979a) hopes to clear up in his theory of governmentality is the notion that questions of government are predominantly, if not exclusively, questions of the macro-politics of statecraft. There are, rather, Foucault claims, multiple 'lower-order' categories of government; one may reasonably speak of the government of the family, of the workplace, of one's relationship to one's self and so on. This broader usage of the concept, as Dean (1999) puts it, 'gives particular emphasis to issues of the government of human conduct in all contexts, by various authorities and agencies, invoking particular forms of truth, and using definite resources, means and techniques' (p. 2). Government thus refers to any calculated direction of human conduct; its 'jurisdiction' includes a focus on the smallest micro-politics of day-to-day life in addition to more obviously macro-political issues that we would typically associate with the administrative apparatuses of particular state governments. Using the notion of government in this way gives 'particular emphasis to issues of the government of human conduct in all contexts, by various authorities and agencies, invoking particular forms of truth, and using definite resources, means and techniques' (p. 2).

Despite that such micro-political forms of government may be immanently separable from macro-political forms of government, *these two typically work in conjunction*, in often unpredictable relations of combination. Such combinations are difficult to predict, and should not be understood as planned, or predetermined. They do not connect in any simple, one-to-one or linear way. In fact, such combinations often seem to work in *discontinuous* or *indirect* ways. However, and this is the vital point, the micro-politics of government nonetheless typically work to *support* and *extend the overarching agendas of macro-power*. Here it starts to become possible to point to what governmentality might mean, namely the overarching rationality behind the use of *multiple* forms of government; an awareness of how the conjoined effects of lower-order (micro-political) forms of government work to support the broadest agendas of the state.

In many sixteenth century political texts, claims Foucault, the 'arts of government' came to be considered in relation to a wide range of issues, from educational questions on the government of children, from the government of individual souls and lives, to questions of the monarch's government of the state, to even issues pertaining to the government of *one's self*. We are here concerned with an ever-expanding set of potentially governable objects; power, furthermore, is diffused broadly, and multiple micro-level institutions and sites of social exchange. Less than homogenous power is not reducible to a single figure, namely that of the sovereign or monarch. As opposed to the case in sovereignty, in which virtually all instances of power repeat and extend the sovereign's will, the state of government is characterized by a diverse and immanent network of practices of government which criss-cross state and society. These practices have very different levels of application, and very different forms, this is why one speaks of an 'arts of government'. As Foucault (1979a) puts it:

> practices of government are, on the one hand, so varied that they involve a great number of people: the head of the family, the superior in the convent, the teacher or tutor in relation to the child or the pupil, so that there are several forms of government among which the Prince's relation to his state is only one particular mode; and on the other hand, all these governments are internal to the states of society.
>
> (p. 9)

What we start to find in an 'arts of government', argues Foucault (1979a), is continuity between various levels and types of power which may often seem totally autonomous. This continuity works both 'upwards' and 'downwards', 'upwards' in the sense that the person who governs must first learn how to govern *him/herself* correctly, and 'downwards' in the sense that the head of a family will know how to look after his family, and in the sense that individuals, in general, under the socio-political power of the state, will behave correctly. We have then not only a more plural form of power than in eras of sovereignty – a wider collection of objects – we have also a far more heterogonous functionality – a broader set of combinations of various orders of power. Governmental activity is heterogeneous, pervasive and multiple, coming to apply, as Dean (1999) notes, to a complex of people and things. It is no longer a case simply of the sovereign's possessions and territory that concern power; there are now innumerable objects, relations and capacities that come to bear the vested interests of governmental power.

In opposition to the self-justifying notion of sovereignty, the ends of government rest in something beyond itself, in what Foucault (1979a) refers to as *the disposal of things in the most correct and efficient manner*. In the case of government, it is not simply a matter of maintaining the authority of an unquestionable, final and categorical law – as in the case in sovereignty – it is rather a question of arranging things and people always towards their most profitable and productive outcomes. The logic of government is that of the ever-changing, and ever-tactical, orientation of people and things towards relations of greatest benefit. The ends of government for Foucault (1979a) now lie not simply in ruling itself, or in increasing the sovereignty of the ruler, but in improving the condition of the population, in increasing its wealth, its longevity, its health as a whole; power is now intent on growing and ordering this set of resources, it 'exerts a positive influence on life ... endeavour[ing] to administer, optimize and multiply it, subjecting it to precise controls and comprehensible regulations' (Foucault, 1980c, p. 137).

The notion of the 'population' hence emerged as a crucial focus of governmental attention. 'Populations' came to be seen as possessing not only their own regularities (their own rates of death and disease and so on), but also their own intrinsic and aggregate effects; it became possible to speak of the defining characteristics, habits, activities and tendencies of a given population. In short, to measure, predict and monitor the population in all its different dimensions, facets and peculiarities became an absolute imperative of governance.

Disciplinary bio-power – governmental bio-politics

In referring to the importance of 'power's relation to life', Foucault (1980b) is drawing on another important conceptualization of modern power, namely the notion of bio-power, which, as its name suggests, takes as its responsibility, the exhaustive and large-scale 'administrating of life'. In the late seventeenth and early eighteenth centuries, claims Foucault (1979a), the great political technologies of Western modernity came to adopt a radically new logic, and, accordingly, assume new forms of implementation. What had been a 'power of death' – the sovereign's right to take away the life of his or her subjects – thus becomes a 'power of life', the state's responsibility to care for and enhance the life-processes of its citizens.

It is crucial to grasp the significance of the notion of bio-power, and, likewise, to appreciate the breadth of what is included within the scope of the 'bio-political'. Dreyfus and Rabinow (1982) speak of bio-power as the name Foucault gives to the increased ordering of *all* realms under the guise of improving the welfare of the individual; bio-politics, by contrast, is to be understood as the *calculated life-management of human populations*. The role of the state is a crucial factor in bio-politics, a fact made clear in McNay's emphasis that the domain of bio-politics includes *all processes of life* – in the sense of the vital biological processes of propagation, birth, mortality, disease, life-expectancy and so on – which come to fall under its supervisory and regulatory controls.

Discussion 6.2: Distinguishing bio-power and bio-politics

Although Foucault at times appears to use the terms 'bio-power' and 'bio-politics' interchangeably, it is worthwhile – especially given how influential these notions have proved to be (as in the work of Agamben (1998) and Hardt and Negri (2000), to cite just two examples) – to focus briefly on how these two terms might be differentiated. At a basic level, one might understand bio-power as the generic category of which bio-politics is a variant. Foucault's comments towards the end of *Society Must be Defended* add to this distinction. Bio-power, he argues, emerges, towards the end of the seventeenth century, from a disciplinary focus on the anatomo-politics of individual bodies, and is typically localized to the institutional confines of schools, hospitals, barracks and so on. Medicine and health interventions had a crucial role to play here – as Kistner (2003) is right to highlight – defining standards for physical and moral life-conduct of individuals in relation to society. In the course of the eighteenth century, however, as the importance of regularizing normalization grew, it became necessary to compliment the disciplinary targeting of individuals with a broader point of application: the life of the species as a whole. There is, in effect, both a 'zooming-in' and a 'zooming-out' of power; a movement, in other words, in the logic of power, from the meticulous attention paid to individual bodies, to a concern with the body of the population. Singular *and* collective life came under the influence of power in the respective forms of bodily technologies of discipline and bio-political technologies of regularization. Bio-politics can thus be understood as that type of bio-power that targets collectivities, constituting its subjects as 'a people', 'a nation', 'a race' (Foucault, 2003a). Or, in Lazzarato's (2002) terms of emphasis: whereas bio-power begins with the body and its potentials, and seizes life and 'living being' as its objects, bio-politics is always necessarily a form of government, it involves a government–population–political economy relationship (for more on this distinction, see Rabinow and Rose, 2003).

Power's new preoccupation with the various forces of life effectively means, as Lazzarato (2002) stresses, that a new ontology of power is established. Foucault (1978a) makes this point plainly: so thoroughly have contemporary methods of power and knowledge assumed responsibility for the control of processes of life and health, that – for the first time in history – biological existence is reflected in political existence. Our political existence is thus inseparably attached to out vital biological functions, both as individuals and as members of a species body. Put simply, there is no question of the body, its health, its betterment, no question of biology, disease or well-being, which is not also a political issue; biology and power have hence become inseparable. More than this: life and power themselves have become inseparable – it is exactly through the regulation of life and life-processes that power exercises its influence, that it guarantees its hold upon us. It is power's increased preoccupation with the process of life that has so massively widened its jurisdiction, which has resulted in its saturation of virtually all aspects of everyday existence. It is likewise this factor that has so dramatically extended the interventionist warrants, the spread of different disciplinary techniques and apparatuses of power. Similarly, this taking charge of life has meant that power has been able, with remarkable success, to possess and manoeuvre the discourse of rights as the basis of its own legitimacy:

> It was life more than the law that became the issue of political struggles... The 'right' to life, to one's body, to health, to happiness, to the satisfaction of needs, and beyond all the oppressions or 'alienations,' the 'right' to rediscover what one is and all that one can be, this 'right'... was the political response to... [the]... new procedures of power.
>
> (Foucault, 1978a, p. 145)

A series of important parallels are thus evidenced between the demarcated domain of disciplinary power, and the broadening rationality of bio-power. Among these is an interest in technical and technological means of implementation, the recourse to humanitarian discourse and, of course, a preoccupation with normalization. In fact, these are not so much parallels as continuities, given that Foucault will eventually (1994) come to speak of 'disciplinary bio-power' as a singular, although diversely realized, system of power. In his own terms, we have here two series that share a normalizing agenda, 'the body-organism-discipline-institutions series, and the population-biological processes-regulatory mechanisms-State' (2003a, p. 250). The normalizing society, moreover, 'is a society in which the norm of discipline and the norm of regulation intersect along an orthogonal articulation' (p. 252). This ascendancy of normalization does not mean

> that the law fades into the background, or that the institutions of justice tend to disappear, but rather that the law operates more and more as a norm, and that the judicial institution is increasingly incorporated into a continuum of apparatuses (medical, administrative, and so on) whose functions are for the most part regulatory.
>
> (Foucault, 1978a, p. 144)

Foucault here is more tentative, less categorical in discussing the prospective role of sovereignty than he was in the era of *Discipline and Punish*. Certain sovereign mechanisms remain important features within the overall scheme of bio-power; the institutions of justice and law, for example, maintain a fundamental role, even if the joint influences of bio-political and disciplinary intervention typically precede them. One begins to appreciate the gains Foucault makes by interposing these two models. On the one hand, we have a mode of power that functions on the capillary level of individuals, optimizing their capabilities, and integrating them, via the route of a self-regulating subjectivity, into systems of economic control. On the other, we have an operation of power that comes from 'the top down', that focuses on regulating and predicting the 'species body'. The latter is a technology of reassurance and security which looks to biological processes rather than to single bodies and that attempts to protect a whole social body from internal dangers, and does so by gathering a massive corpus of data on the resources, capacities and problems of the population. The concept of disciplinary bio-power, as Dreyfus and Rabinow (1982) are quick to point out, is hence able to link together the various political technologies of the individual, the knowledge-producing efforts of the human and social sciences and the structures of state domination. This conglomerate notion of 'disciplinary bio-power' hence usefully enables Foucault to join 'bottom-up' and 'top-down' flows of power while maintaining an emphasis on technical and tactical imperatives. Similarly, it posits the importance, within governmental regimes, multiplicity of diverse and multi-modal forms of control working in conjunction in a joint and complementary way without necessarily being arranged in any systematic or intentionally orchestrated manner. This stands to reason: the expansive mandate of administering human life in the broadest possible sense would mean that a successful regime of government need rely on a wide range of semi-autonomous technologies, on a web of disciplinary and bio-political effects, which while made up of often discrete components, while not strictly synchronized or even networked, can nevertheless work in a mutually coherent manner. What this conceptualization requires, however, is the provision of a relay, a 'go-between', connecting micro- and macro-'physics' of power; Foucault provides this with the notion of 'apparatuses of security'.

Discussion 6.3: Towards a genealogy of modern state racism: *Society must be defended*

Having made reference to psychoanalytic approaches to racism as a means of emphasizing the possible shortcoming of critical, historical and discursive modes of critique, it seems useful to provide a brief sketch of how Foucault's most important engagement with this topic, namely that of his 1975–1976 Collège de France lectures, *Society Must be Defended*. Foucault begins the lectures with a restatement of his view that the field of power is fragmentary, diverse and changing. Complex in its components, such a field is made up of an 'unbalanced, heterogeneous, unstable, tense set of force-relations' (p. xviii). Hence the usefulness of the 'schema of war' as a mode of conceptualization that renders power-relations in the terms of a model of perpetual conflict, looking for 'the principle of intelligibility of politics in the general form of war' (p. iv). This model has certain advantages: it allows us to understand how 'relations of force' might possess a strategic coherence, indeed, a kind of 'tactical rationality' despite their chaotic multiplicity. Here Foucault inverts Clausewitz's famous assertion that 'war is politics continued by other means' in order to make the more provocative claim that 'politics is war continued by other means'; he thus draws our attention to the fact that everyday regimes of social ordering share the objectives of warfare, certainly inasmuch as they hope to attain practical relations of control, subjection and docility.

The 'schema of war' is not Foucault's invention; it is a mode of analysis that he lifts from a variety of earlier political texts where it is applied as a means of understanding historical processes. Foucault credits this notion with an unusual 'insurrectionary power'. His hope is not only to apply the formula methodologically, as one aspect of his analytics of power, he also aims to trace its genealogy, thereby telling us something about the origins of State racism. This principle of the perpetual war within society, the idea that the civil order is continually characterized by the tensions, tactics and divisions of an internal battle, has, he claims, developed from the notion of a 'war between races'. This is an idea that gives rise to two broad types of historical interpretation: the revolutionary idea of class struggle and the racist idea of biological racial duality. Foucault deals with each of these in turn.

In opposition to the predominant function of history in Medieval and Roman times – that of praising and aggrandizing power – the rationale of 'a war of the races' was, initially, and most fundamentally, a resistance to sovereignty, be it that of the monarch, the class system, or of Imperialistic domination. As such, argues Foucault, the idea of 'race struggle' originally develops as a political narrative *designed to refute notions of the 'divine' or 'natural' right power.* The notion of the 'war of the races', in fact, is considered one of the roots of the class struggle itself, a claim that Foucault substantiates with reference to the writings of Marx. There is something genuinely revolutionary about this notion, certainly inasmuch as it draws attention to the history of a people's enslavement or servitude; it may in this respect be linked to the use of nationalist sentiment in the anti-colonial struggle. Importantly, we need to bear in mind here that the idea of 'race' when it first appears historically, is for Foucault, something far closer to the solidarity of an oppressed group, class or nation. Indeed, 'race' up until this point has not been attached to any essential or biological meaning – this will be the prerogative, argues Foucault, of the socio-biological sciences of the nineteenth and twentieth centuries and the technologies of government that seek to utilize them. Although Foucault does not discuss it in any great detail, the Colonial project is clearly a key factor here, lending considerable density and force to the biological and cultural essentialization of the category of race.

The racist idea of biological racial duality – moving now to Foucault's second point of focus – is largely coterminous with the rise of the modern regime of bio-power. This notion of race is a component within a rationality of power that takes the population as its target, and the development and cultivation of its life as its overall objectives. At this point the notion of 'race struggle' is transformed into the racist idea of 'racial purity'. There is something like a tragedy in the politics of resistance that occurs here: a resource of dissidence, an instrument of solidarity against various types of oppressive sovereignty is contorted into one of modernity's most characteristic, and most atrocious, forms of social logic: the racist notion of inherent biological racial superiority.

The twentieth century has presented us with a heinous pairing of bio-power (that aims to protect and strengthen the population of a state) and state racism (that rests on conceptualization of the biological superiority of one race over another). Apartheid is one example of this, although the genocidal project of Nazism is closer to Foucault's historical frame of reference. In the era of bio-power, claims Foucault, power loses the indiscriminate 'function of death' – indeed, its primary mandate is now safeguarding and improving life. Under such conditions, the only way to justify state sponsored programmes of ethnic persecution or genocide is through appeals to the rationality of racism. Hence the imperative to kill is today acceptable only on the basis of the elimination of a threat to a given population; the right to cause death is permissible only on the promise of life to a given populace. Modern states seeking the right to wage war, or to take life, will continue to produce forms of racism and/or social prejudice so long as they are operating within the broader ethos of bio-power that gives such distinctions an urgent political meaning.

Whereas the discourse of the 'struggle between races' was initially a weapon to be used against oppressive forces, ultimately it came to be assimilated within a discourse of racism that turns *on exactly the oppressed groups* who may have otherwise utilized the logic of 'the war of races' in their defence. 'Racism' argues Foucault, 'is, quite literally, revolutionary discourse in an inverted form' (p. 81). We should not be surprised thus that racism in its modern forms contains a utopian element, or that it mimics the solidarity of oppressed. For Foucault we do not grasp the internal logic of racism without understanding this fact: in modern racism we have an inversion of the revolutionary into the oppressive.

Apparatuses of security

Foucault (1980e) uses the designation 'apparatuses of security' – or, alternatively, 'dispositif' to describe the various semi-autonomous techniques of government necessary to the regulation of the modern state. Such apparatuses, described by Foucault as the *essential technical means of governmentality*, are established in response to a situation of crisis, as a means of addressing a problem of social control. Apparatuses, furthermore, are:

> thoroughly heterogeneous ensemble[s] consisting of discourses, institutions, architectural arrangements, policy decisions, laws, administrative measures, scientific statements, philosophical, moral and philanthropic propositions; in sum, the said and the not said, these are the elements of the apparatus. The apparatus itself is the network that can be established between these elements.
>
> (Foucault, 1980e, p. 194)

Rabinow and Rose (2003) add a useful gloss to this depiction, describing the apparatus as:

> [a] device oriented to produce something – a machinic contraption.... [of the] control and management of certain characteristics of a population...The elements composing or taken up in [such] a

network apparently could be anything...the elements in an apparatus...[are] joined and disjoined by a strategic logic and a tactical economy of domination operating against a backdrop of discursive formations.

(pp. 10–11)

What is helpful about these descriptions is their emphasis on a loose – and indeed, immanently separable – co-ordination of the ways and means through which the powers of government come to be applied. As both the above descriptions impress upon us: there is a fundamental irregularity, an apparent incompatibility of components at the heart of the dispositif's strategic conjunctions. Rather than a principle of disorder, this factor of unevenness is an effective condition of possibility for the functioning of the apparatus. Despite that each aspect of such an ensemble may be put into play by very different types of people or activities, despite that each such aspect may well maintain a highly divergent, even mutually incompatible, set of functions and capacities, they are, even while retaining an effective kind of autonomy, nevertheless able to work in concert. A shifting assemblage thus of diverse yet complementary components that all contribute to an over-riding unity of effect; we have here something like an under-coordinated machine of power.

By entailing the prospect 'of a kind of strategic *bricolage*', as Rabinow and Rose (2003) nicely put it – a tactics, that is, of unconventional combinations – the apparatus's lines of conduction become difficult to predict, to thwart, or disentangle, and hence give rise to unanticipated effects. Apparatuses hence are kinds of joiners, diagonal lines of connection cutting across, combining formal dissimilarities. They are hinges, one might say, between the knowledge of spoken and written discourse, and the materialization of this knowledge within the immanent sphere of everyday practice; hinges also, perhaps more accurately, crucially, between macro- (and structural) and micro- (individualized and interpersonal) modalities, between state and capillary forms, between formalized and spontaneous events of power. The immense flexibility of governmental power that Foucault draws our attention to is enabled precisely in this way, through the means of such varying and often unexpected articulations. Although strategic intent may be read retrospectively across such an unorthodox combination of elements, the overall efficacy of this arrangement cannot be said to be strictly predetermined, prearranged. The apparatus's conductions of power through a social body may thus be characterized as *under-determined in its co-ordinations*, although *over-determining in effects, in efficacy*.

The analytical importance of the notion of apparatus lies in the fact that it enables us to bring into focus a regularity of functioning across different component parts of an effective ensemble; it shows up composite patterns of power-relations that we may not otherwise be able to discern. We are not limited in our analyses to forms of a similar type – to a single level of analytical categories (of class, institution, culture, psychology, etc.) – but are able to read 'diagonally' across such types.[1] The understanding of the apparatus draws our attention to the plasticity of governmental power, which, as I have emphasized, is enabled precisely though the articulations the apparatus makes possible. The sophistication of the composite model of power that Foucault offers us has much to do with the fact that power here is not strictly reducible; broken up into the combined effects of a mobile constellation of variable components – as a current, a vector enabled by such an array of forces – power is difficult to definitively isolate, or substantialize.

In considering apparatuses, Foucault is less intent on analysing, per se, the different institutions and mechanisms of state power than in getting a hold of the specific type of political rationality that the state has produced in these ancillary apparatuses. In the examples of such apparatuses that Foucault will go on to give – the police, the pastorate, discussed below – he is not looking to localize forms of power, to tie them to definitive, concrete elements as was the case in his analyses of disciplinarity. He is attempting rather to isolate the concepts, assumptions and procedures common to distinctive rationalities which come to diffuse themselves throughout a given culture in such ways that they come to be intuitively activated in a variety of autonomous settings. This, incidentally, makes for a useful distinction between apparatuses and technologies. The latter, as a category of analysis, is strongly focused on exactly the minutia of the concrete instrumentation and mechanization of institutional applications of power; the former, by contrast, is far more concerned with broader political 'logics'. Foucault's intent is to evoke the breadth of the 'implementational logic' of governmental power; his objective is to emphasize the spread of this power, its existence and 'rootedness' across social networks, to reiterate that a given type of power cannot be fixed by studying it in any one situation or context. Apparatuses are exactly cases in point of such rationalities. The fact of their functioning as rationalities – an affirmation of Foucault's assertion that power is not a 'thing' or possession, but rather a relational force – helps explain the ease with which they are spread throughout a given social and historical domain.

It is worth making a methodological aside in this respect, emphasizing that if we are to adequately grasp a given type of power, in all its potential breadth, then it is not enough to study it only in one situation, to fix it in only one implementational form. It is in this connection that Foucault (1990) claims that

> those who resist or rebel against a form of power cannot merely be content to denounce violence or criticize an institution…What has to be questioned is the form of rationality at stake. The criticism of power wielded over the mentally sick or mad cannot be restricted to psychiatric institutions; nor can those questioning the power to punish be content with denouncing prisons as total institutions. The question is: how are such relations of power rationalized? Asking it is the only way to avoid other institutions, with the same objectives and the same effects, from taking their steed….
>
> (p. 84)

This, of course, is by no means to dispense with the methodological injunction of engaging relations of power in as much specificity and localizing detail as possible; it is simply to point out that one should also be aware of how the logics, intentions, strategies and procedures of such specific sites and relations of power come to support and conduct one another. Not just the fine-grain analysis of the micro-physics of disciplinarity then, what is required also is a panoramic perspective on governmental 'architectures' of power. That is, we should trace the implementation of power not only *vertically*, in linear relations of control, but *horizontally* also, in lateral or sideways relations; we need understand the laterality of given relations of control.

To serve, protect and love

The first general apparatus, or 'rationality of state', that Foucault discusses is that of the 'police'. This may seem unsurprising in the sense that such an apparatus would be absolutely central in terms of the implementation of a successful regime of government; what is surprising, however, is the unusual historical inflection Foucault gives the term. Importantly, Foucault is not speaking merely of the institutionalized office of the police as we commonly understand the term, that is, those civil servants whose specific job it is to prevent and investigate crime. He (1990) speaks about 'police' in the sense of a utopian governmental project – as present in the works of French and German political thinkers of the seventeenth and eighteenth centuries – as a set of administrative concerns over people and things, over the relationships between (in the broadest sense) men, property, produce, exchange, territory and the market.

This particular notion of the police was very broad, encompassing, amongst other things, the maintenance of religion, the upkeep of morals, health, public safety and amenities, trade and so on. Everything, in short, with a bearing on how people lived, and with a bearing on the problems, diseases and accidents that befell them, lay within the scope of police concerns – anything, that is, that could be grouped under the broadest interpretation of the state's mandate to 'protect and serve' its people. Perhaps the most obvious contemporary equivalent to this notion would be the portfolios given to the various members of a State's parliament. This would seem an apt comparison, given that Foucault (1990) claims that the true object of the police at this time was 'man' [*sic*] in all his/her capacities, concern not only over how he or she might survive, but over how she or he might be improved, expanded and developed.

At a slightly more general level, one might understand the job of the police as to do with the articulation and administration of techniques of bio-power in a way that increases the state's control over its inhabitants. What is striking about this approach is the degree to which the police were understood as adopting undoubtedly positive functions within society, such as fostering working and trading relationships between persons, encouraging 'modesty, charity, loyalty, industriousness... honesty' amongst the citizens of a nation (Foucault, 1990, pp. 77–78). However, although a prime objective of the police was to keep the population healthy and happy and to improve the quality of life wherever possible, this would be done in order to ensure a higher priority: enabling the state to increase its collective power, to exert its strength in full. This is the central paradox underlying the notion of the police which Foucault outlines when he defines the aim of modern government, or state rationality, namely to 'develop those elements constitutive of individual's lives in such a way that their development also fosters that of the state' (p. 82).

Discussion 6.4: Colonial discourse as apparatus

One of the foremost attempts to outline the nature and functioning of colonial discourse – itself a type of apparatus – is to be found in the work of Homi Bhabha

(1994). The issue of the stereotype is of central importance here; it is understood by Bhabha as a major discursive strategy of colonial discourse, as, in the words of Childs and Williams (1997), the cardinal point of colonial subjectification for colonizer and colonized alike. At points in Bhabha's writing the notion of colonial discourse appears to lose analytic precision, to risk becoming – in view of the layered set of descriptions he offers – something of an anomalous concept. Aware of this problem, Bhabha (1994) focuses, in the celebrated 'The other question', on specifying the 'minimum conditions and specifications of such a discourse' (p. 70). Colonial discourse:

1. functions, strategically, to create a space for 'subject peoples' through the production of particular forms of knowledge;
2. produces types of knowledge through which surveillance is exercised and through which complex forms of pleasure/unpleasure are incited;
3. authorizes the strategies of colonial rule by the production of stereotypical knowledge of colonizer and colonized, two orders of knowledge assessed and evaluated according to fundamentally different criteria;
4. maintains the racist objective of construing the colonized as a population of degenerate types on the basis of racial origin;
5. justifies conquest and works to establish systems of administration and instruction;
6. marks out a 'subject nation' and then appropriates, directs and dominates its various spheres of activity (Bhabha, 1994, p. 70).

What this list of features makes abundantly clear is that colonial discourse is not to be reduced to spoken or written words, to practices of textuality. By contrast, Bhabha characterizes colonial discourses as first and foremost an *apparatus of power,* 'that turns on the recognition and disavowal of racial/cultural/historical differences' (p. 70). With this concept, as we have seen, Foucault was attempting to grasp the loose but nonetheless efficacious combination of multiple different forms or implementations of power – from types of speech and types of knowledge, to the material constraints and productions of institutions and everyday social practices – that nevertheless worked in tandem to produce overall effects of control.

Bhabha understands the role of knowledge within colonial discourse in a flexible way, viewing it always within the context of *reciprocal exchanges* with material, institutional, administrative measures of power from which it is never wholly autonomous. I mentioned this because although Bhabha understands stereotyping colonial discourse from a variety of conceptual perspectives – as an instance of ambivalence, as following the route of fetishistic disavowal, to give a psychoanalytic example – his application of the concept remains, arguably, loyal to its Foucauldian underpinnings in as much as it seeks to emphasizes the strategic spread and efficacy of a type of power which has no one single mode of operation. To be sure: the complex and multifaceted interaction of knowledge and power means that knowledge is a component of force in a wide array of practices, institutions, styles of thought, kinds of pleasure and modes of government. It is clearer then why Bhabha draws on the notion of the apparatus: exactly to emphasize the heterogeneous interchange between knowledge and control so characteristic of the colonial world. Colonial discourse thus, in the words of Childs and Williams (1997), 'constructs a knowledge of 'subject peoples' through which it authorizes its rule, installs racial differences, and produces the colonized as entirely knowable' (p. 123).

A second apparatus – or rationality – of power named by Foucault is the pastorate. The pastor, he comments (1990) is not a magistrate, nor prophet, nor educationalist, nor sovereign, nor benefactor, even though the influence she/he holds over their followers contains elements of all of these leadership roles. This is because at its most basic, the pastor's role is that of a guardian, a spiritual overseer. The model for this kind of guardianship is that of the shepherd in charge of a flock, a role which has several constituent components. First, the shepherd needs to watch over his/her flock with scrupulous attention, to ensure their salvation through 'constant, individualized and final kindness' (Foucault, 1990, p. 69). Pastorship is hence, a salvation-based form of power; more than this, it is a kindly power, one predicated on the provision of love. Secondly, given that the shepherd is an intermediary of a greater power or knowledge – typically that of God – a kind of unquestionable authority comes to characterize his/her leadership. Thirdly, the pastor is understood as bearing a kind of responsibility or accountability for the flock. As reiterated by Dean (1999), the pastor is bound by a particularly complex moral tie to each member of the flock, a tie which includes his charge of properly knowing each member. This is an in-depth and individualizing knowledge that runs deep; the shepherd needs to know of the needs and deeds, the sins and wishes, *the contents of the soul*, of each member of the flock. Foucault (1982) explains: 'this form of power cannot be exercised without knowing the inside of people's minds... exploring their souls, without making them reveal their innermost secrets. It implies a knowledge of the conscience and an ability to direct it' (p. 214). Lastly, the pastoral relationship should result in a developed form of conscience in its subjects, in the gradual use and understanding of a series of techniques of self-examination, by which they come to know themselves better, and implement upon themselves the lessons of the pastor.

As Foucault discusses in *Abnormal*, the need to access the 'private sins of the individual' thus came to be combined with technical elaborations that would ensure its success. The classical techniques of self-examination and the guidance of conscience were hence transposed into a Christian thematics, observes Foucault (2003b), a change which established a link between a thorough knowledge of one's self, and an honest confession to someone else. The techniques of examination, confession, guidance and obedience, were crucial components of the effective functioning of pastoral power. As Dean (1999) rightly insists, the pastoral relied on those techniques that enabled the pastor to formalize a knowledge of the individual's secret inner existence.

The strictly religious form of the pastorate may seem to have lost much of its sway in modern society; Foucault, however, draws attention to the diffusion of the rationality of the pastorate. Emblematic of the gentle functioning of power, this notion of pastoral guidance is what lies beneath our modern ideas of a caring treatment. One has in mind here, as in the case of the contra-bond discussed in Chapter 1, those forms of attention and regulation that are motivated by a heart-felt duty or 'calling' and that operate via the provision of a type professional love – the role of the nurse, the teacher, the doctor, the therapist all spring to mind – even as they further the ends of disciplinary bio-power. The rationale and procedures of the pastorate have moreover come to be exercised by a variety of groups and institutions stretching from traditional structures (such as families), private ventures (of philanthropists, benefactors, non-governmental organizations), and of course, to structures of the state (various public and disciplinary institutions, welfare offices and so on). Clearly, the objectives of these secular 'pastorships' are no longer that of leading people to their salvation in the next world; their secularized goals of salvation are now to be found in ensuring the promises of better health, well-being, wealth, security and protection. So pervasive and extensive is this rationality that Foucault (1982) refers to it as the predominant form of the individualizing power of modernity.

Discussion 6.5: Governing stereotypes – colonial apparatuses of discourse and affect

Directly quoting Foucault, Bhabha (1994) draws attention to the fact that

> the apparatus is essentially of a strategic nature... a matter of a certain manipulation of relations of forces, either developing them in a particular direction, blocking them, stabilizing them, utilizing them... The apparatus is

thus always inscribed in a play of power, but it is also always linked to certain coordinates of knowledge which issue from it but, to an equal degree, condition it. This is what the apparatus consists in: strategies of relations of forces supporting and supported by, types of knowledge.

(Foucault, cited in Bhabha, p. 74)

This understanding of the apparatus is particularly useful within the context of the colonial situation. The collateral investments of knowledge in power and power in knowledge are crucial here, certainly in view of how colonial power 'seeks authorization for its strategies by the production of knowledges of colonized and colonizer' (p. 70). Also important for Bhabha is the idea of power as 'strategies of relations of forces'; this is a conceptualization that resists the binary division of mutually exclusive categories – of one all-powerful group who simply controls another which is devoid of power – and does so in favour rather of a far more complex and diverse field of multiple relations of power and resistance. What the concept of the apparatus allows for, furthermore, is an understanding that multiple (formal and informal) types of power combine in a network of diverse elements, whose various forces – no matter how seemingly haphazard – nevertheless maintain the general ascendance of colonial rule. The analysis of the apparatus hence proves particularly useful in tracking the flexibility and diversity of racism; it offers, indeed, a useful means of apprehending the multiple racisms of the Apartheid State, for example, whose real force cannot – as suggested above – be reduced to its legislated or structural forms alone.

Clearly then for Bhabha, the operation of evaluative and racist knowledges occurs alongside reference to systems of administration, in conjunction with the architecture of a wider regime of control; what we have in colonial discourse is 'a form of governmentality' (p. 70). Bhabha's use of this concept of governmentality helps link the idea of the stereotype – not just a quirk of social discourse or an internalized psychological operation – to the politics of nation and peoples. Colonial discourse, for which the stereotype is a dominant strategy, is 'a form of governmentality that in marking out a 'subject nation', appropriates, directs and dominates its various spheres of activity' (p. 70). It is important to emphasize the domain of influence, indeed the level of impact Bhabha has in mind when speaking of the stereotype. We have here a forceful aspect of racist governmentality which is simultaneously discursive and affective, which works both as relation to knowledge and a moment of fetishistic disavowal. Just as Foucault forewarns against a division of the domain of the individual from the broad field of governmental influence – because the individual is exactly a resource of government – so Bhabha disallows the separation of the stereotype from the governance of a 'subject people'. The notion of an 'instrumentality' is important here: it forces us to acknowledge how a particular 'mentality' functions as a political instrument at the level of individuals and larger social groupings alike. It benefits us here to maintain a staggered level of analysis, a 'joint focusing' on the stereotype as it applies both to the individual colonial subject and a broader 'subject peoples'. The implication posed by this point is that the affective and indeed psychical operations pertaining to the individualized dynamics of the stereotype are functional also towards the consolidation of far broader historical and political forces, be they those of colonialism or contemporary forms of nationalism.

'States' of individuals

Welding a politics of the state to a politics of the individual, Foucault's account of the apparatus is able to accommodate both top-down and bottom-up flows of power. Tracing the flow of power first from the top down: the idea of 'the police' provides the rationale behind the distribution of a variety of 'officers' of the state throughout the population under the guise of service ('police' here, of course, in the broad sense of 'officers' working to the ends of the state's objectives of 'serving and protecting'). Tracing the flow of power from the bottom up: the idea of the pastoral relationship provides the impetus, within the rationale of the personalized guidance of individual subjects, for individuals to voluntarily 'give themselves up to power', to follow its injunctions, to concede willingly and truthfully to its technologies, its requests for self-examination, disclosure and normalization. It is in respect of this bottom-up flow of power that Foucault argues that 'Generally speaking I think one needs to look... at how the great strategies of power encrust themselves and depend for their conditions of exercise on the micro-relations of power' (1980e, p. 199).

It is precisely this connection of individualizing and totalizing qualities of power that best evokes what Foucault (1979a) means by 'governmentality'. It is again important to reiterate – especially given the argument I will go on to develop – that governmentality works on the basis of the adoption of multifarious techniques of government not necessarily immanent within the state itself. There is, furthermore, no strictly causal link between these strategies and a centralized state power; their connections are often circuitous, indirect and *dispositional*. The link between individualizing and totalizing forms of power – despite being almost unfailing reliable – cannot simply be qualified in the terms of a one-to-one, input-output model of causality. This is not to say that the 'co-operation' between totalizing and individualizing measures of power is purely fortuitous or coincidental. These articulations exist in a state of uncoordinated synchronization; extremely complex in nature, they maintain an impressive dependability, both because of the sheer number of 'minor governments' – minor offices of power and regulation spread throughout different levels of the populace – and because of the heterogeneous and strategic nature of these links.

The example of apartheid is again instructive here. The full impact of this racist system is grasped not simply through a listing of its official governmental policies, or by cataloguing its ideological commitments and their various institutional manifestations. The tenacity of apartheid racism must instead be grasped through the great network of various racisms it made possible, through an infinitely complex web made up of the varying and indirect combinations of interpersonal and structural forms which then came to be played out across multiple institutional, discursive and psychological levels. This is not simply a case of *reciprocation* – in the sense of mundane transactions of micro-political life substantiating and affirming larger structures of power – it is a relation of *fundamental reliance* inasmuch as the downward flows of totalizing state power are dependent upon individualized, interpersonal, and, I would add, *intrapersonal* modalities of power. The paradox of effective governmental power is that it requires a minimal degree of free play at these lowest levels. As Bozzoli's (2004) analysis of the shortcomings of the apartheid State suggest, the attempt to legislate, codify, to *structure* virtually all aspects of informal, micropolitical social life, ultimately made apartheid's racist system of power overly rigid, inflexible, less than proficient at adaptation and less than able to muster creative or spontaneous responses to challenges to its logic.

Foucault (1982) argues against a trend in sociological and historical understandings of the state in which the powers of individualization have been neglected; in doing so implies not only a further connection between disciplinary and state power, he also, I think, opens up the possibility for a Foucauldian analysis of the governmental articulation of psychological forces. Foucault's (1982) contrasting position, anticipated above, is that the aim of modern government is to develop those constitutive elements of individuals that foster the overall strength of the state. What *makes* individuals – precisely that part of power that personalizes and individuates – is what extends the powers of the state:

[W]e should [not] consider the 'modern state' as an entity which was developed above individuals, ignoring what they are...but on the contrary as a very sophisticated structure, in which individuals would be shaped in a new form, and submitted to a set of very specific patterns... [W]e can see the state as a modern matrix of individualization.

(Foucault, 1982, pp. 214–215)

The state, simply put, is never reducible to structural mechanisms of control; it should not be viewed as antagonistic to the cultivated particularity of distinctive subjects; it requires the free-play of their personal freedoms, the bottom-up support of their independent 'self-makings'. The analytical challenge at hand is that of grasping this interface between individualization techniques and totalization procedures.

This talk of 'self-making' signals a vital aspect of government that I have thusfar neglected, namely the factor of *self*-government. Mitchell Dean calls particular attention to this facet of the governmental control. Not only does he define government as 'an assemblage of practices, techniques and rationalities for the shaping of the behaviour of others and of oneself' (1999, p. 198), he also breaks questions of government down into three interlocking domains: of state, of other persons and of the self. Similarly, he returns to the definition of government as 'the calculated direction of human conduct', to qualify that 'conduct' here refers not only to *activities* – leading, guiding and directing – but also to *self-referential qualities* – reflexivity, self-attentiveness, self-awareness and comportment. So it is not simply that governmental power targets the stuff of psychology – our desires, aspirations, interests, beliefs and behaviours – it is also the case that such psychological faculties are the instruments through which it is affected. There is in government an undeniable aspect of 'self power', as one might put it, *an acting of self upon self.* My intention here is to play up the intrinsically psychological nature of this dimension of government. We return thus to the distinction posed in Chapter 1 between *psychology as a produced set of concepts and reality-effects,* and the *psychological activation of power.* As is no doubt apparent, I am of the opinion that both are crucial factors in the operation of power; we need ask not only what *psychological contents* are produced by self-government, but what are *structures and processes* of the psychology of self-government.

While it is true that I have already touched on Foucault's engagement with certain 'identity-effects' of power, with the notion that the subject turns themselves into a subject of power (see discussion of soul-effects in Chapter 1), it is important to note how the later Foucault seems both to amplify these contentions, so much so that he presents the distinguishing focus of his very last work as that of 'the way ... a human being turns himself – or herself – into a subject' (1982, p. 208). There is also a slight change of position in work of this period: it is no longer simply that power has an outcome that might be qualified in terms of subjectivity, identity or self; it is now the case that power involves these qualities – which indeed are mechanisms – as indispensable components in the maintenance and spread of power over populations. Nikolas Rose (1991, 1996a) is the key figure to have developed Foucault's work in this respect, attending particularly to the micro-functioning of government-ality within the field of power that subjects constitute over themselves. This idea of the instrumentation of subjectivity is crucial, not only insofar as it leads us to examine the role of psychological technology in the cultural production of normalized, self-regulating individuals (as in the work of Rose) – an approach which seems inadequate to accom-modating the complexity of human subjectivity – but also inasmuch as it opens up a route of enquiry for thinking about exactly what this approach lacks. It lacks a means of thinking the political complexity of subjectivity as an instrumentalized array of forces.

Discussion 6.6: 'Micro-sovereignties': A missing category in the conceptualization of power?

It is interesting to note that a chief component in both of Foucault's examples of an apparatus is of 'officer' or agent of sort (police as officers of the state; pastors as agents of guidance). Foucault is thus making room in his account for those qualified or professional experts and practitioners who might, in a limited capa-city, be said to dispense or conduct power. In his earlier analyses, such as that of *Discipline and Punish*, Foucault tended to shy away from such a conceptualization; he did not want to reduce the complexity of power, the anonymity and general-izability of disciplinary measures, simply to an institutional interchange between agent and subject of power. Such a conceptualization seemed to resemble too closely a sovereign notion of power: authority embodied in a single figure, or, worse yet, the image of a monumental institutional force reproduced, in largely homogenous ways, by multiple agents of the state. Clearly Foucault did not want to privilege a top-down model unable to do justice to the bi-directional flows of modern power and inadequate to understanding the practical autonomy of pastoral and disciplinary representatives.

This notwithstanding, the 'officers' mentioned in Foucault's examples of appar-atuses do possess instrumental elements of both sovereignty and agency. Not only do they possess a formidable degree of contextual authority (a kind of micro-sovereignty), they also do play an indispensable agentic part in extending normalizing agendas. This proved a sticking point in my own analysis of the power of psychodynamic psychotherapy (Hook, 2001); what category of analysis might properly evoke a sense of the situational power of these figures, without returning to the motifs of sovereignty and agency so clearly rejected by Foucault? Despite then being fully aware of the conceptual implications that Foucault's earlier analyses wished to avoid, it seems that the later Foucault tentatively allows for – and indeed needs – an analytical category of something like an 'officer' in his analytics of power. Consider the following:

> Between every point of a social body . . . between the members of a family, between a master and a pupil, between one who knows and one who does not, there exist relations of power which are not purely and simply a projection of the sovereign's power over the individual; they are rather the concrete changing soil in which the sovereign's power is grounded, the conditions which make it possible to function.
>
> (Foucault, 1980d, p. 187)

Furthermore, a point that Foucault's theorization of the Psy-function (see Chapter 1) anticipates:

> The family, even now, is not a simple . . . extension of . . . the State; it does not act as the representative of the State in relation to children, just as the male does not act as its representative with respect to the female. For the State to function in the way that it does, there must be, between male female, and the adult and child, quite specific relations of domination which have their own configuration and relative autonomy.
>
> (1980d, pp. 187–188)

Clearly then, despite a reticence to reduce the power of these relationships to a model of sovereignty, there *is* a variety of sovereignty – in the sense of the exercising of kinds of practical authority, in relations of relative dominance or control – at work at specific and/or points of the social body. These points are not merely projections of facets of a sovereign's power. Rather they are distributed 'points of attachment' that allow the power of government to take hold: 'micro-sovereignties' of localized and specific authority and dominance, whose continued presence, far from expendable, makes the broader architecture of state control possible. This notion of 'micro-sovereignties' proved invaluable in my own work in highlighting the asymmetrical nature of the power-relation embodied in psychodynamic therapies, a relationship in which the psychotherapist comes equipped with highly distinctive forms of agency and authority. The question then is whether enough attention is paid within Foucault's analytics of power – despite

his consideration of the sovereign-like functioning of the family and his awareness of pastoral and police roles – to developing a category of analysis adequate
to the task of capturing the particularity of such 'micro-sovereignties'.[2] Focussing more intently on such an intermediary domain would not only afford us
a distinctive and valuable analytical vantage-point, it would also enable a more
developed understanding of the interchange between macro- and micro- forms of
power.

The instrumentation of subjectivity

It is appropriate now to return to the definitions of technologies of
subjectivity and self offered at the beginning of this chapter, to expand
and amend them such that they might be applied to the work of conceptualizing racism as a type of technology of subjectivity.

At a basic level, technologies of subjectivity – here I still follow the
basic contours of Rose's treatment – may be understood as regimes of
living that arise in response to the problem of *how to be* in various facets
of one's life. Rooted in a self-disciplining agenda, they necessarily entail
a set of regulative practices and involve attempts to alter, shape and
better the self in accordance with the recommended ideals of experts.
This can be put more strongly: these technologies – indeed, these kinds
of *subjectification* – involve the operation of a type of power that connects
the norms of authorities to the motivating ideals we have of ourselves.
This is not simply a case of superimposition; effectively we are only
able to assume, to realize selfhood through such technologies of practice and understanding. What accounts for the extraordinary cultural
sway, the deep personal significance of such technologies is that they
deal with the apparently essential qualities of an inner, defining psychology of substance; anchored in the profundity of interiority, they bring
with them the trump-card of inner truth, and hold out the promise
not only of actualizing our selves, but of attaining the better selves we
can be.

We may understand technologies of self as the *subjectivization* of technologies of subjectivity, indeed, as the personal integration of such
frames of knowledge and practice within the private ethical systems of
singular subjects. At this level of analysis one is concerned with internalized techniques of self-management, with the devices and dialogues of
the intrapersonal relation of better knowing, mastering, improving and
caring for the self. Rose (1991) emphasizes not only that these objectives
need be embodied in evident practices, but also that 'they are always
practiced under the actual or imagined authority of some system of
truth' (p. 29). It is worth briefly turning to Foucault's own discussion

of technologies of the self; not only does it provide a slightly more flexible description, it also provides a means of fleshing out the ethical dimension of such practices:

[T]echnologies of self... *permit individuals to effect* by their own means or with the help of others *a certain number of operations* on their own bodies and *souls, thoughts, conduct, and way of being*, so as to transform themselves in order to attain *a certain state of happiness, purity, wisdom, perfection*, or immortality.

(1988a, p. 18)

I have clearly italicized aspects of Foucault's description so as to highlight those aspects I wish to emphasize; we can, as such think of such technologies along the following lines: a series of self-implemented operations, directed at one's thought, conduct and general way of being, with the aim of the transformation or maintenance of certain ideals of happiness, purity or perfection. Foucault's (1988a, 1988c) concern with a hermeneutics of the self takes in a wider sweep of historical examples than is outlined by Rose. Foucault allows that certain modes of self-examination are possibly more concerned with thought than action; the technologies of self in question are not always linked to, or codified by, disciplinary knowledge and procedures (obviously not, given the historical scope of his examples); the outcome of ascetic practices of self, furthermore, are often qualified in thoroughly idiosyncratic terms – there is thus no necessary recourse to the ideals of experts – such as those of a particular style of living, an aesthetics of self, or indeed, an *ethics*.

For Foucault (1988c, d), the 'conduct of self-conduct' evidenced in technologies of the self amounts to an ethical engagement. A gap is thus opened between the general structure of given technologies of subjectivity and their individualized activation and/or rearrangement, between *normative* morality and ethical individuality. Self-examination, self-guidance or self-regulation directed toward the ends of betterment is thus thought by Foucault to constitute ethical activity. Rose (1996a) is instructive: 'Ethics... is understood in terms of specific 'techniques of the self', practices by which individuals seek to improve themselves and the aspirations that guide them' (p. 95).

One should note a point of disconnection here: never strictly correlative to or simply derived from technologies of subjectivity, technologies of self are rather indirect, deferred or personalized variations thereof. This is an issue of some significance, for as Rose (1991) stresses, the instrumental government of subjectivities cannot be assigned any direct or one-to-one correspondence with larger structures of political power. Those pastoral and disciplinary experts who play their part in the formulation of technologies of subjectivity cannot be said to collude with the state in trapping or controlling individuals, at least not in the context of modern liberal democracies, where explicit limits are placed 'upon direct coercive interventions into individual lives by the power of the state' (p. 10). The contradiction of freedom to be appreciated here is that 'governments of subjectivity' demand that 'authorities act upon the choices, wishes, values, and conduct of the individual in an indirect manner' (p. 10).

Surprisingly, Foucault's implication in speaking of ethics in this respect is that there is a degree of personal freedom to such practices of the self. In those technologies of self which allow some latitude in how one experiments with, remakes, or alters the self, he identifies the potential for non-normalized forms of self-regulation; hence the idea of 'making oneself as a work of art' (Foucault, 1988c). Although this appears to contradict Foucault's earlier work, it is worth heeding the qualifications to his argument. Foucault advances that the Greek injunction to 'care for the self' came to be gradually superseded by another injunction, more overtly moral in nature, the Christian imperative of 'knowing the self'. The latter is more closely associated with apparatuses of regularization and normalization, particularly given that disciplinary self-knowledge necessarily occurs through the mediation of an other, a disciplinary or pastoral agent, or a matrix of systematic knowledge and prescriptions. Hence the (ideal) difference between moral and ethical systems: whereas the care of the self permits for variation across rigid moral parameters – an ethical care of the self is precisely *creatively* rather than formulaically exercised – modern normalizing society offers us more codified, formalized, categorically set templates for the practicing of self. The care of the self thus by no means represents an uncomplicated zone of liberation. At each point of its practice – assuming such a creative ethics of self is even thinkable within normalizing disciplinarity – the care of the self runs the risk of being superseded, domesticated by more homogenous systems of disciplinary bio-power.

Discussion 6.7: The sovereignty-discipline-government complex

Having introduced the ideas of the arts of government, disciplinary bio-power and apparatuses of security, it is necessary to explain how Foucault links each of these semi-autonomous models of power. The notion of governmentality as the overarching rationality behind the use of multiple modes of government, provides just such a basis of articulation. These modalities of power are not merely indicative of different types of society; they should rather for Foucault (1979a) be seen as constituting a triangle of operations, the 'sovereignty-discipline-government' complex, which takes the population as its primary target, apparatuses of security as its essential mechanisms, and disciplinary technology as it instruments. As Dean (1999) puts it, the 'problem space of rule', as it coalesces from the beginning of the nineteenth century and appears for the next two centuries, is one defined by three lineages:

> The first is that of sovereignty which, having first taken a juridical form, is democratized and anchored in the rights of the legal and political subject. The second is that of discipline which, having arisen in the practical techniques of the training of the body, becomes a generalized regulatory mechanism for the production of docile and useful subjects. The third is that of government, which having first arisen in the 'dispositional' problematic manifest in police and reason of state, becomes a government of the processes of life and labor found at the level of populations and in which the subject is revealed in its social, biological and economic form.
>
> (Dean, 1999, pp. 102–103)

Although each of these paradigms of power has enjoyed its historical period of ascendancy – they are taken to have developed in a definite historical sequence – the dynamic functioning of modern power is characterized by aspects of all three such 'lineages' of authority and control. One of the assets of this model – Foucault's attempt, in other words, to expand the concept of power to government – is that it makes it possible to include a variety of conceptualizations of power into a broad theory of social regulation. As McNay (1994) suggests of the theory of government, it now becomes possible, in speaking of relations of power, to more clearly distinguish between forms of violence, spheres of relative control and authority, macro forms of domination and control, subjectivized elements of power, and the micro-politics that characterize relations between individuals.

The 'sovereignty-discipline-government complex' might be represented diagrammatically as a 'triangulation' of modalities of power. By *'sovereignty'* I refer to prohibitory, law-based forms of power modelled on the relation between a sovereign – a figure of vested authority and practical power – and their subjects. Although such a notion of sovereignty could not be understood to fully encompass the working of apparatuses – which are too diverse in form and articulation to be reduced in this way – it is clear that this logic of power does inform the 'micro-sovereignty' discussed above, that is, the role of everyday 'officers'/officials who exercise limited relations of control and authority over ordinary citizens in specific contexts. By *'disciplinary bio-power'* I refer to the 'micro-physics' of an individualizing power rooted in the body and productive of psychologies, whose impetus is to care for, correct and better the life, health and humanity of problematic subjects. This is a crucial part of the 'instrumentality' of govern-mental power; we are concerned here with the technical means which come to be implemented through the various moral orthopaedics of discrete human technologies. In speaking of *'government'*, following Dean (1999), I have in mind a range of calculated and rational activities that employ a variety of techniques so as to influence the conduct of individuals. These activities maintain definite but shifting ends and endeavour to shape conduct principally by working on the desires, aspirations, interests and, I would add, *affects* of subjects. This category of control is hence inclusive of the notions of technologies of subjectivity and of self.

These are clearly non-discrete categories; apparatuses of security are certainly aspects of government (involving the 'protect and serve' agenda of the state) and yet also entail kinds of micro-sovereignty, as, of course, does discip-linary bio-power. Bio-politics would represent another clear point of overlap; an extension of disciplinary bio-power on the one hand, it shares with govern-ment the same object of management, namely the population. In addition then to an initial triangle, representing a basic configuration of power – the unified effects of governmental, sovereign and disciplinary modalities in roughly equal measures – we might imagine the superimposition of another triangle, representing the combinations of such modalities (*bio-politics* emerging between disciplinary bio-power and government, *apparatuses* emerging between government and sovereignty, and, perhaps, the category of *disciplinary micro-sovereignty* emerging between the modalities of disciplinarity and sovereignty) (Figure 6.1).

It is necessary to offer a series of challenges to and variations upon this outline of technologies of subjectivity and self offered; unless we do this, it will remain an insufficient means of conceptualizing racism's affective technologies of subjectivity and self. A first point of difference: surely the professional authorities and experts that shape the general structures of presiding technologies of subjectivity need not only be explicitly discip-linary agents or experts of the soul? Despite the disciplinary specificity that Nikolas Rose maintains on psy-professionals, he does allow that a variety of political and pastoral leaders may play their part in setting in place the normative cultural ideals that will ultimately ground techno-logies of subjectivity. We may extend this: a broader array of popular

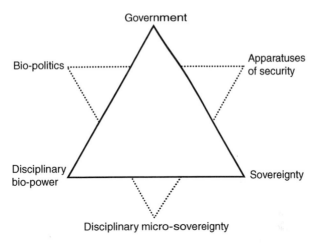

Figure 6.1 The sovereignty-discipline-government complex.

representations, images and impressions, what we may guardedly refer to as the cultural imaginary, that is, wide range of public fantasies and ideals – which themselves play a powerful anchoring role in the psychic life of communities (Jacqueline Rose, 1996) – may be said to inform this process, and to do so in less than rational or transparent ways.

Secondly, the norms that Rose emphasizes in his description of technologies of subjectivity should not perhaps be viewed only in the delimited sense of the explicit, normalizing objectives of disciplinary bio-power (hard as it is, admittedly, to delimit the range and force of such objectives). Surely, a more varied and everyday field of socio-political values also play their part in such a normalizing process; one might take as an example here the cross-section of populist discourse and hegemonic sentiments that come to be employed even in governmentally-endorsed rhetorics of national pride and patriotism (I discuss an extended example below). Another emblematic case in point is provided by the idea of 'whiteness' (also discussed in more detail below), 'whiteness' understood here as the implicit and undisclosed norm, as a discursive force-field of unspoken values and commitments, against which a variety of cultural differences, indeed cultural 'deviances' are measured and assessed. It would appear apparent then – and Bhabha's (1994) extension of the notion of governmental apparatuses along the lines of colonial, stereotyping discourses and identifications aids us here – that the norms of subjectivization we are dealing with need not be formalized by the standards of human science knowledge. As in the case of colonial discourse, or its 'post'-colonial variations, we have, as Bhabha has argued, a formidable network of knowledge, indeed, an apparatus, encompassing, as in Said's (1978) model of Orientalism, formal and informal, latent and manifest components; such hegemonies more than adequately serve the knowledge function that Rose's conceptualization calls for. Moreover, as in the case of racism, and commonplace racializing knowledge, the force of social mythologizing at hand often requires a different order of relationship with truth than that entailed by certified human scientific disciplinary knowledge. Similarly, there are endless intuitive formulas and tactics of self–other positioning that condition racializing modes of interaction; that these habituated ways of being cannot be definitively linked to contemporary disciplinary or institutional bases of knowledge, by no means diminishes their strategic or instrumental nature. Such actions and stereotypes are clearly elements of a forceful set of discursive practices; potentially codifiable according to a racist system of values, such psychological points of activation are clearly able to play their part as elements within the ensemble of an apparatus of governmentality. An aligned consideration: the irrational intensity, indeed, the *force* of norms is not, surely, only a question of rational prescription and conscious activation? How norms and ideals enter our circuits of imagination, behaviour and belief – their tenacity, their intuitiveness, their sublime or unconscious aspects – seems to require a more varied, a more sophisticated depiction of the 'apparatus' of psychological subjectivity than Rose allows for.

So then despite that it risks the cohesion of Rose's application, might we not opt to move beyond the disciplinary particularity of a demarcated focus on institutions, agents and modes of knowledge, positing a more variable, a more complex cultural terrain of discursive influences on routines of self-knowledge and self-practice? Are we to assume that such a transmission of values and ways of being requires a precise institutional and disciplinary home? Can we not imagine rituals of performance and identification, relays of public practice and display that also equip their practitioners with rudimentary rules of behaviour, with basic social technologies of identification and being? Do these not provide us with paradigms of practice and experience – indeed with formulas of belief, action and response – that enable subjects to negotiate certain social tasks and to identify salient life-ideals, and to do so in often remarkably passionate ways? I am thinking here of an array of activities in the production of 'Britishness', for example, from the well-defined behavioural codes of sports spectatorship (with its particular modes of dress, its circuits of action, expression and celebration), to the formalized commemorative and memorial behaviours that link past and present modes and achievements of Britishness, to an assortment of demonstrative actions, gestures and significations advocated by Britain's prospective Prime Minister, Gordon Brown, and other Labour MPs (the wish to formalize St George's Day as a means of celebrating Englishness; calls to embrace the Union Jack; the idea of 'a flag in every garden'; the hope of a 'British Day' as equivalent to the 4th July celebrations in the United States; the aim to increase the prominence of citizenship ceremonies and so on (Blunkett, 2005; Wintour, 2006). In a world of heightened nationalist, patriotic, or indeed, racist values, it is conceivable that these are the kinds of identifications, the general idealized formulas of behaviour and belief, that supply historically specific technologies of (nationalist, British and potentially racist) subjectivity.

Admittedly, the availability of such procedures and well-defined parameters of subjectivity depends on certain conditions. It may in fact be wholly dependent on a climate of intensified ideals, on extreme programmes of political rhetoric and agitation that are successful in inflaming passions and evoking attachments. This is perhaps why Paul Gilroy is more willing to speak of *fascism's* technologies of self rather than of racism's technologies of self: the demonstrative, indeed, *dramaturgical* quality of fascist politics, its accoutrements of imagery, iconography and ostentation, the very intensity of the identifications and exclusions it sets in place, makes it a political form more suitable than most to incur discrete technologies of subjectivity. This I think is a fair point, as is the cautioning that such technologies of subjectivity – given the overlapping co-ordinates of identity that makes up a subject – would always exist in intermingled rather than pure or discrete forms. There are certainly different combinations of technologies of subjectivity that intersect in individual technologies of self. An affective technology of racism should not thus be seen as encapsulating all of a subject's modes of self-knowing and self-practicing (although it may certainly inflect and influence virtually all of them); this is clearly not how we should seek to apply such an analytical frame.

Psychological technologies

I wonder though, does this objection – the idea that certain political forms are more suited than others to installing distinctive technologies of affect – not, ultimately, lead us astray? For one, does it not make the mistake of assuming that in our 'post-ideological' era such signposts of identity, such structuring parameters of desirable subjectivity, are any less present than in previous eras, despite that they may now be better rationalized, better protected, more subtle, more healthy, more advantageous, than the crude ideological dramaturgy of earlier orders of power? Furthermore, is this not to underestimate the extent to which our everyday subjectivities are *already technologies?* Is it not, in other words, to underplay the fact that subjectivities emerge within specific co-ordinates of power that provide them with modes of self-knowing and locate them relative to the norms that make the practice of identity meaningful? My position would be that our subjectivities are always already informed by techniques and strategies, by multiple rules, codes and habituated patterns of being – never simply our own – that mobilize assumptions of what is positive and desirable, that become intuitive, automatic.

What is interesting about the above argument – that certain political conditions lead more easily to the formalization of technologies of subjectivity than others – is that it makes apparent the assumption that some subjectivities are technologized and others less so. Surely if we are uncomfortable with notions of a natural psychology unconditioned by power – hard not to be, after Foucault's genealogical critiques – then we need confront the possibility that technologization is a precondition for the emerge of modern subjectivity in the first place, certainly so in the sense that subjectivity requires the co-ordinates of location dictated by norms and associated modes of self-knowing, protocols of self-conduct, guidelines – even if only ever implicit, performative and behavioural – of how to be as a particular type of subject. If it is to be possible to bring a Foucauldian analytics together with a type of critique which takes seriously the role of psychological functions in the conduct of power – something I treat as a critical imperative – then our aim is not to isolate a series of natural psychologies, but rather to identify a variety of instrumentalizable *psychological technologies* that play their part in the life of power. Psychological technologies – rather than natural psychologies – should be our critical presumption and our analytical focus. In the notion of an affective technology of racism then, extending this suggestion, we have a means of capturing not the whole of a racist persona, but an array of (often subliminal) 'procedural' elements, a means of tracing the flow of conventionalized formulas and affects of racism as they come to be conducted through an individualized ethics.

My suggestion that technologies of subjectivity/self potentially in some way underwrite all behaviours should not be read as a means of pointing to the redundancy of this model of conceptualization (suggesting hence that it 'goes without saying'). On the contrary – and this perhaps more than anything is the point of this chapter – this model opens up a unique analytical perspective on the mechanisms, procedures, the instrumentation and strategy that underlies all aspects of psychological and behavioural life. It provides a means of making visible a kind of human instrumentation which varies from one socio-historical context to another and which draws on a different set of innovations, tactics and techniques in order to fulfil various tasks and objectives of power. This does pose a slightly different question: if virtually the entire range of the psychological is a technologized domain – grounds for the activation of power, open, in other words, to the conduction of forces of government – what then are the minimal criteria of identification required to speak meaningfully of technologies of self, required to differ-entiate one technology of self from another? Under what conditions of analysis can we start speaking of a coherent technology of self?

Perhaps one response is to start with the types of critical discursive and genealogical analyses discussed in Chapters 3 and 4, to identify key discursive forces, and, likewise, key governmental agendas, arrays of apparatuses, types of political rationality – also, crucially, the partic-ular ideals of normalization – and to ask what particular goals, flows of conduction are being prioritized. There may be innumerable possible technologies of subjectivity and self, but they surely require a minimum degree of co-ordination – complex as such a point of articulation might be – with such larger technologies? Furthermore: is it viable to speak of the system of values, self-knowledge and self-conduction – the prospective technology of self, in other words – as attaining the weight, the influence and function of a personalized ethics?

Protocols of being

Such objections as to when it is appropriate to apply the notion of tech-nologies of subjectivity and self are useful also inasmuch as they point to the fact that affective technologies of subjectivity require not only a particular alignment of affective forces, but also, surely, a set of formaliz-ations, that is, concrete prescriptions of *how to act*, protocols of *practical political being*. This directs us towards a prospective shortcoming of the notion of racism as an affective technology of self. Rose's conceptualiza-tion certainly does pose a problem here, not in view of the imagined system of truth that makes a necessary point of reference or authentication – what we might call the 'racist imaginary', that is, ongoing (post)colonial myth-ologies of racial difference are more than adequate to this task – but rather in terms of the particular *techniques* of knowing, caring for and mastering the self such an affective technology presumably entails. Personal racism seems, surely, to lack the procedural and technical components required by a technology of self? Where is its precise vocabulary of terms, its techniques of implementation, its distinctive exercises and strategies; where might we locate the expertise of tactical and technical mastery; where indeed is the element – as one might put it – of protocol in inter- and intra-subjective 'technologies' of racism?

These are astute comments, and they demand more than one level of response. The crucial component that these comments identify as missing is the rational didactics of consciously applied rule systems. While this factor must not be ignored – Rose's (1996a) emphasis on rules is surely appropriate for the applied focus of his work – is it not the case that something akin to the 'disconnector variable' so crucial in thinking the working of apparatuses and understanding the rationality of governmentality, is again necessary here? Would we not indeed make the error of assuming an overly simplistic model of subjectivity – and indeed, human causality – if we understood the conduction of power through subjects as simply rational, linear, as an uncomplicated 'downloading' of ideals and protocols of behaviour that remain largely unchanged in their transmission and reactivation? This interchange between structures and subjects, discourse and subjectivization, between technological 'protocols of being' and the vicissitudes of identification and action cannot be reduced in this way; these interchanges introduce a series of disruptions, not only of rationality and transparent self-knowledge, but of intention, indeed, of conscious awareness and overdetermined action as well. That a designated protocol of racist behaviour – in the sense of co-ordinated techniques, strategies, skills, rules and design – is not overtly apparent, does not mean that certain technologies of being are not present. This notion of racist technologies of subjectivity/self is applicable, I would argue, even if the protocols of subjectivity in question appear less than systematically codified and are not directly accessible to verbal or discursive consciousness, even, indeed, if they appear only in the terms of habituated activity and response, only along the lines of affective patterning and positioning.

Pierre Bourdieu's notion of the habitus assists us in this respect. Bourdieu (1988), as is well known, directs our attention to the orientation of bodies in space, to aspects of demeanour and posture, to cadences of voice, movement and poise that remain grounded in the routines of a particular place or cultural location, that of the habitus. There is thus a repertoire of appropriate actions, gestures and behaviours rooted in the habitus, a pervasive *etiquette of conduct* which features not as a set of conscious prescriptions of action, but as a far more intuitive array of orientations, conducts, self-presentations and dispositions. This bodily, behavioural and situational range of signals and normativities makes for a regularizing collectivity of sorts, a habituation within parameters of minimal variation that is predicative, prior to (or in addition to) explicit representational or discursive formalization. So while, ideally, it is conceivable that one may set oneself to the task of listing the tacit, subliminal, performative rules in question, it remains nevertheless true that these orderings of conduct never need to be codified, recorded or even consciously learnt – certainly not at the level of explicit discursive formulation. It is at this level of bodily response and habituated action, in subliminal, apparently 'pre-discursive' demeanours and dispositions that I would suggest we need to locate the protocol factor, the rules of particular technologies of self.

Here I think it is worth returning to Bozzoli's (2004) contention that what ultimately disenabled apartheid was its overformalization, exactly the overprescription of its racist logics and policies to the point of the eradication of any looseness and flexibility in the system. The 'rationality' of this racist system of power, its ability to work through unprepared articulations, dispositional conductions, was effectively crippled precisely at the point that the formalization of rules compromised the spontaneity, the immediacy and the 'creativity' of its quasi-independent activations. Much the same is true I would wager of effective technologies of political affect; they need to retain a degree of free-play, a modicum of flexibility and variation in their operation. There needs be a disconnection here between the concrete, literal implementation of rules, and the dispositionality of their articulation within the terms of individual conduct; what I think we see here, to echo an earlier phrase, is an underdetermined (or non-deterministic) arrangement of initial influence that yields an overdetermined set of political effects.

It is imperative not to underestimate the complexity of the affective or psychological functioning under consideration. Rose's model is itself to be criticized for not appreciating the discontinuities and breaks, the breadth of 'differential articulations', involved in the apparatus of psychological subjectivity – a relay of indirection and dispositionality if ever there was one – an apparatus that is duplicitous, divided, often incongruous even unto itself. We are returned to a cardinal maxim of psychoanalysis: as important as rational precepts and rulings may be, they can only go so far in understanding the motivational life of human subjects. Two interesting possibilities arise in connection with the issue of psychoanalytic understandings of human motivation, and how they might enable one to extend the idea of technologies of subjectivity and self. First, should such technologies only be oriented towards aimed-for ideals, toward objectives of truth and betterment; might they not equally be arranged around images of dread and aversion, around points of denigration and disgust? What is the negative end of the scale of such subliminal regimes of being; can we not – *must* we not – factor hate and fear into their schedules of motivation? This is a possibility I have discussed elsewhere (Hook, 2006), that racism, as affective technology, may be read, along the lines of Krisetva's notion of abjection, as an 'operation of repulsion' (Butler's (1997) phrase). Secondly, might the ideals of technologies of subjectivity and self be understood not merely at the level of basic life objectives, but also at the less rational, even sublime level of passionate attachments and investments that typically accompany notions of ideal-ization? Psychic life, notes Leader (1996), always involves a striving after some ideal. How though does this difficult relationship between the ego and ideal (already touched on in Chapter 1) – which, for psychoanalysis, always involves qualities of failure, guilt, repetition and avoidance – extend the complexity of the model offered by Rose?

A further criticism of Rose's work on technologies of self becomes apparent at this point. His reticence to make reference to any form of psychological conceptualization means that he cannot engage with some of the most powerful dimensions of human subjectivity, indeed, with perhaps *the* crucial means through which ethical practices of self come to be entrenched, stringent personal ideals, obeyed, transformed into, beyond the constraints of ordinary rationality. (Is this not a measure of a truly disciplined or truly ethical subject that they remain within the confines of a particular injunction despite that rationality, or the dictates of gratification – or indeed social conformity – with demand otherwise?). I have in mind the prospect that technologies of self, as imparted from given technologies of subjectivity, may be repeated, internalized and identified with in a more robust, more tena-cious and less rational way than Rose allows for, as *unconscious* aspects of our relation with ourselves. Without this supplementary level of explanation it becomes difficult to account for the full irrationality and intensity of such procedures, for the fact that they come to be chained into patterns of affective reward and punishment, guilt and gratification, deeply routed, as it were, in a personalized set of social ideals, values and behaviours which exist not merely on the surface of conscious intentions and goals but also symptomatically, in irrational actions, in the form of fantasies, in modes of phobia and enjoyment. The inability to ever fully know or control self – which for psychoanalysis remains a constitutive impossibility – might be exactly the paradoxical condition of possibility that makes these practices so endlessly extended and repeated.

III

Sentimentalities of state

Having clarified a series of critiques and possible extensions of the model of technologies of subjectivity/self in line with how it may provide a framework for the promulgation of racial (and indeed, racist) values and positioning, I turn now to a series of illustrations of what I take to be the governmental conduct of affective commitments and values, which while not always racist in and of themselves, nevertheless hold a powerful racializing potential.

'The role of government', writes former British Home Secretary David Blunkett, 'is to assist people through the uncertainty and transitions of their lives', particularly so in the world of the twenty-first century, 'an era born of globalization, with greater insecurity and instability than ever before' (2005, p. 21). An antidote to anxieties of this sort, he claims, lies with the project of linking both identity and a sense of belonging to a commitment to nationhood and a modern form of patriotism. Moreover (and here it is worth quoting him at length):

> [We need] a clear view of British values, stemming from both our history and our beliefs as a people ... [A]n open, adapting society needs to be rooted, and Britain's roots are ... anchored in a sense of duty and a commitment to tolerance ... [There is] a golden thread twining through our history of common endeavour in villages, towns and cities ... Britishness is defined not on ethnic and exclusive grounds but through shared values, our history of tolerance, openness and inter- nationalism ... [Such a] vision embraces the diversity of our state and unites us through our values, history, culture and institutions ... I have long argued for a self-respect and respect for others, and an under- standing of our identity and sense of belonging ... [W]e need a glue that holds us together. We need to be able to celebrate our nationality and patriotism ... without narrow nationalism and jingoism ... [H]ow though do we affirm our Englishness ... in a new way? By celebrating our culture, from the music of Vaughan Williams and Elgar to the poetry of ... Wilfred Owen and Philip Larkin and the quintessentially English humour of Tony Hancock ... by celebrating our landscape, our heritage

of Victorian cities, our history...The left...has shied away from the politics of national identity...[However] debating our identity and sense of belonging is not to be nostalgic, but to address the world of the 21st century.

Why are David Blunkett's comments, penned for *The Guardian* as part of the run-up to Britain's 2005 general election, apposite regards my concerns here? Well, first, Blunkett quite unabashedly links strategies of government to the management of a particular order of sentiment. His comments suggest the degree to which contemporary modes of governmentality need concern themselves with the political vocabulary of emotion, with *affective* forms of political capital. Blunkett leaves little room for doubt: a prime task of liberal–democratic government is to manage the affective forces of the nation, to lend them a certain narrative coherence and – provided one is foolhardy enough to follow his lead – to channel them along the intertwined routes of patriotism, national pride and cultural essentialism. These comments, and the broader agenda of which they are a part, pose an intriguing problem of political causality; they imply, a complex – even discontinuous – pattern of political influence in which governmental measures endeavour to direct, to shape all sorts of social life, down even to questions of emotional ties and passions.

A second striking element of Blunkett's commentary is the degree to which he frames it as a description of the constitutive values of the British left. This is more than a little odd, certainly inasmuch as Blunkett's particular brand of political sentimentality seems more easily associated with the politics of the British right, particularly in its utilization of a quasi-essentialism of an Englishness of 'longing and belonging' and the differential rights of cultural access that such a discourse puts into play. What is one to make of this disconcerting parallel, where a key manoeuvre of the right, namely its valorization of Englishness and the grounding of such an Englishness in the certainties of history, culture and land, becomes a tactic of the multiculturalist left? More to the point, might we question whether Blunkett's valorization of a select English past and present – 'a golden thread twining through our history of common endeavour' – works to tacitly code for whiteness, or, if not 'whiteness' *per se*, then something like it, such as the artefacts and values of a less inclusive time and culture? The tactic we may accuse Blunkett of, in other words, is that of employing a set of discursive extensions and derivatives of a historical form of 'Englishness' for whom 'whiteness' stands as an unspoken yet inescapable common denominator.

Affective dis/junctions

It would seem clear that in engaging Blunkett's comments we are not dealing with a straightforward example of racism, or an overt racist 'technology of affect'. If anything his comments would seem an example of an affective technology of *nationalism*, or, more accurately yet, Britishness, although it is true, as Jacques (2005) makes plain, that ardent forms of nationalism may be considered as amongst racism's most powerful concomitant forms. I think it is worth considering the role of affect in this respect as a kind of relay, which both *disconnects* a certain order of statements from a potentially racist or exclusionary reading, and that also *reconnects* what is spoken of within today's rules of discourse with older and more questionable presumptions of exclusion.

Discussion 6.8: Affected 'whiteness'?

It is worth questioning whether Blunkett's ideals of Britishness might be linked to lingering hegemonies of benefit and disentitlement, querying whether, indeed, a differential rights of cultural access are put into play by many of his terms of reference. In this respect, it seems interesting to experiment with the notion of 'whiteness' as a relay of affect, or indeed, as an 'affect position'. I have employed such a notion of 'whiteness' elsewhere (Hook, 2005b) as a means of making apparent certain post-imperial patterns of aggrandizement, objectification and exclusion, as a means, in other words, of conceptualizing hegemonies of white privilege which exist in tacit forms, as extensions, variations and sublimations of historical forms of white racism. My objective there was to grapple with, as in Blunkett's commentary, an unarticulated common denominator that always returned to stabilize talk of Englishness. The affective nature of this silent denominator of 'whiteness' means that it is more a function of what is *felt* than what is *said*, more a passionate attachment, a partly unconscious identification rather than simply a factor of discursive consciousness – hegemony, we might say, in its affective form. A silent denominator of this sort works by speaking to prior assumptions; it is able to operate in an unformulated, prepredicative yet nevertheless powerfully *felt* way. This denominator is perhaps best understood, in terms reminiscent of Adorno, not as a single value or term of identification, but rather as a shifting constellation of elements existing in a virtual rather than a substantive or essential manner.

'Whiteness' thus may be approached as a relay of affect able both to discon-nect a certain order of statements from explicitly racist connotations (on the basis that affects are implicit, often less than rationally, discursively explicated) and yet able to *reconnect* allowable social declarations of exclusion with more questionable assumptions (the passionate nature of 'affect positions' dictating *where* one belongs, *what* one loves, *who* one hates and so on).

There are at least two strategic reasons to employ such an affective notion of 'whiteness'. First, to demonstrate that the strong conduction of affect managed by many post-imperial and neo-liberal forms of governmentality – calls for patriotic unity, displays of national pride and so on – often entail a powerful racializing element by virtue of the particular cultural norms and histories they prioritize. Secondly, thinking of 'whiteness' along the lines of an 'affect position' directs our attention to certain regular patterns, routings of affect, where, despite a degree of latitude regards the rules of discursive formalization, there is nevertheless a general bounding and conducting of affective forces (of belonging, entitlement and exclusion) towards a series of governmental ideals.

I can cite another example of affect as the unspoken connector bridging what is spoken of to a more questionable ideological set of values of *what is heard*, what is understood or *affected*, namely the Conservative Party's 2005 election slogan: 'It's not racist to impose limits on immigration'. This slogan was quickly followed by a response from the Commission for Racial Equality warning party leaders against inflaming racism during electioneering. As was made clear by one commentator: no, it may not be necessarily racist to impose limits on immigration, but to turn debates on asylum and immigration into key political rallying points in an election year – racialized and racial-izing debates if ever there were any – is certainly to pander to racism (Kennedy, 2005).

A series of questions present themselves at this point. What is the political utility of the rhetorical discontinuity we see at work in these above examples that disavows the right while nevertheless affirming some of its most elementary themes (in Blunkett's case), and that denies racism yet nevertheless stokes the flames of racialized sentiments of entitlement and exclusion (in the case of Tory electioneering)? What is the principle of disjunction at work here that enables the speaker to put into play an order of political sentiment whose foreseeable derivations and populist codifications – formulas of the 'England for the English' sort – which they are nevertheless able to distance themselves from? What indeed is, in Blunkett's words, 'the glue that holds us together', what is the bonding agent, the means of binding in question, often present more in the force of a feeling than in the codification of a proposition? Furthermore: how might we understand the implementation and management of the affective forms of capital that are linked to strategies of idealization and elision and that come to play their role in the substantiation of imagined communities?

Discussion 6.9: 'Psycho-technics' and the instrumentalization of affect

Adorno's notion of 'psycho-technics' provides an important theoretical precedent for my concerns with instrumentalized affects. 'Psycho-technics' refers to a means of psychological manipulation – particularly that of *fascist* propaganda, never for Adorno separable from the issue of racism – a type of manipulation which remains entirely calculated and highly rationalistic in nature even while inducing effects that are profoundly irrational. '[T]he irrational gratifications which fascism offers' Adorno remarks, 'are themselves planned and handled in an utterly rational way' (1991, p. 18). Clearly Adorno is conceptualizing a far more explicit form of racism that I am; rather than with overtly fascist rhetoric, my concerns lie with the insidious entitlements of a nationalist mode of identification which seemingly operates as a strategy of government. Nevertheless Adorno's approach throws into perspective, by means of contrast, at least three elements of the approach I am trying to develop. For a start, the affective technologies of racism that I propose we investigate cannot be reduced to a programme of psychological manipulation, as is the risk in Adorno's conceptualization. My intent is not to develop a primarily psychological account; it is rather to offer a grid of analysis that focuses on a political technology that inevitably involves certain affective or psychological components.

The element of discontinuity comes next. Adorno is certainly right to point to an element of calculated rationality in how fascist/racist sentiments come to be conducted (or, more aptly perhaps, *affected*) through communities, just as he is right in making the case that such a strategic rationality can be profitably analysed. What he seems to be missing is an understanding of the appropriate 'disconnector' that needs to be brought to bear in such operations. His account seems inadequate to grapple with a discontinuous (or indirect) form of racism that operates *only via a relay component* that severs directive or declarative political forms (like the contents and the discursive force of overt racist propaganda) from the 'ethical' micro-political practices of self through which racist logics come to be replicated at the level of the individual subject.

Thirdly, my account also differs from Adorno's 'psycho-technics' in respect of issues of agency. The 'intentionality' of affective technologies of racism does not fit within the confines of the agency of the single political actor. Or to put things slightly differently: this is not the best level at which to scrutinize their efficacy, or to track their ongoing effects. This points us back to the Blunkett commentary: the conduction of particular political affects that his rhetoric hopes to achieve, while intentional to a degree, may nevertheless be said to exhibit an operational logic which far outstrip Blunkett's his own contribution. Crook (1994) provides us with an instructive link here in criticizing the individualism of Adorno's notion of 'psycho-technics': 'Adorno can give no account of the knowledge-base from which this rationalistic calculation proceeds beyond a certain commonsense shrewdness' (p. 25).

In contrast to Adorno, I am interested in racism as an affective instrumentality of government that comes to be managed through a tactics of indirection and discontinuity. The tacit mode of racism that I have in mind is only 'completed', and only provisionally so, by a preserve of affects that respond to strategic forms of political discourse; issues of singular agency are thus sidestepped. This is a form of racism which remains intermingled with, and obscured by, a series of acceptable values. Apparent always through implication rather than explication, loosely articulated and immanently deniable, it appears as something less than racism at its point of enunciation despite that it often takes on a profound affective force at many of its points of address.

The array of concepts I have introduced above – the circuitous governmental conduct of conduct, the idea of *affective* subjectivities, amenable to conduction, informed and shaped by the strategic incitements of a discursive and governmental field – provide a promising way of understanding these problems of political causality. This framework supplies a means of comprehending the oblique routes, the spontaneous articulations, along which such affective forces come to be channelled. More than this, it holds the prospect of a unique analytical perspective on contemporary neo-liberal and post-imperial forms of governmentality. In the example cited above, we have components of just such a functioning: the attempt, by the state, to marshal a potent set of affective investments which follows the route of powerful identifications – indeed, powerful *subjectivizations* – along the lines an exclusive history of nation, culture or heritage. We have here an example of a voice and strategy of the left, and by extension, an operation of neo-liberal democratic governmentality, which requires the workings of a technology of affect – the conduction, in other words, of a carefully consolidated quantity of political sentiment – and which does so with reference to a preserve of attachments and belongingness, to a carefully cultivated identity of likeness.

My argument, as such, is that canny forms of governmentality are able to utilize particular kinds of affective capital – say for example subliminal forms of white identification and white racism, what I guardedly refer to as 'whiteness' – which can be played out, deployed for political gain despite remaining unowned by the parties (or the governments) who would thus profit. Although the avowal of explicit forms of racism cannot be considered a viable tactic of neo-liberal, democratic strategies of governmentality, the profit to be gained in the attenuation of racism's subsidiary or less explicit forms, the effects of their diffused articulation should not simply be glossed over. Such a 'pararacism' (for want of a better term) is apparent always through implication rather than explication. It remains so loosely articulated (and immanently deniable) that it appears as something less than racism at its point of enunciation despite that it often takes on the affective density of racism in how it is received at various of its points of address.

It is clear, in reference to Blunkett's commentary above, that a far more detailed and sustained analysis is called for than I have offered here. My objective has simply been to signal that certain of the tools given us by Foucault and Rose provide a basis to conceptualize racism as an extension of a hegemonic 'whiteness'; these instruments allow us to think racism as an affective 'instrumentality' of state that comes to be managed through a tactics of indirection and discontinuity. They enable us to grasp something of the dispositional and contingent interchange between forms of the subject and forms of the state which allow for racism, or its lingering historical effects, its re-configured forms, to remain in constant movement. Such a mode of explanation permits for the fact that such forms of racism are captured neither in the strategic incitements of a particular strand of political rhetoric, nor in historically and ideologically weighted forms of subjectivity, but in how each sets in motion a dynamics of implication for the other, most apparently perhaps through the conductor of affect. There is, as it were, a 'sharing relationship' at work here, a constant de-agenting pattern of circulation that ensures that neither singular subject nor isolated instance of governmental discourse can be identified as solely responsible for racism.

The approach I am suggesting is able to tell us about the social formalization of a particular rationality of government – thinking here of the discourses of national identity and their tacit codings for race as employed by the party politics of many liberal democracies – and the fierce individualization of these sentiments, that is, the 'affected' and stylized inscription of such logics within psychological subjects in formulas of affect, in personalized patterns of meaning, loss, value and threat. Such an approach, furthermore, provides a speculative basis for bringing together a mode of critical 'psychological' enquiry – psychological inasmuch as it focuses on the political utilization of affect – and a Foucauldian analytical frame.

Discussion 6.10: Racism in dispositional arrangement

I have argued above that contemporary modes of governmentality involve a strong conduction of affect, a streaming or encouragement of particular affective bonds, and that such conductions involve dispositional arrangements of ambiguous caus-ality and agency. An intriguing example of a governmental attempt to instrument-alize affects of nationalist fervour can be drawn from Asia. The weekend of 16th March saw a series of massive anti-Japanese protest marches throughout China, taken by many to be the largest example of mass political since the Tiananmen Square demonstrations. The Chinese government took steps to maintain the orderliness of such 'patriotic' rallies; nevertheless as journalist Jonathan Watts observed:

> The ambivalence of the authorities was apparent in an unusual text message sent out in the name of the Shanghai public security office by China mobile. 'Demonstrations need prior permission. Public displays of patriotism must be orderly, reasonable and legal. Express your patriotic feelings in a right manner,' it said.
>
> (Watts, 2005a, p. 19)

Watts' (2005a, 2005b) articles on these events pose a relation of uneasy collu-sion between the government and the protestors. The Chinese government, he intimates, had much to benefit from here certainly so inasmuch as the rallies redirected a focus of protest that had until very recently been addressed to the government itself. News about the rally was broadcast by the Shanghai radio station. Furthermore, riot police steered protestors away from Tiananmen Square and towards the Japanese embassy 'where they stood idly by as the demonstrators stoned the windows' (Watts, 2005b, p. 21). Shanghai police not only approved the demonstrations, they actively encouraged them, Watts argues, especially given that many among the millions who received the text message that called for people 'to show their love for their country in a law-abiding way . . . took it as a green light to join the demonstration' (p. 20).

How do we configure our own affective responses?

The examples I have supplied in support of the notion of racism as a technology of affect have thus far focussed more on the fact of *governmental conduction* than on the technical issues of self-management. While I am unable to offer any detailed discussion of this facet of affective technologies of racism here (although see Hook, 2005b, 2006), I think it does help to provide a brief illustration of some of the points at hand. In order to do so, let us turn to a description Ian McEwan offers us, in his novel *Saturday*, of a character's response to a car accident of which he considers himself blameless:

> Above all, there swells in him a peculiarly modern emotion – the motorist's rectitude...the thrill of hatred, in the service of which various worn phrases tumble through his thoughts, revitalized, cleansed of cliché: just pulled out, no signal, stupid bastard, didn't even look, what's his mirror for, fucking *bastard.*
>
> (2005, p. 82)

Just the page before, McEwan describes the murky flux of this character's background thoughts, the sense his character has of things on his mind, thoughts yet to be 'unwrapped into syntax or words' (p. 82). This, McEwan notes, is mentalese, a preverbal form of language 'a matrix of shifting patterns, consolidating and compressing meaning in fractions of a second...blending it inseparably with [a]...distinctive emotional hue' (p. 81). This comparison between two adjoined forms of thought and affect is interesting; it implies that a failure of originality often characterizes moments of passion. The unsteady dividing line between the background noise of thoughts that remain unformulated in words, and the well-worn phrases through which we make instances of affect socially intelligible to ourselves, appears to function here as a threshold of socialization.

There is a paradox at hand: despite that the subject may feel a sharp sense of differentiation – a vivid rush of individualization *in* the moment of affect – the affective routine in question is typically of a profoundly formulaic sort. The same may be said of the affective dimension to particular instances of racism, acts which are at the same time intensely personalized and yet also somehow anonymous, at least in the sense that they are rooted through a third position, a locus and reference point of speech and meaning that we might designate as Other. It is as if an Other's words and emotions are employed in the stylized thoughts and reactions of racism – borrowed words and emotions, borrowed formulas of response – that are lent a substantializing emotionality and verbal/practical inflection by the racist. Regards the stylized performance of affect, let us refer back to McEwan's description of his character's response to the crash: what we witness is a social moment, one in which a set of social formulations provides the character with the terms of his outrage.

The phenomenology of affect which comes into play here, the sense of veracity and of groundedness that the affective moment lends to experience, is perhaps best pegged as the 'ego ontology' of sudden feeling, that is, *an affective grounds of belief* which feels deeply singular and individualized despite that it comes from an Other. There is a resonance here with the post-structuralist notion that a discursive utterance employed by the subject is something less than its own authentic creation. We may speak here of an affect-position: it is not just that 'the subject is spoken', but also that the subject is *affected*. Edward Said's (1983) useful formulation apropos the Foucauldian notion of discourse – referred to in Chapter 3 – is of some use in extending this idea: 'Above and beyond the possibility for saying something' he notes, 'there is a regularizing collectivity called a discourse' (p. 186). One is tempted to adapt this formulation: above and beyond the possibility for feeling something in a purely idiosyncratic or individualized manner there is a regularizing collectivity, a motivated channelling of emotions – the interposition of an Other horizon of intelligibility and appeal. In the case of the calculated conduction of certain sentimentalities for political gain such an interposition can be understood within the terms of an affective technology, be it one of nationalism or of 'Englishness', or, as in our case, of an insidious mode of racism which is typically underpinned by both these concomitant forms of attachment.

Discussion 6.11: Racist affective technologies of subjectivity

Although, as already noted, I am unable to develop these ideas in any detail here, it does help, I think, to provide a sketch of how one might go about further conceptualizing racist technologies of affect. Such technologies of affect – kinds of technologies of subjectivity that are subsequently taken up as affective technologies of self – should not be viewed as crudely deterministic in their influence. Nor should they be understood as simply dominated by the strict controls of rational governance. There is within them, as in the dispositionality of apparatuses, a type of free-play between top-down and bottom-up forces; such 'instrumentalities' of racism must be viewed at the level of the complex relations attained between subjects and their material and symbolic structures.

If we are to take seriously the challenges posed to historico-discursive conceptualizations of racism (Discussion 6.1), then I think it helps to make recourse to psychoanalysis or another developed account of affect. Let us turn to Fanon's most psychoanalytically oriented work as an example. I maintain that we can derive from *Black Skin, White Masks* something like an affective technology of phobia. This is a technology that is racist inasmuch as it takes 'blackness' or some other designator of racial identity as its principle of generativity, as the phobogenic object – Fanon's term (1986) – at its centre. An element of this sort would seem indispensable to most forms of racism, which require not only the exaggeration of a perceived threat, but also that this exaggeration takes on an excessive and persecutory quality.

Such a technology of phobia should not be conflated merely with a politics of fear. This is in part due to the remarkable levels of ambivalence that underwrite the phobogenic object, which remains crisscrossed with relations not only of dread, disgust and fear, but also, for Fanon (1986), with relations of attraction, fascination, exoticism and desire. A remarkable form of inversion and condensation characterizes such affects, one in which we may discern a perpetual vacillation between unreasonable portions of derision and envy. As Fanon rightly insists, a highly coveted and valued quality is isolated in the racial other: the Muslim's supposed proclivity to violence, the Jew's assumed ability to accumulate wealth, the threatening virility and athleticism attributed to the black man. This attribute is then transformed into a persecuting quality, the single stereotypical element to which the figure in question can be reduced to. All of these elements need to remain in place if we are to understand anything of the volatility of racist affect: the multiple paradoxes of fear and yet attraction, hate yet desire, abjection yet idealization.

Another way of playing up the anxiety of such relations and the potentially catastrophic threat of perceived difference at work within them is with reference to the notion of castration. Fanon's psychoanalysis of colonial racism is, I think, heavy with the unstated presence of exactly such a mechanism; Bhabha's (1994) enticing explanation of stereotypical otherness on the basis of the model of fetishism of course assumes it. I mean to evoke the concept of castration not in the vein of the more literalized applications that have so often been ridiculed and criticized, but in a more figurative manner. In speaking of castration I am talking about an element of subjectivity that has been socially-valorized and loaded with narcissism. This element of subjectivity is typically anchored in the body, although not necessarily so, presumably though it features as a marker of difference within the visual or aural field. I have in mind an element of subjectivity which functions as a vehicle of pleasure, identity and self-investment alike, an element that represents a kind of 'extinction of subjectivity' when threatened. Importantly, the stakes of loss involved here are seemingly calamitous, at least from the perspective of the threatened subject. For them, the threat is that of the collapse of a narcissistic or 'solipsistic' image of the world of me (or of others like me), be that a world of masculinity, a world of whiteness, or a world of the look and sound of Englishness. The widespread valorization of whiteness (Seshadri-Crooks, 2000; Hill, 2004), I think, and the explosiveness that characterizes the perception of whiteness (or Britishness) as somehow imperiled, requires a mechanics of this sort. This is a 'tactics of castration' that is not castration anxiety itself, but perhaps rather a set of political sentiments arranged in a structure or pattern of affect of an analogous sort. In fact, in terms of the argument I have developed thus far, it makes far more sense to speak of a *technology of castration* than to think of castration as a necessarily universal element of a metapsychology.

'Affect positions'

There is also another factor to consider here: the fact of the 'follow-through emotion' that arises as a consequence of the symbolic registration of an event. The fictional extract above demonstrates something of this knock-on effect; McEwan appears to understand how the act of linking the burgeoning emotion (of anger) to a series of subjective co-ordinates (the blamelessness of the protagonist, the recklessness of the other driver) can aid in reflexively *amplifying the affective response*, and, indeed, in providing a kind of *retroactive justification for it*. We can extend these reflections on the ambiguities of causality in affect with reference to Leader's (1996) observation that the performance of an emotion – even if the performance is of a feigned sort – is frequently enough to induce the emotion in question. This idea, that the 'going through the motion of emotion' is enough to *actualize* the emotion reiterates the well-known James–Lange theory, the idea that mimicry of an affective expression may secondarily produce that affect.

Two lessons then about the operation of affect that tell us something about how affects come to be instrumentalized in particular technologies of subjectivity and self. First, rather than the sole preserve of the affected protagonist – the emotional deduction derived from the individualized terms of their experience – there is something *affected* in such instances of feeling. Affect, in other words, is not the creative or original function of the psychology of its agent, it is rather of a piece with a greater social whole. It runs along a circuit of social intelligibility and value – a broader affective technology of subjectivity – in which the agency of the subject's feeling is but one moment, the moment when the pulse of this charge might be said to pass through them.

Secondly, in opposition to the standard assumption that an affect is given rise to by an external event, we need to bear in mind the possibility of a causative loop, the fact that a growing affect may be amplified – or retroactively *caused* – by the symbolic registration of a particular event. There is a type of reverse causality at work here: the retrospective causation of warranting particular relations of entitlement, belonging and exclusion on the basis of the 'proof of affect' of how real such relations feel and hence must be. The disjunction – always relative, never complete – between explicit, predicative *discursive* pronouncements, and the less codified domains of affective positioning (of passionate attachments which remain unstated if not largely unconscious in nature) is of some importance here, certainly inasmuch as such a 'proof of affect' can often be used as evidence of the reality that it plays its part in constructing *without this feeling like a contradiction*. So the proof that black men are violent is in my fear of them, the proof that women are coquettish is my attraction to them and so on. It is important to acknowledge here that we may ready our affective postures in how we position ourselves in given social encounters. We may as such assume certain 'affect-positions' (fear, anger, irritation and love) which then become the proof of affect for a given ideological proposition, for a categorical relationship of entitlement, exclusion, belonging and so on. That I feel threatened by an influx of immigrants is proof enough of their moral dubiousness, proof enough also of why they – and others like them – should be prevented any rights of access.

What, we should thus ask, is the constructive role of the deployment of certain 'affect–positions', what are the characteristic object-relations that they entail and that they generate (*where* to belong, *what* to love, *who* to hate, *with whom* to identify)? We have here, I think, a mode of affective construction that plays its part in binding imagined subjects and communities – as in Blunkett's nationalist rhetoric of belonging – to the questionable 'essences' of place, history and nation. This is an oblique mode of subject production able to affect passionate attachments – and equally powerful divisions – that often speak louder than words and that typically feel as if they predate the immediate history of either subject or community. In the question of affect, we are dealing with an elusive, powerful, and, more importantly yet, instrumentalizable aspect of subjectivity, indeed, with a factor of subjectivization that can be taken up as a component part of an affective technology (of, say, racism, xenophobia and nationalism) which may be linked in turn to a strategy of governmentality. It profits us here – given this movement between rational and affective registers of analysis – to think about the consolidation of affect-positions. I have in mind here the case of certain patterns, regular routings of affect, where, despite a degree of latitude regards the rules of discursive formalization, there is neverthe-less a general bounding and conducting of affective forces toward a series of ideals.

Affect, as a property of power, should not be regarded as secondary or incidental, as merely the by-product of other modes of political activity. Nor should this property be viewed, as in Adorno's psy-technics, as existing only within the performative domain of manipulative politicians. Such utilizations of affect should be approached, as I have tried to show above, as instrumentalized avenues along which quite precise political aims may be pursued. These avenues, furthermore, allow for apparent disconnections of agency, causality and intention-ality and they cannot be reduced to narrow individualizing or psycholo-gical frames of analysis. Despite such difficulties and complexities – and here the point of my argument – such lines of influence are deserving of the technical analysis of any complex political technology composed of heterogeneous forms and entailing disjunction and discontinuity as basic elements of its operation.

Regularized affective formations

Just before closing, I think it is worth offering some brief comments on the bringing together of Foucauldian analytics and select psychoana-lytic concepts, something I have suggested above without being able to discuss in any real detail. This endeavour of bringing psychoana-lytic and Foucauldian forms of analysis together brings with it a series of prospective benefits and dangers. On one hand, it recognizes rather than dismisses the importance of psychoanalysis as a tool of political analysis. Psychoanalysis, I would argue, provides a rich set of terms that enable us to offer vital descriptions of the functioning of a political rationality *that is not always rational*. On the other hand, recourse to the terminology of psychoanalysis brings with it a series of concerns, not the least of which is the risk of a certain epistemological slippage, the unintended essentialization of certain psychical mechanisms of racism, which is just what the framework of technologies of subjectivity/affect had hoped to avoid.

Of course, not all lines of psychoanalytic critique are equally prone to such effects of reification; many, such as the Fanon example cited above, maintain a degree of antagonism towards ahistorical or univer-salist trends of interpretation; others, notably Lacanian orientations, heed the constitutive role of symbolic structures. If the framework I am suggesting is to work, it will, furthermore, be imperative to draw a distinction separating the *contents* of affect from the *processes* of affect. My suggestion would be that there are certain regularized 'operating systems' of affect, coherent processing forms, *formations of affect* that attain a level of durability. Such processing forms do not maintain a fixed or ahistorical set of contents, but are rather supplied by a variety of political and discursive systems. This is crucial because it is the difference between assuming the inevitability of racism as a form of psychic defence common to all humans, and the injunction to examine the particular way that hate comes to be socially organized. Making a distinction of this sort is, of course, no affront to Freudian psychoanalysis, which advances exactly such a gap in the domain of sexuality, where there can be no predisposed sexual object or sexual aim. This is an important lesson I think for how hate comes to be operationalized, and loaded with a certain order of representations.

The model of racism that I am speculatively advancing – that is, racism as affective technology of subjectivity and self would thus need to assume that there are kinds of routings, channellings of affect that take on regularized forms, and which are amenable to the exploitation of various political and discursive systems, which are themselves thus reinforced in the process. It seems to me that Foucauldian approaches to governmentality, and the associated scrutiny of human technologies have for too long neglected the question of affect.

I am sympathetic, for reasons outlined in Chapter 4, with the argument that the ostensibly psychological notion of 'affect' appears incompatible with a Foucauldian frame;[3] this certainly is the case if one takes this concept to bring with it the presumption of an essential interior that exists beyond the jurisdiction of power. Then again, I do not subscribe to the view that affect should be located exclusively within the bounded parameters of individual interiority, nor do I believe that this concept necessarily entails the trappings of the epistemology of humanism. I share thus Rose's (1996b) suspiciousness towards any theory that commits us to a reliance on the belief of a human nature. I appreciate also the pertinence of the Deleuzian concept of the fold as Rose employs it inasmuch as it 'suggests a way in which we might think of human being without postulating [an] ... interiority' (p. 142). The theme of fold, the idea that what is 'inside' is merely an infolding of an exterior, is a useful illustrative figure, one of considerable importance to the overall argument that I am advancing, certainly inasmuch as it helps us avoid 'binding ourselves to a particular version of the law of this interiority whose history we are seeking to disturb' (p. 142).

Nevertheless, those utilizable elements of the human subject, those 'instrumentalities' of the human subject that might guardedly be referred to as 'psychological' or 'psychic', the very elements that Rose's analysis would eschew – 'Is it possible…that one might write a genealogy of the subjectification without a metapsychology? I think it is' (p. 142) – remain, it seems to me, crucial dimensions in the conduction of power.[4] It seems to me that if we are willing to accept that affect is indeed a human capacity – which, to press the point home, is neither simply localizable within the parameters of the individual psychological subject, nor the point from which a series of psychologistic or liberal– humanist presumptions necessarily flow – if we are willing to accept this, then we must accept that affect can be utilized, 'resourced' by types of power which generate and produce it, even as they conduct and extend and its forces.

Perhaps in this respect we should follow the model set by Foucault in his genealogical prioritization of the body. The objective here, as I have already noted, is not to substantialize a transhistorical entity, but rather to examine the forces of the body as anchoring points of power's corporeal implementation. The same may be true of affect – affect approached thus as a set of forces that act as anchoring points for power's psychological implementation – an idea which brings with it two interesting suggestions. The first of which is that we need to treat psychoanalysis as an ally of Foucauldian analytics – albeit an uncomfortable or unexpected ally – one which provides a sophisticated vocabulary with which we may grasp the micro-functioning of a political instrumentation of affect. The second suggestion is that such an initiative is critically sustainable only on condition that, simultaneously, we concern ourselves with writing the genealogy of affect, a genealogy within which the conceptual language of psychoanalysis will presumably play a large although by no means singular role.

In closing, one obvious objection to the idea of racism as technology of affect: surely the notion of governmentality involves a greater degree of rational calculation than this account allows for? Here it seems helpful to refer to Foucault's earlier methodological imperative to be aware that highly strategic implementations of power are not always reducible to a clearly delimited agency (as discussed in Chapter 2). The intentionality of power – and here Foucault's account may benefit from a psychoanalytic turn – may be more complicated and overdetermined than models of intention that presume only the objectives of rational calculation.

Conclusion

In what has gone above, I have introduced a series of interlocking notions – the ideas of an arts of government, disciplinary bio-power, apparatuses and the bio-political – so as to 'complete' the outline of Foucault's conceptualization of modern power offered in Chapters 1 and 2. This leaves us not only with an advanced conceptual framework, but with a variety of analytical perspectives. I have also, in keeping with Foucault's hope that his writing might be a touchstone for further critical experimentation, offered a series of thoughts on how related notions – the dispositional arrangements of governmentality, technologies of subjectivity/self – might be applied as means of apprehending contemporary forms of racism as they have been animated within given governmental agendas.

This conceptualization of racism as an affective technology of affect – as of yet little more than a provisional sketching of ideas – begs a series of questions: what particular theory of affect will be applied; does this handling of the notion of affect rely too much on a model of discursive structuring; if affects are in part unconscious, then how exactly are they prone to rational management? It also poses some promising lines of investigation: given that racism may be said to perform an ordering function tantamount to that of a personalized ethics, given that a racializing system of values is often asserted and defended with the same moral fervour, the same conviction and passion as fundamental ethical commitments, how then might the notion of racist technologies of self – racism, that is, as personal 'ethics' – illuminate this quality of interpersonal racism?

Admittedly, this notion of racist technologies of subjectivity/self is still at an early stage of conceptualization. Why I have included it here is so as to argue, extending my concerns in Chapter 1, that a Foucauldian project that takes power as the object of its critique cannot concern itself only with the historical formation of psychology, but must look to various of its functions as precisely the instrumental, historically specific components that make human power-relations possible.

Notes

Introduction

1. See, for example, the 1987 republication of his *Mental Illness and Psychology* (originally published in 1954).

1. Disciplinarity and the production of psychological individuality

1. This emergence, from a bodily surface of experience, of certain repetitions and learnings, that is, of a 'soul-effect', is a process which has more than a passing similarity to Freud's genesis of the ego, which is always bodily in origin, and which arises as the result of physical sensations on the surface of the body.
2. Admittedly, Foucault does list a series of equivalent terms: 'self, consciousness, conduct, whatever it is called' (1977a, p. 305).
3. This, I hardly need note, is not always an easy distinction to draw. Nor is it a distinction necessarily qualified by the absence or presence of conscious volition; subjectivization need not, in other words, occur along strictly voluntary lines. The fact that subjectivization – subjectivation is Butler's (1997) preferred term – recapitulates subjectification also makes it difficult to potentially difficult to clarify a causal sequence.
4. One may compliment this list of rudimentary psychological operations. Each of the operations listed here (self to potentiality, self-consciousness before the ideals of power) presumably requires the involvement of a third element, that is, recourse to an 'other' of power, by which I mean to allude to what is sanctioned or proscribed by the most immediate representative of current disciplinary priorities. In the absence of completely clear-cut directives, psychological engagement with this 'other' would surely involve an element of presumption or imagination: an imagination of power, one might say, which is not completely explained by structural factors. My intent here in implicating the possibility of an interpersonal interaction between agent and subject of discipline is simply to suggest that a greater degree of psychological complexity is very possibly at hand than the determining function of panoptic structure.
5. It is interesting to note that this psychological aspect of disciplinarity, an element which surely, vastly, amplifies and extends the efficacy of such technologies, is eluded to in Jeremy Bentham's original writings (quoted by Foucault), in which he describes his design of the Panopticon. This architectural structure is said to constitute a 'new mode of obtaining power, of *mind* over mind' (cited in Foucault, 2006, p. 74, emphasis added). This is an arrangement in which a physical force takes on a sort of immateriality so that the process of power – here following Foucault's paraphrase – 'passes from mind to mind' such that we have an interplay between Herculean strength (lent to those who govern an institution) and 'the pure ideality of mind' (p. 76).

6. This, interestingly, is not to discount the fact that animals can be disciplined – which of course they can – but in a far more rudimentary manner.
7. Of course, Foucault does not set out to offer an account of psychological subjectivity, so to criticize him on the basis of a model implied by his account is – despite the value of such an undertaking – not to imperil the whole of his notion of disciplinarity.
8. Although the consideration of such forms of resistance remains an imperative – for Butler (1997) it guarantees 'the incomplete character of any effort to produce a subject by disciplinary means' (p. 89) – it is a resistance that can only undermine, it 'remains unable to rearticulate the dominant terms of productive power' (p. 89).
9. One can in fact extend this retort: is it not the case that individual psychological difference is simply *retroactively* identifiable; might this not be the reason that, from our perspective, such individual differences appear, paradoxically, to pre-empt their own construction. Furthermore, is the very fact that there appears to be a kind of doubling not a function of our own historical location, which cannot adequately imagine a 'before' of individualized psychological difference?
10. This is not to deny the obvious point that it is *already* a function of power that certain phenomena come to be recognized as significant differences as opposed to others; the issue at hand is to ask what is the additional type of consolidation, what are the complimentary dynamics of power that give particular discursive objects such a forceful historical reality?
11. Unlike 'extension', 'animation', 'cultivation' and 'promotion', Foucault's talk of *production* implies a kind of total creation. As is by now apparent, I would suggest that one of the above terms would be more appropriate, although this would notably lessen the drama and force of Foucault's argument.
12. Indeed, as I have tried to show above, the professionalization, the disciplinarization involved in the former is easier to historicize, to tie to definite historical periods, than is the latter.
13. The notion of 'psychological formations' nicely captures the ambiguity of the issue at hand; it leaves undecided whether the disciplinary formations in question are psychological – fashioned from the stuff of psychology – or whether they are the 'psychological formations', the effects *formed* by, and through, disciplinarily.
14. It seems naïve – to pose for a moment a different line of query – to believe that any mode of power to which humans are successfully subjected could completely dispense with a *psychological* dimension of operation. If this were not the case, surely human and animal subjects would be controlled, brought under the thumb of power in precisely the same kind of ways?
15. I mean here to refer to operations of subjectification and subjectivization alike.

3. Discourse, knowledge, materiality, history: Foucault and discourse analysis

1. There is a good deal of methodological and conceptual variation in the discourse analytic work stemming from these two influential models of

analysis. Rather than scatter my attentions over a diverse spread of applications, the tensions that will be isolated here will be those between Foucault
and the initial discourse analysis methodologies of Parker (1992) on the one
hand, and Potter and Wetherell (1987) on the other.

2. Foucault's perspective on madness here, as stemming from his reading of
Descartes in *Madness and Civilization* (1965), is by no means uncontested.
Perhaps his most well-known detractor in this respect is Derrida, whose
Writing and Difference (1978) takes strong exception to Foucault's conceptualization of the relationship between madness and reason. Derrida is particularly
concerned with Foucault's earlier suggestions of the possibility of a 'dialogue'
of sorts between madness and reason (see also Whitebrook, 2005).

3. It is worth noting here that Foucault's views here on 'the forbidden speech
of politics and sexuality' stand in stark contrast to his later comments in *The
History of Sexuality Volume 1* (1978a), where he asserts that 'nothing has ever
been more spoken than sexuality itself'.

4. I note that while Said (1983) suggests that such a 'regularizing collectivity'
might be somehow overcome, Foucault (1981a) declines to endorse such a
position, preferring for the most part to emphasize the 'unthinkability' of
that which lies beyond such systems of regularization. In Said's own words:
'[U]nlike Michel Foucault, to whose work I am greatly indebted, I do believe in
the determining imprint of individual writers upon the otherwise anonymous
collective body of texts constituting a discursive formation like Orientalism'
(1978, p. 23).

5. This relationship between discursive and material relations of power appears
to be much like the relationship between power and knowledge for Foucault
(1977a). The power-knowledge complex points our attention to the endlessly
circular relationship between relations of power and knowledge, relations
which are mutually reinforcing and which substantiate and extend each other
in complex ways.

4. Foucault's 'philosophy of the event': Genealogical method and the deployment of the abnormal

1. This is not to ignore the fact that Foucault features prominently in certain
descriptions of discourse analysis (see Fairclough (1992, 1995)). Similarly it is
not to ignore the fact that the analysis of large-scale discursive formations did
not feature as an objective of Foucault's archaeological works whose project,
following Davidson (1985), was 'to isolate the level of discursive practices and
to formulate the rules of production and transformation for these practices'
(p. 227).

2. 'Critique' here, as throughout this book, is meant in a way distinct to any sense
of either globalizing theory or totalizing history – both of which genealogy
is explicitly opposed to – hence Foucault's preference for the qualification of
'*local* critique'. Foucault's use of the term here should thus be understood in
opposition to its application in Marxism.

3. Wariness towards assumptions of sameness across contexts does not mean
that genealogy automatically discredits recurrence as a category of analysis.
On the contrary, the genealogist must be sensitive to the recurrence of events,

not, however, 'in order to trace the gradual curve of their evolution, but [rather] to isolate the different scenes where they engaged in different roles' (Foucault, 1977a, p. 140).

4. One recalls, in respect of the latter, here Foucault's deriding remarks, discussed in the previous chapter, on those forms of analysis that privilege the domain of signifying structures.

5. Or in the somewhat ambiguous note with which Foucault ends his essay on genealogy: 'the critique of the injustices of the past by a truth held in the present becomes the destruction of the man who maintains knowledge by ... the will to knowledge' (1977a, p. 164).

6. One might propose here that a return to Nietzschean genealogy, less ill at ease with a certain order of 'psychological' formulations than Foucault's, might serve as a model here.

7. One might offer a variation on this point: if a given genealogy is working well, it should *appear* to be enforcing a 'counter-ontology'. It should appear to advance a different possible view of 'how the world is', a view opposed to the social, epistemological and philosophical universe that we inhabit. This, after all, is part of its function, to return many of our everyday orientations to knowledge, many ordinary discourses, in an unfamiliar way. True as this is, the clear proviso is that genealogy needs to stop short of the goal of writing alternative ontologies.

5. Space, discourse, power: Heterotopia as analytics

1. One might attempt to illustrate this point by pointing to the apparent distinction between 'place' and 'space' (as does Chaney, 1994), the idea thus being that 'places' are those delimited sites that have become thoroughly imbued with a particular set of social values and behavioural norms, with a practical 'social identity of function'. As useful as this is in drawing our attention to the formidable discursivity of particular places, certainly by contrast to those social 'spaces' whose function and value is not as rigidly demarcated, it should not lead us to presume the existence of an asocial form of space that exists outside of discursive registration.

2. These distinctions between different kinds of gated communities often breaks down in practice, especially in South Africa, where large-scale gated communities – sometimes referred to as 'security-parks' – tend to encompass all of these functions.

3. One should be wary of extrapolating too wildly here: gated communities do not always exhibit as homogenous cultural and demographic populations as one might imagine, as Rossouw (2001) points out.

6. Governmentality, racism, *affective* technologies of subjectivity/self

1. One sees in the notion of the apparatus a convergence of Foucault's favoured analytical themes: the unconventional combinations of *bricolage* that he discusses apropos heterotopia; regularity over a field of diverse formal

elements, that is, the conjunction of forces and power-events of different kinds working in concert; furthermore, the prioritization of horizontal 'sideways' patterns of analysis in opposition to vertical, linear (depth) traditions of analysis.

2. *Psychiatric power*, it is true, offers a series of observations on the personal tactics of influence employed by psychiatrists (the modes of dress, demeanour and appearance most suitable to the curative task at hand); interesting as such comments are, they are not typical of Foucault's methodological approach.

3. Although, interestingly enough, Foucault does, in *Abnormal*, make reference to affect, and not merely as a conceptual or discursive construct, but as a factor of motivational force (cf. Foucault, 2003b, pp 264–266).

4. Rose clearly hedges his bets here: declaring that no *meta*psychology is necessary in the writing of the genealogy of human subjectification – a position I agree with; this is clearly not the same as ruling out all descriptive recourse to psychological language (which is effectively what I am arguing for). I should emphasize here that Rose's is not an uninformed rejection of psychoanalytic conceptualization. For one, he makes mention of Norbert Elias's view that a psychoanalytic psychodynamics provides a material basis for the inscription of civility into the soul of the social subject. He also notes that the analytical route opened up by the strategic utilization of psychoanalytic concepts is, for many, required in order 'to avoid representing the human being as merely the passive and interminably malleable object of historical processes ... [and] if one is to have an account of agency and of resistance' (1996b, p. 142). Ultimately, however, this is a view he rejects on the basis that it requires the adoption of a particular (humanist, disciplinary, non-historical and psychologistic) way of understanding the human being.

References

Abrams, D. and Hogg, M.A. (1990). The context of discourse: let's not throw the baby out with the bathwater. *Philosophical Psychology*, 3 (2): 219–225.

Adorno, T.W. (1991). The psychological technique of Martin Luther Thomas's Radio Addresses. In J. Bernstein (Ed.), *The Culture Industry: Selected Essays on Mass Culture*. London: Routledge, pp. 66–79.

Afary, J. and Anderson, K.B. (2005). *Foucault and the Iranian Revolution: Gender and the Seductions of Islamism*. Chicago: University of Chicago Press.

Agamben, G. (1998). *Homo Sacer: Sovereign Power and Bare Life*. Stanford, CA: Stanford University Press.

Anonymous (1998). *Buyers can Design Their Own Homes*. http://.bday.co.za/specials/collage/z5.htm.

Ariès, P. (1962). *Centuries of Childhood*. London: Jonathan Cape.

Armstrong, D. (1990). Use of the genealogical method in the exploration of chronic illness. *Social Science and Medicine*, 30: 1225–1227.

Bannister, P. (1995). *Qualitative Methods in Psychology: A Research Guide*. Buckingham: Open University Press.

Best, S. and Kellner, D. (1991). *Postmodern Theory Critical Interrogations*. Hong Kong: Macmillan.

Bhabha, H.K. (1994). *The Location of Culture*. London and New York: Routledge.

Blakely, E.J. and Snyder, M.G. (1999). *Fortress America: Gated Communities in the United States*. Washington: Brookings Institution Press.

Blunkett, D. (2005). For far too long we have left patriotism to the extremists. *The Guardian*, March 19, p. 21.

Bourdieu, P. (1988). *Outline of a Theory of Practice*. Cambridge: Cambridge University Press.

Bowman, B. (2005). *Children, Pathology and Politics: Genealogical Perspectives on the Construction of the Paedophile in South Africa*. Unpublished PhD thesis. Johannesburg, SA: University of the Witwatersrand.

Bozzoli, B. (2004). *Theatres of Struggle and the End of Apartheid*. Johannesburg: Wits University Press.

Bremner, L. (2000). Crime and the emerging landscape of post-apartheid. In H. Judin and I. Vladislavic (Eds), *Blanc_Architecture, Apartheid and After*. Rotterdam: NAi Publishers.

Bulhan, H.A. (1985). *Frantz Fanon and the Psychology of Oppression*. New York and London: Plenum Press.

Burman, E. (1990). Differing with deconstruction: a feminist critique. In I. Parker and J. Shotter (Eds), *Deconstructing Social Psychology*. London: Routledge.

Burman, E. (1991). What discourse is not. *Philosophical Psychology*, 4 (3): 325–342.

Burr, V. (1995). *An Introduction to Social Constructionism*. London: Routledge.

Butchart, A. (1997). Objects without origins: Foucault in South African socio-medical science. *South African Journal of Psychology*, 27 (2): 101–110.

Butchart, A. (1998). *The Anatomy of Power European Constructions of the African Body*. London and New York: Zed Books.

Butler, J. (1997). *The Psychic Life of Power: Theories in Subjection*. Stanford, CA: Stanford University Press.

Caldeira, T.P.R. (1996a). Building up walls: the new pattern of spatial segregation in Sao Paulo. *International Social Science Journal*, **147**: 55–66.

Caldeira, T.P.R. (1996b). Fortified enclaves: the new urban segregation. *Public Culture*, **8**: 303–328.

Chambers, I. (1994). Leaky habits and broken grammar. In G. Robertson, M. Mash, L. Tickner, J. Bird, B. Curtis and T. Putman (Eds), *Travellers Tales: Narratives of Home and Displacement*. London: Routledge.

Chaney, D. (1994). *The Cultural Turn*. Hong Kong: Routledge.

Cheng, A.A. (2000). *The Melancholy of Race: Psychoanalysis, Assimilation and Hidden Grief*. New York: Oxford University Press.

Childs, P. and Williams, P. (1997). *An Introduction to Post-Colonial Theory*. London: Prentice Hall.

Clarke, S. (2003). *Social Theory, Psychoanalysis and Racism*. Houndmills, NY: Palgrave.

Cohen, P. (2002). Psychoanalysis and racism: reading the other scene. In D.T. Goldberg and J. Solomos (Eds), *A Companion to Racial and Ethnic Studies*. Malden, MA: Blackwell.

Connor, S. (1989). *Postmodernist Culture*. Oxford: Blackwell.

Crook, S. (1994). Introduction: Adorno and authoritarian irrationalism. In S. Crook (Ed.), *Theodor W. Adorno: The Stars Down to Earth and Other Essays on the Irrational in Culture*. London and New York: Routledge, pp. 1–45.

Dainfern Promotional Brochure (DPB) (1999). Dainfern: Johannesburg.

Davidson, A.I. (1985). Archaeology, genealogy, ethics. In D.C. Hoy (Ed.), *Foucault: A Critical Reader*. Oxford: Basil Blackwell, pp. 221–233.

Davidson, A.I. (2003). Introduction. In M. Foucault, V. Marchetti and A. Salomoni (Eds), *Abnormal: Lectures at the Collège de France 1974–1975*. London and New York: Verso, pp. xvii–xxvi.

Davis, M. (1992). *City of Quartz: Excavating the Future in Los Angeles*. New York: Vintage.

Dean, M. (1994). *Critical and Effective Histories: Foucault's Methods and Historical Sociology*. London and New York: Routledge.

Dean, M. (1999). *Governmentality. Power and Rule in Modern Society*. London and New Delhi: Thousand Oaks, Sage.

Deleuze, G. (1988). *Foucault*. London: Athlone Press.

Derrida, J. (1978). *Writing and Difference*. London and Henley: Routledge and Kegan Paul.

Dews, P. (1984). Foucault's theory of subjectivity. *New Left Review*, **144**, March–April: 72–95.

Dixon, J.A. and Durrheim, K. (2000). Displacing place-identity: A discursive approach to locating self and other. *British Journal of Social Psychology*, **39**: 27–44.

Dolar, M. (1999). Where does power come from? *New Formations*, **35**: 79–92.

Dreyfus, H.L. and Rabinow, P. (1982). *Michel Foucault Beyond Structuralism and Hermeneutics*. New York: Harvester Wheatsheaf.

Eagleton. T. (1991). *Ideology: An Introduction*. London and New York: Verso.

Eribon, D. (1991). *Michel Foucault*. Cambridge, MA: Harvard University Press.

Evans, D. (1996). *An Introductory Dictionary of Lacanian Psychoanalysis*. London and New York: Routledge.

Fairclough, N. (1992). *Discourse and Social Change*. London: Polity Press.

Fairclough, N. (1995). *Critical Discourse Analysis: The Critical Study of Language*. London and New York: Longman.

Fanon, F. (1986). *Black Skin, White Masks*. London: Pluto.

Feltham, O. and Clemens, J. (2003). An introduction to Alain Badiou's philosophy. In O. Feltham, and J. Clemens (Eds), *Infinite Thought Truth and the Return to Philosophy* (by Alain Badiou). London and New York: Continuum.

Fink, B. (1995). *The Lacanian Subject Between Language and Jouissance*. Princeton, NJ: Princeton University Press.

Finlay, W.M.L. (2007; in press). The propaganda of extreme hostility: denunciation and the regulation of the group. *British Journal of Social Psychology*.

Foucault, M. (1965). *Madness and Civilization: A History of Insanity in the Age of Reason*. London: Tavistock.

Foucault, M. (1970). *The Order of Things: An Archeology of the Human Sciences*. New York: Pantheon Press.

Foucault, M. (1974). Human nature: justice versus power. In E. Fons (Ed.), *Reflexive Water: The Basic Concerns of Mankind*. London: Souvenir Press, pp. 135–197.

Foucault, M. (1977a). *Discipline and Punish: The Birth of the Prison*. London: Penguin.

Foucault, M. (1977b). Nietzsche, genealogy, history. In D.F. Bouchard (Ed.), *Language, Counter-memory, Practice*. New York: Cornell University Press, pp. 139–164.

Foucault, M. (1977c). History of systems of thought. In D.F. Bouchard (Ed.), *Language, Counter-memory, Practice*. New York: Cornell University Press, pp. 199–204.

Foucault, M. (1977d). Nietzsche, Freud, Marx. In D.F. Bouchard (Ed.), *Language, Counter-Memory, Practice*. New York: Cornell University Press, pp. 139–164.

Foucault, M. (1977e). What is an author? In D.F. Bouchard (Ed.), *Language, Counter-Memory, Practice*. New York: Cornell University Press, pp. 113–138.

Foucault, M. (1977f). Revolutionary action: "Until now". In D.F. Bouchard (Ed.), *Language, Counter-Memory, Practice: Selected Essays and Interviews*. New York: Cornell University Press, pp. 218–233.

Foucault, M. (1978a). *The History of Sexuality: An Introduction, Volume 1*. New York: Vintage House.

Foucault, M. (1978b). *I, Pierre Rivière, Having Slaughtered my Mother, my Sister and my Brother...A Case of Parricide in the 19th Century*. Harmondsworth: Penguin.

Foucault, M. (1979a). Governmentality. *Ideology and Consciousness*, 6: 5–21.

Foucault, M. (1979b). My body, this paper, this fire. *Oxford Literary Review*, 4 (1).

Foucault, M. (1980a). Two lectures. In C. Gordon (Ed.), *Power/knowledge: Selected Interviews and Other Writings by Michel Foucault*. New York: Pantheon Books, pp. 78–108.

Foucault, M. (1980b). Truth and power. In C. Gordon (Ed.), *Power/knowledge: Selected Interviews and Other Writings by Michel Foucault*. New York: Pantheon Books, pp. 109–133.

Foucault, M. (1980c). Powers and strategies. In C. Gordon (Ed.), *Power/knowledge: Selected Interviews and Other Writings by Michel Foucault*. New York: Pantheon Books, pp. 134–145.

Foucault, M. (1980d). The history of sexuality. In C. Gordon (Ed.), *Power/knowledge: Selected Interviews and Other Writings by Michel Foucault.* New York: Pantheon Books, pp. 183–193.

Foucault, M. (1980e). The confession of the flesh. In C. Gordon (Ed.), *Power/knowledge: Selected Interviews and Other Writings by Michel Foucault.* New York: Pantheon Books, pp. 194–228.

Foucault, M. (Ed.) (1980f). *Herculine Barbin: Being the Recently Discovered Memoirs of a Nineteenth-Century French Hermaphrodite.* New York: Pantheon.

Foucault, M. (1981a). The order of discourse. In R. Young (Ed.) (1981), *Untying the Text: A Post-Structural Anthology.* Boston: Routledge and Kegan Paul, pp. 48–78.

Foucault, M. (1981b). Questions of method. *Ideology and Consciousness,* 8: 3–14.

Foucault, M. (1982). The Subject and Power. In H.L. Dreyfus and P. Rabinow (Eds), *Michel Foucault Beyond Structuralism and Hermeneutics.* New York: Harvester Wheatsheaf, pp. 208–226.

Foucault, M. (1985). *History of Sexuality: The Use of Pleasure, Volume 2.* Harmondsworth: Penguin.

Foucault, M. (1987). *Mental Illness and Psychology.* Berkley, CA: University of California Press.

Foucault, M. (1988a). Technologies of the self. In L.H. Martin, H. Gutman and P.H. Hutton (Eds), *Technologies of the Self: A Seminar with Michel Foucault.* Amherst: University of Massachussets Press, pp. 16–49.

Foucault, M. (1988b). The political technology of individuals. In L.H. Martin, H. Gutman and P.H. Hutton (Eds), *Technologies of the Self: A Seminar with Michel Foucault.* Massachusetts: University of Massachusetts Press, pp. 145–162.

Foucault, M. (1988c). *The Care of the Self: The History of Sexuality, Volume 3.* New York: Vintage Books.

Foucault, M. (1988d). The ethic of care for the self as a practice of freedom. In J. Bernauer and D. Rasmussen (Eds), *The Final Foucault.* Cambridge, MA: MIT Press.

Foucault, M. (1990). Politics and reason. In L.D. Kritzman (Ed.), *Michel Foucault, Politics, Philosophy, Culture, Interviews and Other Writings 1977–1984.* New York and London: Routledge.

Foucault, M. (1993). Space, power and knowledge. In S. During (Ed.), *The Cultural Studies Reader.* London and New York: Routledge, pp. 161–169.

Foucault, M. (1994). The birth of biopolitics. In P. Rabinow (Ed.), *Michel Foucault Ethics, Subjectivity and Truth: The Essential Works of Michel Foucault 1954–1984 Volume I.* New York: The New York Press.

Foucault, M. (1997). Utopias and heterotopias. In N. Leach (Ed.), *Rethinking Architecture: A Reader in Cultural Theory.* London: Routledge.

Foucault, M. (2003a). *Society Must be Defended: Lectures at the Collège de France 1975–1976.* M. Bertani and A. Fontana (Eds). London: Allen Lane.

Foucault, M. (2003b). *Abnormal: Lectures at the Collège de France 1974–1975.* V. Marchetti and A. Salomoni (Eds). London and New York: Verso.

Foucault, M. (2006). *Psychiatric Power: Lectures at the Collège de France 1973–1974.* J. Lagrange (Ed.). London and New York: Palgrave.

Foucault, M. and Trombadori, D. (1991). *Remarks on Marx: Conversations with Duccio Trombadori.* New York: Semiotext(e).

Frosh, S. (1989). *Psychoanalysis and Psychology Minding the Gap.* London: Macmillan.

Gandhi, L. (1998). *Postcolonial Theory.* New York: Columbia University Press.

Genocchi, B. (1995). Discourse, discontinuity, difference: the question of 'other' spaces. In S. Watson, K. Gibson (Eds), *Postmodern Cities and Spaces.* Oxford: Blackwell.

Gergen, K.J. (1999). *An Invitation to Social Construction.* London: Sage.

Gilroy, P. (2000). *Between Camps: Nations, Camps and the Allure of Race.* London: Penguin.

Gilroy, P. (2004). *After Empire: Melancholia or Convivial Culture?* London and New York: Routledge.

Glaser, B.G. and Strauss, A.L. (1967). *The Discovery of Grounded Theory Strategies for Qualitative Research.* Chicago: Aldine Publishing Company.

Gough, B. and McFadden, M. (2001). *Critical Social Psychology: An Introduction.* Basingstoke: Palgrave.

Gordon, C. (1980). Afterword. In C. Gordon (Ed.), *Power/knowledge: Selected Interviews and Other Writings by Michel Foucault.* New York: Pantheon Books, pp. 229–259.

Hall, S. (1992). Race, culture, and communications: Looking backward and forward at cultural studies. *Rethinking Marxism,* 5 (1): 10–18.

Hardt, M. and Negri, A. (2000). *Empire.* Cambridge, MA: Harvard University Press.

Heather, N. (1976). *Radical Perspectives in Psychology.* London: Methuen.

Hepburn, A. (2003). *An Introduction to Critical Social Psychology.* London/Thousand Oaks/New Delhi: Sage.

Hetherington, K. (1996a). The utopics of social ordering: Stonehenge as a museum without walls. In S. Macdonald and G. Fyfe (Eds), *Theorizing Museums, Sociological Review Monograph.* Oxford: Blackwell.

Hetherington, K. (1996b). Identity formation, space and social centrality. *Theory, Culture and Society,* 13: 33–52.

Hetherington, K. (1997). *The Badlands of Modernity: Heterotopia and Social Ordering.* New York: Routledge.

Hetherington, K. (1998). *Expressions of Identity: Space, Performance, Politics.* London: Sage.

Hill, M. (2004). *After Whiteness Unmaking an American Majority.* New York and London: New York University Press.

Hook, D. (2001). Therapeutic discourse, co-construction, interpellation, role-induction: psychotherapy as iatrogenic treatment modality? *The International Journal of Psychotherapy,* 6 (1): 47–66.

Hook, D. (2002). *The Power of Psychodynamic Psychotherapy.* Unpublished PhD Thesis. Johannesburg: University of the Witwatersrand.

Hook, D. (2005a). A critical psychology of the postcolonial. *Theory and Psychology,* 15 (4), 475–503.

Hook, D. (2005b). Affecting whiteness: Racism as technology of affect. *International Journal of Critical Psychology,* 16: 74–99.

Hook, D. (2006). 'Pre-discursive' racism. *Journal of Community and Applied Social Psychology,* 16: 207–232.

Hook, D. and Bowman, B. (2007). Paedophile as event: Tenets of genealogical analysis. Unpublished manuscript.

Hook, D., Harris, B. and Landsman, C. (1999). Suffering bodies – moral orthopaedics of the body & soul. In M. Terre Blanche, K. Bhavani and D. Hook (Eds), *Body Politics: Power, Knowledge and the Body in the Social Sciences.* Johannesburg: Histories of the Present Press, pp. 132–156.

Jäger, S. (2001). Discourse and knowledge: theoretical and methodological aspects of a critical discourse and dispositive analysis. In R. Wodak and M. Meyer (Eds), *Methods of Critical Discourse Analysis*. London: Sage, pp. 32–62.

Jacques, M. (2005). The Middle Kingdom mentality. *The Guardian*, 16 April, p. 17.

Kendall, G. and Wickham, G. (1998). *Using Foucault's Methods*. London: Sage.

Kennedy, H. (2005). Pandering to racism. *The Guardian*, 16 April, p. 18.

Kistner, U. (2003). *Sovereign Power and Bare Life with HIV/Aids: Bio-Politics South Africa style*. http://wiserweb.wits.ac.za/PDF%20Files/biopolitics%20-%20kirstner.

Kozulin, A. (1990). *Vygotsky's Psychology: A Biography of Ideas*. Cambridge, MA: Harvard University Press.

Lane, C. (1998). The psychoanalysis of race: an introduction. In C. Lane (Ed.), *The Psychoanalysis of Race*. New York: Columbia University Press.

Landman, K. (2000a). An overview of enclosed neighbourhoods in South Africa. *CSIR Building and Construction Technology*, BP 449, BOU/ I 187.

Landman, K. (2000b). Gated communities: an international review. *CSIR Building and Construction Technology*, BP 449, BOU/ I 186.

Lazzarato, M. (2002). From biopower to biopolitics. *Pli*, **13**: 100–111.

Leader, D. (1996). *Why do Women Write More Letters than they Post?* London and Boston: Faber and Faber.

Lees, L.H. (1997). Ageographia, heterotopia and Vancouver's new public library. *Environment and Planning D: Society and Space*, **15**: 321–347.

Lyon, D. (1994). *Postmodernity*. Milton Keynes: Open University Press.

McEwan, I. (2005). *Saturday*. London: Jonathan Cape.

McHoul, A. and Grace, W. (1997). *The Foucault Primer*. New York: New York University Press.

McKenzie, E. (1994). *Privatopia: Homeowner Associations and the Rise of Residential Private Government*. New Haven: Yale University Press.

McNay, L. (1992). *Foucault and Feminism: Power, Gender and the Self*. Cambridge: Polity Press.

McNay, L. (1994). *Foucault: A Critical Introduction*. New York: Continuum.

Macey, D. (1994). *The Lives of Michel Foucault*. London: Vintage.

Macey, D. (2000). *Dictionary of Critical Theory*. London: Penguin Books.

Macey, D. (2004). *Michel Foucault*. London: Reaktion Books.

Marks, D. (1993). Case-conference analysis and action research. In E. Burman and I. Parker (Eds), *Discourse Analytic Research: Repertoires and Readings of Texts in Action*. London: Routledge, pp. 135–154.

May, T. (1993). *Between Genealogy and Epistemology: Psychology, Politics and Knowledge in the Thought of Michel Foucault*. Pennsylvania: The Pennsylvania State University Press.

Mbembe, A. (2001). Ways of seeing: Beyond the new Nativism. *African Studies Review*, **44** (2): 1–14.

Miller, J. (1994). *The Passion of Michel Foucault*. London: Flamingo.

Mills, S. (2003). *Michel Foucault*. London and New York: Routledge.

Nietzsche, F. (1899). *A Genealogy of Morals*. London: Fisher Unwin.

Nietzsche, F. (1983). *Untimely Meditations*. Cambridge: Cambridge University Press.

Oliphant, L. (2001). Claims of racism stain Dainfern. *Saturday Star*, March 3, p. 5.

Parker, I. (1989). *The Crisis in Modern Social Psychology and How to End It*. London and New York: Routledge.

Parker, I. (1992). *Discourse Dynamics: Critical Analysis for Social and Individual Psychology*. London: Routledge.

Parker, I. (Ed.) (1999). *Deconstructing Psychotherapy*. Sage: London.

Parker, I. (2003). *Critical Discursive Psychology*. Houndsmills: Palgrave Macmillan.

Parker, I. (2004). *Slavoj Žižek: A Critical Introduction*. London: Pluto Press.

Parker, I. and the Bolton Discourse Network (Eds) (1999). *Critical Textwork: An Introduction to Varieties of Discourse Analysis*. Buckingham: Open University Press.

Parker, I. and Burman, E. (1993). Against discursive imperialism, empiricism and construction: thirty two problems with discourse analysis. In E. Burman and I. Parker (Eds), *Discourse Analytic Research: Repertoires and Readings of Texts in Action*. London: Routledge.

Parker, I. and Shotter, J. (Eds) (1990). *Deconstructing Social Psychology*. London and New York: Routledge.

Parker, I., Georgaca, E., Harper, D., McLaughlin, T. and Stowell-Smith, M. (1995). *Deconstructing Psychopathology*. London: Sage.

Pidgeon, N. (1996). Grounded theory: theoretical background. In J.T.E. Richardson (Ed.), *Handbook of Qualitative Research for Psychology and the Social Sciences*. Leicester: BPS Press, pp. 75–85.

Pidgeon, N. and Henwood, K. (1996) Grounded theory: practical implementation. In J.T.E. Richardson (Ed.), *Handbook of Qualitative Research for Psychology and the Social Sciences*. Leicester: BPS Press, pp. 86–101.

Posel, D. (2001). Race as common sense: Racial classifications in twentieth-century South Africa. *African Studies Review*, **44** (2): 87–113.

Potter, J. and Wetherell, M. (1987). *Discourse and Social Psychology: Beyond Attitudes and Behaviour*. London: Sage.

Potter, J., Wetherell, M., Gill, R. and Edwards, D. (1990). Discourse: noun, verb or social practice? *Philosophical Psychology*, **3** (2): 205–217.

Purvis, T. and Hunt, A. (1993). Discourse, ideology, discourse, ideology, discourse, ideology... *British Journal of Sociology*, **44** (3): 473–499.

Rabinow, P. and Rose, N. (2003). Foucault today. In P. Rabinow and N. Rose (Eds), *The Essential Foucault: Selections from the Essential Works of Foucault, 1954–1984*. New York: New York Press, pp. vii–xxv.

Ransom, J. (1997). *Foucault's Discipline: The Politics of Subjectivity*. Durham: Duke University Press.

Rieber, R.W. and Robinson, D.K. (Eds) (2004). *The Essential Vygotsky*. New York: Kluwer Academic/Plenum publishers.

Riggs, D.W. and Augoustinos, M. (2004). Projecting threat: Managing subjective investments in whiteness. *Psychoanalysis, Culture & Society*, 9: 219–236.

Rose, J. (1996). *States of Fantasty*. Oxford: Clarendon Press.

Rose, N. (1991). *Governing the Soul: The Shaping of the Private Self*. London and New York: Routledge.

Rose, N. (1996a). *Inventing Our Selves*. London and New York: Routledge.

Rose, N. (1996b). Identity, genealogy, history. In S. Hall and P. du Gay (Eds), *Questions of Cultural Identity*. London: Sage, pp. 128–150.

Rossouw, S. (2001). Living behind the barricades. *Mail & Guardian*, January 12–18, p. 6.

Said, E. (1978). *Orientalism*. New York and London: Routledge and Kegan Paul.

Said, E. (1983). *The World, the Text and the Critic*. Cambridge: Harvard University Press.

Said, E. (2003). *Freud and the Non-European*. London and New York: Verso.

Seshadri-Crooks, K. (2000). *Desiring Whiteness: A Lacanian Analysis of Race*. London: Routledge.

Shepherdson, C. (1998). Human diversity and the sexual relation. In C. Lane (Ed.), *The Psychoanalysis of Race*. New York: Columbia University Press.

Simons, J. (1995). *Foucault and the Political*. London and New York: Routledge.

Smart, B. (1983). *Foucault, Marxism and Critique*. London: Routledge and Kegan Paul.

Smart, B. (1985). *Michel Foucault*. London: Ellis Horwood and Tavistock.

Soja, E.W. (1989). *Postmodern Geographies the Reassertion of Space in Critical Social Theory*. London: Verso.

Soja, E.W. (1995). Heteropologies: A remembrance of other spaces in the citadel-LA. In S. Watson and K. Gibson (Eds), *Postmodern Cities and Spaces*. Oxford: Blackwell.

Soja, E.W. (1996). *Thirdspace: Journeys to Los Angeles and other Real-and-Imagined Places*. Oxford, United Kingdom and Cambridge, United States: Blackwell.

Stoler, A.L. (1995). *Race and the Education of Desire*. Durham and London: Duke University Press.

Tamboukou, M. (1999). Writing genealogies: an exploration of Foucault's strategies for doing research. *Discourse: Studies in the Cultural Politics of Education*, 20(2): 201–218.

Tamboukou, M. (2003). Genealogy/Ethnography: finding the rhythm. In M. Tamboukou and S.J. Ball (Eds), *Dangerous Encounters: Genealogy and Ethnography*. New York: Peter Lang, pp. 195–216.

Tamboukou, M. and Ball, S.J. (2003). Genealogy and ethnography: fruitful encounters or dangerous liaisons? In M. Tamboukou and S.J. Ball (Eds), *Dangerous Encounters: Genealogy and Ethnography*. New York: Peter Lang, pp. 1–36.

Taylor, C. (1984). Foucault on freedom and truth. *Political Theory*, **12** (2) May: 152–183.

Toscano, A. (2005). A brief history of fanaticism. *Is the politics of truth still thinkable?* Paper delivered at Conference, Birkbeck Institute for the Humanities, Birkbeck College, London, November 25.

Tuffin, K. (2005). *Understanding Critical Social Psychology*. London/Thousand Oaks/New Delhi: Sage.

Van Zyl, S. (1990). Explaining violence in South Africa: some psychoanalytic considerations. Paper presented for the Centre for the Study of Violence and Reconciliation, University of the Witwatersrand, Johannesburg, October 31.

Van Zyl, S. (2003). The creature on the couch versus the citizen on the street. It's published in the Journal for the Psychoanalysis of Culture and Society (*JPCS*), 8 (1), Spring 2003.

Vygotsky, L.S. (1978). *Mind in Society the Development of Higher Psychological Processes*. Cambridge, MA: Harvard University Press.

Walkerdine, V. (Ed.) (2002). *Challenging Subjects: Critical Psychology for a New Millennium*. Basingstoke: Palgrave.

Watson, S. and Gibson, K. (1995). Postmodern politics and planning: a postscript. In S. Watson and K. Gibson (Eds), *Postmodern Cities and Spaces*. Cambridge: Blackwell.

Watts, J. (2005a). China braced for mass protests. *The Guardian*, April 16, p. 19.

Watts, J. (2005b). Violence flares as the Chinese rage at Japan. *The Observer*, April 17, pp. 20–21.

Wertsch, J.V. (1985). *Vygotsky and the Social Formation of Mind*. Cambridge, MA: Harvard University Press.

Wetherell, M. and Potter, J. (1992). *Mapping the Language of Racism, Discourse and the Legitimation of Exploitation*. New York: Harvester Wheatsheaf.

Whitebrook, J. (2005). Against interiority: Foucault's struggle with psychoanalysis. In G. Gutting (Ed.), *Cambridge Companion to Foucault*. Cambridge: Cambridge University Press, pp. 312–347.

Winnubst, S. (2004). Is the mirror racist? Interrogating the space of whiteness. *Philosophy and social criticism*, 30 (1): 25–50.

Wintour, P. (2006). Brown: Remembrance Sunday should become 'British Day'. *The Guardian*, January 14.

Willig, C. (1999). Introduction. In C. Willig (Ed.), *Applied Discourse Analysis*. Buckingham: Open University Press, pp. 1–21.

Willig, C. (2005). Commentary on 'Genealogy, discourse, "effective history": Foucault and the work of critique'. *Qualitative Research in Psychology*, 2: 32–33.

Wolberg, L.R. (1977). *The Technique of Psychotherapy*. New York, San Francisco, London: Grune and Stratton.

Young, R. (1981). Introduction to Foucault's 'The order of discourse'. In R. Young (Ed.), *Untying the Text: A Post- structural Anthology*. Boston: Routledge and Kegan Paul, pp. 48–49.

Young, R. (1990). *White Mythologies Writing History and the West*. London and New York: Routledge.

Žižek, S. (1998). Love Thy Neighbour? No, Thanks! In C. Lane (Ed.), *The Psychoanalysis of Race*. New York: Columbia University Press.

Index